A BOOK AROUND THE IRISH SEA

A BOOK AROUND
THE IRISH SEA
History without nations

David Brett

Wordwell

First published in 2009
Wordwell Ltd
Media House, South County Business Park, Leopardstown, Dublin 18

Cover design: Ger Garland
ISBN: 978-1-905569-36-6

British Library Cataloguing-in-Publication Data.
A catalogue record for this book is available from the British Library.
This publication has been funded under the Heritage Council's 2009 Publication Grant Scheme.

The author is pleased to acknowledge the assistance of the research funds of the University of Ulster in completing this book.

Editor: Alicia McAuley
Book design and layout © Nick Maxwell, Alicia McAuley
Photographs by the author, unless otherwise stated
Printed by Graficas Castuera, Pamplona

For Mary Fitzgerald and Robert Towers

CONTENTS

ONE
By way of introduction

We must stress that in the life of peoples external events and conditions exercise a decisive influence upon the internal constitution.
— Otto Hinze

Sea areas: Fastnet, Irish Sea. Steady north-west. Four moderating to three. Visibility good.

GANNETS, PUFFINS, CORMORANTS, ETC.

Figure 1. Sea birds.

Somewhere fathoms down is Sarn Badrig, the undersea ridge that runs south-westward from Cader Idris, dipping down under Cardigan Bay, built, so fishermen said, to make a saintly way across to Éire. It is in fact the remnant of a glacial moraine from 20,000 years ago, when the bay was full of grinding ice. At very low water stretches of this reef can be seen just emerging from the sea, several miles out, and there are reports from the eighteenth century that the remains of houses were found upon it. There are extensive submarine forests along the coast in which tree roots from 10,000 years ago can still be found.

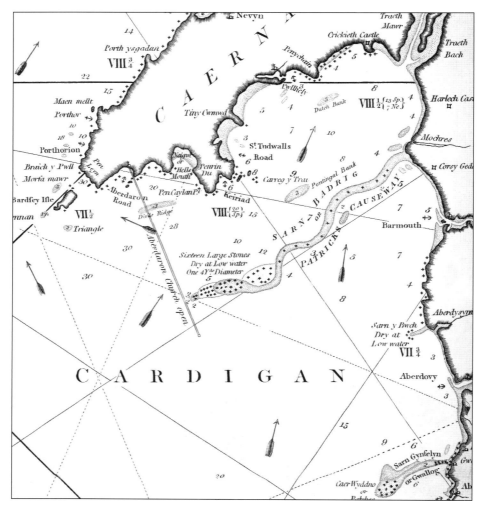

Figure 2. Sea chart of Cardigan Bay, showing the three main reefs or *sarnau* that project into the bay and that gave rise to the story of the Cantre'r Gwaelod — the lost country swallowed by the sea.

***

Meanwhile, back on watch … cold hands and empty stomach. In the galley John is preparing a hot drink that cannot come too soon. Flashing lights in the corner of the eye: hallucinations … or trawlers?

To the east, a lightening: from pitch to pearl.

(At the moment I am the deckhand and occasional helmsman of a 35 footer outward bound from Strangford Lough to the Pool of London.)

Nothing will make me into a good helmsman. I lack the trembling sensitivity that takes transmissions through the wheel and foot and cheek as the hull, the sails, the rigging, surge and lurch from one crest to another. But this is easy enough, and steady, and securely boring: to stand braced in the cockpit, peering under the boom or through the stays into the grey light, sensing the wind on my cheek and, with one eye on the tell-tale, scrying forward. These are not busy waters, but there are enough large ships coming up from the south to demand alertness on the watch. And when they come, they come quickly.

***

So much of travel today is spent in airborne capsules of aluminium and plastic that the physical fact of location is lost. Is that the Mersey? And it is, and those the docks, and that the flat elbow of Wirral. And then, almost at once, we are over central England and the angle of the cabin roof is tilting forward.

Fylde slides below;
the main coast sidles inboard
like a broken promise.

Illustration 1. The early morning ferry prepares to take off from Belfast Harbour.

The capsule effect has been brought to sea level in the catamarans that ply between Belfast and Scotland — the nastiest form of transport yet devised, which unites the worst of airline rhetoric with the ambience of an amusement arcade. All sense of sea is lost.

For the true, physical, experience of travel the only crossing is the night boat from Belfast to the Mersey, which maintains the ancient rituals of the sea — as well as its physicality, its unexpectedness and its monotonous brutality. A whole night hiding behind Ellan Vannin waiting for the wind to moderate merely to force seven, the lumbering trucks swaying and creaking within the creaking and swaying of the blundering ship. Birkenhead in a March dawn: salt, diesel, wind and the white birds crying after. Sometimes the Maidens look like the ships they have drowned.

Is there a place for a book on this? A book that would not be a journey across flat space but deep into time through the portal of a place?

**

There is a song that used to be heard when Irish people were winding down after a good night's drinking:

> The sea, the sea …
> Long may it roll between England and me.

The sentiment rests on the assumption that seas divide and separate, but if the historical and spatial truth were better grasped we would perceive that, as a human realm, the sea precedes the land — that, as the great occasion of exchange and meeting, it is the uniter of peoples. But it is a uniter that makes differences apparent. And what is more, it is far from being a defensive moat. Until the advent of modern warfare to have a long sea coast meant to be highly vulnerable to invasion. These islands demonstrate that proposition. We penetrate one another, inextricably.

The subject of this book is that stretch of water generally called the Irish Sea, and its shores, considered as a place of exchange and meeting, as a zone of interaction, as a fact of geography and history that precedes mere nations. Question: since we are accustomed to the idea of a Mediterranean culture, why not to a culture and history of our own inland sea? Answer: because the idea of nationality gets in the way.

The problem of imagination is not unlike that called, in *Gestalt* theory, the 'figure/ground shift'. The sea in question is shown in Figure 3. Which is the figure and which is the ground? Which is positive and which is negative? We choose how we see. Either/or.

Here we are speaking merely of the outlines of things, but figure/ground relations touch on the foundations of human consciousness.[1] Everything we think about is made up in this way, from our earliest and most explorative mental processes onward. 'What is this in my hands?' thinks the tiny child, who, knowing nothing of blankets, realises only that they are not skin. A world begins to condense and solidify under her fingers. A figure steps out from the ground.[2]

Figure 3. The Irish Sea, disconnected from the north Atlantic and sketched out with a felt-tipped pen.

***

And so, as I struggle to keep alert in the quarter-light of early day, out of the ground of pearly grey a figure of shadow begins to form into headlands and hills. St David's Head; Ramsey Island; the Bishops and Clerks. And a low spiky hill of granite that 60 years ago was the first mountain I ever climbed by myself. The last few feet were steep rock and my heart was pounding.

***

The reasons why the sea is called Irish is itself a question. It might just as well have been called the 'Manx Sea' or the 'Welsh Sea'. (Indeed, it was so called by the Manx and the Welsh. But we are writing in English.) I surmise that this is because it was so named by Greenwich cartographers who were mindful of the old — Tudor — couplet:

He who would England win
must with Ireland begin.

How much of Irish history has grown out of that perception?

I have come across no classical names for this stretch of water. Pytheas the Greek, as he sailed north towards Orkney about three centuries before the birth of Christ, gave it no name that has survived. Neither did Ptolemy, compiling his geography more than a century later, although he listed some identifiable names and places. And before Pytheas, Himilco, a Carthaginian sailor whose lost log book (picked up two centuries later by the Roman Avienus) refers in a plausible way to the land of the 'Hierne' and a place still further north — 'a rough country with frequent thickets and harsh cliffs, where mountains threaten the sky'.[3]

It is hard to suppose that the ancient mariners had no name at all for so important a northward firth. Perhaps in Pytheas's day — and earlier — it had such a name as 'the Inner Passage' for those who were looking for a (relatively) quiet sail from Biscay to the northern seas in search of fresh sources of copper and tin (without which bronze could not be made). For Strabo and Diodorus Siculus it might have been the 'Mare Britannicum'. But I shall go along with the term 'Irish' because it does not seem to offend anyone.

A similar question hangs over terms such as 'the British Isles'.[4] Is this a neutral geographic description or an ideological construct? For people living on the largest of the islands it is more or less neutral. But for the Irish, the term 'British' is inextricably associated with the Anglo-Scottish enterprise of empire and ceased to be neutrally descriptive long ago. For this reason the term 'British Isles' is something that, if British visitors are sensitive, they will consider before using in Ireland. But this is difficult for Irish natives, since every atlas uses the term without embarrassment. I propose to use 'the Islands', and to recall from time to time 'Britain and the islands adjacent', and 'the island beyond Britain' — geographical designations deriving from late-classical times. But there are, as we shall see, difficulties in every name. There is, in fact, no neutral name for this arm of the ocean. There is no such thing as a neutral name.

This Irish Sea acts as a kind of inland waterway, linking many parts, extended further inland by navigable rivers and canals. These linkages form the vertebrae of this book. They constitute a large part of the experience of being British (whatever that might have been, is or may be) and, largely and consequently, that of being Irish, Scottish, Welsh etc. England, it seems to me, is largely defined against 'the continent' more than against other parts of the Islands — of which most English people are ignorant or neglectful (though when you speak to them they almost always say something like, 'but my grandfather was Scottish', as if that were some kind of excuse or explanation).

And now it occurs to me that there is a good case for claiming a North-Sea culture somewhere along the same lines. Such a way of thinking — by way of shorelines — precedes the nations that squat along the shores. We begin to imagine writing a history without nations.

The issue of things, peoples and places and their proper names is a sub-theme in what follows. Whenever it is not pedantic to do so I shall try to refer to people and their places by the names they themselves used. Thus, I shall often refer to Anglesey (a Viking name), as Mon, to the Isle of Man as Ellan Vannin (an eighteenth-century anglicised form of the Gaelic Eilean Mhannain), to Ireland as Éire and to Scotland as Alba (it was Alba before it became Scotland). England I shall usually call England (the name given by the Norse Vikings to what Anglo-Saxon speakers called Englelond). What is now called Wales became Cymru (meaning approximately 'our people') to make a fifth-century distinction between the P-Celtic-speaking peoples of Wales, Strathclyde, Rheged and Cornwall and the speakers of the Germanic tongues that had taken over the easterly lands. (It was the tongues that did the taking over; the people largely stayed put.) In Latin, this Cymru approximated to what Roman governors and administrators meant by Britannia, and it perpetuated itself as far north as Cumbria, Cumbernauld and the Cumbrae Islands. For these P-Celtic speakers, England was Lloegre, the lost land (lost, that is, to another tongue).

This matter of names is no small matter for whoever lives in Northern Ireland, since there remains a persistent doubt as to where we are and what we are called. Do we live in the United Kingdom, Northern Ireland, Ulster, Ireland, the Six Counties or (in a comico-fanatical version) the Occupied Six Counties? Of all these designations, 'Ulster' is by far the oldest and most to be revered, but of course the six counties of Northern Ireland are not the same as the nine counties of Ulster, and have still less to do with ancient Uladh. 'Northern Ireland' is the most recent and contentious name along this shoreline and its legitimacy rests mainly upon the conviction of a majority of its inhabitants (though many of them obstinately refer to themselves as 'Ulstermen' and 'Ulsterwomen'). In this respect, the naming question is political to its very core. I repeat: there are no neutral names.

The notion of 'Celticness' and the 'Celts' I shall usually avoid altogether, since as a self-description it was never used by anyone before the eighteenth century and then only used in a context formed by long-outmoded racial theory.[5] As such it has a disreputable history and many contemporary historians deprecate its use. It does, however, make good sense in well-defined cases, as when we speak of the Celtic Church and, of course, of a family of languages. It is, moreover, a designation much used by the north-westerly inhabitants of the Islands to distinguish themselves from the south-easterly lot; this distinction, which is essentially a matter of sentiment, not history, needs to be respected out of courtesy. For the real historical inhabitants, however, I prefer to use the term 'Gaels', Irish or Scottish. These are the people who in historical times have spoken and speak the Q variants of Celtic, often called Goidelic, as opposed to the P variants, often called Brittonic, spoken by the Cymri and the Bretons and the ancient populations of Kernow. How these relate to the idea of Picts and Pictish (or Pritennic) is obscure beyond description.

The issue of the naming of peoples is, as Simon Bolivar said of the politics of Peru, intricate and horrible no matter how considered. Popular history, still in thrall to nineteenth-century ideas of race and nation, continues to believe that 'peoples' are formed by a common racial character (nowadays masquerading under the guise of genetic inheritance) in which biological descent is expected to tell us something useful and permanent about particular societies. The critical historian, however, is likely to treat a 'people' as something fluid, a shifting group brought into being by political forces and given identity by language and textual means, in chronicles and other kinds of story.[6] In this respect, 'nations' are narrative devices and 'peoples' are constituted by how they have been described by others as often as how they have described themselves. In this context the question, 'Who was a Celt, a Briton, a Pict or a Saxon?' depends on who is asking and on when, where, why and in what language the question is being put and the answer given.

These are the perennial problems of any kind of history that accounts for origins. They turn up all through the following book because at least part of my hope would be to write an account of the past that would, by incorporating a degree of criticality (that is, a reflection upon sources, concepts and terms), create something like a new kind of popular history written in a scholarly but non-academic manner. This may be a forlorn hope, since there are really only two classes of people — those who are seek questions and those who seek answers. But it lies behind what follows, which scrambles along in a fumbling way like a man in a bag.

**

Where shall we draw the limits?

My Irish Sea is that stretch of water between, in the south, the line from St David's Head to Carnsore Point (in navigational terms, between Tuskar Rock and the South Bishop lights, now coming up to the south through opalescent haze) and, in the north, from the Mull of Kintyre to Fair Head. But I retain for myself the right to discuss such places as the islands of Iona, Rathlin and Caldy and to venture around the corner south-west from Carnsore Point into Waterford Harbour. I wish also to write now and then of Arran and Bute which, while usually considered as lying within the Firth of Clyde, are strategically and geologically enmeshed with the Irish Sea. Sections of what follows will have to do with, in the north, Argyll and Lorne, as well as the crossing of the Severn Sea into Kernow and Armorica. I allow myself to visit Glasgow and even, briefly, Manchester. Navigable rivers and canals extend the sea and help to form the scope of my survey; half a chapter is devoted to them. When I deal with events and journeys by land I allow myself a latitude with respect to my distance from the sea, but we shall never be far from salty water. (There are a number of good reasons for including Cornwall and the Isles of Scilly, but my reason for excluding them is that I do not know them and they are too far away to cycle through. The nearest I have been to either was to sail round the point of Land's End one misty evening, but we were preoccupied with dodging a tanker and in the mist our captain identified the Eddystone Lighthouse as the periscope of a submarine.)

I have also excluded, for reasons of brevity, any extended study of Dublin and Liverpool. Such enterprises have already been undertaken by others.

As a fact of physical geography, the Irish Sea consists of a number of shallow basins, ridges and deeper troughs, full of shifting tides. Because it is open to the Atlantic at both ends, the sea in effect receives an extra inward tidal flow which generally shifts northward and runs out by the North Channel and round the great spur of Fair Head in a powerful current as the whole sea ebbs. Off most of the promontories there are formidable tide-races, which include the sound of Ynys Enlli — Bardsey Island — around the tip of the Lleyn Peninsula and the brisk rips between Skomer, Ramsey and the head of St David's. Another strong current runs up the Antrim coast, while the Menai Strait runs like a great river that goes now this way and now that. Navigators in ancient times must have used these currents rather like slingshots, to propel their craft by careful timing. The rocks known as the Bishops and Clerks that lie off St David's Head appear, as the tide surges past them, to leave wakes of foam like a fleet of great battleships.

These physical facts only seem unimportant to those who dismiss the impositions of nature upon human life as irrelevant and like to think only of 'discourse' and 'culture'; yet the affinities between Ulster and southern Scotland (to take a tendentious example) rest, quite literally, upon geological foundations. The obvious similarities of the indented coastlines of western Scotland, south-western Ireland, south Wales and the coasts of Cornwall and Devon, Brittany and Galicia have a common origin in the rising and falling of lands and waters, and have some common human consequences.

Moreover, the shape of the Mor Iwerddon, as it is known in Welsh, and its coastline continues to alter to this very day. Fields and even towns have been swallowed by water or buried in sand; bays and bights have filled up with mud and detritus. There is always something provisional about the coastline. There are major examples of this, of which the fate of Chester is one. From a major port in the fourteenth century it declined to a river quayside by the seventeenth, and the great anchorage of the Hoyle Lake, which was used by everyone from the Romans to the Vikings to the Tudor navies, was replaced by sandbanks. The weight of trade passed from the Dee to the Mersey. The port of Bannow, which Norman adventurers used as a base from which to impose themselves upon Éire, sank under the dunes during the sixteenth century. And there are other, minor examples, such as the fourth-century oratory of St Piran of Cornwall, which suddenly reappeared from its sandy grave in 1836.

In the long run, everything is provisional — even, as we have already noted, the figuration of Bae Ceredigion, from whose shallow waters may be heard the sound of the sunken bells of Cantre'r Gwaelod.

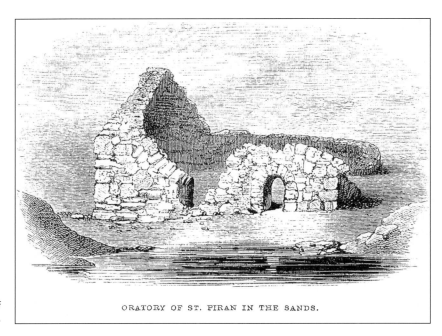

ORATORY OF ST. PIRAN IN THE SANDS.

Figure 4. Oratory of
St Piran.

And what about the temporal limits?

Well, I have decided to limit myself to recent history — that is, post-glacial times. There is no doubt there was a human population before the last great Ice Age and that its remains and traces can be found in several parts, but frankly I find it hard to relate to these people. Those very ancient times exist in a world that is wholly dependent on the scholarship of others, or mere fancy, and neither of these positions attracts me.

We also need to consider the weather, which plays a large part in history.[7] The Irish Sea may well be considered a calm water, being largely surrounded by land, but those who sail upon it will testify differently, for the weather is very changeable, especially in its northern half. Ask the 130 who drowned when the Stranraer ferry went down off the Copeland Islands in 1953. Ask the 450 who drowned when the *Royal Sovereign* broke in pieces on the coast of the Isle of Man in 1859, laden with Australian gold. Think of the *Tayleur* of Liverpool, the grandest ship then afloat, which went down on her maiden voyage with 370 passengers in 1854; or the East Indiaman that collided with Lambay Island and left a trail of blue-and-white porcelain and a black cabin boy as her sole survivor. And where is the fleet of Sir Cloudesley Shovell? Gone to flotsam with King Philip's five armadas.

Weather has its own part in human history and we ask ourselves whether, if the Spanish or French fleets had possessed better pilots for sea areas Shannon and Fastnet, history might not have been very different. South-westerly gales have much to answer for, including, perhaps, the continued existence of the British state.

Small harbours and large bays are common and, if you can see anything at all, there will usually be land in sight to one quarter or another. The intervisibility of the coasts has meant that no great navigational initiative was required to cross from one coast to another; from very early times, indeed, 'we find the Irish Sea a busy thoroughfare of criss-cross routes'.[8]

And what sort of craft were they that plied these routes? This is a subject for the marine archaeologist, but for the most part I would like us to think of two main classes of ships — the lean and the plump. The lean are epitomised in the slender, deadly longships of the Viking raiders: these were craft you could pluck up, carry onto the land and turn into houses. The plump are those built for cargoes, of which the prototypes were the heavy galleys the Veneti built, and which Caesar describes so exactly in his *Commentaries* — brutes of heavy oak fastened with iron chains and bolts, driven by leather sails.

***

No sooner has one conceived of the idea of a book than one learns that what one took for one's own has already been co-opted by bigger and better men. The kind of prefiguring I had been doing had, I discovered, already been done for me by Barry Cunliffe[9] and before him by Fernand Braudel.[10] In studying — indeed, inventing — the idea of an Atlantic identity and situating it within the arc from Cape Farewell to the banks of Morocco, Cunliffe created and ordered a way of looking at his topic from which I have had to learn and which I have partly had to follow. But my intentions are significantly different. In taking what Braudel has called the 'longue durée' view, Cunliffe has chosen the vast sweep of prehistorical settlement as his starting domain, and from that stepped forward into the fourteenth century. He has little to say about the subsequent extension of the Atlantic community into the new found lands. And he has nothing whatever to say about the North Atlantic Treaty Organisation, which for the past decades has given military shape to a geopolitical unity and in fact springs out of much the same deep connections from which have been constructed centuries of strategy and power play.

My purview is smaller, informal and more neighbourly, and thus more personal. Even, it occurs to me, existential. I write as the grandchild of emigrants who, setting foot on land at Liverpool, found themselves travelling against the sun and so invested themselves in Yorkshire. As an unborn child I rolled across on the night boats between Liverpool and Dublin in my mother's swell. My world is a historical world that contains men with cases in their hands and women with babies on their backs. As a growing child I used to think of geography as the Cambrian coast. Windy summers were spent facing Ireland. Now, at 70, my home is in Ulster. This space is my space and this time my time.

Braudel, unlike Cunliffe's spatialised picture, took a historically distinct era, the reign of Philip II of Spain, but found that he could not encompass even a few decades without resorting to a geological timescale — not just for scene setting, but to help create a structure for explanation. All through his mighty book the relations between mountain and coastal plain, between plain and sea and between sea and island repeat themselves in transformations. They are not a backdrop to the scene but actors in the play. Here, too, current, tide, wind, headland, island, sandbank, estuary and anchorage play their parts.

This book has no single historical focus; I prefer to think of its centre being a question — 'What is it to live and die along these shores?' I shall look at that question in terms of *longue durée*, of what Cunliffe refers to as 'the underlying consistencies that bind communities together and the rhythms that moderate their development over long periods of time'.[11] Around these coasts a long succession of human organisations developed, overlapped one another, succeeded one another, exterminated one another and left their traces impressed on and coursing through one another. What has it felt like to live in this layer cake, to burrow through it like a little weevil? And what has been the inner life of these organisations that our species builds like dykes against the terrors of death and disorganisation? No human experience ever quite vanishes and, just as our very early childish adventures remain with us, to be repeated in different forms and reinterpreted under adult circumstances, so histories are inscribed into the present and pass through this existence into the next. The dimensions of time and space cannot be separated in real life, because life reflected upon has thickness and duration and we are merely its latest instance.

This book focuses upon specific locations. I have proposed to myself to make journeys all around the Irish Sea, by varied means, though mainly by bicycle. I have designated a number of sites which will enable me, from their particular point of vantage, to write a history that is topocentric in character, in which time is felt through the experience of places explored. That might be a stage towards a history without nations.

**

My sites follow a definite movement through time as well as space — that is to say, they are placed along temporal as well as spatial coordinates and move towards the present day. However, I reserve the right to describe and comment on anything that pleases or interests me and captures this multidimensional attention. All are places that have been and are important to me and have been part of my formation.

For an excursion into the most ancient sea-ways and wanderings it makes sense to begin my book with a visit to the chambered grave of Carnanmore at the north-easternmost corner of Ireland and the nearby hillside of Tievebulliagh, from which great mounds of flint were dug, shaped and exported up and down the coasts. This is the sea of the stone-ways, whose medium of interchange was the axe, and its other sites lie in Cumbria and north Wales. Here I pause to think of these ancestors and their ancient languages.

I also propose to spend a little time with the Romans and consider how they viewed this sea, and my brief point of vantage is a Roman fort on a low hill overlooking the Solway Firth where, as a child, I stood to watch repeated squadrons of aircraft practise their machine-gun and bombing runs across the sand. I can hear their detonations to this day.

My third site lies at the other end of the Irish Sea — the ancient ecclesiastical site of St David's — as headland, town, cathedral and monastery. From there we look out on a Mor Iwerddon of priests and monks and hermitages, and of the spread of missionaries, scholars and scribes. This is the sea of the book ways, the roads of the cup and the bell. From this place we peer out north towards Ynys Enlli and Whithorn Bay and into the Firth of Clyde. So we arrive at the great monasteries of Bangor and Iona. How much of Irish history, we will ask ourselves, is an extension of Welsh history? What sense does it make to distinguish them, and on what grounds?

Looking outward from Ellan Vannin we share perspectives with the Vikings and a world in which raiding and trading left their characteristic marks upon the shore, in names and settlements and marketplaces. This world went some way towards obliterating the priestly perspective of the Mor Iwerddon, overlaying one strata of human experience with another, much as the fire and dust of volcanic basalt cover the mild and sea-laid chalks of Antrim. With Ellan Vannin we also partake of the world of the *re* Innse Gall, the lords of the Isles, of Somerled, Kishmul and the Clan Donald, who acknowledged no nation.

Being English born I have never been able to share the Irish attitude to the Norman invasions. The Normans were not English, whoever the English were then. Indeed, they treated the wretched Anglecyn with even less consideration than, subsequently, the English treated the Irish: England was to Normandy as Ireland became to England. It takes a long time to get rid of your conquerors; perhaps you have to become them. That, at least, is what seems to have happened in Scotland very early on, since the establishment of the feudal kingdom of Scotland followed a broadly Norman model, staffed by French- and Flemish-speaking knights brought in peacefully by David I. And the Normans were Vikings in suits, whose Frenchified manners were no deeper than a coat of mail. The Irish Sea is rimmed around with their fortresses of every age and kind, and they constitute another layer, which is well surveyed from Carnsore Point. And this introduces another minor theme of the sea and its book — architecture. Buildings, of whatever age or size, speak of their inhabitants as clearly as any text. They stand against time as they stood against enemies.

I have also been spending some time on a roundabout watching the traffic passing north and south between Belfast and Dublin. This is a very good viewpoint from which to survey the several armies that have passed this way, each attempting to define relations between the various peoples of the sea, from ancient Cuchulainn onward by way of the brothers Bruce to William of Orange. From here we can look out at the war fleets of the fourteenth century that pursued one another up, down and across the waters between here and Anglesey and observe the savage, muddy campaign fought up and down the Moyry Pass by Mountjoy, the lord deputy, in what resembles a Tudor battle of Passchendaele.

But the only proper place from which to view the Irish Sea in its military/naval aspect is from the top of Nelson's column. And I do not mean the one that stands in Trafalgar Square, but the one that stood, until it was exploded, in O'Connell Street, Dublin. From this precarious position it becomes immediately obvious that British–Irish relations (from the most ancient times as well as in the modern period) are founded on the paramount need of the Anglo-Scottish states to maintain control over the Irish Sea by any means whatsoever. I choose that phrase with care and deliberation. And this remains the case, as anyone who sees a Trident submarine whale its way past Rathlin, nosing up its great hill of water, will agree. This enables me to bring into play the geopolitical approach to the Irish Sea proposed by H.J. Mackinder in his discussions of the defence of the realm.

My eighth location is a lock gate on the Newry Canal, which I open to make my way into the world of the eighteenth-century engineer who expanded the sea into the countryside by way of the water-roads. The connection between Lough Neagh and the Irish Sea is by far the oldest of all the summit canals of the Islands on whose connecting towpaths you can cycle, with a few interruptions, throughout the lands. The canal system, linked before long to rails, was the transport that more than any other created a modern Ireland and is coeval with the idea of a united Irish nation in a contemporary sense — a state still unachieved. These were the veins and arteries of flight and exile, of import and export, the systole and diastole of capital.

This leads on naturally to an excursion into shipbuilding, the infernal trinity of Belfast, Glasgow and Liverpool and the relations between them as seen from the summit of the Dargan Alps (a mountain range of scrap iron). Belfast, in effect, is an incomprehensible town without its connection to the other two and the profound difference between Belfast and any other Irish city must take cognisance of the moment when the first keel was laid on Queen's Island. From this followed a huge interchange of skills, people, capital and goods between all three, creating not three cities but one place. In this chapter I concentrate largely upon steel, architecture and colossal technology, and its concomitant — the movement of whole populations. For a brief while the Irish Sea was a site of world-historical importance.

So we see the Irish Sea as a trade area, which, beginning in flint and metals and books, graduated by way of dogs and horses into oak and leather and thence into flax and butter and beef, distributed by canals (then rails and then roads) that ran from Limerick to London by way of the sea crossings, and finally into the trades of today.

One of the heartening developments of recent years has been the revival of otherwise rather sunken little ports such as Dundalk, Drogheda and Warrenpoint into a new prosperity based upon the container-lorry/ship system. This has been a factor in the belated modernisation of Ireland and a force for peace and normalisation (whatever we think we mean by that) north of the border.

For most of this, my main transport has been the bicycle as made by Claud Butler — 'hand crafted in England' — the sort of machine for which, when I was 15, I would have gladly died. Several journeys, though, have been by car and one memorable trip was taken by yacht.

Firstly and lastly we climb together, on foot, up the winding stair of Scrabo Tower, from where, on a clear day, we can see across to Kintyre and up to the head of Loch

Illustration 2. Scrabo Tower, one of the great outlook towers of the Islands, built by Charles Lanyon, who went on to become Belfast's premier nineteenth-century architect, an engineer and a politician. Needless to say, the actual cost greatly exceeded the estimate, but it is a truly prodigious folly that appears from nearby like an Atlas rocket on its launching pad (see also Chapter 10).

Lomond, eastward over the Galloway Hills and over to Man, and southward as far as Wicklow. The sun glints off the distant snow; the sea brims at its bounds. It may be, we reflect, that the life of cities such as Belfast, Dublin, Glasgow and Liverpool is inscribed in the geopolitics of their sites and locations — that another name for the sea is Fate.

***

At least that is the idea. But no plan survives contact with the enemy and what I have now is a writing significantly different from what I imagined at the outset. This is hardly surprising, since the objects of knowledge are constituted in and by our search for them. Two themes have come to the fore, which existed at the start but have swelled.

The first is language. I find that I have been unable to make sense of the Cuan Éirinn without regarding it as a linguistic zone in which several languages and families of languages (and their scripts) have contended for local supremacy. In this book, languages largely replace peoples as Ariadne's thread through the labyrinth. This has to be the case if we understand the stable genetic inheritance of the inhabitants. According to a recent study, the Institute of Molecular Biology, Oxford has established a common DNA going back to the end of the last Ice Age, shared by 99 per cent of a sample of 6,000, confirming that successive settlements of Celts Saxons, Vikings and Normans did little to change that make-up. The previous concept of successive invasions and settlements, of the 'drive to the west' associated with notable historians of the past, is thrown into confusion when we learn that the genetic material contained in certain 8,000-year-old human bones are found to be virtually identical with that of contemporary men and women still living near the same site. This has been further supported by substantial studies linking genetic and archaeological kinds of evidence.[12] The supposedly 'natural' concept of racial groupings has to be replaced. It now makes very little sense to talk about Celtic, Germanic and Nordic incomers displacing the indigenous populations and each other. Ethnicity is not a genetic category; I take it to be cultural and therefore overwhelmingly, but not exclusively, linguistic. What was displaced, if anything, was the foremost language of whatever human group was in charge — what I am calling the language of record. The underlying population structure changed little more than the geology.

It is frankly absurd to deduce cultural conclusions from biological evidence when we know how quickly and easily cultural — and especially technological — practices spread. Arguments that mix evidence from documentary sources with those from material culture and then from genetics are always going to be hard to sustain, just as to make comparison between fishes and oranges and tulips is logically precarious. They take radically different kinds of evidence and so must produce different kinds of conclusions, which cannot be mutually coherent, though they may support or weaken one another.

I assert, as an *a priori* condition of writing and reading this book, that what brings coherence to history is place; it is only under the heading of topography and the conditions enforced upon us by location in space that the numerous aspects of human life in time can be given logical coherence. It is place that makes human life possible:

> Not to be in a place is to be nowhere and to be nowhere is to be nothing.[13]

***

The second large theme that has emerged from my earlier intention is geopolitical and the topic that we now call 'state formation'. Sitting uncomfortably on the vanished tip of Nelson's column in Dublin I read two books that have found their way into the following pages. G.R. Sloan in his *Geopolitics of Anglo-Irish relations in the twentieth century* (1997) had already trodden ground that I intended to walk upon, and he very usefully introduced back into circulation the ideas and arguments of Halford John Mackinder, whose book, *Britain and the British seas* (1902), described the British state, in its evolution, as a response to geographical conditions.[14]

Mackinder's immediately relevant concept is the division of Atlantic Britain into 'the seas of the oceanic border' (from Orkney to Kerry), 'the British Mediterranean' (The Irish Sea) and the 'marine antechamber' (the south-western approaches). He describes the Irish Sea as a 'land-girt quadrilateral, wholly British, whose four sides are England, Scotland, Ireland and Wales'; the North Channel is 'not merely British on both sides, but also remote from all foreign shores. It is set midway along the "back of Britain", a private entry as it were to Liverpool and Glasgow.'[15] Mackinder, writing in the run-up to the First World War, shows himself keenly aware of the importance of controlling these waters, and, with respect to successive blockades and submarine warfare, events proved him exactly right. Sloan's interest lies in developing these insights and relating them to the successive treaties and 'peace processes' since 1921. Yet the issue of the defence of the realm is notable by its absence in most discussions of contemporary Northern Ireland. I write as someone who has picked up the bullets from his front garden that hailed about the roofs at night, as one who has stood by gravesides and wept.

I am also very well aware of the historical and contemporary debate about what has been called 'state formation', and I have used both formally and informally books such as *The British problem* c. *1534–1707: state formation in the Atlantic archipelago* edited by Brendan Bradshaw and John Morrill (1996) and, in a more polemic vein, Tom Nairn's *The break-up of Britain: crisis and neo-nationalism* (1977). These tend to advance a view of the Islands that is archipelagic by intention, as opposed to nation-centred views, be they Anglo-Britannic or Hibernian. But none of these does justice to what I take to be the real experience, which is based on location.

I am strengthened in this approach by my growing conviction that the best way to analyse contemporary English experience is to begin with the assumption that England should be regarded as the first *ancien régime* of the industrial epoch.

***

At the time of writing a great corpus of studies is appearing from such publishing houses as the Four Courts Press in Dublin and from many university departments. I have not been able to keep pace with it. I even find hints of 'Irish-Sea studies' as an academic category and wonder if I am not premature.

These Irish Sea studies have grown, it appears, in two main stages. We have some preliminary studies led by archaeological writers and societies, of which *The Iron Age in the Irish Sea province*, a set of essays edited by Charles Thomas and published by the Council for British Archaeology (1969) is the first, and *Irish Sea province in archaeology and history*, edited by Donald Moore (1970) is the second. Both of these, and some accompanying writings, employ the idea of the cultural zone or province in a way I find persuasive and congenial. This wave of interest has been followed 30 years later by a second, less speculative and more securely founded; titles here that have been the most important to me include the collection of essays edited by Brendan Smith entitled *Britain and Ireland 900–1300: insular responses to medieval European change* (1999) and most recently Benjamin Hudson's *Irish Sea studies 900–1200* (2004). Several conferences and study schools have been held. Some of these have centred themselves upon the Isle of Man as a suitable venue and focus. At the very last moment, when I had agreed the form of this book with the publisher, another new study was put into my hands. R. Andrew McDonald's *Manx kingship in its Irish Sea setting 1187–1229: King Rognvaldr and the Crovan dynasty* (2007) is so readable and relevant that, were I a serious pedant, I would have felt compelled to write at least one chapter afresh. However, it seemed to confirm that my general stance conformed to an existing tendency in these studies, so I overcame the temptation. All these and many others have been swept up or sipped at, without attempting to include everything.

Among the many matters I have made a decision to exclude have been the city histories of Dublin, Liverpool and Belfast, considered as topics in themselves. Others have done this better than I ever will have time to do. For my part, living in a town and at a time when one might be shot for merely walking on the wrong side of the road, this book represents something of my own journey towards understanding just where I now find myself in both space and time.

And with that in mind I have determined not to drown myself nor my reader in scholarship, nor to fear imprecisions that in other circumstances I would abhor. To quote Johan Huizinga and his foreword to *Homo ludens*:

The reader of these pages should not look for detailed documentation of every word. In treating of the general problems of culture one is constantly obliged to undertake predatory incursions into provinces not sufficiently explored by the raider himself. To fill in all the gaps in my knowledge beforehand was out of the question for me. I had to write now or not at all.[16]

And with that in mind I put foot to pedal and press.

Notes

[1] In H. White (1973) *Metahistory: the historical imagination in nineteenth-century Europe*, Baltimore: Johns Hopkins University Press, p. 30 *et seq.* the author distinguishes different stages in the creation of an historical topic. The first stage he calls the 'prefiguration' of the field. The historian must 'constitute [the field] as an object of mental perception … it must first be construed as a ground inhabited by discernible figures'. This is an essentially poetic act which he describes as 'preconceptual' (therefore, prelinguistic). This field is then conceptualised according to modes of 'argument', 'emplotment' and 'ideological implication', and in accord with tropes and conventions of discourse. This process enables us to turn the data of the historical record into a structure of explanation by way of a historical narrative. In blunt terms, we have to imagine something as a whole before we can study it in pieces.

[2] There is a further note to add. The use of a felt-tipped pen has eroded the coastline as surely as the tide; Man, Anglesey and Arran are not as prominent as they should be and something strange has happened to the Ards Peninsula. The plump edge of the felt has reproduced itself in the rounding down of coastal incidents. The means of representation has become part of what is represented in the process of reproduction. This is a lesson for the historian.

[3] Cited in B. Cunliffe, (2001b) *The extraordinary voyage of Pytheas the Greek*, London: Penguin Books.

[4] There is an excellent discussion of this problem in N. Davies (1999) *The isles: a history*, London: Papermac.

[5] This is a real can of worms opened and fondled by such scholars as Malcolm Chapman, Simon James, Ruth and Vincent Megaw, J.D. Hill and others great and small. Of great value is P. Graves-Brown, S. Jones and C. Gamble (eds) (1996) *Cultural identity and archaeology: the construction of European communities*, London: Routledge. The latest and most complete study of these problems is J. Collis (2003) *The Celts: origins, myths, inventions*, Stroud: Tempus. Of great value is the epilogue to S. Oppenheimer (2006) *The origins of the British: a genetic detective story*, London: Constable.

[6] I am here indebted to E. James (1989) 'The origins of barbarian kingdoms: the continental evidence' in S. Bassett (ed.) *The origins of Anglo-Saxon kingdoms*, London: Leicester University Press, pp. 40–51.

[7] A very useful book here is P. Dark (2000) *The environment of Britain in the first millennium AD*, London: Duckworth.

[8] N.K. Chadwick (1970) 'Early literary contacts between Wales and Ireland' in D. Moore (ed.) *The Irish Sea province in archaeology and history*, Cardiff: Cambrian Archaeological Association, p. 73.

[9] B. Cunliffe (2001a) *Facing the ocean: the Atlantic and its peoples, 8000 BC–AD 1500*, Oxford: Oxford University Press.

[10] F. Braudel (S. Reynolds, tr.) (1949, repr. 1972) *The Mediterranean and the Mediterranean world in the age of Philip II*, London: Collins.

[11] Cunliffe *op. cit.*, p. vii.

[12] See especially B. Sykes (2006) *Blood of the isles: exploring the genetic roots of our tribal history*, London: Bantam, and Oppenheimer *op. cit.* for the most recent state of this discussion. See also Chapter 2.

[13] C. Benson (2001) *The cultural psychology of self: place, morality and art in human worlds*, London: Routledge, p. 10.

[14] H.J. Mackinder (1902) *Britain and the British seas*, Oxford: Clarendon Press.

[15] *Ibid.*, pp. 12–21.

[16] J. Huizinga (1938) *Homo ludens*, Haarlem: Tjeenk Willink.

TWO
I put foot to pedal and press

The bicycle is a device for turning vertical pressure into horizontal movement by means of wheels, cranks and chains. The pressure needs to be regular and steady, which is why it is such a good means of transport for the older sportsman. No shocks. No bumps. No pain. The foot bone connects to the pedal plate, the pedal plate connects to the pedal crank, the pedal crank connects to the chain wheel, the chain wheel connects to the sprocket wheel, the sprocket wheel connects to the back wheel and the back wheel going to go to around. Them wheels, them wheels, them round wheels, them wheels going to go around …

And here we go again.

The cycle of time runs backwards as we pedal forward and I find myself ten years old once more, mounting my old black-enamelled Raleigh. By 13 I was quartering the Plain of York on a green Lenton Special in Reynolds 531 tubing. By 14, Cumbria was not too far. Head down, bum up. Go for it. At 18 I was into cyclo-cross, that fearless mixture of fell-running and mountain biking. And after that into plain pounding foot-running — mountain marathons and, what is worse, the solitary, terminal game of what I now learn is called 'ultra-running'. My best run, which I still wonder at, was from the Kirkstone Pass Inn above Ambleside to Dick Hudson's on Ilkley Moor in 23 hours. I could never be bothered to calculate how far it was or how many thousand feet I'd climbed, but it was all off road and non-stop. I remember again pounding over the last three miles of heather, expostulating with my feet: 'Come on, you worthless bastards! Do your thing!'

But before that …

The Meanwood Beck flows down a long valley towards the centre of Leeds; the slopes are well wooded and gouged by worn-out quarryworks. The beck itself is constantly interrupted by old weirs, leats, flumes and goits that fed the broken mills and watered the wasted and overgrown gardens and their black ornamental ponds. The quarries, now thick with oak saplings and entangling brambles, contained ruined sheds, rusted wheels and mossy cogs of iron, as well as steep faces of blackish stone. Climbing these crags gave me a taste for danger and myself and my companion, a ginger-haired boy called Sandy, spent long days pursuing risk.

The beck itself, which was almost a small river, could be followed several miles beyond the city limits, past an aqueduct to a set of dams and fish-ponds, now totally abandoned. We sailed upon these oceans on improvised rafts, returning home cold and wet and muddy and entirely pleased with ourselves.

But I also blame my aunt, who favoured long country walks, thermos flasks and guidebooks, for whom no journey was complete without an ancient church or grange and who would not admit to fatigue or sore heels; and who was convinced that a tramp through the rain was as good as a stroll in the sunlight.

And so here we are, on the coast road north of Larne, still hammering out the miles. Them wheels, them wheels, them round wheels, them wheels going to go around …

***

Part one: Sea-ways and stone-ways: looking south from the private entry

A sublime resting place tops the hills above Fair Head, looking eastward across the North Channel to Kintyre and northward to Islay and beyond. You walk uphill from the road a mile or more over tussocky grass, leaving at your back the coastal defence installations on the bluff of Greenanmore, until the contours widen and you follow a broad, almost level, ridge south to a mound of rocks. The mound, when you reach it, is a few yards across and contains several greater rocks forming a chamber and a fallen passage aligned on the setting sun.

Illustration 1. The cairn of Carnanmore, visible for 20 miles, is revealed as a passage grave when approached. a) The passage has fallen in but the chamber is intact and provides a trim shelter against the cold wind.

Left: b) The floor and roof are perfectly level slabs; the walls are neatly laid in course. Right: c) The empty tomb. Looking out to all azimuths, the chambered grave of Carnanmore is visible from all points of the horizon, but leads into the dark. One of the larger rocks is marked with carved circles and other designs that are hard to make out and one requires a certain faith to decipher them.

And who was it that lay in this tomb?

Was it a chief person of whatever group or tribe inhabited this corner some 5,000 years ago? We should not assume it was a man, since many female bones have been found in other passage graves. Nor should we assume it was one person only; chamber graves have been used as communal resting places into which the bones of the clan have been collected. What the westward alignment means I do not think we can say; the usual alignment of ancient monuments, as I understand it, is towards the dawn of the winter solstice, several points to the south of east. But whoever it was, and whatever office this person may have held, his or her burial was certainly invested with a heavy symbolism. For not only is this a magnificent site, but it overlooks the northern entry to the Inland Sea.

This strait is the northerly equivalent of the Strait of Dover, a waterway into ocean that for thousands of years warlords, chieftains, sub-kings, *jarls* of Norway, Scottish kings, the British state and the North Atlantic Treaty Organisation have sought to control, employing to that end any means whatsoever. On Rathlin Island, where now the seals lie on the shore to sun themselves, a thousand O'Donnell women and children were massacred to assert control of this strait. On Rathlin (which turns like a little cog between the wheels of Alba and Éire) was located the first radio station devoted to the shipping news (1898). The first transatlantic wireless telegraphy station was established at Macrihanish on the Mull of Kintyre in 1905. Twice in the last century the North Channel bore warships, convoys of supplies and troops and, during the last round of the great European civil war, Campbeltown in Kintyre, just across the way, was the centre for training in anti-submarine warfare. Air patrols across the north-western approaches were conducted from Macrihanish, Antrim and Derry, and the 20 or so airfields of Ulster were the main landing strips for US aircraft on their way to airfields in Great Britain. Fragments of lost Liberators and Flying Fortresses litter the heathery headlands of Kintyre and Islay. This is strategic ground, and therefore holy ground.

Looking eastward from Carnanmore through the squalls, you can just make out the profile of Alba's south-westerly tip — a rocky hill of no outstanding form but high enough to catch low-flying warplanes looking for Macrihanish and, some years ago, a helicopter bearing a man I knew. He and his companions were scattered over the scorched heather among shards of aluminium and steel. The scar of it remains there still. To this day the northern door of the Irish Sea, which Halford Mackinder described as a 'private entry',[1] carries unimaginable destruction under its gun-coloured water.

Pytheas the Greek, on his circumnavigation of the islands, passed this way around 300 BC. His mission was to explore the northern seas with a view to seeking new trade for the Greek colony in Massalia (now Marseilles). Setting sail from the mouth of the Garonne he passed along the coast and, like countless others before and since, went by Brittany and Cornwall on the inner passage north. We know that he took some sort of latitude reading from the sun's height, and Barry Cunliffe argues persuasively that he may have done so a second time from the Isle of Man, and then from Stornoway, before striking east through the Orkneys.[2] After sailing the North Sea, and conceivably visiting Jutland, he returned through the channel back to his starting point and wrote a report that was much copied and miscopied by later writers. Ptolemy in his geography described the inhabitants of Kintyre as the Epidii, the people of the horse, either because they bred the small fleet ponies used by Scottish armies until the seventeenth century or because the horse was their emblem. The name still lasts in Kintyre as MacEacheran. Southend, its last village, may figure in the Roman road atlas known as the *Ravenna Cosmography* as Rauatonium, but that is an obscure business.

Looking south from the tumulus on Carnanmore, the dead would have peered out at a broad plateau, then sparsely grown over with hazel and oaks in its shallow folds. This high land extends southward as far as Belfast, but is underpinned and surrounded by chalk slopes and flat-bottomed valleys which debouch towards the sea in a series of bays and beaches now occupied by substantial villages. On successive headlands there are precipices and landslides through which we see again into the structure of the earth: above, basalt; below, chalk. This gives a wonderfully picturesque and unusual coastal landscape. But what it gave the former inhabitants was a readily available supply of flint nodules and access to other hard igneous rocks such as the dark, dense porcellanite that lies within the scarps of Tievebulliagh, Rathlin Island and in some other locations. During millennia the stones of Antrim were the nearest supply of sharp edges for the whole northwest quadrant of the Islands. This was the Mesolithic Sheffield, which had already lasted millennia when the cairn of Carnanmore was built.

As you go south over the tumulus you can cut down to the main road across a wearisome bog and on the other side you find a track, in origin a very old track indeed, that leads down to the level floor of Glendun. At the foot of this valley is a small settlement, Cushendun, standing upon what was once the beach. This is now a curious little village, with a tiny bar and several houses built at the start of the twentieth century by Clough Williams-Ellis in his distinctive style. (He built another Irish-Sea village at Portmeirion in north Wales.)

Cushendun has a claim to being among the oldest inhabited places in all Ireland. On this old beach site, numerous flint instruments have been found, some crude in form, others executed with greater skill. Classifying these objects is intricate and dating them difficult, but they are certainly among the oldest artefacts of this part of the world, dating from around 9,000 BC.

It is not my intention to make a great distinction between the Stone, Bronze and Iron Ages, not least because we ought to think of them as interpenetrating and overlapping in time. The use of stone tools did not cease when bronze became available, nor did iron render bronze unusable. We should not assume any great caesura between one stage and the next. Any one group might be living, technically, in all three at once. The idea of an 'age' is not so much a feature of reality as a device to help us think and classify.

Illustration 2. Flint beds in the chalky cliffs of Garron Point.

This beach and its environs continued to be occupied, despite changes in the sea level, for the next 9,000 years and was part, along with a few other sites in Wales, the Isle of Man and the coast further south, of the first of the cultures of the Irish Sea. There is some evidence, from the relative lightness and small size of the tools found, that the first people were primarily shore-scroungers and beachcombers, making a fairly easy living from oysters, catching fish for their supper and moving inland for nut-picking in season. Hazel bushes covered the land and provided an important source of food. They left occasional finds of harpoons and other fishing gear made from antlers and bone; they also used pins and awls (perhaps for making skin clothes and hide boats.) Heavy implements of the kind that might be used for tree-felling only appear at the end of the first period of settlement, when we move into the Neolithic times, and these came from the nearby crag of Tievebulliagh.

A name has been given to this early culture — the Larnian. Those who know Larne are given to smile at this, for the town and ferry-port has (alas) a deplorable reputation for sectarian violence and illegal distillation. But I invite them to reconsider: Larne may well be the first capital of 'Auld Erin'. There are Larnian settlements most of the way down the east coast of Ireland, as well as across the water, though few have been found inland. This strongly suggests a maritime society. One notable centre of population was Strangford Lough, south of Belfast, which is ringed with ancient oyster middens and flint grounds described as Mesolithic. This region was inhabited by these Larnians for a very long time, from around 8000 to 4500 BC and the period seems to have included many sub-periods and changes, which has led one writer to conclude that 'a single settlement pattern for the Mesolithic for the whole of Ireland is thus highly unlikely and settlement patterns were probably a feature of adaptations to local environments and the availability of food resources'.[3] In other words, they wandered about a bit, changing as they wandered.

Frank Mitchell compares the Larnians with the aboriginal inhabitants of the New South Wales coast, who lived in this way until recently;[4] they remind me of the coastal tribes of western Canada, who speared the salmon one month, gathered oysters the next and lived a semi-nomadic life up and down the shorelines, meeting now and then for grand competitive feasts. (What a life!)

As these Larnian people grew in population and ambition — and came under the influence of newcomers with new languages, who also taught new skills — they morphed into a society generally known as the Clyde-Carlingford culture. It was these folk who piled up the hollow hill at Carnanmore and cleared back the forests. Their stone axes were heavy and polished smooth for cutting down trees.

The prehistory of this little region was first written by flint collectors, who found it immensely fertile ground. There are places where you can scarcely lift a sod without turning up the little sharp fragments that indicate that here some person once chipped and shaped and sharpened. As a result, early studies of ancient life in Ireland stressed this coastal element and it was only quite recently that the inland settlements were identified and then excavated. When the chambered grave of Carnanmore was made, the centres of social life and development had in fact passed southward and inland. But as long as men used stone and flint tools this coast was a centre of industry and trade, serving the peoples of what is now Ireland, and large parts of Scotland and beyond, with knives, scrapers, arrowheads and axes, and exporting them southward as far as Kent and Dorset, and possibly across the 'Sleeve' into continental Europe.

And this pyramid (for that is what the cairn of Carnanmore is), like every other pyramid from Giza to Yucatán, is an assertion of organisation in the face of death, implicating the one in the other.

* * *

Continuing south from Cushendun you arrive at the entrance to the small valley of Glenaan. The slopes hereabouts are full of ruined farms and neglected paths — an old country, long inhabited, that once was prosperous, not least in ancient times, to judge by the frequency of monuments and raths and the existence of a substantial promontory fort on the rocky heights of Lurigethan. The Tievebulliagh 'axe factory' is marked prominently on the Ordnance Survey map; it is best reached by taking a long bog road up the side of the valley for about three kilometres and then striking off south across the hillside to a prominent scar on the flank of the mountain, where there has been recent quarrying.

Tievebulliagh is a shapely hill as seen from the coast: a cone, with one precipitous flank. This cliffy part is the edge of the Antrim basalt, composed of bands of hard rock interrupted by bands of a substance that hardly merits the name of rock — something like compressed gravel, a crumbly chocolate-coloured breccia. As a result, the cliffs are unpleasantly loose and preceded by steep screes and a glacis of shaley grass. At the foot of these slopes, directly below the highest point of the mountain, is an area of hummocks and dells that look like what they are — the spoil-heaps of an extraction industry. By searching about in the last tailings of scree or in the entries of rabbit holes you soon come to recognise what you are looking for — blackish shards of porcellanite made in the chipping process by which blocks were roughed out for polishing and sharpening elsewhere.

The title 'factory' is a misnomer; this was, properly speaking, a quarry. My companion and I found the mother lode by following up the trail of fragments, keeping to the left of the main scree run. Most of the scree is of the upper basalt, a brownish stone of no interest to the toolsmith or knapper, but that which we followed was a deep bluish grey in colour. It came in flakes that had been split off, leaving very sharp, tough edges. Where the steep grass gave out at the foot of the rocks we found a declivity backed by a small outcropping of this stone lying as a stratum underneath

Illustration 3. a) The shapely hill of Tievebulliagh. The main scree slope comes down to a gravel working reached by a path; the main quarry face is above a grassy shelf to the left of the scree.

Illustration 3. b) The main quarry face is above a grassy shelf to the left of the scree, where the hard porcellanite underlies the crumbly basalt (within the white lines). Porcellanite was formed when a fine clay, made from mineral rich deposits of volcanic dust, was impacted and heated by lava flowing over it. It is, in effect, a naturally occurring ceramic.

Illustration 4. The Malone hoard. Porcellanite can be finely worked and polished. Varying in length up to eight inches, these beautiful tools gleam with a sooty black lustre (reproduced courtesy of National Museums, Northern Ireland).

the crumbly basalt. The lie of the land around it suggested that there had been a more extensive rock face at an earlier time, now covered up with earth and detritus.

According to Hallam Movius, 'axes made from this material are superior to flint examples; the rock is harder and less friable than flint, hence a better and more lasting cutting edge can be produced'.[5] What is more, the rock can be given a fine polish. Not surprisingly, there was an extensive trade in tools made from it. They have been found densely all over north-eastern Ireland, and less frequently further south, as well as in the Isles of Man and Arran, in Kintyre and Galloway and in the Hebrides. There is a very fine example of a heavy axe in the little museum at Kilmartin, just north of the Crinan Canal.[6] There is a group of finds from north of Aberdeen and others scattered over England as far as Kent.

Tievebulliagh axes were favoured because they were well suited to cutting down trees.[7] They were probably designed with this in mind and form part of a general move towards making larger and heavier tools for agricultural use and in connection with house-building and possibly boatbuilding. Unlike flint, porcellanite edges do not splinter, so they remain sharp; they form very rugged blades. Nevertheless, some examples are of such beauty and excellence of finish that one wonders if they might not have been made as presentation pieces in formal exchanges of goods and as presents between different families or clans. The collection of axes found at Malone, Belfast, now in the Ulster Museum, is so splendid a hoard as to suggest this idea. Or perhaps they were a travelling tradesman's bag of samples.

I take the desire for perfection, embellishment and decoration to be a disposition not unlike the faculty of language and counting, immanent in our nature. Without it we would not be complete human beings.[8] Just as there are no societies that do not speak or count, so there is none that does not decorate, embellish or make patterns. Aesthetic perfection of this fundamental kind acts as a marker of humanity. Donald Brown includes the decoration of artefacts, along with gossip, lying, making metaphors, binary distinctions and a fondness for sweets in his list of 'human universals'.[9] But any one instance of perfect work or completed decoration (or any other 'universal') always exists in some local context of social meaning, which is always going to be particular. In the late Bronze Age, stone axes came to form part of a cult, to appear in burial mounds and clearly to stand for some abstract power or authority. This carried over into Roman times and was revived by Italian Fascism. In the semi-mythical stories that appeared in the early middle ages particular symbolic weapons (usually swords) were so particular as to be given proper names — 'Excalibur', 'Durendal', 'Nothung' — which denote their power of bestowing rule upon their possessors. In looking at these axeheads are we witnessing a stage in the creation of authority?

In his study of Scandinavian flint daggers, Jan Apel has argued that the late Stone Age's transition into the early Bronze Age was accompanied by a complex of differentiating social structures, which included the creation of specialised objects. It is certain that the skilled and difficult work of creating shaped flint daggers or polished stone axes 'required an apprenticeship system in which the knowledge and know-how of dagger making was transmitted from one generation to the next'.[10] Their very existence has bearing on the division of labour, the creation of social and cultural capital and, ultimately, of social complexity and inequality. Skill of this order is not value free but embedded in social usage and cultural belief. Apel and his colleagues have argued that we are dealing with a specialised class of workers, conceivably a hereditary caste. We may imagine within this a further division of labour between the hewers, shapers and polishers, prospectors and traders.

***

The use of stone rather other than flint was a feature of the Irish Sea area, for we know of at least five other sources of tools made from non-flint rock along its shores. These were Craig Llwyd on Penmaenmawr Mountain in north Wales and a smaller site on Mynydd Rhiw in the Lleyn Peninsula. There was another site on Lambay Island, north-east of Dublin, where there is an outcrop of porphyry, and yet another in the Prescelly Mountains of Pembrokeshire. Arran was a source of the volcanic glass obsidian, which was also used. Above all was Pike O'Stickle above the Langdale Valley in Cumbria. This was, perhaps, the greatest of all non-flint quarries.

***

Cut to Langdale

Behind the inn at the head of Langdale is a series of rocky walls and buttresses, which provide climbs and scrambles at all levels of difficulty. They are warm and south facing, but lead up to bleaker and steeper terrain. Below you, as you climb, you can see into the level meadow of the upper dale — golf-smooth turf cropped by sheep and a broad gravelly stream bed. Ahead, steep rocks loom up. A concatenation of boulders has to be surmounted by stretching and bridging movements. Then a wall, and then a knight's move onto and across and up a slabby cliff. It is smooth here, with holds well polished by generations of boots and sweaty hands. It feels, briefly, like a serious situation: pause and consider. But at this standard of climbing you can be confident that good edges, cracks and ledges are never far away and, before long, I am scrambling upward on mixed grass and rocks as fast as I can. There is a marvellous keen exhilaration to be had from climbing steep rock alone, for the level of concentration must be high and always sustained, and it is through impassioned intensity that life gains value.

At my back are the wooded hills around Windermere and a view of sea towards Morecambe Bay. Bright sun — a shade too bright and clear — and mixed clouds moving swiftly. Now, as I start to walk along sheep-trods towards the foot of the upper cliffs, comes a brief spotting of rain.

***

The way to Gimmer Crag is by a narrow path that skirts the slope above the rocks and, almost level, leads you around the hillside to the foot of a large tilting mass that intimidates the soloist. All the more so since, on that day, it was slowly drizzling. I arrived at the foot of what is called the 'original route' to find it repulsively slippery and not suitable for the unprotected. Having the idea that the weather would improve later in the day I was in no mind to go valleywards, so I descended a little and started to pick my way along the scree and boulders below the crag, looking up now and then to identify features and routes for another day.

Past the main buttresses of Gimmer Crag comes a series of more broken heather-covered crags and steep ground, slit with gullies and clefts. This was unpleasant terrain, but I knew that the furthest bulge of crags had something like a ridge up one side of it, so I continued scrambling over boulders and scree towards the foot of the peak marked as Pike O'Stickle.

And so it was that, clambering up into a stony bay of the hillside, I found a large shallow alcove of grey-blue rock and a great quantity of splinters or shards lying in the back of the alcove and scattered all about.

***

And today, 50 years later, it is much the same. The scree is as tiresome, the heather as inhibiting and the rocks as steep and vegetatious as ever. Here I am, still managing the broken ground well enough and coming round the foot of a ridge into a wide bay of scree. This scree consists mainly of sharp splinters of fine-grained rock, which has the tint watercolourists call Payne's grey — the colour of shadow. And at my feet, and on my table as I write, are leaf-shaped blades of rock, very sharp along the edges. Some of these edges appear to have been worked into well-considered curves for cutting or scraping. There are also many tiny fragments, some of which, again, appear to have been shaped. The trouble is that the rock undoubtedly shatters into these shapes naturally. It is not easy for the untutored eye to tell the artefact from the accident. I give up turning over likely fragments, empty my pockets of all except a few, and toil on upward and across.

After a struggle I am across the scree slope and tucking myself under the craggy wall of Pike O'Stickle. There are three or four places where blocks have been torn out of the slope and there is much shattering. All around are great boulders of grey epidosite. I keep on up the loose, now looser, talus and find, quite unexpectedly, above on my left, a cave or mine hole. It is much too well shaped and smoothed off to be natural, though the cave behind the entrance leads into a natural cleft. All around are splinters and shards. This can only be the place.

* * *

Illustration 5. View of Pike O'Stickle and Gimmer Crag from Langdale. The Neolithic quarry site is at the head of a long pale scree gully, composed of chipped and shattered rocks, that leads down almost to the valley floor.

The quantity of splinters and fragments lying in this trench is very great. This was, over thousands of years, a major industrial site. The way the upper gully cuts back into the plateau above and the absence of any large stream suggests that it was systematically excavated by many generations of workers. Thousands of tons of rock have been moved. And since there are other smaller sites discovered on the Langdale peaks (and, one suspects, others waiting to be discovered) one has to imagine this moorland scene, 5,000 years ago, as a well-organised enterprise. It would have acted as a generator of social structures.

Once again, we are in the world of conjecture, but it is certainly the case that Langdale was the centre of an export trade around the sea coasts and up into Argyll. There is even a record of one Langdale tool being found near Gydnia on the Baltic shores of Poland where (I suppose) it was being traded for amber.

Illustration 6. Langdale: an opening in the gully wall below the summit. Epidosite splits easily into sharp flakes that litter the bed of the gully. While some are natural, others are certainly not.

The map of trade from Antrim can be laid over the map of trade from Langdale.

So the sea-ways of the Irish Sea were as much a conduit of objects as of people. What went out were stone tools, finished or roughly shaped; what came back were such goods as amber (from the Baltic region), jet (from North Yorkshire), fine goods of whatever sort, ceramics, in time metals, and always skills and experience. Against the steady state of most prehistoric society we have to set a countercurrent of mobility, in which both men and objects travelled widely and with them their skills, both manual and intellectual. This mobility should never be underestimated.

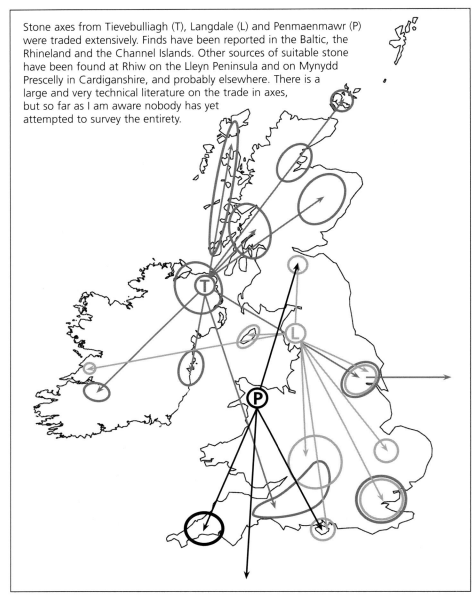

Stone axes from Tievebulliagh (T), Langdale (L) and Penmaenmawr (P) were traded extensively. Finds have been reported in the Baltic, the Rhineland and the Channel Islands. Other sources of suitable stone have been found at Rhiw on the Lleyn Peninsula and on Mynydd Prescelly in Cardiganshire, and probably elsewhere. There is a large and very technical literature on the trade in axes, but so far as I am aware nobody has yet attempted to survey the entirety.

Figure 1. Map of trade. The extent of Tievebulliagh's trade can be shown on a map originally made by E.M. Jope but reprinted by Frank Mitchell in his admirable 1986 book, *The Shell guide to reading the Irish landscape*.

* * *

The serious traveller will wish to visit the other nodes on this network, principally Penmaenmawr, the rocky headland that juts against the shore between Bangor and Conwy on the coast of north Wales. This great hummock has been mined, tunnelled and quarried for millennia and now it is one mass of scar tissue. There are so many sites, active and ancient, that the profile of the mountain has been radically altered; it now resembles a mouthful of broken teeth. At its western end is a scarp known as Craig Llwyd, where there is another source of tool-quality stone. However, despite wandering up and down over rocks and bracken, I was unable to find it.

And now, trekking over the long humpback of Ellan Vannin, I can look out from Snaefell and take in, with a turn of the head, the sea-ways and stone-ways of the Neolithic men who quarried out the scarps of Tievebulliagh, Pike O'Stickle and Penmaenmawr and who later grubbed for metals in the rocks of Anglesey and Orme. And I can apprehend, at once, directly and sensuously, the unity and scope of my subject.

Illustration 7. Craig Llwyd and Penmaenmawr. Penmaenmawr, all scars and furrows, with Craig Llwyd to the right above the trees overlooking holiday cottages. Behind the skyline is a vast quarry. There are several mine levels and a diagonal rail track, with an old mine building on the crest.

* * *

In time the trade in flint was overlaid by a trade in metals; what we now call Anglesey was a main local centre for copper mining. Bronze-Age excavations have been traced on Parry's Mountain and at several places along the coast. They form a tourist venue at Llandudno. There were also copper deposits in Snowdonia and Cumbria, while tin was available two or three days' sailing away in Cornwall. Tin and copper mixed make bronze. Gold could be found in Wicklow and Snowdonia. Iron was being smelted in several places.

Illustration 8. Dawn rises over the Rock of Dunaverty and the lifeboat station, Southend, Kintyre. The castle extended over the plateau to the left, where ditches and embankments can be traced.

It is not surprising that the north-eastern corner of Ireland has been the site of many finds of Bronze-Age cauldrons, swords, horns and implements of every kind, including the magnificent flesh hook of Dunaverney, found a few miles from Carnanmore, an ornamented gaff of bronze, silver and wood which may once have supported a grand liturgical cauldron and been used at ceremonial feasts. This remarkable object is decorated with a pair of ravens and a family of elegant swans and dates from around 1000 BC. These and other highly ornamented pieces frequently incorporate gemstones, jet and amber, and the trade in these goods interlocks with the others.

The Clyde-Carlingford culture was to have a long life, persisting into historical times as Dalriada, a zone lying astride the North Channel. It prolonged itself into the lordship of the Isles, sometimes ruled from Ellan Vannin. It remained a definite political zone as late as the English Civil War and afterwards, ruled by the Clan Donald.

***

Part two: on the mull

The action of the cycle is smooth and steady; the road is flat. The sea beside the road is quiet and the traffic light. Keep the legs turning and you get there. Keep the legs turning and you dream. The automatic pilot takes control and he will get you wherever you want to be.

Any fit person can cycle all day provided he or she does not hurry, but that person must be tolerant of his or her own company and willing to enjoy the movement of the mind for its own sake. This in turn means trusting the pilot and having presence and alertness just below the surface so that the instant it is required you have full attention to the matter in hand.

This may be an enormous truck passing you at 70 miles an hour, trailing a sucking gale, or a large ragged wheel-smashing pothole just ahead. And then there are sheep. The sheep is a creature whose intellectual capacity is small and the little mind it has is not easily made up. It is hard to share the roadway with sheep, because they are always uncertain as to which side of the road is theirs. Sheep are large and solid, and to collide with a sheep would be a heavy experience. There are a lot of sheep on these coastal roads.

There are also dogs, just as unpredictable, but with added malice. Some are well known. There is one creature given to frenzied pursuit. On the first occasion he nearly brought me down because the road was wet and the farm gateway slippery with dung. My scalp was prickling and my temples sweating by the time I had got out of his range. Now I have learned to expect this brute and, as he leaps out, so I increase my speed, but not so fast as to leave him behind. He pounds along three paces from my left ankle, snapping and slavering, until suddenly he deflates on the verge. One afternoon he will drop dead, and I shall turn and laugh.

There are people like that dog, always raging. So I keep the legs turning, turning, turning vertical pressure into forward movement so that I do not rage — so that the movement of my mind is quiet, comprehensive and never too deliberate.

* * *

There are places which, both in their history and their present condition, provide epitomes of much larger themes: such a place is Campbeltown, over the water in Kintyre.

I first arrived there limping and in winter, with my knee stitched and stapled together by the nurses of Oban General Hospital, and my experience of Kintyre is misted over by delirium and shock. I had contrived to fall most of the way down a large snowy mountain. My first night was spent in the back of the car at the highest point of the steep road leading down to the lighthouse on the mull. My idea was to get good dawn photographs across the channel into Antrim and of the ridge of Carnanmore, but the next morning was full of an icy cloud that hid every view in mist and furred every rock in rime. The road down to the mull was out of the question, for I could scarcely walk a step. I retreated to the town and a seaman's breakfast on the windswept quay. My second visit was two years later in brilliant winter sunshine.

***

The light of Kintyre is peninsular, like that of Cornwall or Orkney. More sky than land or sea. A Grecian blue tending to silver. The south of Kintyre is such a singular district that it deserves to be known much better, and I cannot help myself writing as if for an imaginary tourist with a bicycle.

Take your cycle along the coast road right around to the townland of Southend. Observe the dramatic hump of Davaar Island and think, 'What sort of name is that?' As you turn south the lower and more pastoral shape of Sanda comes into view. Sanda was a hermitage and port of call for the wandering followers of St Ninian, and later a redoubt for the Norsemen. The dawn is now up and across the links you will see a tower of rock. This is the Rock of Dunaverty.

This is the place where chieftains of Dalriada maintained a fortress and where in AD 712, according to Irish annals, there was a siege when those chiefs fell out. Here Robert Bruce made his headquarters before going on the run to Rathlin. Dunaverty Castle was also the last refuge of royalist forces in Scotland during the civil-war period; the garrison, awaiting transport to Ireland, was massacred by the troops of the Covenanter General Sir David Leslie, at the urging of a minister of religion.

Illustration 9. Warrior, with shield and spear, Southend, Kintyre.

Not far away, continuing along the coastal road, there is an old graveyard and ruined chapel from the thirteenth century. Among the many and varied tombstones there is a small eroded grave slab, depicting a warrior. This is probably a piece from the sculpture workshops of thirteenth-century Iona or Loch Awe. It is similar in design, though much smaller than similar carvings at Saddell Abbey, further north along the eastern shore.

On a rock nearby are the remains of another (possibly older) shrine and a pair of carved footprints. One (facing east–west) is certainly ancient, named after St Columba, and is possibly an old inauguration site. It was an ancient custom of these people that, to be inaugurated as a ruler, one took possession of the land by placing one's foot upon it. Here, perhaps, men stood to become the rulers of Kintyre. The other footprint is, alas, an addition by one Daniel McIlrevie, stonemason, in 1856.

Roman artefacts have been found nearby, in caves. This may well be the place where Agricola landed in the summer of AD 82 and where he decided that Hibernia was not worth the trouble of invading (see Chapter 3).

Cycle back to Southend. On the hills above the townland there is at least one large Bronze-Age enclosure/fort and probably more. Do not go back to Campbeltown but turn left to Macrihanish and its huge runway. This has some claim to being the longest landing strip in Europe, if not the world, and it was built as part of the NATO strategy of controlling the waters of the north Atlantic. From here vast aircraft cruised the Arctic sky.

Coal was mined near here as early as 1500, and during the nineteenth century both a small railway and a short canal were used to bring the coals to Campbeltown, whence they were shipped to Clydeside. Traces of both can be found in several places.

Campbeltown, when you get there, is a curious place — unusually imposing for its location, with architecture of real distinction. The changes in its name denote its adventures from a Gaelic townland to its present status.

As Gaelic Ceannloch Cill Cieran (the head of the loch of Ciaran's chapel) it was scotticised into Kinloch KilKerran: the change of name signified the creation of a royal burgh. This transformation (in 1597) meant that it was now directly under Scottish royal jurisdiction, depriving the Clan Donald and their allies of a strategic asset. By 1607 the Campbell earl of Argyll received a lease of all the lands thereabout, with an undertaking to expel all the Catholic and Gaelic-speaking MacDonalds, whom the Privy Council considered to be 'the schoolmaisters and fosteraris of all barbaritie' and permission 'to plant a burgh to be inhabited by Lowland men and trafficking burgesses'.[11] Most of these incomers were from Ayrshire and all were Presbyterian. The new town, when it was built, had a large kirk by 1643 and was called Lochhead.

The number of distinctly lowland names in the parish register doubled between 1665 and 1685. Campbell-town, as it had now become, was in fact a plantation town that grew in parallel with the Scottish and English plantations in Ulster, constructed by successive Campbell lords of Argyll and the monarchy with the intention of subduing the Catholic Gaeltacht. And it was in 1685 that the earl of Argyll began his revolt against the 'papisticall' rule of King James, by reading out (in the main street) a proclamation to:

> the Gentlemen, Burgesses and Commons of all sorts now in arms … with the concurrence of their true and faithful Pastors, and of Several Gentlemen of the English Nation joined in with them, for the defence of their Lives, Rights and Liberties, and the recovery and restablishment of the true Protestant Religion.[12]

Campbell-town, like any Ulster plantation town, was now a nest of radical Presbyterianism.

During the eighteenth century it became a run-down sort of burgh, of which someone wrote:

> That life went on in such a place
> cast a shame on the human race.[13]

Its economic heyday, however, was the latter part of the nineteenth century, and its apogee was 1906, when three major hotels, a gentleman's club, a library and a splendid tenement block were completed. The town had become a sort of colony of Glasgow, reached by sleek pleasure boats that ran up, down and across the Firth of Clyde. Supporting this prosperity was the use of the loch by the collected fishing fleets of the west coast, the packing of their fish, the building of these fishing boats, whaling, and a great growth in distillation — whence comes, I suppose, a drinking song:

> Campbeltown Loch I wish you were whisky —
> I would drink you dry.

There were 34 registered distilleries; now there is but one.

This whisky was being downed in the gentleman's club, the three hotels and, more discreetly, in several expensive residences designed by H.E. Clifford. These buildings are characteristic of Glasgow's Art Nouveau in its sober moments and are part of that architectural school which I comment on later — the architecture of the Irish Sea.

Campbeltown's cinema has a good claim to be Scotland's oldest surviving picture house — a little and very early Art Deco building, dated 1913. There are a number of hotels that now depend largely on the passing herring fishers and yachtsmen, to whom the loch is an important anchorage. In the 1930s another hotel was built at Southend. This was large, splendid and modernist, looking out over Dunaverty and Antrim, but it came too late. No sooner had the doors opened but the war intervened. It became

Illustration 10. The gentleman's club, Campbeltown, designed by H.E. Clifford in 1906 — one of several sober but stylish buildings in the town, designed in its glory days between 1896 and 1906. Clifford (1852–1923) had an extensive practice in his younger days, working on many large commissions in Glasgow, of which Pollockshields Burgh Hall is the best known. In Campbeltown he also did a tenement building, some houses and Lochhead Distillery. The club, like most of his buildings, is in a deep red sandstone quarried in Ayrshire, easily brought in by boat.

a hospital facility for the Royal Navy, full of the burnt and frozen survivors of the north Atlantic; shortly after the war, in a time of austerity, it was abandoned. It remains a roofless oddity that stands beside another nineteenth-century ruin — a pile of quality masonry, now much reduced, whose origins are obscure to me.

However, the moment we leave Campbeltown we re-encounter the older strata of Scottish history.

To the north of the town, about seven miles away, lies the little Saddell Abbey, a ruin set among trees of great beauty. Here there are two memorials that commemorate the two aspects of Kintyre. One, a carved slab done in the Iona style, displays a Viking warship, the insignia of the lords of the Isles. The abbey was founded by Somerled, the great Scotto-Norse warlord. The other commemorates Colonel Donald Campbell, who died in 1698. His name is surrounded by a trophy of drum, pikes, swords, muskets and flags; mixed in with them are the arms of the men that he had defeated — the Gaelic long axes, pikes, arrows and bows.

***

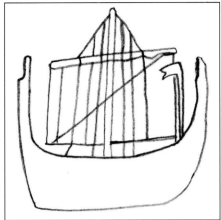

Left: Illustration 11. The triumphs of the Campbells over the Macdonalds are celebrated in death: a mausoleum at Saddell Abbey.
Right: Figure 2. Somerled was here: the longship glyph of the *re* Innse Gall, carved on a gravestone at Saddell Abbey.

I do not want to conclude this purview without visiting the most ancient layer of all. I mean the Picts. They left no writings, so we are hard put to ascertain just who or what they were or did. The Romans distinguished them from the Scotti and St Columba had to employ a translator when he was converting them, so I think we must conclude they were not Gaelic speakers. Irish sources refer to them as the Cruithin, who had been expelled from Antrim; they were excellent carvers of stone and builders of forts. Their sculptures are all associated with Christianity: large beefy crosses and deeply incised slabs that have a quality all their own. Though the iconography is usually recognisable, the treatment of figure and surface is distinct and, like the taste of coffee, almost indescribable without using lists of adjectives. But what are described as 'vitreous forts' were probably built by the Picts. One of them is found north of Campbeltown on the eastern shore.

The little island at the tip of Carradale Point is crowned with a fort whose remains consist of a grassy hollow enclosed by a wall made from a material rather like the glassy slag that used to be found on the sides of coal tips, or like the clinker that collects in the bottom of coke ovens. This is the glue that holds the boulders together and it seems to have comprised the core of a drystone rampart, the loose stones largely having been removed or thrown down.

The slag is immensely tough and creating it required kiln-like temperatures. What is remarkable, however, is the size of the molten body achieved. It is not hard to conceive of conditions in which clay, ash and various silica-based rocks could be fused together, and we know the old men of Kintyre worked metal, since they left traces of iron smelting along the beaches. It is not a large step, conceptually, to see how the tough slag left in the process might be reused, nor how correct packing of rocks, clay and resinous timber might be used in a flue-like arrangement to achieve a very hot flame. But the 'vitreous' forts of the later Iron Age remain to be wondered at. They, like the brochs to be found up and down the coasts as far as Orkney, are a very serious kind of building that speaks of a people of skill and pertinacity. The conclusion must be: never underestimate your ancestors.

Illustrations 12 and 13. Carradale Island fort and its wall. The glassy slag of the 'vitreous' fort can be seen. The core of the rampart, when exposed, is found to be made of fused rocks. The fort itself occupies most of a small island.

***

Part three: but who were they?

The picture is not clear or simple. It used to be thought that the arrival of settled agriculture in north-western Europe coincided with the arrival of a 'Celtic horde', speaking an Indo-European tongue, from central and eastern Europe. But the discovery of field patterns at Ceide in Mayo, which are certainly about 5,000 years old, puts this in doubt. Archaeological finds of recent years, now backed up by much more accurate dating techniques and verifiable genetic evidence (as opposed to racial and racialist assumptions) have effectively destroyed the older concept of successive waves of migration and of the movement of whole and cohesive 'peoples' to such a degree that the concept of Celticness appears to be undermined and discredited except in some restricted cases.[14]

It seems to this writer, finding his way through both the learned and the popular histories of these times and places, that the difficulties of interpretation arise from the assumption that an ancient culture, to be a culture, had to be unified by a shared language, a shared technology and shared agricultural methods. To have one was to have the others and thus in time to constitute a natural group, as a 'nation'. In order to make an archaeological science conceivable, such an idea was probably necessary, but can it survive the actuality? We are now, I think, more attuned to the untidiness of the actual than we were a few decades ago. Perhaps we were always more like we are today than we thought. A master-narrative of racial shifts and accompanying technical advances is too single and simple. The sites we are visiting were used for several thousand years — longer than all the rest of European history put together and then doubled — and we ought to tolerate some imprecision. Moreover, the racial categorisations of the past become vicious when imported into the present and amalgamated into national stories.

We can, however, give some answers to the general question, 'Who are our ancestors?' These answers can be categorised as genetic, linguistic and archaeological. Nor should we discount the legendary. However, these cannot amount to a coherent single story because they derive from different categories of evidence.

Genetic

At the time of writing there is a great deal of work being put into establishing the genetic origins of populations and, so far as I have been able to ascertain, all point in greater and lesser degrees towards genetic similarity and stability; the 'nations' and 'peoples' of the Islands are genetically essentially one and one only.[15] But this 'one' is the product of several admixtures, mostly prehistoric. At the risk of reducing a mass of complicated evidence of several kinds, itself already the product of previous reductions, I propose that we can usefully think as follows.

At the height of the last Ice Age, when most of the Islands were well buried in glaciers, the human population had fled and left very little behind. Most of northern Europe was a semi-polar desert, not unlike Baffin Island or Novaya Zemlya. Our ancestors took refuge well to the south, in what is now Spain, or in Italy and parts of the Balkans, and in the regions now covered by the Ukraine, north of the present Black Sea, then a large lake.

When the last great Ice Age began to retreat, northern Europe was repopulated from two of these shelters, Italy and the Balkans being largely cut off to the north by the frozen Alps and Carpathians. One large migration followed the Atlantic seacoasts (which were not, of course, quite where they are today). Others came by land across what is now Poland and the Baltic areas.

The first major thaw began around 17,000 years ago and this set in motion a large population of people. These were returnees — old Stone Agers, whose forebears had held the land many thousands of years before. The major group to enter what is now the Islands came from the Iberian shelter. Genetic analysis of human remains very strongly suggests that they came from the Basque region (indeed, to this day the particular genetic pattern that passed into north-western Europe can be found in 90 per cent of Basque males).

This 'Iberian' pattern designated as *Ri* contained several related sub-patterns that can be found in different broad locations. For example, the genetic sub-pattern known as *Rib-14* can be found principally in the western half of Ireland, while the *Rib-15c* pattern centres on Cornwall. *Rib-16*, however, largely moved up into the Netherlands and what was then the great north-European plain — now largely populated by herrings. Here, in time, they encountered migrants from the Ukrainian/Balkan refuge, designated *I*. To this day, these easterners can be traced along the east coast of England (though they reached Ireland and, curiously, Stephen Oppenheimer's map gives them a little enclave around what was to be the Pale.)[16] Other *Rib* groups crossed northern Europe and moved into Scandinavia and the Baltic area, encountering other people bearing the *I* gene flow. It is important to understand that the *R*, *I* and other gene flows are not actual persons, still less ethnic groups, but classes of genetic material which, handed on from family to family, both precede and outlive the individuals.

Around 13,500 years ago this burst of activity and movement ended as the ice stopped its retreat. We must assume some depopulation, as our ancestors developed a very slow-motion form of the Spanish holiday, but some hardier souls stayed on and were able to increase again when better weather came around and to receive reinforcements from the south.

There followed another long period of steady warming up, with greater inundations of the low-lying lands (11000–8000 BC). During this Mesolithic time, the population was augmented from the east, as settlers originating from the Ukrainian refuge (the Russian equivalent of the Spanish holiday, to this day) crossed the great plains and arrived in the English midlands, which were, of course, one with what we now call Germany and Poland. There was no simple way from Kiev to Coventry because the thawing of the Alpine and Carpathian glaciers turned the Don, Dnieper, Vistula, Danube, Oder and Rhine into immense torrents. When these torrents reached the sea they created delta zones of giant proportions across the Dogger Bank. Their banks were thick forest most of the way, full of bears and wolves. And of course we are dealing with small bands of nomads moving slowly forward year by year.

This second, eastern flow of genetic material was extensive but, it seems, never as large as that from the Iberian refuge, which recommenced around the same time. New arrivals of the *Ri* lineage ensured that a very large number of Islanders now carry the original Iberian gene pattern, no matter from where they came, because they united with those who had survived from the earlier immigration. Ultimately, this comprised 45 per cent of our traceable male lines, though looking in detail we find an east–west division of genetic sub-patterns. Oppenheimer remarks of the main south-western route that:

> The decision of whether to go north east, right up the Seine/Channel basin, and explore the 'European' side of Britain or just continue along the Atlantic facade marks the first step in a pattern of recurrent geographically determined relationships that still divides England genetically and culturally from the rest of the British Isles.[17]

It is important that we do not mix these distant genetic origins with anything we might wish to call Anglo-Saxon or Celtic today. Those are concepts that belong in a different logical category.

The Mesolithic population expansion (some writers call it a population explosion) was followed by another period in which relatively colder weather returned. This lasted another 2,000 years until the sudden warming of the Neolithic period brought sea levels up to something like today's. The genetic flow continued, with new Iberian *Ri* groups in northern Wales and parts of the south coast of England.

The *I* lineage, originating in the Ukraine area, was now prominent in Scandinavia and the low countries, with forerunners in East Anglia. These now became part of extensive migration from all parts of Scandinavia during the Bronze Age. They followed routes that are, not surprisingly, much the same as those followed recurrently by Vikings and others — one course down the east coast and another through the Hebrides and into the Irish Sea. In fact, there has been continuous gene flow from Scandinavia and the Baltic ever since the late Mesolithic period, generally to be traced in the eastern half of the Islands, but also coming into the Irish Sea by the 'private entry' to the north. From the perspective of Carnanmore we have to understand that the ancient men who built the cairn were part of a genetic domain that was already, significantly, Nordic. This Scandinavian element supposes what we already guess — the existence of maritime, even oceanic, skills among the early inhabitants of Norway, long preceding any Vikings.

There also appears a set of genetic markers that was hitherto exotic, probably from north Africa and the eastern Mediterranean. This group *E3b* is widely found in England and Wales, and especially in north Wales, where it seems to be associated topographically with the mining of copper. Associated with this is another group, *J2*, which follows a similar route but is not found in Ireland. Oppenheimer writes that the evidence 'suggests that there was a long trail of Neolithic gene flow into mainland Britain from the central and eastern Mediterranean via Spain, perhaps bypassing France'.[18]

He even envisages a 'Spanish colony' in north Wales that connected back to Galicia, another copper-rich district. Himilco the Carthaginian was presumably part of this trail, while Pytheas the Greek went on much the same quest, taking in France in order to bypass Carthaginian settlements in Spain and Portugal. We are entitled to imagine a long trade war between the controllers of the two different routes. The Roman destruction of Carthage (in 146 BC) was perhaps the very last stage in this rivalry.

What is striking is that the gene flows that entered the Islands in the Neolithic period (when the beach at Cushendun was a busy place) did not cross the Irish Sea in any large quantity. The increasing population in Ireland was mainly part of gene flows that had already arrived in Mesolithic times.

The general conclusion has to be, on the basis of DNA taken from people alive today, and tracing the results back in time by well-established methods, that the genetic mix of the population of the Islands is pretty much now as it was in 7500 BC. Accordingly, the idea that there were pre-Roman invasions, followed by more in the fifth or sixth century, Celtic, Anglo-Saxon or Nordic, bringing in different peoples in large numbers, is not tenable: they were already here. Moreover, it is better to think of the general movement of people in post-glacial northern Europe as being south to north rather than east to west.

But knowing that, what do we know?

For my part, approaching this topic with a mind formed by the study of design and architecture, I incline to the spread of practices rather than of peoples and, in historical timescales, practices change us. Older people learned new skills from newcomers who were, perhaps, few in number. How far did individuals travel and so bring back new thinking and new practices? To what degree did skilled craft-workers travel to barter their skills? And to what degree were skilled craft-workers considered as desirable booty, as slaves to be kept or traded on?

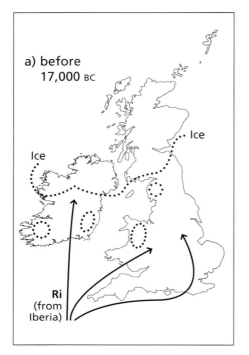

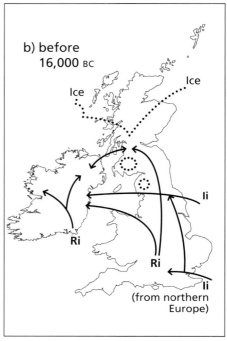

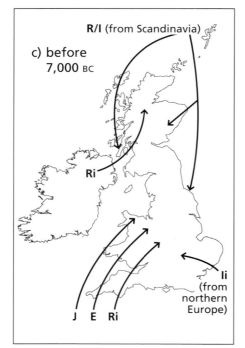

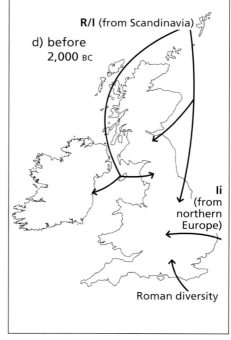

Figure 3. Four maps of gene flows (after Oppenheimer).

Linguistic

Much the same can be said of languages: they are easily acquired and spread and need imply nothing about the origins of the speakers. They follow trade as much as they follow peoples. Consider again the spread of English along trade routes and railways and the speed with which immigrants into Britain and the United States have acquired it. The speakers of English and 'the English' are entirely distinct categories.

So what language were our forebears speaking to each other as they laboured to build the cairn of Carnanmore? And does this define who they thought themselves to be?

The comparative method of studying languages, which can be worked backward to reconstruct languages now lost, is considered reliable provided we do not rest all explanation upon it. Two unrelated languages can still affect one another's development by being spoken side by side. (A good modern example of this is modern Hungarian, which is essentially one of the Finno-Ugric tongues of central Asia but, being surrounded by Slavic and Germanic languages, has acquired a very large vocabulary from them. The visitor skips through the language by leaping from one guessable word to another.) On this comparative basis two possible 'trees' have been devised to account for the two basic types of Celtic language being used in the Islands when we enter historical time (that is, with the Roman invasion of Britain). These

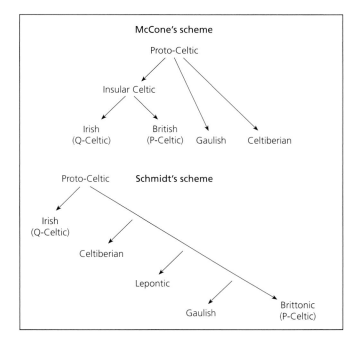

Figure 4. Figure of language derivation.[19]

basic types are usually designated as P-Celtic or Q-Celtic, referring to the use of the p sound which is elsewhere a q or k sound.

The most commonly used tree is that suggested by Kim McCone, which puts Gaelic (Q-Celtic or Goidelic) and Welsh (P-Celtic or British or Brittonic) close together, as divisions of a supposed 'insular Celtic', which is distinctly separated from Gaulish and the Celtiberian language of ancient Spain. Opposed to this is an alternative 'tree' argued by Karl Horst Schmidt, which places the two Celtics (P and Q) much further apart. Both assume the existence of a 'proto-Celtic' language but in the absence of concrete examples this may well be a logical requirement of this kind of theory rather than a feature of reality. We may feel that McCone's thesis is intuitively more obvious because it puts the two languages spatially closer together, as they are in geography, but these diagrams are about language derivation, not space. Neither has either of them anything to do with genetic derivation nor any specified historical dimension.[20]

One difficulty in both schemes is their mode of linear presentation, which suggests a clarity and directness missing in reality. A tonal presentation, in shades of grey, might be closer. The time dimension, without which these figures can't really be useful in historical accounts, demands a three-dimensional diagram. But these must lie outside the flat pages of a book. My poor understanding of these matters seeks a plastic conception of languages and their growth and mutual relations, such as we might use to model the way in which a chaotic interstellar cloud of gas and debris condenses into a solar system and finally establishes orderly relations between different fields and different objects. This does not require that there ever was a proto-Celtic that anyone actually spoke; in such a model proto-Celtic is the whole nebula out of which the several languages finally condensed. However, we ought to try.

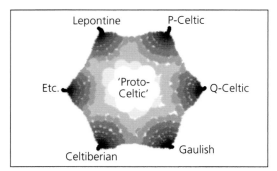

Figure 5. A tonal diagram of languages 'condensing'.

But even this diagram cannot avoid constructing spatial relations between languages that cannot help but imply forms of relationship that have nothing to do with the actual matter of the language.

Jackson and some other deep scholars of these difficult matters have designated what they call Pritennic, which is assumed to have stood in a similar relation to Pictish as Brittonic stood to Welsh and Goidelic to Gaelic. Most assume that this putative Pritennic was an Iron-Age language closer to P-Celtic than Q-Celtic. One can certainly point to similarities between Welsh and Pictish place names, and the Q-Celtic-speaking St Columba had to use an interpreter when preaching to a Pictish gathering; so perhaps the Picts were more P-Celtic than Q-Celtic. Older ideas that Pictish contained pre-Gaelic or even Basque elements have now been abandoned. What we also know (or seem to know) is that Q-Celtic-speaking Irish records treat the Picts as Cruithin, who were held to have been in Ireland before they — the Q-Celtic-speaking Gaels — drove them out. But this driving out is an obscure matter; it may mean not much more than that one language supervened upon another among the same group of people. If this is so, the builders of Carnanmore were people we would probably call Picts.[21] And we must never forget that what we are mainly dealing with is the language of record: the language of annals, and legends written down later, and the language of law. These are often substantially different from the general speech of a community, which may also comprise two or three parallel tongues, and languages of class and status. If we want to map them our model is closer to that of geological maps.

We are now approaching a way of estimating these pyramidal ancestors.

Genetically, they are the distant descendants of the distant inhabitants of the Iberian shelter-lands, who moved up slowly and in fits and starts along the Atlantic coastline, taking advantage of lower sea levels. They carry genetic material of, principally, an *Rib* kind. Those on the western shore are slightly more homogeneous because they received fewer new gene flows in the Neolithic period — from 6000 BC. There is, however, a definite Scandinavian-based inflow of *I* genes and some more exotic elements, just such as one would expect round a strategic strait (for example, contemporary Singapore).

Linguistically, the early Islanders were within that proto-Celtic nebula of speech-ways from which the modern Celtic languages condensed. We can call these Pictish, so long as we know how little that really means.

And where would we want to place Manx, or Cumbrian? To describe the Irish Sea as a zone of contention between different languages assumes that the tongues under discussion were all sufficiently distinct to merit their own names. In some cases, and on formal occasions, they might well be, but in the day-to-day interchanges of people about their business, perhaps not. I am reminded of days spent in Balkan villages, where the language you spoke was more or less defined by the way you were facing; or of parts of the higher valleys in the eastern Alps, where you might begin a sentence in Italian and pass through a sort of German, only to end in Romanche.

***

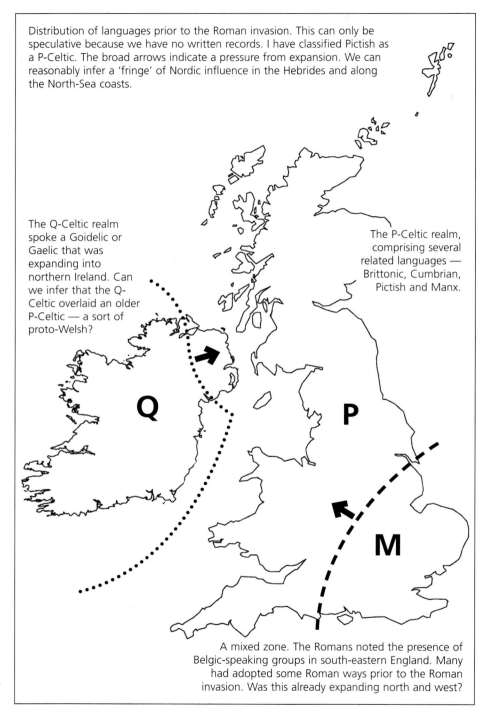

Distribution of languages prior to the Roman invasion. This can only be speculative because we have no written records. I have classified Pictish as a P-Celtic. The broad arrows indicate a pressure from expansion. We can reasonably infer a 'fringe' of Nordic influence in the Hebrides and along the North-Sea coasts.

The Q-Celtic realm spoke a Goidelic or Gaelic that was expanding into northern Ireland. Can we infer that the Q-Celtic overlaid an older P-Celtic — a sort of proto-Welsh?

The P-Celtic realm, comprising several related languages — Brittonic, Cumbrian, Pictish and Manx.

Q

P

M

A mixed zone. The Romans noted the presence of Belgic-speaking groups in south-eastern England. Many had adopted some Roman ways prior to the Roman invasion. Was this already expanding north and west?

Figure 6. Four language maps.

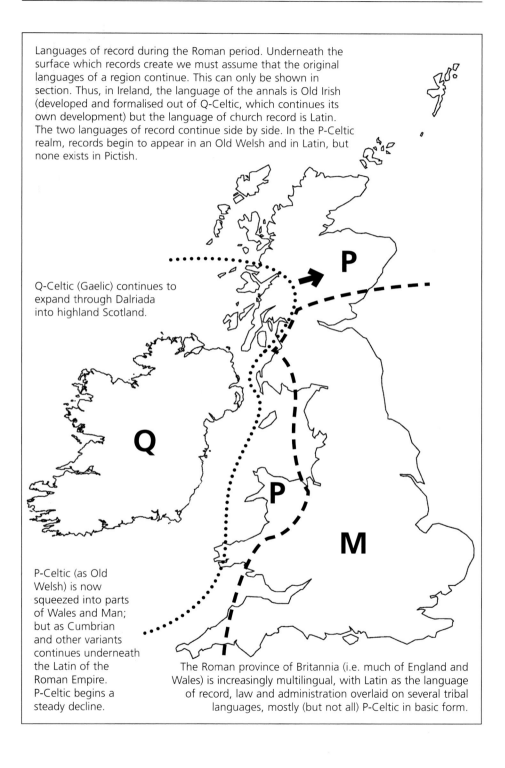

Languages of record during the Roman period. Underneath the surface which records create we must assume that the original languages of a region continue. This can only be shown in section. Thus, in Ireland, the language of the annals is Old Irish (developed and formalised out of Q-Celtic, which continues its own development) but the language of church record is Latin. The two languages of record continue side by side. In the P-Celtic realm, records begin to appear in an Old Welsh and in Latin, but none exists in Pictish.

Q-Celtic (Gaelic) continues to expand through Dalriada into highland Scotland.

P

Q

P

M

P-Celtic (as Old Welsh) is now squeezed into parts of Wales and Man; but as Cumbrian and other variants continues underneath the Latin of the Roman Empire. P-Celtic begins a steady decline.

The Roman province of Britannia (i.e. much of England and Wales) is increasingly multilingual, with Latin as the language of record, law and administration overlaid on several tribal languages, mostly (but not all) P-Celtic in basic form.

At the withdrawal of the Roman armies and administration, Britannia reverts to the tribal languages in the more remote areas, but the Germanic languages that always had a substantial foothold in the south-eastern parts begin to spread along the vectors of the Roman road system (perhaps as trade languages). Q-Celtic reaches its point of maximum expansion by becoming the language of record in most of Scotland and the Isle of Man. P-Celtic (as Pictish) is eclipsed, but as Old Welsh enjoys a revival and an heroic literature.

From 800 Norse becomes established in many parts and becomes the language of record in the Hebrides.

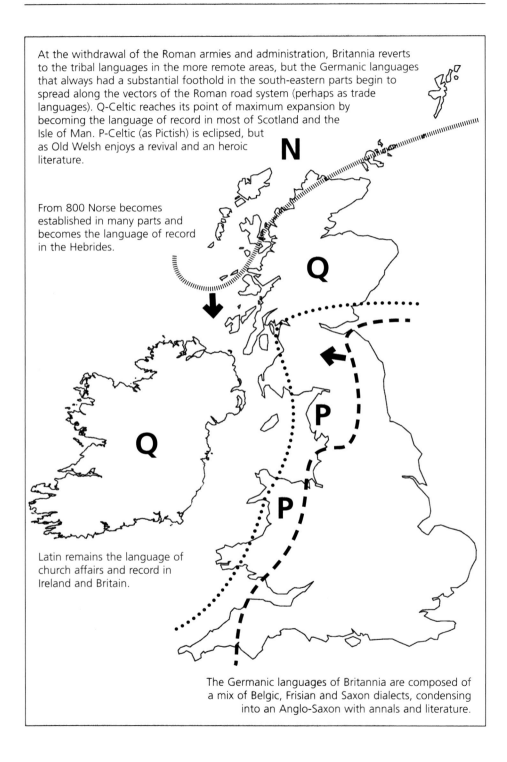

Latin remains the language of church affairs and record in Ireland and Britain.

The Germanic languages of Britannia are composed of a mix of Belgic, Frisian and Saxon dialects, condensing into an Anglo-Saxon with annals and literature.

During the twelfth century, Norman French (with Latin) becomes the language of administration and law for most of the Islands, though the second layer of daily speech remains largely as before. Gaelic and Anglo-Saxon, however, continue as languages of independent record (the *Anglo-Saxon Chronicle* (850–1150), the *Annals of Ulster* (431–1540), the *Annals of the Four Masters* (1632–1636)) and of literature. Anglo-Saxon transmutes into Middle English.

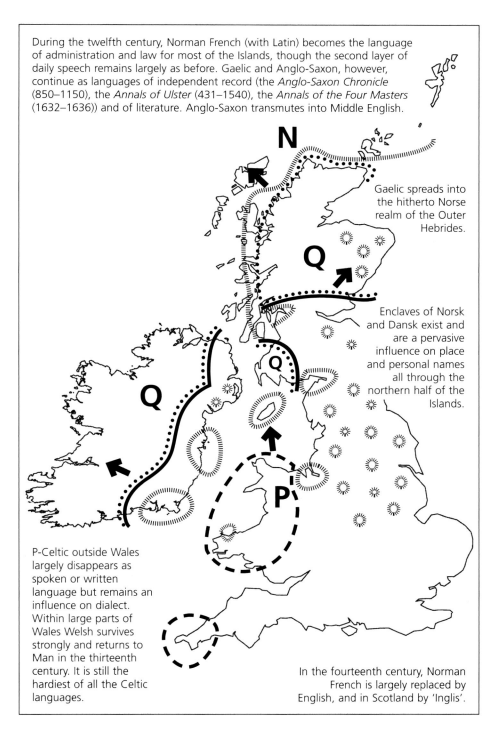

Gaelic spreads into the hitherto Norse realm of the Outer Hebrides.

Enclaves of Norsk and Dansk exist and are a pervasive influence on place and personal names all through the northern half of the Islands.

P-Celtic outside Wales largely disappears as spoken or written language but remains an influence on dialect. Within large parts of Wales Welsh survives strongly and returns to Man in the thirteenth century. It is still the hardiest of all the Celtic languages.

In the fourteenth century, Norman French is largely replaced by English, and in Scotland by 'Inglis'.

One of the matters thrown up by a genetic survey is the light it sheds, or fails to shed, on legendary material. This is frequently in contradiction.

Bronze-Age and Iron-Age rulers and record keepers thought of themselves as folk who, in the distant past, had been wanderers, colonisers and conquerors. To comprehend this we have to look at other kinds of material, the legendary and mythical. We will not expect to find objective fact in this material, but we will find explanatory structures and patterns. These are important because they are artefacts of the mindset by which our forebears sought to explain to themselves who they thought they were.

Around the tenth century AD this material came to be written down by monks, mainly in Ireland. Accordingly, the legendary stories have been appropriated into an Irish history. But it seems more reasonable to think of the originating stories as belonging to a general stock of legendary and mythical material common to all the inhabitants of the Irish-Sea coasts, no matter what language they were speaking or who they thought they were. How many layers, they would have asked themselves, lie beneath the present surface?

The ancient men, whose history was in the register of myth and with no clear sense of linear time, embedded into their storytelling a deep cyclical pattern of periodic flooding and displacement, which had, I surmise, some connection back to earlier, damper times when north-west Europe was being resettled by nomadic bands. John Carey, in an essay entitled 'Native elements in Irish pseudohistory', describes this as a 'framework of successive occupations' which took a definite form around the year 1050 in a text called the *Lebor Gabála Érenn* — the Book of Taking, or Invasions, of Ireland.[22]

The first inhabitants of Ireland, we are told in the *Lebor*, were a clan of many women and few men, led by a granddaughter of Noah (the monks were anxious to fit these legendary events into some kind of biblical chronology). After various misadventures they were carried away by the deluge they had hoped to escape.

The next occupations had an equally difficult time. While there had been but three lakes and nine rivers in all Éire, seven more lakes promptly burst out of the ground. (Knowing the Irish weather, this is highly likely.) Forests were cleared and some sort of order was brought to the primitive landscape in spite of these erupting waters. We may interpret this as what, in fact, the people did when they attempted to occupy post-glacial land. The instance here is Ireland, but the story is a kind of universal, as is its *dénouement*. A fearful gang of beings comes on the scene — the Fomoire, whose malevolence is without limit. These Fomorians are to the settled life of legendary Ireland what Grendel is to the Anglo-Saxon polity — the demonic 'other' with whom no peace is possible. Like Grendel, they are 'Cain's kindred'. As Carey puts it, 'An antagonism comes into being which did not exist before the land emerged from the waters, and existence defines itself increasingly in terms of oppositions and dualities.'[23]

Their name, according to some, suggests sea raiders or sea monsters (that is, they came from somewhere else). But more recent theories of 'otherness' have a political dimension. Any incursive regime demonises its repressed natives and this outermost corner of Europe had become — at least according to legend — a layer-cake of repressed natives. The imagery of Fomorian revenge is evidence of a kind in favour of that model. We shall have to return to the Fomoire from time to time, since they are part of the persecutory and paranoid fantasy of every ruling class. Every aristocracy must build its own barbarians.

After further struggles the human survivors return and, as the Fir Bolg, bring in agriculture. These men sound rather like the Belgae of real history. They also bring a rudimentary political order of provinces and kingship, only to have it snatched from them in turn by magical 'others' — the Tuatha de Danann. These were the people whom the Gaels had to defeat in order to possess the land in peace and it is at this point that we begin to enter pseudohistorical rather than mythical time. These Gaels first saw Ireland from the top of a high tower in Spain. Led by a supposed Mil, these forces stage a Milesian conquest which for the next thousand years was held to be the real story.[24]

We should, of course, be very chary indeed of supposing this to be some kind of folk memory of the Iberian shelter-land, but knowing of the connections in Neolithic times — that is, of the Clyde-Carlingford culture of Carnanmore and the Mull, of the trade in metals as well as in people — then the Milesian notion does not sound as fanciful as it did once. But the essential point is not the truth of the tale but its function. What was the *Lebor Gabála* for?

The monkish compilers of this legendary history were concerned to create a tale that would account for the diverse character of the population of Éire and the adjacent coasts while asserting its continuity and unity. The hitherto oral tradition was being 'fixed' into writing. It was part of the process by which inhabitants of the Islands came to think of themselves as having continuous and varying histories over an organised and articulated time. It did not have to be true to serve its purpose. Its existence demonstrates a degree of cultural common ground among the participants, though they lacked most forms of political commonality. It also creates the categories by which subsequent populations learn to understand who they are by inventing the terms that from then on determine the discourse.

One can see in this, even at a distance of a thousand years, an ideological project — the definition of a people. For this there has to be a sufficient number of people speaking the same language and in touch with one another to make the idea of a group with shared interests conceivable. There also has to be some kind of organising authority. In this case it was the church, in various forms, using in this case the common language of literary Gaelic. (In ecclesiastical matters, the language of record was generally, though not always, Latin.) In the tenth century these conditions came together enough to provide a number of foundation stories. The concept of Alba was clarified into Scotland when Kenneth MacAlpine successfully established a more or less unified kingdom around Perth in AD 1000, which in time came to be backed up by another legendary history (which somehow accommodates Scotland into ancient Scythia by way of Egypt). The Venerable Bede had been doing something of the same in Jarrow, overlooking the German Sea and trying to describe the history of what he could perceive as something he called 'Englelond'. What makes Bede's history different from the *Lebor Gabála*, however, is that it is no longer legendary. Some of his evidence can be checked by other sources. Bede is approaching history in its modern sense. However, Bede's account of the Anglecyn is later interrupted by other tales. Indeed, the uses to which the Arthurian legends and the supposedly Trojan origins of the 'British race' have been put make the *Lebor Gabála* seem like a model of plausibility.

We are here at the very earliest stage in the creation of defined peoples, if not nations, in which the people is first perceived as a figure on a ground. One can thus begin to think about its history, which we create as we enter it. The idea of a common history carries with it (and serves) the idea of an established legitimacy. Conquest divides the people into rulers and ruled; legitimacy unites. The annals, chronicles and king-lists that incorporate these legendary accounts legitimise a *status quo* and begin to establish states or proto-states.

With this goes the definition of languages. To what degree does this definition, which takes place largely within texts, form nations, which have boundaries? It seems we can begin to construct them retrospectively, though how they were experienced at the time is another matter altogether.

In the post-Roman centuries, when these histories were being compiled, large parts of southern Cymru were inhabited by Q-Celtic speakers. Mon (or Anglesey) was linguistically disputed territory. Galloway was partly Q-Celtic speaking; likewise the Inner Hebrides. And a large part of what is now England was a P-Celtic-speaking realm until the sixth century, although Oppenheimer and some other scholars argue that there was already a substantial Saxon presence along the east coast.[25] Within all realms we have to envisage several sub-languages and dialects and the degree of mutual comprehensibility is something we can hardly assess. It is very likely that the languages we know now condensed as unifying trade languages rather than beginning as indigenous tongues of definable populations. It would often, perhaps usually, be the case that rulers spoke one language and the ruled another. In England this was the case until the fourteenth century. The first king of England to conduct business in English was Edward I. In the west of Ireland two languages were spoken widely until the great famine of the 1840s; then Irish Gaelic went into decline. In Scotland, Gaelic went into steady decline from clearances and the movement of the population into industrial areas. In the eighteenth century, as part of the mapping of Ireland and Scotland by British-army surveyors, place names were extensively anglicised. Any map of zones we make is two dimensional, whereas the linguistic reality is three-dimensionally layered by status and function. Who is saying what to whom? Bearing that in mind it still seems worth including a few language maps from time to time. But the altering surface map of languages demands a simultaneous section through language use at any one site at any one moment, which reveals its layers, just as a mineshaft reveals the sections of the strata.

Place names provide one way of assessing this kind of sectional map. According to T.J. O'Rahilly, we can infer from place names in Ireland that there were four layers of Celtic speakers that relate approximately to the stages of the *Lebor Gabála*.[26] The Priteni are the earliest people, who became known to the Romans as Picti and to the later Irish annalists as Cruithin. These enter historical time as inhabitants mainly of what is now Scotland, but there are repeated allusions to them as having been expelled there from what is now Ulster. They are followed by the Fir Bolg, who may or may not be cognate with the Belgae. Julius Caesar describes them as a people of Germanic origin who were settled on both sides of the English Channel. If this is so, and the Fir Bolg are the same as the Belgae, then the ancient Celtic lands were at least partly Germanic. However, Roman accounts are probably no more or less accurate than are early European accounts of the inhabitants of the new world, which took little notice of the major differences which Sioux, Apache and Iroquois perceived among themselves.

A third of O'Rahilly's layers is provided by the Lagin arriving in Ireland and western Britain from what is now Brittany, being what Romans referred to as Gauls. Caesar, in his account of his wars in Gaul, describes their prowess as shipbuilders, and we may imagine them reaching Ireland, the Irish-Sea basin and the western fringes of Scotland directly by way of Biscay, without needing to pass through central Britain. One section of this people, known in Irish history as the Domhnain, were known to the Romans as the Dumnonii. They were inhabitants of what is now Devon and on place-name evidence it seems likely they got as far as Dumbarton. These groups, or at least their rulers, since we are not talking about large migrations, were P-Celtic speakers.

The fourth and most recent of these Celtic-speaking incomers was (according to O'Rahilly) what is termed Goidelic — that is, Gaels; they were Q-Celtic speakers. These may have been Gaulish peoples who came directly to Ireland and parts of Scotland from Gaul, perhaps as late as the time of the first Roman expeditions (that is, 50 BC). These may have been the people who displaced the Cruithin. But a very large hole is shot in this thesis by the genetic arguments that conclude that there was very little immigration into Ireland in the times supposed by O'Rahilly. As Oppenheimer puts it:

> It is becoming difficult to find archaeologists and historians who still accept the idea of a Celtic migration to Ireland. There is, in any case, no genetic evidence for an Iron Age

migration from my analysis ... the specific lines I have identified do not reach the Atlantic fringes of Britain, let alone Ireland.[27]

But there is no good or necessary reason for supposing that genetic maps fit or should even be expected to fit over linguistic maps, let alone technological maps. That would be to impose a theoretical order where none need exist.[28]

In addition, other authorities have found O'Rahilly's account unconvincing, notably Myles Dillon and Nora Chadwick in *The Celtic realms* (1967).[29] Still others argue that Q-Celtic was an older form of language than P-Celtic, which may indicate an Iberian origin for the later migration, thus supporting the otherwise discredited Milesian story.

Moreover, place-name evidence does not always fit with archaeological datings, which have now become very much more accurate than they were in O'Rahilly's day. Radio-carbon and dendrochronological evidence appear to contradict linguistic evidence about dates at several points; there seems no doubt that the population of the Irish-Sea coasts was, in fact, a great deal more culturally diverse than used to be thought. For example, the distribution of hill forts in Ireland bears slender relation to the finds of Celtic jewellery, yet both used to be thought of as typically 'Celtic'.[30] The widespread use of Celtic ornament through the Anglo-Saxon world is hard to account for in ethnic terms; within Ireland, finds of La Tène metalwork, usually regarded as the *fons et origo* of Celtic ornament, largely occur in the northern half of the island and not in the south. This is more easily understood if we regard the spread of style as independent of ethnic origin, as the product of trade and taste and fashion more than anything else.

Greater difficulty yet arises when we try to fit linguistic maps over technological and other maps and then try to deduce political consequences from the results. It cannot be otherwise, because the attempt to create historical accounts on ethnic lines involves mixing categories of evidence. Ethnicity is not a natural fact but a kind of aspiration or ideology. It is a process in which people try to define themselves against others by projecting backwards into an imaginary past.

The origins of peoples can never be a neutral matter. It is, as I have written elsewhere, 'a nexus around which concepts of race, nationality, history and culture continually circle'. This is especially the case with nineteenth-century notions of Celticness. It is also important in the story of the idea of Englishness, since this largely begins in the adoption of a supposed Germanic heritage. This particular racial (and racialist) myth has been usefully summarised by MacDougall.[31] But it begins with Bede's initial description of the arrival of Angles, Saxons and Jutes, based on a partisan account by Gildas (see Chapter 4). How these in turn map onto the spread of the English language is yet another difficult matter, to which I will have to return later.

It is important to try to get this matter straight, because on it much depends and around it much blood and ink are spilt. I return to what I have written before (slightly adjusted) because at present I don't think I can say it better.

> There is a family of languages that we call Celtic because peoples we call 'Celtic' speak them; even if the relation between the speakers of Celtic languages and the 'Celts' need be no closer than the relation that exists between the speakers of English and the 'English'. Likewise there exists a consistent body of art and craftwork that we all call 'Celtic art', even if, as developed through time, we have to keep qualifying it as 'La Tène', 'Hiberno-Saxon' or 'insular' and acknowledge Romano-British, Viking, Coptic and other sources. These classes are, separately, real and concrete phenomena produced by real and concrete persons and, in principle, questions about them separately are decidable because they are within the same logical categories; but how 'Celtic art' maps onto 'Celtic languages' and the peoples known as 'Celts' is a very obscure and messy affair indeed ... study of language, art and human geography under the heading 'Celtic' is fine so long as we don't assume a transcending and unifying identity between the three fields, because that assumption is part of the nineteenth-century identification of culture with a unity of language and race and nation.[32]

Much the same may be said of Anglo-Saxon and indeed any other supposed national grouping. What has happened is that the demand for simplicity has led us, and continues to lead us, into mistaking words for realities. By qualifying different phenomena (artefacts, genes, languages) with the same adjective (Celtic, Anglo-Saxon etc.) we endow them with spurious unity.

The men and women who ruled or came to occupy the domains of the Clyde-Carlingford culture and other stretches of the Irish-Sea coasts spoke, by 100 BC, a mixture of languages which to the north and west were generally Q-Celtic and to the east and south P-Celtic. One imagines an Irish-Sea *patois* or Celtic Creole of which Manx may be the relic. Into this was injected, at different times, the *argot* of the Roman army and the Latin of the church, and later Norse, Danish, Northumbrian and the Anglo-Saxon tongues. Northumbrian Anglian evolved towards Scots, as Mercian and other Anglian evolved towards Old English. Over this, in time, was spread a Norman French that became the language of government for most of the coastal lands from about AD 1100. The degree of mutual comprehension among speakers of these languages can only be speculated upon. For these reasons I propose to consider the banks of the Irish Sea in terms of plural language communities that have emerged over millennia and continue to exist and evolve. Their plurality is a matter of place but also of time and status. This complexity has by no means gone away and now underlies the universal use of modern English as the bedrock underlies the soil.

When we look at these ancient sites, and learn about them from the different kinds of findings they offer, we cannot fail to comprehend the Irish Sea as a zone of complex interchanges and trades — which the sleeper on Carnanmore has watched through millennia.

Notes

[1]   H.J. Mackinder (1902) *Britain and the British seas*, London: Heinemann.

[2]   B. Cunliffe (2001b) *The extraordinary voyage of Pytheas the Greek*, London: Penguin Books.

[3]   T. McErlean, R. McConkey, W. Forsythe *et al.* (2002) *Strangford Lough: an archaeological survey of the maritime cultural landscape*, Belfast: Blackstaff Press for the Environment and Heritage Centre, p. 45. A wonderful book.

[4]   F. Mitchell (1986) *The Shell guide to reading the Irish landscape*, Dublin: Country House.

[5]   The move inland may well have been required by a major climatic event 4,200 years ago, in which the extensive oyster beds in nearby Strangford Lough were destroyed. Just what it was or why this event took place is unknown, but it brought down the Mesopotamian kingdom of Sargon I, as well as a Chinese dynasty, and is dateable from evidence within the Greenland ice.

[6]   H.L. Movius (1942) *The Irish Stone Age: its chronology, development and relationships*, Cambridge: Cambridge University Press, p. 222.

[7]   Out of 22 stone axes that were geologically tested, seven were of Antrim provenance and five were from Cumbria. See R. Butter and D.C. Lyons (1999, 2nd ed.) *Kilmartin: Scotland's richest prehistoric landscape: an introduction and guide*, Lochgilphead: Kilmartin House Trust.

[8]   D. Brett (2005) *Rethinking decoration*, Cambridge: Cambridge University Press, p. 6 *et seq*.

[9]   D. Brown (1991) *Human universals*, New York: McGraw Hill.

[10]   J. Apel (2001) *Daggers, knowledge and power: the social aspects of flint-dagger technology in Scandinavia 2350–1500 cal. BC*, Uppsala: Uppsala University, p. 14.

[11]   As quoted in Kintyre Civic Society (2003) *The Campbeltown book*, Campbeltown: Kintyre Civic Society, a compendium of local history.

[12]   *Ibid.*

[13]   *Ibid.*

[14]   See especially S. James (1999) *The Atlantic Celts: ancient people or modern invention?* London: British Museum, for the summary of these arguments. See also M. Chapman (1991) *The Celts: the construction of a myth*, London: Macmillan, and D. Brett (1996) *The construction of heritage*, Cork: Cork University Press. The most thorough dismantling of this Celtic story, however, is J. Collis (2003) *The Celts: origins, myths, inventions*, Stroud: Tempus. See also S. Oppenheimer (2006) *The origins of the British: a genetic detective story*, London: Constable, Part 1. Oppenheimer summaries the problem as 'wrong myth, real people'.

[15]   And indeed, no sooner had I finished this paragraph than two books appeared which broadly confirm its hypothesis: B. Sykes (2006) *Blood of the isles: exploring the genetic roots of our tribal*

history, London: Bantam, and Oppenheimer, *op. cit.* What follows here is heavily dependent on Oppenheimer.

16   Oppenheimer, *op. cit.*

17   *Ibid.*, p. 154.

18   *Ibid.*

19   Adapted from *ibid.*, p. 77, Figure 2.4.

20   *Ibid.*, p. 206.

21   These matters are best approached by way of F.T. Wainwright (ed.) (1955) *The problem of the Picts*, Edinburgh: Nelson, and more recently M.J. Ball and J. Fife (1993) *The Celtic languages*, London: Routledge.

22   J. Carey (1995) 'Native elements in Irish pseudohistory' in D. Edel (ed.) *Cultural identity and cultural integration: Ireland and Europe in the early middle ages*, Dublin: Four Courts Press, p. 48.

23   *Ibid.*

24   There is a judicious and lively non-specialised account of these matters in S. O'Faolain (1947) *The Irish*, London: Pelican Books, Chapters 1 and 2.

25   See Oppenheimer, *op. cit.*, Chapter 7, and Chapter 4 of this book.

26   T.F. O'Rahilly (1946, repr. 1971) *Early Irish history and mythology*, Dublin: Dublin Institute for Advanced Studies.

27   Oppenheimer, *op. cit.*, p. 242.

28   English has become a world language, spoken by people without any 'genetic' connection to England.

29   M. Dillon and N.K. Chadwick (1972, 2nd ed.) *The Celtic realms*, London: Weidenfeld and Nicholson, pp. 5–6.

30   James, *op. cit.*, pp. 94–6, summarising the work of J.D. Hill in several articles and B. Raftery (1994) *Pagan Celtic Ireland: the enigma of the Irish Iron Age*, London: Thames and Hudson.

31   MacDougall, H.A. (1982) *Racial myth in English history: Trojans, Teutons and Anglo-Saxons*, Montreal: Harvest House.

32   Brett, *op. cit.*, p. 138.

THREE
Stone, bronze, stone, steel

North of Saddell Abbey the road undulates above the shore, with long views across the Kilbrannan Sound to Arran. The terrain is mainly reedy pastures and forestry. I write that it undulates, but what I remember was uphill, steady and prolonged, into a brisk northerly wind. Up the page of the map also, which gives the sense of going against the grain of the land. Down the page, down the hill. Down, while I am going up.

The sound is bleak and choppy, Arran streaked with cloud. Head to the wind. Vertical becomes horizontal. Switch to automatic pilot.

Who is it that I pursue? Clio, to whom I am enslaved? And beyond Clio, her mother, Memory. It is time to reconsider the Muses. It is also good to think of history as a form of the imagination, which, with music and her sisters, fills the dreaming mind as the cycle turns. It also feels right to consider any form of representative imagination as female, since we have to do here with those parts of the mind that have symbolic gender.

As a nervous and bereaved little boy I was surrounded by clever women who were always talking. There may well have been nine of them, with my mother and her sisters and their several female friends and relations who filled the house with their paraphernalia and noise, with their clothes, their moods. They always seemed to expect interest and attention, respect and enthusiasm; and learning. They were learned themselves, in a way. I had to be learned too, in a way. A little-Jesus-in-the-Temple sort of kid. Our family games always seem to have been quizzes.

Men were generally of grandfatherly age and visiting, in uniform.

Only now, of a grandfatherly age myself, do I seem to have become an adult male. When I got to school age this proved something of a problem: I recall a number of small girls whom I admired immensely but dared not approach. Has anything changed?

So it goes on. Press down, go forward. Lean into the wind.

***

On the Roman shore

I have no precise recollection of having seen the Roman sea fort near Allonby when I visited it as a child. Then it was no more than hummocks in a field. But I do recall the strategic vista that it offered across the firth and the recall is entangled in the memories of childish fantasy — of a time in which every man I knew of, with the exception of my grandfathers, was in uniform and the sight of the sentry on his watch was ubiquitous. I can scarcely think of that fort without that memory of a man in a greatcoat leaning against a palisade and looking into the night. The British-army greatcoat, being so thick and stiff, transforms a man into sculpture so that he loses particularity and becomes the Universal Watchman. Aeschylus got him spot on:

> I ask you, gods, relieve me at my watch
> A long year's living the life of a dog
> on the rooftree of the house of Atreus.
> I have watched the conclave of the stars
> storm-bringers, lamps of summer night
> the shiners nailed into the black.
> I know their rising and their setting.
> and now I am waiting for the flare
> that will carry the report from Troy.
> — Aeschylus, *The Oresteia* (my adaptation)

Illustration 1.
Crosscanonby Milefort near Allonby, Cumbria. The fort looks down on salt-pans dating from the eighteenth century.

In fact we know a good deal about the watchman and his way of life, since the site of the Crosscanonby Milefort was recently excavated and many very ordinary finds (of hearthstones, pots, utensils and the like) were made. It has even been designated (like the rest of the coast) a UNESCO World Heritage Site, and its contents have been published. None of this was excavated in 1944 and, though I recall having had the ditches pointed out to me and admiring the possibilities of the view, nothing more than green grass was then visible at our feet.

Now the fort has been excavated, tidied up and signposted. Wooden posts indicate a gate; there are finely dressed ashlars. There is a square perimeter of ditch. I now learn that this was a position of leftfield defence to prevent incursions from across the Solway aimed at outflanking the wall, part of a coastal defence line stretching as far south-west as Ravenglass (which the Romans called Glannoventa and used as a naval base).

What I do remember was a Hurricane flying no more than 50 feet above our heads down the full length of the shoreline. It was ochre-grey below, as I recall, and its very rivets were visible. I remember a streak of black oil and the smell of hot engine. We shrank into the grass and then turned around to see how it climbed over Allonby village (then as now a rather bleak line of houses beside the dunes) and turned northward in a rising parabola; then it dived again and roared over the muddy estuary waters at wave height, machine-gunning a target craft that could be seen on most clear mornings suffering the same fate, swerving over the waves surrounded by spray and showers of its own fragments. After high tide my little brother and I would find long belts of empty brass cartridges along the shore.

The numerous birds that strutted on the mud and sand in search of shellfish took no notice of these frightful incursions but continued to strut stiffly or, from time to time, to run and swoop. My aunt told me that these birds were oystercatchers; this seemed unlikely to me, since I did not think that oysters could run. The behaviour of the birds and that of their prey did not seem to match one another.

In those days nearly every wood in the north of England was filled with Nissen huts, bunkers and obscure shacks. Long lines of trucks would travel slowly up and down the land, apparently without purpose. Every piece of waste ground was being employed for something called 'training' and my brother and I were fortunate in that our immediate stretch of beach was unencumbered by concrete traps and wire entanglements. The Solway coast, ever since Roman times and into the present, has been laden with warlike preparations. Not far across from where we were staying, but inaccessible on its northern shore, was the little industrial village of Eastriggs, created in the First World War as a vast munitions factory almost wholly staffed and inhabited by 30,000 women making bombs and shells. The sexual adventures of these women remain as grandiose folk memory. This activity (and doubtless its popular reminiscence) was renewed in the Second World War and has never entirely vanished. Carlisle remains a garrison town and Spadeadam, in the moors beyond, was the site of Britain's experiments with rocketry.

Illustration 2. Edward Longshanks: his monument.

Even the brewery was run by Her Majesty. In 1944, the whole region was a camp.

The Solway is, with the possible exception of Salisbury Plain, the most militarised stretch of country in the Islands. As Hadrian's Wall declines towards the sea and slowly sinks into marshland it becomes a designated footpath and cycle-way. A short way below the village of Burgh-by-Sands (which was itself the Roman fort of Aballava), on the damp water-meadows, you can find a monument to Edward I, who died here in 1307 on his way to hammer the Scots. His body was laid out in Burgh Church, a heavily fortified old structure that seems to have been made out of parts of the Roman fort. All the villages along the latter end of the wall's track are built with nicely cut sandstone blocks. Beyond the monument, at the water's edge (visible in the photograph above, to the right) is a large concrete blockhouse and gun emplacement, whose likely function was to prevent commando raids on the vast ammunition stores that were made and kept around the village of Eastriggs and the northern (Scottish) bank of the river in both world wars. This monument to Edward, which was set up in 1803, replaced a much earlier one, built in 1685. This square mile contains notable militaria from AD 150 to 1300 to 1940.

Well before that it had been the site of camps and barracks from all centuries. In AD 100 it was also busy, with the road going north from Carlisle (Lugovalium) into Caledonia, and the wall to the east. Roads ran south towards Chester (Deva) and south-west to Ravenglass (Glannoventa) before heading off over the mountains to Hardknott (Mediobognum), Ambleside (Galava) and Lancaster (Lunium). Glannoventa was a considerable place to judge from its remains and from inscriptions that identify its purpose as a naval base from which a fleet patrolled the Irish Sea. This stretch of coast is, throughout, a heavily romanised district, though it was always a remote corner of the empire — a sort of north-west frontier.

Illustration 3. Ravenglass Bathhouse. The fort of Glannoventa lay in what is now dense woodland on the low hill above Ravenglass Station. Its only substantial remains are this bathhouse, which has somehow survived almost unquarried. Traces of a road can be found along the beach but incoming tides have washed away the westward wall of the fort. The substantial bay is now very shallow but may have been very much more useful in AD 150.

Illustration 4. The fort of Mediobognum in the Hardknott Pass is an altogether more solid remain, substantially restored with foundations for many stone buildings and a large stone perimeter wall. It stands on a magnificent site overlooking Eskdale and facing the Mare Hibernica.

Illustration 5. The heated bathhouse, Mediobognum. The fort is recorded as equipped for a cohort of 500 men (Dalmatian troops were on station at one time, with administrative and technical support).

* * *

My father, in his day, was also part of the vast enterprise called war and to hoard cartridges and other spent munitions was a way of knowing what he was about. I acquired quantities of empty cartridges of different calibre, bomb fragments and, above all (to be admired and envied by my schoolfellows), a complete German incendiary bomb, minus its flammable contents. This had little to do with my father directly, since he was guarding an airfield in Assam under much warmer circumstances, and this one had fallen, ineffectually, on the Leeds district of Meanwood.

It was to avoid objects like this that we had taken ourselves off to the windy banks of Solway, never expecting to live within the constant sound of heavy machine guns and aerial attack.

We two boys were not allowed to wander out towards the sea lest we encountered an unexploded device. My mother was preoccupied by all the munitions lying randomly about this coast. For my part, aged seven, the thought of a bomb was exciting, but the idea of quicksands, about which she also warned us, was truly terrible. The shores of the firth were composed of turf, shingle and, below the tideline, a mixture of white sand and a blackish rank mud that smelt very unpleasant. To drown in these sloughs would have been an unspeakably horrible fate, which I often imagined. It still returns to me in dreams.

The sea, in turn, gives up its dead in the form of abandoned phosphorous bombs which every now and again (more than 60 years later) float upward from their graves in the North Channel, where they were dumped after the war. They now provide the children of the Antrim coastal villages with dangerous amusement, and they have been known to burst into a slow and sodden flame.

It seems that every time we sought to exchange the night-time bedlam of the West Riding for rural peace, we found ourselves at the mercy of flying pieces of metal. The worst of these had been 'one of our own' — a stray ack-ack round that wasted an apple tree in a country garden a few feet from our door. Of this I only remember a shallow crater in the brown earth, filled with a rust-coloured water.

In the summer of 1943 my mother and a woman friend had obtained the key to a beach cottage just below Crosscanonby Fort. Nothing of it now remains but a cracked foundation of concrete in a tangle of brambles and gorse just above the high-tide mark. Striding with difficulty through the spines and spikes it took me several minutes to locate it. Behind this ruin and the coastal road a low hill rises — perhaps an ancient sand dune. When I saw it again I remembered the red earth and the steep tangled vegetation, and I remembered how abrupt it had seemed when I struggled to reach the crest all those years ago. The foreshore was also encumbered by a circular enclosure which, I now learn, is all that remains of an old salt-extraction industry that may have existed in Roman days. The imperial legions, like all troops, depended upon salt beef for their rations.

Then (I think it was in early May) there had been a view across to the Lakeland Hills that seemed to my young eyes enormous and very distant, and I can still recall with perfect exactness the view across the firth to the mirror image of those hills, the cone of Criffel in Galloway.

***

> Over the wall the north wind blows
> I've lice in my tunic and a cold in my nose.
> — W.H. Auden, 'Roman wall blues'

Whoever looked out from the fort in AD 300 was most probably a co-opted local man.

The recorded inhabitants of the immediate area of Allonby were the people known to the Roman army as the Carvetii, or 'stag people'. These were a clan or tribe living in the Eden Valley and its environs. They were sufficiently distinct to be given their own administrative unit, or *civitas*, but were essentially a branch of the Brigantes, who were a confederation of clans. That collective name, in P-Celtic, probably meant 'the hill people', and their main territory covered Cumbria, the Yorkshire Dales, most of Lancashire and parts of the Plain of York. As a confederacy the different parts of the Brigantes were widely spread; there were also Brigantes across the Mare Hibernica in

Leinster. There is strong evidence that the more prosperous regions of what is now West Yorkshire had regular contact with agricultural southern Britain and with the metalworkers of the Hallstatt and La Tène cultures of central Europe. The Carvetii, however, still seem to have lived an older style of life, as their name suggests, neglecting the crops in favour of stag-hunting.

According to Tacitus, who wrote the story, when the Romans first encountered them, the Brigantes were ruled by a high queen named Cartimandua. This lady, whom Tacitus described as having a 'noble lineage', saw advantage in welcoming Roman assistance and was made a client and pensioner of the imperial rule. We also know that she faced an uprising of clansmen led by her own consort, called by the Romans Venutius, and that she refused to support the later uprising of Boudicca. We also know that she divorced the irascible Venutius and married his armour-bearer, one Vellocatus. A tribal civil war ensued, with the Romans backing Cartimandua and, of course, profiting from the division. By AD 72, General Agricola reached the line of the wall. Before long the land north of Deva and Eboracum (York) was gridded with major and minor highways and studded with forts, large and small. Villas and farms followed.

Recent studies have concluded that the wall was, in effect, a much more complicated affair than it now appears. Hadrian's Wall, as we have it today, was the spine of a defensive zone spreading north and including several other lines and limits, as far north as Perth, built at several times.

Carlisle itself was always a place of significance, being in the armpit of the land below Strathclyde. There was a defended Iron-Age settlement of some kind here when the Romans arrived, whose name is supposed to have been the *caer* or fort of Lywelydd. To this the Romans gave the name Lugovalium. It stood on the low rocky bluff above the river where the castle now stands. This in time became Caerluel, thence Carliel and finally Carlisle. Agricola, when he arrived with his men, chose as his camp a site on the banks of the river, presumably to secure the crossing place, where his men constructed a bridge. What came into being was a military cantonment and supply depot around which the town of Carlisle began, as a native marketplace and shanty-town that grew up in the lee of the wall. One imagines a rowdy, ramshackle gathering of saloons and general stores, a muddy field set aside for a cattle market with booths and brothels — a sort of northern Tombstone. The wall began as a ditch-and-rampart earthwork and was rebuilt in stone only after AD 122. It extended some way along the southern side of Eden Estuary below Carlisle.

This was land that was waterlogged and liable to floods and high tides, with many lagoons and swamps. Today it has been tidied up and dykes have been built to contain the waters, but it was still an obstacle to armies into late-medieval times. The estuary also lacked navigable channels. The quayside at Port Carlisle is a product of the railway and canal system, being the last seaward point to which an embankment could be built, but it is also close to the last few stones of the wall. Here, at Bowness (which seems to be built almost wholly from stones of the same size as those used in the wall), the Romans had some kind of port or naval supply depot and a substantial fort called Maia; and only a short distance from here, further down the coast, the inlet of Skinburness was an important supply point for the armies of Edward I as he hammered the Scots. Carlisle, which was intermittently besieged by Scottish armies during the Wars of Independence, survived uncaptured because the garrison could always be supplied by sea. At Bowness there was also a railway viaduct intended to carry the line over into Annan in Scotland, but it was damaged by a build-up of ice in 1875 and never fully recovered.

* * *

Our sentry was probably a member of a force assigned to coastguard duties. Piracy and raiding were habitual and continuous up and down the coasts. The imperial command extended to two fleets, one (the Classis Britannica) for the channel, and another (of which almost nothing is known) that was based on the Severn Estuary and patrolled the Irish Sea. Both of these required servicing and helped to create industries and disseminate skills. There was also a system of watchtowers, beacons and coastal defences, the largest trace of which is the site of a tower on Holyhead Mountain and the fort beside Holyhead Harbour.

Illustration 6. The fort beside Holyhead Harbour, which in time became Caer Gybi, is still in good condition, but how much of the walls are truly Roman remains uncertain. It consists of a rectangular enclosure of rough stone, around 15 feet high, with corner towers. In Roman days it was beside the anchorage and therefore an important calling point for trading vessels and for the Roman *classis*. It now contains two churches, both old, one of them dating from the ninth century. Gybi was a protégé of St David and from his monastic settlement (see Chapter 4).

We should not underestimate the speed and efficiency of watchtowers for fire and semaphore-like signalling. In the nineteenth century a connection was established between Holyhead and Liverpool such that a message could be passed within minutes (in good weather), using a simple code, from one station to another along the north-Welsh coast, to Hilbre Island off the Wirral and thence to Wallasey. We may assume that the Romans could do much the same, from much the same succession of cliff and hilltops, and we may imagine (without evidence) a chain of beacons that stretched from Holyhead to the wall, by way of the north-Wales coast and Ravenglass, taking in Crosscanonby Milefort (which was integrated into the wall's own signal system) that would reach the North Sea.

* * *

To include the Romans in this book I have to treat them not as a people but as a form of civil life. The Romans of the empire, and especially of the later empire, were not an ethnic group: they were a new form of political affiliation, a citizenship that was given as a reward, and a status to which one might aspire or which one might resist. Romans, and of course Roman soldiers, came from a very many places and races. The number of Latin-speaking and Latin-born Romans in Britain was very few, but a great number of Britons became Roman citizens or, in Tacitus's terms, friends of Rome. He wrote of these people that 'the toga was often to be seen among them'.[1]

The army was multicultural in the extreme; it was a matter of policy to move soldiers far from their home countries. Among the legionaries along the wall we can find soldiers from all over Europe and even further afield. At Corbridge there is a tombstone to one Barates from Palmyra and his British wife, while in a graveyard at York were found skeletons of unmistakably African character beside the remains of their local womenfolk. At least one detachment on the Solway coast came from northern Gaul; others came from the Adriatic. How many of these buried legionaries found their way here along the army roads from west Africa, Tripoli and the Lebanon? And what of the Sarmatic cavalrymen who served in the very last years of the empire? For these reasons we should think not of the Romans but of the civil condition of 'romanitas'.

And if they were multicultural they were also multilingual. Each legion and each century (a hundred men), being composed of ethnically similar conscripts or mercenaries, had its own internal speech. What held them together for command purposes was the army's own version of Latin. As Norman Fairclough comments:

> A language has been jokingly referred to as 'a dialect with an army and a navy', but this is a joke with a serious undercurrent. Modern armies and navies are a feature of the 'nation state' and so too is the linguistic unification or standardisation of large politically defined territories which make talk of 'English' or 'German' meaningful.[2]

Indeed, as John Creighton observes when dealing with this epoch, 'the first important point is to get away from the concept of clearly defined languages'.[3]

Whatever was being spoken by the indigenous Carvetii under the heading of Brittonic or P-Celtic, we can be confident it was not one simple monoglossic phenomenon. We have to assume a huge variation from region to region and probably from social status to social status. The idea of 'standard' languages is an unintended consequence of print culture — of, finally, typesetters, whose conventions we have all had to follow. (William Caxton was, in point of fact, the first person to notice this problem.) Were we to walk through Britannia at this period we would find the language changing every few miles in greater or lesser degree, according to whom we were speaking and about what. These conditions are common today in India and, indeed, in the country districts of the Balkans. A Macedonian friend reckoned she could walk to Danzig without changing her speech and still be able to make herself understood, provided she stayed close to the demotic of wherever she happened to be. The importance of Latin to the army was functional — it gave them a single, unified language of command *that nobody else had*.

Full participation in *romanitas*, however, required deep changes in the character of individuals and peoples involved. The military/industrial habits of accuracy, conformity and efficiency were rewarded and reinforced. The notions of clan and kindred (on which a tribal society, by definition, depends) were consequently weakened. Though evidence of this kind is very hard to find or identify, the transformation would also appear in such concrete but almost unmentioned matters as personal hygiene and body language, just as it does to this day in comparable circumstances. It may be useful to think of the transformation involved as being from the tribe to the instrumental collective. By this latter term I mean an organisation with specific purposes to which everything else is, finally, subordinated.

In the army (and of all collectives, the army is perhaps the most instrumental) the basic tribal/familial loyalties were replaced by the family of the legion. Individual soldiers were integrated into a hierarchy of units; these units were permanent and had a history and a title (the fourteenth legion, for example, was given the title Martia Victrix in honour of its success against the revolt of the Iceni). The individual was thus part of a supra-individual body, loyal principally to itself and its name. The legion was supported by a permanent commissariat and a semi-industrial supply chain that worked at all times of the year; this in turn was supported by an effective tax and contribution system exacted from the inhabitants by a civil service. Legions had their own farmlands and ranches, which set standards of systematic husbandry and storage to the less capable native peoples. The citizens themselves, in a new province like Britannia, were frequently retired soldiers who had been granted lands, no matter where they came from; or they were co-opted local magnates and their dependents whose fortunes were now bound up in those of the army and the administration. This is how long-lasting empires gain, spread and maintain their power. The imperial system also perpetuates itself by providing institutions and ways of action that continue after the formal empire is withdrawn. The last cases of this system were the post-Cromwellian settlements of Ireland, which took root to such an extent that the Stuart kings did not dare reverse them.

This concatenation of institutions and practices was stitched together by two further features, almost unknown to the P-Celtic-speaking Britons of the north-western half of Britannia — written communications and coinage. Both information and wealth were generalised and made abstract, uniform and fluid.

A certain impersonality of mind and action flowed from adherence to these abstracted and supra-individual loyalties. The further abstraction of value from goods into cash is comparable. These are matters enmeshed in urban life and trade; none of them sits well with kin-based tribal society based on barter, which had now become, from the urban, imperial perspective, peripheral. Between those lands touched by Roman ways and those that lay beyond the Limes Romanus (the limits of the empire) we imagine a gulf of mutual incomprehension opening up. The people who inhabited the rest of the Islands and had never stopped speaking their P- and Q-Celtics, nor encountered a bureaucrat, had a rich social life of their own and a powerful and self-sustaining sense of who they were, but the way in which they articulated the world was incompatible with Roman measurement, written texts and records and the Roman concept of land ownership, which was individual and familial. In the Gaelic/British world, land was not owned individually but was the collective patrimony of the clan as a whole, the *tuath* or *tud*. There were several ways of holding land available to a Roman but they did not include the collective.

There were, of course, rebellions against imposed *romanitas* and incursions by displaced or irreconcilable clansmen. But despite their furious energy, few of the rebellions came to anything. Tacitus, as usual, sums the matter up:

> the barbarians, happiest when looting and unenthusiastic about real effort, bypassed the forts and garrisons, and headed for the places where they knew the largest amounts of undefended booty lay. Something like 70,000 Roman citizens and other friends of Rome died in the places mentioned. The Britons took no prisoners, sold no captives as slaves, and went in for none of the usual trading of war. They wasted no time in getting down to the bloody business of hanging, burning, and crucifying.[4]

This was the Iceni led by Boudicca. But when they met up with the Roman main army, which had stayed aloof while the clansmen went on their rampage, the result was total defeat by a force perhaps one eighth their size. This set the military pattern from then on, through the Norman occupation of Leinster to Culloden, with few exceptions. What the Romans possessed was permanent organisation in depth.

Tacitus's term 'barbarians' is descriptive rather than pejorative: the barbarians were those without *romanitas*. They were the people who could not make real (i.e. sustained and purposive) efforts; they demanded instant gratification. They could not understand how war might be an extension of 'usual trading'. Organisation in depth requires regularity, efficiency and conformity. Several Roman histories, including Tacitus's own book, evince admiration for the barbarian virtues of courage and independence rather in the way that European writers have admired and romanticised the 'Orient' or native Americans. But this relationship, which Edward Said has described as an 'a discourse that is … produced and exists in an uneven exchange with various kinds of power'[5] is really more about Roman culture than it is about 'barbarians'. This is a relationship observable in every imperial/colonial situation, current or defunct (and not least in that between Britain and Ireland).

A sentry on the wall or among the Solway dunes or looking out from the headlands of Wales was a component of an organisation, not a tribe nor a clan. He had behind him a network of roads, camps, forts and supply dumps. He had signal towers, despatches and reports. And he was paid in cash. His was a new kind of social existence.

***

Governor Agricola used his coastal forces to good effect in the invasion of Strathclyde. The whole campaign, which came to fruition in AD 84 when the Caledonii were brought to heel in the far north-east, was a series of combined operations described by Tacitus:

> Agricola was the first to make the fleet a factor in his resources and it made a fine display as it followed his advance. The war was pushed by sea and land simultaneously, and often infantry, cavalry and marines shared their rations in a joint celebration … The Britons, as was learned from prisoners, were amazed at the presence of the fleet: it seemed as though the secret places of their seas were being laid bare, and the last asylum barred against the vanquished.[6]

The general, as a young legionary commander in charge of the twentieth legion, had also been in charge of the Irish-Sea fleet and well understood the conduct of combined operations. Agricola probably crossed from Maryport and Ravenglass into Galloway and proceeded up the coast supported by his fleet. By this means he avoided the shallow bays and estuaries around Dumfries which, cutting far into the land, provided awkward obstacles to armies, then and since. The soldiers were set ashore, one imagines, directly near Stranraer — probably on the sands of Luce Bay, which is still in use as a military training ground. They and the fleet could then command the North Channel from a fine harbour at Loch Ryan. From there they could pass directly to Kintyre and continue up and around the coast of Scotland from promontory to peninsula without undertaking a prolonged land campaign. This was the method of advance employed by Agricola's former superior, Paullinus, against the Ordovices and others, when the aim was to conquer centres of resistance in Mon. It has been followed ever since by commanders advancing along a broken coastline (compare the Allied advance up the peninsula of Italy in 1944 and the landings during the Korean War). But the campaign as a whole was partly inspired by Agricola's curiosity about Ireland.

Roman interest in Hibernia was mainly geographical: they had the idea that it came close to Spain and was somehow squeezed into the Bay of Biscay. The governor formed the impression that Hibernia could have been conquered by a mere legion with some local back-up forces and that this would have strategic advantage because the whole of the north-western world would then be included in the empire. His view, as reported by Tacitus, was that 'Ireland, lying between Britain and Spain and easily accessible from the Gallic Sea, might serve as a very valuable link between the provinces'.[7] But to Agricola's (or Tacitus's) chagrin, the emperor declined to commit troops and ships to any invasion plan.

However, from the perspective of this project, it was a very significant decision. It split the populations of the Islands into those directly acquainted with the Roman state and those to whom Roman civility was something that took place elsewhere. Hereabouts lie the origins of the prolonged differences between those who knew *romanitas* at first hand and those who became part of what was once called the Celtic Fringe.[8] But the matter on the ground was never simple. Interchange could not be avoided because all inhabited the same space, the space of the sea-ways. The inhabitants of the east coast of Ireland were closer to those across the water than they were to those a day's ride inland. Moreover, there were large settlements of Q-Celtic-speaking Gaels in both north and south Wales and all were part of existing trade relations that predated Roman times.

The Isle of Man was visited by Roman patrols, who called it Monapia. The island was not occupied, though an inscription was left, along with a number of coins and similar items. Perhaps there was a trading post along the lines of those developed by the Hudson Bay Company for Arctic Canada. Military expeditions beyond the Tay took Roman know-how and goods as far as Inverness.

Whether or not there were Roman incursions into Ireland is not securely known and is a subject for controversy among scholars. However, patrols and reconnaissance were a standard part of military prudence, then and now. I think we should assume that the Romans kept a close eye on men and matters across the Irish Sea and that to do this they must have maintained some sort of presence.

A number of Roman-style artefacts have been discovered on Lambay Island, just north of Dublin, which is exactly the sort of location in which such a watching presence might have been maintained.

***

In the first year of the northward campaign Agricola contented himself with erecting a wall between the Clyde and the Forth. This wall was composed of a deep ditch and a high embankment with a fort every two miles, as well as watchtowers and interconnecting roads. It protected the fertile lands south of the Clyde and the lands of Lothian. In tactical terms it was more formidable a construction than the southern wall but was too easily outflanked by sea at either end. It was eventually given up around AD 367 when the legions retreated southward to where Hadrian's wall had already been reinforced. There was also a line of forts and outposts around Perth and Montrose, giving a defensive zone rather than a Maginot-line form of defence.

According to Tacitus, Agricola had a policy of 'romanising' the barbarians of the northern parts:

> by these means many states which up to that time had been independent were induced to give hostages and abandon their hostility … Moreover, he began to train the sons of the chieftains in a liberal education, and to give a preference to the native talents of the Briton … As a result, the nation which used to reject the Latin language began to aspire to rhetoric … the toga came into fashion, and little by little the Britons went astray into alluring vices: to the promenade, the bath, the well-appointed dinner. The simple natives gave the name of 'culture' to this factor of their slavery.[9]

Had Tacitus consulted the watchman on the walls he might well have been less smug. There was a series of raids and incursions around the ends of the northern wall and at least one short Brigantean revolt. In the fourth century these wars gained in scope and success and began to offer a serious challenge to Roman control. The imperial authority in Rome concluded that further extension north and west was not in the empire's best interest. The southern wall was reinforced and built in stone as being a more defensible frontier (from AD 120). These decisions all manifest a recognition that the empire had reached its limits.

The land between the two walls, Altclut or Strathclyde, was a difficult and insecure place to live in but it became a nursery of great churchmen and warlords, of whom St Patrick and St Ninian are the best known today. The fame of the warlords is now known only to those who have worked their way into Welsh medieval romance and the obscure annals of the time, but for two centuries after the withdrawal of Roman rule the kingdoms of Rheged and Altclut (Strathclyde) maintained themselves against everyone else.

* * *

Our sentry, cold and sniffling, has to be treated as a new kind of social being. Without projecting onto him our own complex and onion-layered identities I think we can be sure that he had divided loyalties and a plural sense of being, for which the term 'Romano-British' is a deal too simple. On the British side of the hyphen we have to nest a series of qualifications one within another. His particular way of being Romano-British included being Brigantean and Carvetiish at the same time. When he looked over the water to the dusky forests of Galloway, was he looking at people he recognised as his own or thought of as alien? And what about those others further west, only seen on the clearest of days, but who were only too likely to arrive with unheralded violence? Meanwhile, his *romanitas* was equally diffused or multicentric and consisted first in his adherence to orders and to what Shakespeare calls 'the disciplines of the wars'.[10] The legion was his second home and its good order had to be internalised as an inner discipline or be lost, catastrophically. This meant (and of course I am writing a kind of fiction now) that an authority structure culminating in the distant emperor had to be maintained both internally and externally. It is also important to understand that the Roman army had, by the third century, developed not only its own distinct form of Latin, but also its own Mithraic religion. It was of itself a kind of ethnicity of which our man was a member.[11]

There were matters of the formal culture, particularly as it appears in imagery and architecture, and how this relates the character and location of authority, which I discuss below.

There was also our man's material interest to consider: he was incomparably better off under Roman rule. No longer at the whim of the nearest tribal thug, he might well have been planning ahead, imagining a smallholding on land granted to him by the

Illustration 7. The excavated camp at Segontium just outside Caernarfon is as neatly presented as a parade ground.

commander of his commander. This is to say that his *romanitas* was maintained by the tension between interest and authority. Neither could afford to be weakened lest the whole fly apart. This was a typical colonial situation of willed dependence and divided loyalty.

The mere existence of Roman organisation and its colonial culture along the bounds of the Irish Sea permanently modified everything else along the coasts and its disappearance could not be a simple return to the *status quo ante*. Moreover, our sentry and his fellow coastguards could also be found all along the shores south of Lancaster, which was a notable base, past the fort at Ribchester and through south Lancashire as far as Chester — the great legionary fortress. They were found, too, along the banks of Wales. Southern Wales was, like all the more fertile parts of Britannia, co-opted into the Roman system. There were substantial villas in Glamorgan and Carmarthen was evidently a small town. Central Wales was largely neglected. Further west, as already observed, Holyhead was a naval base of some description with a large stone fort and watchtower, and Segontium, just south of Caernarfon, was an important settlement of which a fully excavated fort remains.

But from a point of view based upon the Irish Sea as a whole, the most interesting aspect of these remoter Welsh outposts — and Segontium was more remote than the wall — is that they were the point of contact between Roman, Romano-British and Q-Celtic settlers and traders from Hibernia. Pembrokeshire, a well-established Irish zone, was, with Anglesey, a locus of interaction. One recent scholar, writing in the journal *Emania*, argues:

> That many aspects of culture were transferred to Ireland from a Romano-British milieu is not in doubt; what is not clear is when and by what mechanism such transfer took place … Dyfed, though extensively Romanised, was also sufficiently close to the Irish culture to allow easy transfer from one to the other.[12]

This in turn has led to a scholarly debate, and a journalistic spree, on the subject of Roman invasions or expeditions into Ireland. Was it possible, some have asked, that Drumanagh Fort on the headland south of the Boyne was actually a Roman military post?

Secure answers are not forthcoming because no proper excavation has taken place because of legal disputes. In addition, the whole matter was diverted by the press into a ridiculous ramp, because, coming as it did when the approach to the Northern Irish peace process was beginning to gather weight, it seemed to be questioning the myth of Irish Celtic specialness on which much nationalist rhetoric depends.

This section of Ireland's east coast, known as the Skerries, is just the place one would expect the Romans to have visited, but direct evidence is lacking.

Barry Raftery, the leading man in these tricky matters, has written that 'Nobody doubts that there were strong Roman influences in Ireland in the early Christian period.

Illustrations 8 and 9. The headland of Drumanagh, beside the sheltered harbour at Loughshinny, is surrounded by the characteristic cliffs of the area; its top is dead level, but contains a long earthen rampart and ditch as well as a Martello tower built to resist Napoleon. The tower looks over towards Lambay Island which contains, in addition to a Neolithic source of porphyry axes and a house designed by Edwin Lutyens, the site of burials in a Romano-British style.

The only point for debate is how these influences should best be explained.'[13]

One possible explanation, put forward by R.B. Warner in a spirit of speculation, is that the Drumanagh site is associated with putative Roman support for an armed incursion by one Tuathal Techtmar, who figures in annals and king-lists as an exiled prince who enlisted Roman arms for his victorious return to native lands in eastern Ireland. Agricola is known to have kept such a figure in his entourage and he is mentioned by Tacitus. Such a stratagem is characteristic of the entire manner in which Roman armies first landed in and then enlarged their hold on Britannia. Warner goes on to speculate that here we may have an example of a hitherto unknown Roman expedition. Possible Roman finds in Ireland do in fact coincide with historical locations to which Tuathal Techtmar can be linked, though to claim more would be 'no more than the merest hypothesis'.[14] To me the idea of a *temporary* Roman outpost on the east coast of Ireland seems wholly likely, and the notion of the 'returning exile' is a typical device of interventionists; it was on the pretext of settling a local dispute that the Romans came to the Islands in the first place.

However, there was regular trade between Ireland and the estuary of Deva. Chester developed into a large military base and administrative centre, with an arena (now being excavated), walls and port facilities. There has been speculation that had Vespasian or Agricola chosen to expand the province of Britannia, Chester might have become a capital city for a combined province of all the Islands, and Drumanagh lies directly on the nearest route from the legionary headquarters into central Ireland. In reply to the obvious question why such an invasion never made its way onto the pages of the annals Warner points out, perfectly sensibly, that it would not have done if it had been unsuccessful. The imperial powers did not want to hear about failures and tended to punish them severely. In British popular history we learn very little about the Afghan Wars and such ludicrous debacles as the battle of New Orleans. Why should Tiber care anything for Liffey? Perhaps any failed intervention was better forgotten than recorded.

But we hardly need to base an account of Roman influences in Ireland upon such vapours. It was the mere existence of so organised an *imperium* upon its banks that spread cultural and other influence across the Irish-Sea area. There was no need for expeditions to bring this about. There are many ways of describing cultural transference but three main topics are obvious and irresistible.

***

The most obvious is religion. It was through the Roman empire that Christian belief reached the Islands and through post-Roman missionaries that it spread; Latin was the learned language of this church and of most of the annals and records in the centuries that followed.

The degree to which, when the Roman legions and administrators left, the Islands stayed Christian remains debatable; there was certainly an organised church in Roman Britain — three bishops represented it at a doctrinal conference at Arles in AD 314. Many Romanised Britons were at the same time Christians. There were certainly centres, buildings, burial plots and shrines. And beyond the Roman domains, in Pictland and in Hibernia, there were Christians of some description; they were at least sufficiently well known to be noted by ancient Tertullian and Origen.[15] The Romanised inhabitants of Dyfed and Anglesey are likely (one can say no more than that) to have played some part in taking Christian belief into Ireland. But after the withdrawal of Roman forces from around 410 intercommunal raiding and a swarm of pirates, Irish, Pictish and Saxon, beset the land so that organised Christian life in many parts of formerly Roman Britain very nearly came to an end and classical learning with it. But not quite. To survive, Christian institutions had to conform to the political norms of the new pagan kingdoms. Whatever may have been the condition of the Christian Church during Roman years, its subsequent history as the Celtic Church was very un-Roman; it had minimal organisation and lacked a consistent central power. Its acknowledgement of Rome as the site of authority was, to say the least, sporadic. In this respect it mirrored the tribal system it served. We visit it during the next chapter but note that Carlisle had a monastery in the seventh century that owed allegiance to the papal system centred on Rome. This was after the synod of Whitby which, in 663, extensively reorganised church governance in England along episcopal lines, with clear structures of authority. The conversion of the southern Angli was mainly conducted *from* Rome as a form of reconquest *by* Rome. But the Augustinian dispensation did not reach across the Irish Sea or far north of the wall for many years.

***

There were also dramatic consequences in the direction of trade and manufacture. The Roman presence dramatically shifted the weighting of trade between the Islands and the continent away from the Irish Sea and the south-west of Britain towards the south-east — essentially, to the Thames Estuary. It has remained there ever since.

In pre-Roman centuries the ancient trade routes from the Mediterranean world towards the Islands lay through the Garonne Gap, north of the Pyrenees, along the course of what is now the Canal du Midi, as far as Bordeaux; much of this could be managed by small boats. Thence cargoes (of wine, olive oil, ceramics and glass, as well as more specialised goods such as dried figs) were embarked on ocean-going vessels to be taken from various anchorages in Brittany and the Loire Estuary to southern and south-western points along the British coast, to locations in Cornwall and Devon and right up the full length of the Irish Sea. Finds of fragments of amphorae — the large pottery vessels made specially for storage in ships — and Samian ceramics have established this very exactly for the first century BC. The ships then returned with tin ingots from Cornwall, lead from the Mendips, copper and gold from Wales and leather and slaves from everywhere. Hunting dogs, iron and silver are also mentioned by the Roman geographer Strabo. There is evidence that raw materials were smelted or cured before shipment so sites like Hengistbury by Poole Harbour were busy with specialised labour in the years immediately preceding the Roman invasion.

A deal of this trade was controlled by the Veneti, a large clan or confederation rather like the Brigantes, who controlled access to the Loire Valley. This helps to explain the war they conducted with Caesar's legions. Caesar himself reported that a large number of private vessels sailed behind his cross-channel war fleet in the hope of pickings and contracts. Supplying the Roman army was an industry and export trade of its own, equivalent to supplying several chiefdoms.

The mere existence of the new province may be presumed to have increased trade immensely — firstly with the inexhaustible demand for materials of war and later, when the legions had established their own foundries and tanneries in Britannia, with goods for the imperial civil servants and the swiftly growing Romano-British market. Before very long, cross-channel trade included fine marbles from Carrara and elsewhere,[16] tiles and exotic woods for villas and temples and fine textiles, not to mention the ubiquitous wine and olive oil. Within Britannia a host of industries developed to service the army and the civil economy. A very large iron-smelting business in the Kentish Weald is the most studied but one would need to include such humble trades as brick-making, unknown to the tribes. The development of brick-making and tile-making on the Roman model was one of the most useful industries in a midland England where good building stone was rare and it helped to set English architecture on its unique course. Our Brigantean friends were also heavily involved in the lead-mining on which Roman architectural services depended. The Yorkshire Dales and the hills above the Eden Valley were major sources of lead and some silver. Copper was there to be mined in the Cumbrian Hills. Lead and gold are still being found at Wanlockhead beside the Roman road between Lugovalium and the northern wall. Our sentry was accustomed to thinking of Lugovalium as a trading centre and *entrepôt* as much as a frontier post.

How far the proto-Carlisle was a port we do not know; during the fourteenth century the anchorage at Skinburness, some ten miles downriver from the town, was an important staging post for supplies on their way to King Edward's army fighting the Scots; and one imagines a similar use made of it by the Romans. But Agricola and his successors had much better land communications than anyone had ever had before and the need for seaborne traffic was accordingly less. Roads encouraged centralised command and the formation of states and, conversely, centralised command produced roads and organisation.

It is certain that the existence of towns in Britannia stimulated trade in Hibernia and among the Caledonii. Unfortunately we have absolutely no idea as to the relative quantities of goods. We do know that trade was to some degree regularised between Britannia and Hibernia and that there were trading posts of some description at Stoneyford on the River Nore in County Kilkenny and on the shores of Dublin Bay. Over and above staple goods, luxury objects in fine metalwork and gems and the craftsmen who made them could and did travel and the workers might themselves become booty. On current evidence no clear and certain distinction can be made between Romano-British, Saxon and Irish designs and workmanship from this period, except where imagery and iconography is concerned. (Briefly, the use of figurative imagery was usually an attribute of Roman design, hardly used in Celtic or Saxon work, which generally employed non-figurative geometric and interlace patterns.) There is an older history that attributes the remarkable skill and beauty of Irish finds to autonomous native craftsmanship and a Celtic tradition, but modern archaeological evidence brings this into question. It stresses that the Islands were, from the point of view of skilled workmanship and technology, pretty much one place and that this place extended into northern Europe and Scandinavia. The internal divisions of this zone have little to do with any subsequent boundaries and it makes little sense to describe technology in national or ethnic terms.[17]

John Creighton, who has studied these matters in great depth and detail, shows that the spread of Roman-style coinage and by its means, classical iconography, provides a vivid and multidimensional picture of what these kind of interchanges meant. These were associated with at least three levels of interchange, the first being political. It becomes clear that the petty kings of south-eastern Britannia were adopting Roman forms and their implied ideology of the ruler and the ruled decades before the Romans' actual arrival. Secondly, this political level was expressed by a visual ideology of figurative emblems — recognisable portraits of the ruler as god. This prepared the way for the figurative imagery of Christianity. This in turn provides a hypothesis for the art of the Celtic Church which, in post-Roman times, reverted to abstract decoration. I propose that, as a general rule, centralised authority demands figurative imagery for its propagation and, in the absence of such centralising power, figurative imagery begins to wither. I have written about this elsewhere, in the context of the Reformation, but I believe we may be dealing with a feature in the typology of cultures.[18]

If I am right in this, and the change from iconic to aniconic culture and back is a real and difficult journey that is intimately bound up in how the world is seen and governed, then we gain some insight into the problems that Iron-Age craftsmen experienced in making images on coins. Creighton's discussion on coins and the representation of authority includes passages on the rituals of metalworking and the putative psychotropic effects of ritual practices connected with early metal technology and how this might relate to the confused transformations of motifs.[19] Approaching the problem from the craftsman's standpoint, creating or copying an image is curiously difficult if you do not know what an image is in the first place, let alone what an image might in fact be depicting. What Creighton and his sources refer to as 'entoptic phenomena', which exist prior to all figuration, are also marks left by characteristic methods of fabrication, which are themselves intrinsically metaphorical.[20] The relationship between craftsmanship and imagery cannot be understood without considering the metaphorical character of *any* process of fabrication. It is difficult for scholars whose concept of knowledge is text driven to step over into the world in which craft is the main and principal driver of world understanding.

***

And, in the same way, as the wheels turn, and I reflect without reflection and think without thought and allow the rhythm of movement to spread through my dreaming mind. I find myself with Clio once again, the Muse of history, daughter of Memory, and with the understanding she brings. You must approach her, just as you must approach every serious study, with a mind emptied of thought, so that she can enter it on her own terms entirely. You cannot command her; you can only invoke her presence.

> Sing in me, Muse, and through me tell …

The Muse is within us already and sings not to us but through us. To speak of the Muse is, in effect, to evoke a psychic function. The function is, at least in part, the suspension of yourself to allow the material to speak for itself. This is how original thoughts come into being. All that we need to do, past a certain stage, is to remain alert. To listen.

Our formal culture always assumes that the Muse is female and this is correct. But She is female in the register of symbolic figures, not of flesh and blood. That men can mistake real women for symbolic Muses is, of course, well known: for every Dante there is a Beatrice, for every sonneteer a Dark Lady. But there is no sustained, established tradition of the male Muse in relation to real women, nor could there be, if I am right, because the Muse is a fraction, or refraction, or reflection or glint of that deep symbolic maternal, that undifferentiated matrix of mind that precedes mind, of thought that is in the world before it is about the world.

This the kernel of the nut, the poetic act by which the whole story is set in motion — a preconceptual flash of understanding that creates and simultaneously illuminates the field within which it is to be understood. This is an apprehension that cannot be spoken of directly because it precedes instrumental or descriptive language. As Julia Kristeva writes, it constitutes the earliest stage of understanding, 'which is not, therefore, cognitive in the sense of being assumed by a knowing, already constituted subject'.[21] It forms the figure that constitutes the ground of its own self-understanding.

The dreaming willingness to immerse oneself in this matrix frees one from instrumental understanding. It produces and sustains an undifferentiated consciousness that exists well before any learned definition of reality. It is the ground from which new definitions flow. It is the only source of new thought.

* * *

Any accurate assessment of what was going on in the Roman centuries also has to take into account a general improvement in climate, which seems to have reached its height around AD 300. With this went a population increase, which was doubtless supported in Britannia by the relative peace and prosperity of the province following the abandonment of tribal ways. There was also a great improvement in agricultural methods, especially ploughing and harvesting, introduced directly by the Roman administrations. These methods reached Ireland around AD 300 and are now regarded as having formed some Irish landscape features, though the steps by which this happened are very little understood.[22]

The farms of the Brigantes may be taken as typical of the general agricultural advance as it impinged upon the more distant P- and Q-Celtic-speaking communities of Britain. A small number of villas existed: that at Gargrave, near Skipton (in the heart of Brigantia) is probably typical; it dates from the later third century and consists of a rectangular stockade with defensive ditch, containing a number of buildings. In an imaginative reconstruction published by Brian Hartley and R. Leon Fitts, these buildings are all of a distinctly Roman type, with tiled roofs and regular windows, built on an orthogonal plan around a symmetrical axis.[23] This is a provincial version of the kind of villa that existed all across the empire. But we know that some enclosures contained circular buildings of a more primitive kind. At Gargrave it is just possible to see, from the air, a rectangular layout of fields and plots — another sure sign of the Roman model. Then, seeking about, archaeologists unearthed heating and water systems and fragments of mosaic and painted walls. Among the Romanised Brigantes there was even a distinct school of pictorial mosaics, using typical Roman images naively transposed into a local style.

* * *

The next great feature of Roman rule that impinged upon the peoples of the Irish Sea was urban life. It impinged without being incorporated. Because both roads and towns were solidly built, the physical evidence of *romanitas* — the villas, towns, and cities (however small they might have been) — lasted long after the Roman armies withdrew. These ruins provided models of what could be achieved and they showed how such buildings could be made. The Romanesque character of so much early church-building sprang directly from Roman traditions, possibly from direct imitation of existing buildings on the same sites and the reuse of pillars, arches and carved work.

For the Anglo-Saxon-speaking world of Englelond, Roman remains were exemplary. A fragmentary elegy remains, usually known as 'The Ruin', in which the poet is wandering through a ruined city (much as Piranesi wandered through the existing ruins of ancient Rome 800 years later):

> *Wraetlic is thes wealstan; wyrde grbraecon …*
> Splendid this building is, though fate destroyed it,
> the city buildings fell apart, the works
> of giants crumbled. Tumbled are the towers,
> ruined the roofs, and broken the barred gate;
> frost in the plaster, all the ceilings gape
> torn and collapsed and eaten up by age …
>
> Resolute masons, skilled in rounded building
> wondrously linked the framework with iron bonds.
> The public halls were bright, with lofty gables,
> bath houses many; great the cheerful noise,
> and many mead-halls filled with human pleasures.
> Till mighty fate brought change upon it all.[24]

Figure 1. 'The porta maggiore' from *The views of Rome* by G.B. Piranesi (1748).

The site in question is almost certainly Bath, whose springs and facilities became derelict early in the fifth century. But the towns, if not their mead-halls, remained in partial occupation for the succeeding centuries, sustaining the concept of urban life into the future. The great agricultural estates with their buildings and villas often survived in altered forms into medieval times.

How far the existence of these ruins affected the imagination of Saxon builders is a matter for the architectural historian. But the earliest monasteries of Britannia, which were coming into existence as the Roman armies withdrew, took their architectural forms more or less directly from Roman sources. At least, we know that St Ninian, in founding his missionary school beside Whithorn Bay in Strathclyde, across from Allonby, had brought with him from Gaul masons skilled in the setting out of arches, in 'rounded building'. The boundary we perceive between Roman building and the Romanesque style is something more like a narrative device than a feature of reality.

Along the line of the wall and at its stations we know that there were large granaries and similar supply bases to serve the army. They survived to be used and adapted by Northumbrian rulers who also, in time, built a church in the Romanesque style and a monastery (by 684) at Carlisle.

The builders of Durham Cathedral did not need to look far for constructional models. The same models penetrated into Ireland, either as direct imitation through the practice of imported skilled masons or through the importation of actual objects. The trade in carved stones, capitols, fonts and the like was a large business in the fourteenth century and there is no good reason to suppose it did not exist in the ninth.

***

Then there is the question of the roads. The system of roadbuilding and road maintenance instituted by the Roman army provided, for the first time in any part of Europe, a means of effective transport independent of wind and tide. The excellence of their construction meant that they lasted well into the tenth century and provided a ready-made infrastructure for whoever was able to seize upon them. The roads implied a civil service and such institutions as a postal system. The conjecture raised here is that it was the possession of the roads, particularly certain key junctions, that enabled the Saxon inhabitants of eastern Britannia to command the movement of trade and provisions across the former province of Britannia and ultimately to impose their languages, outwards from the south-east. It would be useful to remember here how, in 1066, King Harold Godwinson was able to move his army from London to Stamford Bridge in Yorkshire in four days, win a fierce battle and march them back to Hastings just as quickly.[25] This could only have been done on good roads with good bridges. These could not have been maintained without some form of public service and civil administration. A centralised state already existed in many practical respects. Ireland and the Scottish highland regions, on the other hand, had to wait another 1,200 years for an equivalent road system, of which a proverb said:

> If you saw these roads before they were made
> you would lift up your eyes and bless General Wade.

***

And what happened on the Solway and the Irish Sea when the Roman legions withdrew?

What we do know is that the supply of new Roman coinage ceased when the army left, which induced a steady collapse of a cash economy and an inevitable decline in long-range trade. There was now no easy way for wall-dwellers like Barates of Palmyra to repatriate their profits. Because there was now no immediate necessity for surplus production, because there was no large army demanding to be maintained, we can conjecture that there was a retraction of large-scale agriculture. The ranch and villa at Gargrave was abandoned in this period and the last finding on the site was of the use of roof tiles to construct a temporary hearth, made perhaps by a shepherd sheltering in the ruins.

Hartley and Fitts write of 'a total disappearance of new pottery from the major centres previously supplying the north. A coinless, aceramic society is exceedingly difficult to assess archaeologically.'[26]

The decay of the Roman administration led to the rise of post-Roman kingdoms. It appears to this writer, reading through what he can of the chronicles and scholarly accounts of these obscure events, that the kingdoms were post-tribal realms, cut out by individuals and families from the political chaos. In the terms with which this chapter began, what appears to have happened is that the instrumental collective dissolved, no longer having any purpose to fulfil. But this could not mean a return to the tribal *status quo ante*, because the tribal, familial loyalties were dispersed. There was, and is, no way back to old times, then or now.

The subsequent organisation of power in post-Roman Britannia had to be gathered around notable individuals and their war-bands — a reversion to Iron-Age ways without a clear concept of tribe or clan to hold matters together. Taliesin's translator described these rulers as the 'rustler-kings'.[27] Loyalties, as they seem to emerge from the darkness, are to these particular rulers and their followers and not to clans. What *romanitas* achieved, perhaps more than anything else, was the death of tribal society.

Something of the Brigantean realm re-emerged as Rheged, a British kingdom centred upon the vale of the Eden and the Solway coasts. The Carvetii, if they still existed coherently, were now at the centre of a world, albeit a much smaller one. The rulers of Rheged were, for a while, movers and shakers in the fifth and sixth centuries, allying themselves with the rulers of Strathclyde against the Saxon kingdoms of the north-

Illustration 10. Dunragit (Dun Rheged) near Stranraer is a village on the site of a large cursus monument, beside a substantial mound and many other remains, which include the now-destroyed remnants of a Roman cemetery. It lies between the shores of Luce Bay and Loch Ryan at a strategic site which may indeed have provided a strong forward point for any polity based on the Eden Valley and the town of Caerluel.

Illustration 11. Nearby is another large mound, at Innermessan, whose origins are unknown. It has a generally Norman plan, like a motte, and a position designed to command the Stranraer anchorage, but it has not received close attention from archaeologists. Innermessan was once a substantial small town; it was superseded by Stranraer in the seventeenth century and no longer exists.

eastern coast and against Gaelic raiders. Their battles were recorded, commemorated (and greatly magnified) in the early Welsh epics of *Y Gododdin* and the poems of Taliesin and Aneirin.[28]

Taliesin's patron was Urien, the ruler of Rheged, who during the seventh century managed to maintain Rheged as a semi-Christian principality in alliance with

Strathclyde and Dalriada against both Picts and Saxons. His power, and that of his sons, extended into Yorkshire, but he also has a legendary, even mythical, status as one of the figures of the Arthurian romances.

> Men of Catraeth
> at the break of dawn
> arise
> around your triumphant rustler-king.
> For this is Urien, famous leader.
> He keeps the chiefs at bay
> and scythes them down.
> And until I am old and ailing
> in the dire necessity of death
> I shall not be in my element
> if I don't praise Urien.[29]

Indeed, it is in and through early medieval Welsh that we encounter another layer of Roman influence — that which penetrates into dreams. The most direct of these, rooted in a real geography and connected to a real history, is that of the 'Dream of Maximus' (or Macsen Gwledig), as found in the *Mabinogion.* Here we are told of an emperor of Rome who, riding out with his men (32 crowned kings were his company), falls asleep in the noonday heat. He dreams a journey, across the sea, beyond mountains, to an island beyond the islands, where in a wonderful countryside he finds a wonderful castle and at a splendid but mysterious court he meets a dream woman of surpassing beauty. And then he wakes up. We learn that he is now unable to sleep for thinking of her and this wonderful land. His anxious courtiers send out messengers to search for this place and, at length, they find the island beyond the islands. The beautiful maiden in the court is none other than the daughter of the king of the land, which they now realise is Britain, and the court is at Aber Seint — Segontium, which became Caernarfon. She tells them, 'If it is I whom the emperor loves, let him come for me.' They return and the story is repeated a third time as Maximus goes to meet his bride. She, as a virgin, can ask a bride-price and takes at his hand for her father the whole land of Britain from the English Channel to the Irish Sea, three islands and three fortresses, and between the fortresses she causes roads to be built. She comes to be known as Elen Luyddog, Helen of the Hosts, because it is for her and her only that the men of Britain are willing to assemble. And now assemble they must, for the emperor has been too long away from Rome and must return to reconquer his realm, which he can only do with the guile and bravery of Elen's brothers, Kynan and Avaon.[30]

This story, which is touched on again in the next chapter, shares sources and material with Geoffrey of Monmouth and other pseudohistorians and has some relation to the real history of the Roman general known as Maximus who, on returning to Rome with his Romano-British legions, fighting against the emperor, himself became an emperor. In some versions the tale becomes confused with the emperor Constantine, who was proclaimed in Britain and went on to convert Rome to Christianity, so that Elen becomes Helen, the finder of the true cross and Constantine's mother. Thus, in some sense, Rome was converted by the Cymri.[31]

But to recognise fragments of an actual sequence of events refracted through fragments of a fiction is to miss the main point, which is to witness the incorporation of Roman experience into the P-Celtic-speaking world of Britannia. I think we should conclude that when the Roman legions and their administration left, the Brigantes, Novantae, Ordovices and the other British P-Celtic-speaking tribes returned to a much-reduced version of their previous way of life, inheriting the memory of Roman glory because they had a share in it. But the Saxon-speakers mostly living in the east and the midlands inherited the actual infrastructure and the idea of a state. And the spread of Anglo-Saxon kingdoms in Britain soon became coliminal with the former spread of the Roman *imperium*, ran upon the same roads and inherited an idea of central authority.

The province of Britannia had been dismantled into its constituent parts, which now consisted of a reduced Cymru, Rheged, Altclut (Strathclyde) and Kernow. The north-east coast as far as Fife and well inland was variously known as Bernicia or Northumbria. In AD 636 a Northumbrian army had invested Carlisle and briefly occupied the Isle of Man. At around the same time another Anglo-Saxon kingdom, Mercia, had created itself in the English midlands and captured the ruinous old city of Chester. From here the Cymri were enclosed within the long ditch and wall of Offa's Dyke. This undertaking was a task on the scale of any Roman wall and impresses upon us how quickly the Saxon speakers rose from being farmers and mercenaries to ruling the land. King Offa had indeed become a mighty man who issued coins in his name, on the Roman model.

A discontinuous line of fortifications and strongholds was also in place across the southern border of Ulster, from the Moyry Pass in the east to Donegal Bay in the west. How this came about, and for whom, remains an obscure story. The existence of the Black Pig's Dyke has a number of purely mythical explanations — it was supposedly gouged out by the tusks of a supernatural boar, or cast out by a stupendous worm — but on real-world grounds it was an attempt to define and defend the border of Ulster against attack from the south. This places the dyke in a putative struggle for predominance waged by the Gaels against their immediate Pictish or Cruithin predecessors, who still held some of the land around 100 BC. In effect, the current internal frontiers of the Islands were in place far earlier than we might suppose.

***

Meanwhile, on the windswept *vallum* …

> When I am a veteran with only one eye
> I shall do nothing but look at the sky.
> — W.H. Auden, 'Roman wall blues'

Notes

[1]   Tacitus (R.M. Ogilvie and I.A. Richmond, eds) (1967) *De Vita Agricolae*, Oxford: Clarendon Press, is a wonderful source to have to study. Written with the utmost economy, it makes every other author, and certainly this one, feel inadequate. On reading it one soon realises that Tacitus is using the heroic life of his father-in-law as a way of punishing later emperors and the weakness of contemporary Roman manners.

[2]   N. Fairclough (1989) *Language and power*, London: Longman, p. 21., cited in J. Creighton (2000) *Coins and power in late Iron Age Britain*, Cambridge: Cambridge University Press, p. 147.

[3]   See previous note. Creighton, *op. cit.*, Chapter 6 is particularly relevant, though it deals with a strictly pre-Roman period.

[4]   Tacitus, *op. cit.*

[5]   E. Said (1978) *Orientalism*, New York: Pantheon.

[6]   Tacitus, *op. cit.*

[7]   *Ibid.*

[8]   I think it will be clear by now that the author regards this as a historically spurious and deeply repellent notion. There are no fringes to a globe.

[9]   Tacitus, *op. cit.*

[10]   William Shakespeare, *Henry V.*

[11]   The language of the army was a kind of Creole language, so far as we can tell, formally a Latin dialect but capable of absorbing almost anything it encountered. It can still just be heard and read in the Romanche of eastern Switzerland and other Alpine tongues, and conceivably in Occitan and Catalan. But this is the observation of an enthusiastic amateur.

[12]   H. Mytum (1995) 'Across the Irish Sea: Romano-British and Irish settlements in Wales', *Emania* **13**.

[13]   B. Raftery (1996) 'Drumanagh and Roman Ireland', *Archaeology Ireland* **10** (1) (spring), p. 18.

[14]   R.B. Warner (1995) 'Tuathal Techtmar: a myth or ancient literary evidence for a Roman invasion?', *Emania* **13**.

[15]   There are useful summaries of this material as it relates to the eastern shore in: D. Walker (ed.) (1976) *A history of the church in Wales*, Penarth: Church in Wales Publications; A.W. Wade-Evans (1934) *Welsh Christian origins*, Oxford: Alden Press and many other sources. As early as AD 208 Tertullian had written in his *Adversus Iudaeos* of 'districts of the Britons, unreached by

the Romans but subdued to Christ'.

[16] An account of the symbolic values of marble in the Roman provinces can be found in R.M.J. Isserlin (1998) 'A spirit of improvement? Marble and the culture of Roman Britain' in R. Laurence and J. Berry (eds) *Cultural identity in the Roman Empire*, London: Routledge.

[17] This has been summarised from a mass of archaeological detail in L. and J. Laing (1990) *Celtic Britain and Ireland AD 200–800: the myth of the Dark Ages*, Dublin: Irish Academic Press. They describe this book as 'intended for discussion, not as a statement of total conviction on all issues'.

[18] See D. Brett (2004) *The plain style*, Cambridge: Lutterworth Press.

[19] Creighton, *op. cit.*, Chapter 2.

[20] See also Brett (2005), *op. cit.* To investigate this matter would, alas, require writing another book.

[21] See F. Mitchell (1986) *The Shell guide to reading the Irish landscape*, Dublin: Country House.

[22] J. Kristeva (1986) 'The revolution in poetic language' in T. Moi (ed.), *The Kristeva reader*, Oxford: Blackwell, pp. 93–4 etc.; and my treatment of similar material in D. Brett (2005) *Rethinking decoration*, Cambridge: Cambridge University Press, Chapter 3.

[23] B.R. Hartley and R.L. Fitts (1988) *The Brigantes*, Gloucester: Sutton.

[24] R. Hamer (tr.) (1970) 'The Ruin' in *A choice of Anglo-Saxon verse*, London: Faber and Faber.

[25] He was able to move some 5,000 men 230 miles in a four-day 'march'. They must have run the whole way on a good surface. In younger days an enthusiast of mountain marathons, I am astonished at the combination of organised movement, provisioning and fitness this obviously required. To repeat it after a hard-fought hand-to-hand battle with a Viking army, to run all the way back into Kent and then to launch yourself at the incoming Normans, apparently without resting, is a feat indeed.

[26] Hartley and Fitts, *op. cit.*, p. 115.

[27] Taliesin (M. Pennar, tr.) (1988) *Poems*, Lampeter: Llanerch Enterprises.

[28] It goes without saying that the works of both these poets are known through problematic and much later copies, which have set immense editorial problems. But I must take them as I find them.

[29] 'Gwaith Gwenystrad' ('The battle of Wensleydale') in Taliesin, *op. cit.*

[30] For an exceptional modernist take on these legendary figures, see the work of D. Jones, especially (1937) *In parenthesis; seinnyessit e gledyf ym penn mameu*, London: Faber and Faber.

[31] J. Gantz (ed.) (1976) *The Mabinogion*, London: Penguin Books. See the introduction to this volume for sources and background. See also A. Breeze (1997) *Welsh medieval literature*, Dublin: Four Courts Press, Chapter 3.

FOUR
The Bishops and the Clerks

Coastal roads are a mixed pleasure. When small and secondary they can be a delight no matter how hilly or wind-about; but when they are major they are almost always hellish to cycle, being crowded with trucks speeding to catch ferries, whose slipstreams suck you in towards their oiled and dusty flanks, who feed you lungfuls of carbon monoxide and eyefuls of grit.

The picturesque shores of Arran have to be exchanged for the A72 that carries freight from Stranraer into central Scotland. For most of its length this road runs upon foreshore, along the only-just-raised beachline of Galloway. At times you are in spray-reach of the sea, which breaks upon a shallow coast of boulders and salty pasture; at other times you are compelled to follow the steel crash-barriers as the road climbs up headlands such as Benbane and swoops down precariously to the next village or row of holiday shacks. These passages are unpleasant and even frightening because you can be hemmed in by steel edges to the left and whirring walls of rubber to the right, and over the headlands the roads can be unexpectedly narrow and steep so that you have to heave yourself upwards while taking care not to lose a neat line on the road.

That there are unexpected inland cliffs above you would be a pleasure if you had the time to inspect them or to dawdle past the rows of little weekend houses, each with its garden and flowers, ornaments and gnomes. And although there are pleasant small towns such as Maybole or Girvan there is an impetus to get past this stage of our journey. Girvan in particular is a place of serious, gritty character and handsome building, with a good harbour. Pleasant also is the one-street village of Ballantrae, a few miles further south, which has the distinction of two bridges over the one river. The old bridge is a handsome affair in two stone arches, which seem to have been made from the ruins of the castle that stood immediately above it. I sat for a while here, in improving weather, watching the September squalls dissipate over the hillsides. This castle, though now almost entirely ruined and quarried away, is a good deal larger than the usual tower houses of this region. It had a large courtyard, walls and a ditch and suggests (as do several other architectural features of this coast) that Girvan and Ballantrae were, in their day, much more substantial places than they are now.

The hour moves on. Press down again and turn inland to begin the long weary climb over to Loch Ryan. At once, facing inland, the wind is at my shoulder, not in my right eye.

***

Four great headlands jut into and define the Mor Iwerddon: Kintyre, Galloway, Lleyn and St David's. All share a similar peninsular light and weather; hedges, bushes and trees have an eastward slant and their houses offer blank gables to the evening sun.

> Did he hold his course
> mid sleeve
> where, at the wide gusset
> it's thirty-five leagues
> where Mor Iwerddon meets
> Mare Gallicum
> where the seas of the islands war with the ocean, to white
> the horse-king's *insulae*?[1]

> Another time in a lowering and sad evening, being alone in the field, when all things were dead and quiet, a certain want and horror fell upon me, beyond imagination. The unprofitableness and silence of the place dissatisfied me; its wideness terrified me; from the utmost ends of the earth fears surrounded me. How did I know but dangers might suddenly arise from the east, and invade me from the unknown regions beyond the seas? I was a weak and little child, and had forgotten there was a man alive upon the earth.[2]

I took to my ten-year-old heels as fast as I could, and ran homewards. The immediate cause, I recall, was the sensation of crumbling beneath my feet as I walked out over an area of burnt heather; the biscuit earth was breaking up. The proximal cause was perhaps the sheerness of the cliffs and the depths of the water. There was the sense, too, of something of very great age and of Formorian malevolence embedded in the pinkish granite of the rocks that littered the promontory. Between me and my safety rose a rocky hill which, at that moment, loomed over me.

These and similar experiences of terror are not unusual among those who spend their time in desolate places, alone. It is partly a rational fear of danger, but much more, I think, the appalled realisation that, despite what you might think, you are not necessary. These rocks, these water-swells, this crumbling soil, can do without your existence. The sense of the world's indifference can transform into one of its active hostility. The surface of the world will close over you as deep water closes over a dropped stone; the stone continues falling long after the water has smoothed into a glass of unknowability.

* * *

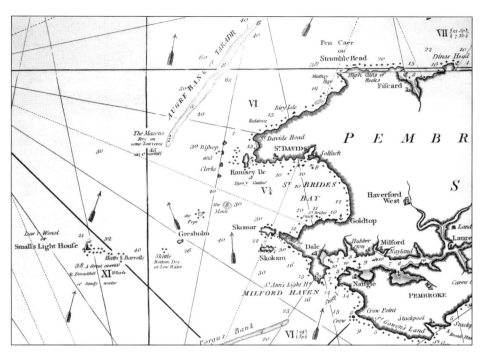

Figure 1. Admiralty chart (*c.* 1790). St David's Head, with the Bishops and the Clerks, not to mention the Monk and the Pope, the four larger islands with Viking names. A note on this eighteenth-century map mentions 'a great overfall and dreadfull whirls of sandy water'. The strong tidal flows make this a tricky coast.

Illustration 1. Traces of a triple-walled promontory fort on St David's Head.

St David's Head is a counterpart to the Mull of Kintyre: a planished landscape of low rocky hills and treeless fields holding, in every windless cranny, dense clusters of bush and undergrowth. A broad strand — Y Traeth Mawr — of white sand and breakers. Low cliffs covered in gorse and scabious. The head itself looks out at islands and rocks — the Bishops and the Clerks — which, as the tide-race runs, trail long wakes of breakers and foam as if they were sailing north followed by the flat hulk of Ramsey Island. The head itself is a compact mass of pale granite split with zawns and fissures in which vast waves suck and bang. On the top of the head is a promontory fort guarded, like its opposite partner on the mull, with a triple palisade. Within are several hut circles. The wall is almost entirely tumbled but one can find small patches where rocks are laid in course.

There are other remains still more ancient on the head: grave-marking cromlechs in an unusual single-post style.

The cromlechs are not the only memorials to the dead. Down by the shore an upright propeller blade and plaque commemorate four American airmen who crashed into Carn Llidi as they prepared to make a landing at RAF Brawdy during the last year of the war. A more comprehensive memorial is kept at the youth hostel nearby and I remember, when spending a summer in the same house, how the farmer recalled the terrible moment when the mountain was drenched in fire.

Like Macrihanish Bay in Kintyre, the military airfield at Brawdy has a secret history. After being an important part of the sea reconnaissance activities in the

Illustration 2. One of the many fine cromlechs to be found on the head.

Second World War it became a part of US submarine intelligence activities under the title of 'oceanographic research unit' and reputedly at the hub of an undersea cable network that enabled NATO forces to track Soviet craft (and even individual whales) as far away as Bermuda. It was until recently the centre for the army's electronic-warfare department.

Illustration 3.
The hut circles on
St David's Head are
numerous enough to
indicate a substantial
population.

* * *

Dewi Sant was born, we are told, to Non, a nun who had been ravished by a local ruler. To give birth she went in shame to a remote byre. At the moment of childbirth a stream gushed forth to form a holy well. His was, in symbolic terms, a sort of virgin birth and it is not surprising that Non is portrayed as a Virgin-Mary figure and has been seen as the patron saint of the raped and abused. On my visit the ruined chapel on the cliffs just south of the town (Capel Non) was adorned with red ribbons and little offerings, to which I added a blue cornflower.

Fully analysed and understood, such a site reveals many layers of meaning which are not yet exhausted. These ancient sacred places set a challenge to secular modernists. How do we account for their power to move us? It has much to do with their careful siting within the landscape; the buildings set off their natural surroundings and never seek to dominate them. They exist because of the place they are in, which they themselves create. Their construction is absolutely simple and obvious, even when very skilled; they do not seek to awe or even persuade us.

Illustration 4. Capel Non: St Non's Chapel. The chapel (now a ruined rectangle of slate) appears to be a medieval building standing on a larger and much older foundation, itself within a Neolithic enclosure marked out by standing stones; a new chapel and a friary have been built nearby. There are other chapels and wells to Non in Brittany, where she is reputed to have died.

Illustration 5. St Non's Well, much restored into an arch. The original was probably a corbelled vault.

When William the Conqueror visited St David's in 1081 he combined pilgrimage with diplomacy, since he also held a conference with Rhys ap Tewdwr, the lord of Deheubarth. He found the old shrine of Dewi Sant to be virtually ruined by Viking raiders and he determined on its renewal. By 1115 the Norman lords of Pembroke had replaced the Welsh bishop with their own man and set him on to build up Tyddewi as a cathedral town and centre for pilgrimage. The new cathedral came to occupy the narrow valley in which it shelters with a large and complicated compound. It seems to hide away from the westerly gales and only the top of its tower can be seen from any distance.

Illustration 6. The cathedral hiding in its narrow valley as if from the Vikings, who had already sacked it eight times by AD 1000.

Sharing the valley is the huge ruined bulk of the bishop's palace, which for opulence and inventive finery puts the prince-bishops of Durham to shame. The bishop's palace consists of a large courtyard surrounded on three sides by ranges of halls, state rooms and apartments. Though it is now extensively ruined, the grandiosity of the elevation is immediately obvious. The roof-height arcades are a special and unusual feature attributed to Bishop Gower (d. 1347) but what we cannot see now is the brilliant colour in which the building was decorated. There is ample evidence to show that the huge formal porch was painted a rich red and that the upper reaches of the walls were embellished in a chequerboard pattern of yellow and purple.

Illustration 7. The bishop's palace.

* * *

There is no part of all the Islands more encastled, bemotted, beringed or embaileyed than Pembrokeshire. Lise Hull, in her admirable short guide (2005), describes 69 fortified places (a number that includes the fortified palaces of the bishops); these castles are principally of Norman origin. But before that, and often on the same site, there were much earlier fortifications, ditches and walls. Some of them are of the greatest antiquity. Many Iron-Age ringforts remain; that would include the triple stockade on St David's Head which was, conceivably, a place of security for troubled times rather than part of a system of domination. Similar promontory or hilltop forts exist on Strumble Head and further north along the Cardigan Bay shore at Ynys Lochtyn and Aberystwyth. Most Norman castles, or those stone castles built by Welsh lords in imitation of their rivals, were placed on older foundations and all began in the first instance as earthworks topped with palisades. Stone castles came as a second generation. Some of these developed into a third or fourth generation, of which kind Pembroke Castle must stand as the finest of all — a mountain range of tilted masonry finally completed in the fourteenth century (see Chapter 6).

* * *

Ireland enters history at St David's Head. At least, it enters that history that is created in and by written texts. The written text implies a consciousness of self, either an individual or a collective self, an 'I' or a 'we', and a reflection upon self that one cannot quite recover from artefacts and the archaeological record. In this respect, though not in others, objects are dumb. To look northward and westward from St David's Head is to scan a domain of learning, of writing and of worship; this is the world of the Celtic Church. The media of interchange become the bishop and his book, the scribe, the reliquary, the crozier and the bell.

As Michael Richter puts it, 'To try and grasp its real significance one has to keep in mind that it still embodies in the early middle ages a persistent prehistoric tradition.'[3] The degree to which this was a unified tradition is another matter. Given that communication by sea was swift and relatively easy, we can assume that unity of liturgy and practice could be acknowledged and observed. But this was a unity cast like a net over some various and distinct clans, each of whom had their own local customs and jealously guarded domains. Not all local churches and monasteries came from or owed loyalty to the same sources. So in practice, on the ground, this unity was probably more notional than actual; and moreover, it was filtered, as we have noted, through a range of dialects and languages.

The documents of this period are ritualistic in character, without regional variation. The annalist's Cymric or Gaelic text was far removed from everyday speech. His Latin was even more so, for this was a late Latin, filtered through traditions and practices already ancient. Furthermore, these texts — these annals, records, genealogies, pseudohistories and king-lists — are, as we have received them, mostly copies of copies, many times transcribed, translated and transformed palimpsests of repeated rethinkings.[4]

There had been a system of writing known as Ogham which, in different versions, existed over much of non-Roman Europe. We know it through carved inscriptions. Its forms and strokes are of a kind well adapted to cutting and striking instruments and they have nothing in common with the cursive qualities of handwriting. The largest zone of Ogham inscriptions exists in southern Ireland and southern Wales, with some extension into south-western England. This powerfully suggests a shared zone of learning but it is some way short of handwriting and ready communication.

Ogham and Roman lettering exist side by side on a few carved stones, though the circumstances of their coming together are not known. A fine example is in the churchyard at Nanhyfar (Nevern) near Aberteifi (Cardigan).

Inside the church there is another stone, now built into a window sill, which commemorates one Maglocunus.

Ogham is a system of writing based upon simple strokes on either side or across a continuous line. It is not, so far as we can tell, a phonetic script, for although it matches with the Latin alphabet it can also function as a counting system and general mnemonic, rather like the quipu system of knotted threads that enabled the Incas to communicate with one another, and perhaps also it is a sign system based upon five fingers. On boulders the edges and corners of the rock stand in place of a continuous line and are cut on either side. This can be seen fairly clearly in the photograph. Of course, the strokes may once have been coloured in for greater legibility. Nearly all actually existing inscriptions are, in fact, names in Old Irish or in a mixture of Old Welsh and Latin. There is a large literature on the origins and meaning of Ogham which runs all the way from the scrupulous to the trashy.

I think this enables us to state with reasonable confidence that this part of the world (anciently Deheubarth) is one of those places where the coexistence of parallel systems of learning and recording enabled something new to emerge. The world of the P-Celtic and the Q-Celtic languages come together with Latin; what emerges is the Celtic Church and, before long, its incomparable calligraphy.

To emphasise the character of this site there is a magnificent cross in the graveyard, set among deeply shading yew trees, that dates from the tenth century and is one of the very finest of its kind. The interlacing would not shame the *Book of Kells*, while on its foot are Roman initials (which I was not able to decipher).

Left: Illustration 8. Carved cross at Nanhyfar.
Right: Illustration 9. Inscribed stone at Nanhyfar. There is Ogham down the left-hand vertical edge of the pillar. Roman lettering on the face appears to read, 'Vitalianus … emereto,' which probably means something like, 'Vitalianus has gone to his reward.' The Ogham gives us just the name 'Vitalani'. The combination of Ogham and Latin script enables us to begin intertranslation, and this and a few other stones have been seen as equivalent to the Rosetta Stone, which enabled us to read Egyptian inscriptions.

We do not know by whom and where the Celtic languages acquired alphabetic writing, but it was certainly inspired by first-hand contact with Roman models and Christian scriptures.[5] It was a process that took time, however, and all documents of this early historical period are, in fact, in Latin, though the letterforms soon took on

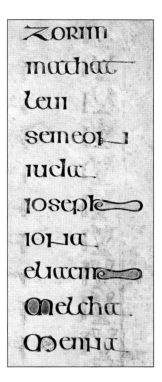
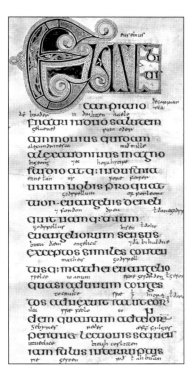

Figure 2. The growth of modern handwriting.
Left: a) *The Book of Kells*, *c.* 800, in half-uncial majuscule derived from Roman script.
Right: b) The Lindisfarne gospels, *c.* 850, in half-uncial majuscule and Anglo-Irish minuscule combined.

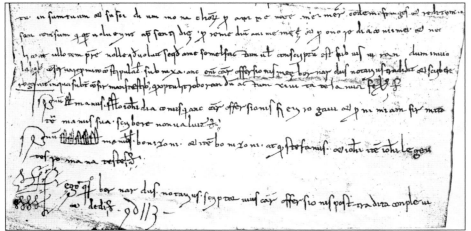

Figure 2. c) A page by Bernardus, notary and writer, north Italy, 1029, in Gothic minuscule.

a cursive and un-Roman quality of their own. More official documents were largely written in the 'uncial' styles, where the letters are formed by broad firm strokes of the pen. Side by side with uncial script there grew up a 'minuscule' tradition, in which the letters are formed with curved lines and flourishes. There are a number of variants of these minuscule scripts, of which the oldest is that of the Celtic Church. In continental Europe the Celtic minuscule is specially associated with the monastic settlements founded by missionaries from Bangor. Sometimes, as in the Lindisfarne gospels, we find the uncial style used for Latin and the minuscule for the translation into Anglo-Saxon, written rather haphazardly between the lines. The advent of minuscule cursive script was also associated with the Carolingian attempt to purify and re-edit ancient Christian texts in order to give them new authority. This in turn, on the pan-European scale, was part of the wider Carolingian attempt to establish state and ecclesiastical authority on a 'modern' basis of monarchy and a civil service.

As Lowe puts it:

> Though scripts seem to move down the ages with the majestic slowness of glaciers, they are not mere carriers of external instruments, but genuine manifestations of their age, bearing the marks of its vicissitudes.[6]

Standing on St David's Head we can align ourselves with the vectors along which a distinctive form of religious practice and belief, and with it a distinctive learning and literary expression, survived and evolved. And it is from the world of Ogham that we derive the first great romance of post-classical Europe, which steps out to us directly into the extreme of modernity.

Figure 3. The first four bars of Wagner's *Tristan and Isolde*.

The story of Tristan and Isolde, which we know through Wagner, comes down to us, like any great river, from several fountains. The composer used Gottfried of Strassburg as his immediate source but Gottfried was adapting from a wide body of work of which at least three early medieval versions exist, these being Norman French in language and character. Behind that is only surmise, but we can infer the existence of an *Ur*-Tristan which, like a great deal of the Celtic Church, transmits into present time a persisting prehistoric tradition. The comings and goings between Kernow and Laighin, the supposed feuds and animosities conducted across what is now St George's Channel, are the shadow of the conflict between P and Q, between the cut inscription and the cursive hand and between the clan and the feudal society. The story affords us a glimpse, through a clouded window of transcription and translation, into a world which is pre-feudal. Just as the 'Dream of Maximus' allows us into the post-Roman world of P-Celtic Britain, so in the story of Tristan and Isolde we are in an evolved but still primal world of loyalties and clans. And at the same time those four first bars, utterly unresolved, throw us into our present lack of resolution.

We can even think of the four centuries or so from AD 350 onward as being a high point in our zone's history which, while not Roman, continued to look back over its shoulder at classical learning and the early fathers of the church. Moreover, the difficulties of moving through the continent beset by Germanic and Frankish armies encouraged the inhabitants of the Irish Sea to look and to travel yet further afield, towards Spain, the Mediterranean and the holy land, and even to Iceland and beyond.

Once again we have to note the facts of physical geography and weather. To stand on the head looking north as the tide floods into the sea is to watch the Bishops and the Clerks set sail, trailing long wakes of foam behind them; it is to have the south-west wind at your back. Ynys Enlli, the Lleyn Peninsula and Anglesey are no more than a long day's sail away. By the next day's sail on open sea you have passed Man and harboured at Whithorn or even, if the weather is with you, found anchorage in Strangford Lough at the island monastery of Nendrum. The following day you can be well up the North Channel in Lamlash Bay, where we find yet another Holy Island, or at the little land of Sanda off the tip of Kintyre. From here sheltered waters will take you into the Clyde and the well-settled populous island of Bute. All these journeys can be done in one-day stages from one safe anchorage to another.

Beyond Bute the sweet waters of Lomond offer you little green islets for your nunnish cell or, if it is the life of action and power you desire, the half-Roman, half-barbaric lands of Strathclyde open up as you advance past the rock of Dumbarton.

> There are hills beyond Pentland and lands beyond Forth.
> If there's lords in the south there are chiefs in the north.

And from there is a way through easy country to the North Sea and the eastern banks of Britain, with still another Holy Island, and beyond. Alternatively, taking a seaward route and rounding the Mull of Kintyre you can follow the water roads to the Firth of Lorne, from which a brisk passage leads across to Iona and beyond. You can go as far as Orkney, Shetland and Iceland if you wish; and from the friendly islands of Lorne it is a short step through the Great Glen to Inverness and the Pictish heartlands. For the church-building missionary or the solitude-seeking hermit the Irish Sea provided the swiftest and safest way north or south, following sea-ways known for millennia.

They also led east and west: the long-established Q-Celtic-speaking Gaels who inhabited parts of Dyfed and Lleyn found no difficulty in moving from one side of the sea to another, so it is not surprising that ecclesiastical sites such as Nenhyfar should be places where intertranslations took place and where script mingled with script.

All the important early church locations are on headlands or islands, as vulnerable as they are defensible. When trouble came from the land an island or a rocky height was the best defence; but when trouble came from the sea the monasteries were like sheepcotes to wolves. At times it seems a wonder that anything survived. St David's monastery (called Mynyw in Cymric, latinised into Mevenia) was a milk cow to the Vikings, who visited it at least eight times and killed two of its bishops.

Still standing on the head, look back south over your shoulder past the islands of Ramsey and Skomer into Milford Haven and beyond. There is another route by sea and land from Ynys Byr into what is now Barnstaple and Bideford, from which a shortish ride will get you to the coast again and Armorica and beyond — to Paris, if you wish, and Rome. This was a link into the central life of Europe, which was never wholly disrupted by the 'barbarian' invasions. It also led directly towards the monastery of St Martin of Tours and his school at Marmoutiers, a great nursery of ascetics and missionary monks. These were the roads travelled by missionaries, bishops and wandering saints, and also by jobbing builders, craftsmen and their goods, the merchants in vellum and pigment and gums, scribes and copyists, and workers in fine metal and gems.

The first missionary of whom we have any record was the man generally known as St Ninian, also as Nynias and (in Welsh) Meugan or Mawgan, Ninus, Ringen and Dingen. Insofar as anything reliable is known about his origins, he was the son of a Romano-British citizen of some education, born probably in the Galloway region, to which he returned after travels and studies. Bede refers to him as 'a most reverend and holy man of the British nation'. His native language was almost certainly a P-Celtic Cymric — that is to say, he spoke an early Welsh (along with Latin, Old French, Greek and who knows what else). He was certainly a follower of St Martin and dedicated his first monastery at Whithorn to his teacher; Candida Casa or the White House, as the church he founded there was known, was considered a direct daughter house of the original.[7] In AD 401, when the Romano-British world was about to fly into pieces, Ninian had in his entourage skilled stonemasons, trained in the Roman methods of laying out arches and building with stone pillars and walls of rubble and ashlar.

Inscriptions in Latin have been found nearby, which attest to the partly romanised character of this nook of the world. At the time of the flowering of Candida Casa, south-west Scotland and the Solway region were under the control of a succession of rulers of some ability and ambition, such as Urien of Rheged and Rhydderch of Altclut (Strathclyde), who successfully maintained Roman order for a few decades after the withdrawal of Roman troops and who conducted campaigns against pagan Picts and the Saxon-speakers, who had a growing polity in Northumbria.[8] It is likely that Ninian's mission to convert the Picts and sustain the church in these difficult times had a political dimension and that he had the practical support of potentates such as the predecessors of Urien. Candida Casa proved a location from which a whole web of connecting churches were founded, a place where generations of monks and priests studied and were ordained and where the ecclesiastical culture of the Irish Sea could find a focus for the next 150 years.

There was a definite Welsh wing to Ninian's campaign. There are several ancient Welsh churches in his name. His close follower St Cadoc founded churches from Perthshire to Brecon and is reported in Brittany and Cornwall as well as Rome and even Jerusalem. He ended his days at the monastery of Cambuslang near Stirling. He also spent a deal of his time in Ireland, founding a monastery somewhere beside the River Liffey. Like many of these saints he had a powerful family to back him up: he is sometimes referred to as a 'prince'. There was also Kentigern, otherwise known as St Mungo, who was forced to leave Altclut in some political reverse and who spent time at the monastery of St Asaph in Powys before being summoned back home to found the see of Glascu. It may well have been his followers who reached the Shetlands, the Faroes and Iceland, to be discovered there by astonished Viking explorers many decades later. (These adventurous men are usually referred to as Irish, but that is to project on to them a misleading category. It seems to me quite likely, if they originated in Clydeside, that they were P-Celtic speakers who held their conversations in Cymric.)[9]

There was also a flow of missionary activity directly from the continent and from Dyfed into Éire. In AD 431, Palladinus of Auxerre was appointed by the pope to be 'bishop to those Irish who believe in Christ', and Gaulish clerics such as St Secundus, St Auxilius and St Iserninus were also active in Ireland. A St Finnian from Llancarfan was busy in the central plains of Ireland around AD 500 (whether he was a Welshman, from his monastery of origin, or an Irishman, from the name he was known by, hardly seems to matter). He was the founder of the important monastery of Clonard.

**

It was always my intention to fit this book within the ambit of a single ride that would take me clear around the Irish Sea in a continuous, many-day marathon. But while we propose, the gods of the 12-winded sky can dispose differently. Torrential rains and equinoctial gales in every week of autumn prevented me. So, viewing the green coasts of Bute from the brown coasts of Arran, I find myself living in memory, returning from winter climbing in the highlands and taking a day off in Rothesay for rest and recuperation.

The town of Rothesay is remarkable for its port and for its castle. The port is like any other, smelling of fish and diesel, but it sits beside a wide natural harbour which looks towards the mainland and is very sheltered. In the winter it is full of fishing boats and MacBrayne's ferries; in summer (although I was never there in summer) it is busy with pleasure craft and cruising yachts. But walk (or in my case that winter, limp) back inland a couple of streets and you find the castle. This is a massive drum-shaped keep of sandstone set within a moat (now a pleasant piece of greenery). This moat was once open to the sea and the tide. I spent most of the morning (which was blustery and cold) investigating and taking photographs of the monstrous hill of stone.

Rothesay Castle was designed and built in the early years of the thirteenth century to consolidate the royal hold on the entries to Clydeside and Glasgow and to put off raids from the further Hebrides and Man or from the lords of Galloway. It was put into the charge of the FitzAlans, who were before long to become the Stewarts — the most significant of the Norman barons employed by the Scottish kings to provide themselves with a power independent of their native aristocracy. In its day the great keep was regarded as a piece of avant-garde military engineering, but no sooner was it built than a Viking army besieged it and chopped a hole in its massive walls. There is a vivid account of this siege in *King Haakon's Saga*. The Vikings returned in 1263 and captured it again; this suggests that the formidable appearance of this building, its relentless symmetry, had more to do with the idea of power than its actuality. The defenders were not able to use enfilading firepower on the attackers, who were able to bring maximum force to bear at any single point on its circumference, with the inevitable result. The keep was then redesigned with four corner towers, but it fared no better in later sieges. There is a conclusion to be drawn from this story — that we should not rely too much on theory, nor worry about appearances.

By now a steady freezing rain was subduing even the raucous gulls on the seafront, and I retired to a bed-and-breakfast establishment and lay down for the afternoon, reading Ross's history of the Stewart dynasty.[10]

The next day was scarcely better but I had still two days before the hired car was to be returned at the airport, so I made a tour of Bute, looking for the ancient ecclesiastical site of Kingarth. At the end of a winding road that insinuated itself between small rocky hills and lochs, with views across the firth to either side, I came to a gate and a sign and a path. William Douglas Simpson attributes importance to Kingarth as an intermediary point between the different monastic allegiances, and this seems very reasonable, for it lies at the confluence of lochs and portages and mountain passes between Iona, Bangor and Strathclyde.[11] There is a chapel and graveyard dedicated to St Blane in a beautiful site between two arms of sea surrounded by rocks and trees. There is a Viking tombstone and a long circumferential wall. The main ruin is a repaired structure of the thirteenth century but another enclosure may date back to the eighth century. But what I remember was its peaceful greenery, its wooded grace, revealed by the bare branches of February.

Illustration 10. Kingarth Monastery, Bute.

***

In addition to the main sites around Whithorn, St Ninian founded several others in Strathclyde and central Scotland. Ninian also maintained a retreat on the island of Sanda just off the Mull of Kintyre, and another on small islets in the Solway where, centuries later, a substantial hoard of gold ornaments was found. Simpson, writing in 1935, identified and listed a large number of Ninianic sites in central and northern Scotland and pointed out that they are close to known sites of former Roman 'lines of penetration' north of the Antonine Wall. He has, moreover, traced out the activities of Ninian's followers such as St Donnan, who was another prolific founder of churches in northern and western Scotland. The foundation of Maughold on Ellan Vannin — visible from Whithorn — was probably another such site.

St Caranoc, Ninian's successor as head of the Whithorn monastery, had extensive connections in Uladh, notably with St Finbar of Movilla on Strangford Lough. This Finbar was in time the tutor of St Columba. And who, we wonder, was the St Molaise or Molash who set up his hermitage in a cave beside Lamlash Bay, Arran? He was, we learn as we study further, of Irish birth but educated at one of the important centres that had grown up in Bute. (But was he also one of the founders of the monastery on

Devenish Island in Lough Erne?) And then there are St Moluag and St Maelrubha, who ranged the Hebrides, founding, among other monasteries, that of Applecross, now remote, but then on the northern sea-ways to Orkney. St Enda was another product of Candida Casa and he sailed round Ireland as far as Inishmore in the Aran Islands around AD 510. And how many others were there, traceable only through jumbled place names, scribal errors, suppositious propaganda and mere fancy?

Looking north from St David's Head with these clerics in mind compels us to think of the Irish Sea and its extensions north and south as a network of vectors along which ideas, men and women, books, techniques and precious objects moved hither and thither, and even to ask whether or not the glorious history of the early church in Ireland was an offshoot of that in Cymru. This network did not evolve spontaneously out of pure missionary zeal, but within and as part of a very obscure and confusing play between different regions and their rulers and sub-rulers seeking to fill the void left by Roman power in Britain and shifts of ruling clans in Ireland.

And cycling up and down the Cardigan coast we constantly encounter their traces.

Illustration 11. Nendrum, an island monastery site in Strangford Lough. It was founded in the fifth century AD by a St Machaoi and continued in good order until 976, when the abbot was reportedly burnt in his own cell. This suggests that the monastery was subject to a Viking raid. Under Norman patronage it became a centre for the Benedictine order and finally a mere parish church, after which it disappears off the record only to be rediscovered (as a 'lime kiln') in the nineteenth century.

***

To get the best advantage from your bicycle, and find out the loveliest spots and those most sacred to the Muse, Mistress Clio of the pen and scroll, it helps to ponder the map and to zig and zag from one deep valley to another. The main coastal road along

Cardigan Bay follows higher ground whenever it can, along the tops of broad ridges which are windswept and which carry large trucks, tractors and cattle wagons. The section between Aberystwyth and Aberaeron reduced me to something like tears, except I was too dry to weep. I wheeled into a large campsite outside Trefriw and found, as I dismounted, that my legs were now unable to carry me and so I fell down in a heap with my Claud Butler on top of me.

Journeys off this road all involve descents and so become very tempting. But when you have come down you must go up again. The descent I made to Cilgerran Castle and the valley of the Teifi was a wonderful half hour of sweeping runs and little lanes, which brought me down to a friendly pub and a compact Norman castle above the river gorge. In Turner's day, when the painter was on one of his tours, this had been an industrial centre: quarries of slate exported their products by sea all along the coasts. Before that the castle guarded the river crossing and marked the highest place sea-going vessels could reach. Before that it had been built by the formidable Marshall family to terrify their neighbours. But this time it provided a place to lie in the sun for half and hour, take photographs and read local history.

The founder of this Marshall dynasty was the fearsome and very able Thomas, who, beginning as a champion jouster, rose through the ranks of feudalism to become lord of Pembroke and arbiter of most of southern Ireland. There is a literature about this man and his career and about how to make a political career by knocking people off horses, by Juliet Barker.[12]

My pack was getting heavy with additional books and maps and the struggle back out of the Teifi Valley and up the hill to a ridge south of Cardigan was long and hard. The road was stupefying in its steepness and the sun never relented. The tar was melting and sticking to the tyres all that afternoon. The next excursion was down a side road to the hamlet of Nevern. The groves of yew in the churchyard gave some shade and coolness but duty required me to look for the extensive hill fort on the wooded crests above. So that day I stepped back and forth between different epochs and found myself, again, with the Celtic Church.

**

Of all the busy characters of the Irish Sea, Patrick is best known, but no one seems to agree where he came from. It has even been suggested, plausibly, that there were two of him. I have decided, for want of more convincing accounts, to follow that of Liam de Paor, who locates Patrick's birthplace as a short distance from Caerluel. This places him securely within Whithorn's sphere of influence, in Rheged.[13] It is perfectly possible that he studied at Whithorn during his early wanderings. His family, too, was in a similar position to Ninian's — Romanised, P-Celtic-speaking Britons holding official positions in the last Roman bureaucracy of Strathclyde and belonging to a Christian community.

The raid in which he was captured and taken into slavery in Antrim was merely one of the many that followed the withdrawal of Roman troops. Escaping, he spent a wandering life in Gaul for some years. He probably completed his Christian education near Marseilles and perhaps also at Tours, but he, in his own writings, gives very few details. What we do know is that, having been made a bishop (where and by whom remains uncertain), he was sent by someone, or he appointed himself, as a missionary and minister to the existing Christian communities of Éire (few and far between but certainly there). From that base he quartered the whole land with legendary success. The place from which he set out to Ireland *c.* AD 432 was possibly either St David's or Whithorn and he built his first church at Saul, near Downpatrick. There is now a handsome neo-Celtic chapel on the spot. However, his great coup was to celebrate Easter on the celebrated hill of Slane, from which the bonfire blazed out to most of eastern Ireland.

Illustration 12. The hilltop monastery of Slane as it stands today. When Patrick celebrated his Easter here (*c.* AD 433) it was a pagan site on a high hill visible for many, many miles and in clear view of Tara where, we are told, the high king and his druids were celebrating their festival of Beltane. His fire challenged theirs. The present structure dates mainly from the sixteenth century, when a Franciscan monastery was built on a much older (and probably prehistoric) site.

The area around Strangford Lough in County Down became remarkable for its range of abbeys and churches. In addition to Patrick's work was that of St Finnian at Movilla, St Machaoi on Mahee Island and St Comgall at Bangor. St Comgall was, it appears, an Irish Pict or Cruithin (that is, a P-Celtic speaker living on the western shore) who founded Bangor Monastery in AD 558. He made missions to central and northern Scotland but his main achievement was to have sent out missionaries and travelling scholars back into continental Europe. St Columbanus and St Gall set out from Bangor in 589 and created several foundations and abbeys across Europe as far as northern Italy, Luxeuil in France, Bobbio in Italy and St Gallen (Saint-Gall in French) in Switzerland became in time great centres of learning that retained their links with northern Ireland. Major manuscripts now in Italy, especially the seventh-century *Bangor Antiphonary*, now in the Ambrosian Library, Milan, were written or copied at Bangor and sent to Bobbio. The music school at St Gallen was directed by a monk with an Irish name. Bangor figured so prominently in medieval church history that when the monks of Hereford were drawing their famous *mappa mundi* in the thirteenth century Bangor was one of only four place names upon it. These were great days on the Irish Sea.

By 580, Candida Casa had come under threat from the pagan Northumbrians who, bent upon rule of land rather than slaves and plunder, had begun to occupy large parts of southern Scotland. At around this time present-day Dumfries was known as 'the fort of the Frisians'. The degree to which the Frisians were invading immigrants or expansionist residents is now difficult to assess, but the archaeological arguments of the Laings and Oppenheimer's evidence from genetic traces strongly suggest that the 'Anglo-Saxon invasion' of Britain is a retrospective invention. They were already there, but were now aggressively expanding their influence into the vacuum left by Romans and by Cymric weakness.[14]

***

There is much obscurity about the details of these ecclesiastical adventurers. Stories of miraculous events and conversions abound and many of these were, we suppose, fathered upon the originals as part of their sanctification. To give an objective foundation to the stories of portents in the heavens and sudden interventions of nature we can point to the undoubted occurrence of severe weather conditions from AD 540, recorded in tree-ring growth and in the deposits of the Greenland ice. The mid-sixth century was a particularly difficult time and it is not surprising that records from that period are scarce and largely legendary.

Simpson writes of the 'disturbed political conditions' and of 'a formidable pagan reaction ... in progress within the Britonic kingdom (of Strathclyde)'.[15] St Kentigern was among those who fled to Ireland or Wales. The conversion, especially that of the northerly Picts, and with it the more general civilising process, could be, and often was, set into reverse. Northern Scotland in particular had to be reconverted by Columba and his missionaries a hundred years after Ninian's best efforts. In this time Ireland remained a region of calm and relatively civilised behaviour.

In the political and military life of P-Celtic-speaking Strathclyde, however, the pagan reaction took form as a struggle between the Dumbarton rulers and those of the Solway, culminating in a war between Rhydderch — 'a wretched man who is quite unable to tell at what hour he may be killed by his enemies',[16] and a pagan warlord named Gwenddolew, who was finally defeated with his Anglian allies near Caerluel in 573. To bring this about, Rhydderch had to rely on Q-Celtic-speaking forces from Dalriada, led by the Aidan who was to become king of Dalriada a few years later. This Aidan was a part of the Gaelic 'invasion' of Kintyre and Argyle that had been taking place. The Dalriadans were (indeed, had to be) an early naval power whose assistance would have been very useful to the beleaguered Rhydderch.

There exists a written account of military use of ships on the Irish Sea in a document of Dalriadan origin, written in Gaelic. The *Senchus Fer n-Alban*, from around AD 750, lists the number of ships and men that could be levied and a number of naval campaigns that had been conducted.[17] That such a document could exist at all demonstrates the existence of a degree of organisation above that of the clan. N.A.M. Rodger suggests the *Senchus* came about in response to a similar level of organisation among the Northumbrians. The system of ship levies, whereby local magnates had to provide galleys and men from their own resources for the use of the clan chief or local king, may have had Roman origins and was certainly very ancient. The Anglo-Saxon kingdoms took it to a sophisticated level of bureaucratic management in the subsequent centuries, and it remained in some kind of existence until the seventeenth century, when the issue of 'ship-money' helped to bring down the English monarchy.[18]

Other notable rulers existed in Britannia, though their deeds are confounded in legend and subsequent invention. One was Cunedda, mainly remembered for driving out Gaelic incursions into Wales, although his origins probably were in Lothian. Cunedda's sons, in some accounts, became major governors and petty kings of most of central and northern Wales. But these brief rulers and their briefer kingdoms are further confounded in stories of Maximus, as related in the previous chapter. But at this point we are well into the world of the first Arthurian stories of Nennius and Geoffrey of Monmouth, and the hallucinatory realm of the medieval *Gesta Romanorum*.

A major difficulty in dealing with this material is that most of it comes to us in the form of compilations, epic poems and histories put together in the eleventh and twelfth centuries, answering to the particular needs of those times. The annalists of the ages that preceded the eleventh century do not seem to have had the concept of an accurate report in any modern sense so, when their lives of saints and lists of kings are reconstructed by later monks — a number of whom, like Geoffrey, were working to late-Norman prescriptions — then obscurity rules.

The first complete and coherent text that has survived this tumultuous period is the *De Excidio et Conquestu Britanniae* of Gildas, a kind of open letter or manifesto addressed to contemporary Christians in the form of a history of recent events.

According to a 'life' written by a Breton monk, Gildas was born *c.* 494, raised in Strathclyde in a Christian household and given a Roman education.[19] He was certainly familiar with the classic Roman texts and wrote in a flowery late Latin; his native language, however, was presumably a Brittonic P-Celtic. His strictly Christian education was acquired at the monastic school of St Illtud, which was either on Ynys Byr (Caldy Island) south of Pembroke or on the Welsh mainland at Llanilltud. The monk's manuscript tells us that Gildas wrote his 'history' in Brittany, but Arthur Wade-Evans makes a case for it having been written on Flatholm in the Severn Sea, where the followers of Illtud had a cell.[20]

Gildas's aim in writing the *De Excidio* (*c.* 545) was to denounce the incompetence and wickedness of recent rulers, to show the miseries of his fellow countrymen as a punishment for their sins and to contrast current times with the peace and wisdom of Roman rule. He despises the barbarian hordes around him, Gaels, Britons and Saxons alike. The one safety for Christians, according to Gildas, is to espouse an ascetic monkish life. He thus figures as a pre-eminent reformer in that direction, helping to set the Celtic churches on the missionary, wandering and hermitic road. He seems to have spent the rest of his life (he died *c.* 570) working to that end. It is certain that he went on a mission to like-minded monasteries in Ireland; he features as a sponsor and ordainer of priests in the Irish records. He was certainly in correspondence on matters of monastic discipline with St Finnian of Movilla. He ended his days in Brittany. Gildas is thus, in many respects, a typical product of the Irish-Sea culture.

He was also responsible for the story that the first Anglo-Saxons were invited into Britain as mercenary soldiers to defend the eastern shores against pirates and would-be invaders. There now seems little doubt that this story has caused both mischief and misdirection. Oppenheimer argues in some detail that these Anglians and Saxonum were already there.[21] Gildas, as a P-Celtic-speaking, Cymric churchman, regarded the pagan easterners as a plague sent from God, as a 'multitude of whelps coming forth from the lair of a barbaric lioness'.

Another figure of the monastic world of the Cymri is St Samson of Dol, who also studied at the monastic school of St Illtud. Samson was of south-Welsh parentage and became one of the most promising graduates of Illtud's academy. He was set to become his successor until displaced by family intrigues. He then figures as abbot of Ynys Byr and as a roving bishop/diplomat in Cornwall, the Scilly Isles, Guernsey and Brittany, where he founded the Dol Monastery. He is also reported to have visited Ireland and to have cured the madness of an abbot near Howth. He is last glimpsed as 'Samson peccator episcopus', signing decrees at a council of Childebert, king of Paris, in 557.[22] Let us note, just in passing, that Dol was the original home of the Stewart family, Norman followers of King David I of Scotland and appointed by him as his stewards.

A name that appears in Samson's story is that of Dubricius, or Dyfrig, to give him his Welsh name. He was without doubt a real person, but his biography has been confounded in the Arthurian material spread about by Geoffrey of Monmouth.

Dyfrig figures in these legendary matters as officiating at Arthur's coronation, as being archbishop of Caerleon (when in fact the Roman metropolitan concept of an archbishop was unknown along these shores). Rather more authentic stories give him a miraculous birth but also place him in the context of a monastic school and as a founder of churches and parishes. At the end of his life he retired as a hermit to Ynys Ennli (Bardsey), where there was a monastery presided over by another pupil or colleague of Illtud, St Cadfan.

The exact nature of the monastic settlement on Ynys Enlli is not clear to me, nor perhaps to anyone. It was well known up and down the Irish Sea as a place of, supposedly, 20,000 hermits' graves. (But, of course, there could hardly have been a community of hermits.) A pilgrimage there was held to be especially meritorious because the crossing was through a fierce tide-race. The island itself is strategically located, as indeed were all the main churches and monasteries of the Celtic Church.

North lies the centre of Caer Gybi in Anglesey. This was founded by St Gybi on the site of the Roman watch station. Gybi was a Cornishman, an associate of St David, who had churches and sites named after him in Pembrokeshire and near Criccieth in the Lleyn Peninsula; he is said to have visited Ireland. The Roman *castrum* is still to be found and in good order, having proved a useful structure; it now contains a much-rebuilt eighth-century one-room church and a fascinating, and also much-rebuilt, later church. It stands on the edge of the docks and the marshalling yards of contemporary Holyhead (see previous chapter).

We know more or less nothing about Illtud himself, save that he was a promoter of learning. He was:

> of all the Britons best skilled in Holy Scripture, both the Old Testament and the New, as well as in every kind of learning, such as geometry, rhetoric, grammar, arithmetic and the knowledge of all the arts; in divination, too, he was well proven and he had foreknowledge of the future.[23]

This curriculum was entirely standard for the time and place, but Illtud was a proponent of ascetic monasticism and his centre was a stopping point for Irish monks on their way towards the continent. It seems likely, then, that (like Nenhyfar) it was also a place of intertranslation, where two or three or more Celtic languages were being mingled with late Latin and in which attempts to set out both P- and Q-Celtics in late-Roman characters were made.

Yet another possible product of Illtud's school was Dewi Sant, or St David (born about 520). Once again, the various 'lives' of this man are plaited with so much legendary and miraculous material that it is hard to credit the rest, but there is no disputing certain main facts. He was born into a substantial Cardigan clan with many and wide connections. There are chapels connected with his mother Non or Nonnita in southern Wales, Cornwall, Devon and Brittany. After receiving education in one or more rather shadowy schools, which may have included Illtud's, David founded a monastery at the place that now bears his name, but was then Mynyw. Official hagiographers portray the future saint as studying in Gaul at the school of St Germanus of Auxerre before returning to found his own centre on the Pembrokeshire headlands. Before he could do this, however, he had to displace a chieftain named in chronicles as Baia Scottus, clearly a Q-Celtic-speaking member of the Scotti, who had either occupied the land after a raid from Ireland or had been one of the original travelling Q-Celtic speakers who had not travelled as far as the rest. Dewi remained at Mynyw for the rest of his life, establishing other centres of learning and piety in Wales, south-west England and Brittany. He had many connections across the sea to Irish monastic houses and we know of a St Maedoc who crossed into Leinster around 600 to found the monastery of Ferns. On Carnsore Point, south of Wexford, there is a ruined chapel which may well have been founded as an Irish outpost from St David's.

What Dewi Sant and his followers had in common with monks across the Irish Sea and at Whithorn was a strict adherence to the most ascetic traditions. His sobriquet was 'the water-drinker'.

Illustration 13. Ruined chapel on Carnsore Point, County Wexford, looking directly across to St David's (date unknown). I have not been able to find anything about this chapel-like building but it is likely to be connected with the nearby monastery at Our Lady's Isle. Carnsore Point was also proposed as a site for a possible nuclear power station—a proposal that was defeated after a vigorous campaign in the 1970s. The same site now houses a large flock of wind generators, which bring the ninth century and the twenty-first together.

There were, in fact, a large number of men and some women who, described as 'saints' in the scant literature, passed their youth in places of learning, adhered to the monastic rather than ecclesiastical aspect of Christianity and became travelling gurus who went by sea and land, starting congregations, building shrines and chapels and leaving their names behind them. Some of these, by virtue of their education and birth, became advisors to chieftains and petty kings. When we learn that they 'founded a monastery', this might mean very little more than that they persuaded a local chief to grant a small enclosure for a gathering of huts and a shrine where several enthusiasts might worship and study together. St Blane's, Kingarth, is a well-preserved example of this type of small monastic settlement. But other saints followed a more ascetic life, working wonders and retiring to the hermit's cell. Their travels, even the well-attested ones, were remarkable: there is a ruined cell upon the barren rock of Sula Sgeir, which just clears the high-tide mark north of the Hebrides; there are others on St Kilda and finally in Iceland. Nor is it impossible that the legendary voyage of Brendan found somewhere far to the north and west.

An eighth-century catalogue of the saints of Ireland describes three stages in the formation of the church in Ireland. The first order derived from Patrick's mission or earlier and were all designated 'bishops'. That enabled them to ordain their followers. The second order were all 'presbyters' ordained by St David, Gildas and St Cadoc; these constituted the Welsh wing of the Irish Church. The third order were presbyters 'who dwelt in desert places and lived on herbs and alms'. These correspond roughly to the fifth, sixth and seventh centuries.

It is clear from all accounts and sources that the organisation of this north-western Celtic-speaking church was informal to a high degree. To be a bishop was not to be a member of a fixed hierarchy nor to be tied to a diocese. There was very little in the way of political organisation that might provide a model or template for an ecclesiastical organisation or vice-versa. The most permanent unit of the Gaelic polity was the *tuath*, or *tud*, a tribal territory ruled (notionally) by a chief, and a bishop was his ecclesiastical equivalent. Only perhaps in the catalogue's second order, which owed its ordination to the Welsh Church, is there any appearance of what we now think of as church governance. There is little sign of sustained obedience to the papacy, though pilgrimages to Rome and even Jerusalem figure in many 'lives'.

***

Returning north we find ourselves confronted by the figure of St Columba (as he figures in Latin). Born to the significant clan of the O'Donnells, Columcille had a deep ecclesiastical education and, like others before him, was well backed by a powerful family. He went on to become a missionary and power-broker all across the northern half of the Islands. He founded his first monastery at Doire and subsequently others at

Durrow and Kells. Then, at the age of 42, we find him going into penitential exile across the water. The reasons for this are obscured by legendary details, but he was involved in a feud between the O'Donnells and the then-high king of Ireland, Diarmuid, which degenerated into warfare.[24] His kinsman, Conall, who was a ruler in Dalriada, offered him a way out.

Setting out in 563 from the mouth of the Foyle, he and his company of 12 monks landed first on Colonsay. He would not stay there because Ireland was still visible (the weather was, evidently, better than usual). His next landfall was Iona, which he could hardly have missed.

Iona is a strategically positioned island and sound which everyone sailing north or south must negotiate. It is large enough to maintain a population (probably 150 monks at its final size) and is separated from the island of Mull by a narrow and intimidating channel. As there are very few anchorages along the rugged south coast of Mull, any small boat (and we are talking now about a 20-foot lath-and-leather curragh) can hardly avoid taking the sound through to the open waters beyond. We should imagine Columba and his men hurriedly taking down their square sail as the current took them so as to row with accuracy through the narrow rocky passage. At low water, with the tide rising and the wind at your stern, this requires delicate judgement.[25]

Columba was a man of great energy and ambition; according to Adamnan in his 'life' the new monastery grew quickly into a thriving centre of learning and self-reliant economy. In addition to scriptural study, Latin, Greek and Hebrew were taught and numerous manuscripts produced and copied in the scriptorium (among the major products we will include at least a part of such masterworks as the *Book of Kells*). But Columba's other function was political. His missionary task was to the probably P-Celtic-speaking Picts, who were besetting the Q-Celtic-speaking inhabitants of Dalriada, his political aim being to reinforce the power of his kinsman Conall and his people. Conall presumably had had this in mind when he had given the island of Iona to the new community. According to Chadwick it is possible that the realm of Dalriada had been set up for the political purpose of denying the Picts access to the Irish Sea.[26]

Douglas Simpson describes Columba as 'always itching to dabble in political affairs … and determined to devote every ounce of his abounding physical and mental energy to assist (his kinfolk) in their task of retrieving their fortunes'.[27]

In 574 Conall died and Columba, in a political and symbolic coup, both decided the succession and then inaugurated the chosen Aidan at Iona. (This was same the Aidan who had fought battles in Strathclyde.) This set a precedent: subsequent Dalriadan rulers were crowned and buried on Iona, which 300 years later became a powerful symbolic site for a newly emerging Scottish state. The effective political centre of Dalriada, however, remained where it had been for millennia — in the area around Kilmartin, the Crinan Isthmus and the Iron-Age fort of Dunadd.[28]

To introduce the name of Dalriada is to open the scholar's equivalent of a creel of crabs. It is hard for the lay reader (such as I) to find a way through the literature, not least because of the nomenclature. For some Dalriada is a region or realm; for others a people — the Dal Riata. This confusion of categories is nicely caught in a passage from Michael Richter's study of Ireland and her neighbours in the seventh century (1999). In a discussion of the origins of the Iona monastery he writes:

> The British Kingdom of Dal Riata had gradually made its appearance as a bridgehead of the north eastern Irish Kingdom of Dal Riata from around 500 onward, but its growth is poorly documented. According to the Irish sources, Iona was situated in the sphere of influence of British Dal Riata, and thus in a political sphere which was decidedly Irish.[29]

As I hope has become clear, the 'zonal' approach to these matters that I am trying to develop suggests that the distinction between British Dalriada and Irish Dalriada is not very fruitful. The north-east of the island of Ireland and the south-westerly fringes of highland Scotland were (and in some respects still are) one place. The inhabitants of Jura, when they want to party or to shop, cross the North Channel to Ballycastle to this day. The Presbyterians of Antrim, seeking freedom of worship in the eighteenth century, would row to Scotland on a Sunday morning, returning after the evening service. Thus the problem of whether or not something is described as Irish or Scottish or British is secondary. Here, certainly, we are dealing with the Irish Sea as a whole and, with respect to Dalriada, with a continuance of the Clyde-Carlingford cultural sphere under new management.

This new management was Q-Celtic speaking with strong connections to Uladh (Q-Celtic speaking) and weaker connections with Strathclyde (P-Celtic speaking); it was in a state of sporadic warfare with Picts to the north and east. The degree to which P-Celtic speakers or what have been termed 'Irish Picts' or Cruithin held sway in parts of Uladh is a very obscure matter indeed. The degree to which there were mutual expulsions and invasions is an even darker matter. But there is a general agreement that there was some movement of population eastward around AD 500, associated with a shift in the balance of power from P-Celtic speakers to Q-Celtic speakers.[30]

***

The year after Aidan's coronation at Iona (that is, AD 575) a large meeting of chiefs and sub-kings was convened, according to annals, at Druim Ceata near Derry, possibly at what is now Limavady, facing the Hebrides. The abbot of Iona attended with a retinue of 20 'bishops'. The meeting had been called by the then-high king of Ireland in his role as *primus inter pares*, with the diplomatic aim of settling the status of the Dalriadan domain. Unfortunately, most of what is known about this event is obscured by contradiction and errors. What seems to have happened is that the two halves of Dalriada (in so far as it was a single polity astride the North Channel) were split apart. The Scottish side became an independent kingdom, except for an obligation to put its fleet at the high king's command when so required. But this supposes the existence of such semi-permanent entities as fleets and kingdoms when perhaps we are dealing with phantoms created by lists and annals written two or four centuries later (some in language so obscure as to baffle the best of medieval scholars). But the existence of a list of kings supposes, without doubt, a conceptual unity in the minds of the annalists, whatever may have been the facts on the ground. The point to be made here, from the perspective of this book, is that events such as the meeting at Druim Ceata, whatever may have actually been the case, came to be seen as an instance of Q-Celtic speakers acting together — as a cultural unity, almost as a polity, though hardly as a nation. This cultural unity was to be appealed to in the fourteenth century as part of the wars between Scotland and England, when the Bruce brothers tried (unsuccessfully) to rally the Gaels and Cymri to their cause.

From around the time of the convention Scottish Dalriada began to develop connections with the Saxon-speaking rulers of Northumbria, some of whom were buried at Iona. These Northumbrians, like Ealdfrith (685–704), took high-born Q-Celtic-speaking wives. The Dalriadans, as we have seen, partook of Anglo-Saxon organisation; there was a great interchange of peoples and practices taking place. The complicated mix of languages, the many gaps in the records and the very different conceptual structure under which they were compiled (not to mention those kinds of history-writing of later years based upon the concept of nations and their identity) seriously interfere with any attempt to get at the reality. Sometimes the student wishes that he or she could devise a vocabulary of terms specially for the task.

It is in and through the shifty, violent and under-politicised world of the seventh century that the learning, artistic quality and vivid humanity of the early churches and their networks of abbeys, monasteries, hermitages and missions travelled and survived. I call this world under-politicised because it had on most occasions insufficient secular organisation to maintain a civic consciousness larger or longer than that of the kindred group. The larger continuity, the long-term view and the ideological constructions of ethnicity were provided and produced largely by the churches and the monasteries. They were the ones who possessed a formal and (within its own terms) universalising language. They kept the records and their partial explanations have generally been taken as true. But that is because they created and controlled the discourse in which events have subsequently come to be understood.

And all this has bearing on the transformation of Alba into Scotland; the matter, of course, is obscure (is there any part of this matter that is not obscure?) but what seems to have happened is that the Dalriadan rulers decamped eastward into

Perthshire and there began to create a pan-Scottish kingdom by amalgamating the Picts, whoever or whatever was designated then or later by that term. These Q-Celtic-speaking rulers, however, continued to look back over their shoulders at their westerly Irish connections. Relics of St Columba were transferred from Iona to Dunkeld at some point in the ninth century to symbolise this shift. In linguistic terms, the new rulers of this 'united kingdom' were Q-Celtic-speaking elite figures on a Pictish and possibly P-Celtic-speaking ground. One scholar gives us good reasons for supposing that 'up to and including the thirteenth century they identified the kingdom of the Scots and its inhabitants with Ireland'.[31] This identification is given a still later expression when Robert I (Robert the Bruce for English readers) addressed the Gaelic rulers in Ireland from his exile in the Hebrides. He appealed to the idea of 'common language and custom … free since ancient times, sprung from one seed of a nation'.[32] But by that time the kingdom of Scotland was becoming a North-Sea power and, except for the brief and violent adventures of Edward Bruce and his army, turning its back on Ireland, and there is no evidence that Irish chiefs in number responded to the appeal.

Nor did Dalriada disappear quickly. The Irish Gaelic language in north Antrim and Donegal remains closer to the Scots Gaelic of Islay than to the Irish of Kerry. As late as the sixteenth century the MacDonalds (Clan Donald) of Argyll claimed to rule large parts of Antrim and frequently did. The last flicker of this was a defeat inflicted on the O'Neills of Ulster by a largely Scottish army near Cushendun in 1613. No, it was not the last flicker, it was the penultimate flare, for during the English Civil War a Presbyterian Scottish army, aided by parliamentarian ships, engaged in a small but very violent campaign up and down the lochs and islands. In fact, later still, the Stewart kings of Scotland waged a war to enforce the obedience of the Gaeltacht of the Hebrides and set the Protestant Clan Campbell to drive the Catholic, Gaelic-speaking Clan Donald out of Kintyre.

The ghosts of the Cruithin are among the many historical vapours plaguing the loyalists of Northern Ireland who, in their wilder moments, identify themselves with those P-Celtic speakers who were expelled from Ulster in the seventh century and returned in the seventeenth like the Jews to Israel. They match themselves with contemporary Israel to counter the IRA's enthusiasm for the Palestinian cause.

***

During Gildas's life and subsequently, the British kingdoms of Strathclyde, Rheged and southern and eastern Britain were being assailed by mutual strife and by Saxon war-bands, progressively pushing further west. The P-Celtic world which, under the pressure of Saxon incursions (actual and linguistic), began to defend itself vigorously and become more conscious of its unity, was now describing itself in annals as Cymru — 'our people'

— as in the modern place name Cumberland and, of course, Wales. Its furthest northern extension was, perhaps, the two Cumbrae Islands in the Firth of Clyde and the town of Cumbernauld near Glasgow. Its furthest point south was Cornwall. In Latin texts this Cymric world increasingly called itself Britannia as opposed to the Saxon Anglia. In Welsh, Anglia becomes Lloegyr — the lost lands.

Gildas's world was cut in two shortly after his death when a Mercian war-band reached the River Dee, refortified the ruined Roman camp at Chester and massacred the monks of Bangor (615). To add to the obscurity of this almost undocumented era, this Bangor was not the Bangor that is, then and now, to be found on the Menai Strait, still less the Bangor in what is now Northern Ireland, but Bangor-ys-Coed, a Bangor-in-the-woods, a few miles south of Chester. The monks had come out *en masse* to urge on the Christian defenders of Cymru against the pagan Sassunaich. This was a misjudgement.

At around the same time Northumbrian rulers extended their power as far as Caerluel and a Northumbrian army invaded both Ellan Vannin and Mon. They also undertook raids into Ireland. We can identify AD 615 as an important date for the culture of the Irish Sea: a new class of language appeared on its shores — a northern *mélange* we now call Anglo-Saxon.[33]

A fine example of Anglian/P-Celtic bilingualism can be seen in the names of two adjacent hills that are visible over great stretches of the Cumbrian and Lancashire coastline and from well out to sea — the summits of Ingleborough and Pen-y-ghent. I recall as a child being transfixed by the sight of Pen-y-ghent, its top covered with snow, and wondering then at its curious Welsh name. It gives me a sharp satisfaction to discover, 60 years later, that I had encountered a remnant of Cymric P-Celtic. Its neighbouring peak is a 'burh' (fort) of the Angles.

We should not suppose that the Saxon world of hordes and war-bands was so very different from that of the Q-Celtic speakers. Nor do I mean to suggest that there was a mass migration. It is important to have firmly fixed in the mind that we are not dealing with large changes in the population. The total number of Romano-Britons (now calling themselves Cymri) seems to have been between one and four million; the most recent claim, by the Laings, for the number of Anglian incomers is initially no more than 25,000.[34] Most of the Saxons were, in point of fact, already there and already expanding their power from the east midlands westward. The Laings' estimate from archaeological evidence is strikingly similar to estimates based on genetic evidence adduced by Oppenheimer.[35] The reason for the Anglo-Saxon success, as summarised by the Laings, was that the collapse and abandonment of the Roman farming system left a void into which they flowed. The Laings further surmise that Anglo-Saxon became the trade language of the forming England. If this is so, the Roman road system (still viable) enabled the language to spread with ease and become very useful. This system of roads focused on the south-eastern corner of the Islands.

We might like to compare it with the very rapid worldwide spread of English in the early nineteenth century, along lines of shipping and railways. Whatever may be the case, the Saxon and Romano-British populations had common rulers by AD 600 and the several brands of Anglo-Saxon had formed the common language of what was now Englelond. To suppose that in some sense the incoming Saxons drove out the Celtic natives is plainly not true, though this remains part of British and Irish popular history. It was the languages of record that were driven out.

***

For this success to attend the Anglo-Saxon language we probably need to look for institutional differences. The Gaelic polities tended always towards segmentation. The larger political units were always conglomerations of little kingdoms, themselves subdivided into smaller kingdoms yet. This was the form under which dynastic expansion took place — by splitting. The same was true of the Cymric rulers: a system known as 'partibility' decreed that sons should have an equal share in the father's legacy. Lise Hull writes:

> In many ways the law of partibility guided the course of Welsh history, for it weakened Welsh resistance against outside invasion and set the scene for the Norman occupation of much of Wales.[36]

In parallel difference, the Saxon kingdoms expanded from the centre without splitting. Anglo-Saxon kings were careful to deny the royal aspirations of their kinsmen; they were then faced with the problem of enforcing their authority from a distance. This is the source of the higher level of organisation all these Saxon kingdoms begin to exhibit. With organisation came centralised bureaucracies, permanent institutions and coinage. These are not possible without sustained central authority.[37]

The degree to which Anglo-Saxon organisation was self-generated, Roman or Romanesque is too difficult and contentious a matter to enter into with any confidence. I am making the following assumption: if it was the case that the Anglian component in Roman Britain was more closely allied with settled agriculture than other components, then it was also more closely enmeshed with Roman organisation. It was, therefore, more or less certain to inherit Roman administrative structures along with Roman brick architecture and roads. I have already cited the example of King Harold's speedy movement of troops (see Chapter 3); to this we should add the astonishing feat of the *Domesday Book*. The capacity to take a census and general national audit could only have been possible when the records were already in existence and the personnel needed to do so available and capable, in an already existing 'civil service'. The smooth brutality and efficiency of Duke William's conquest proceeded just because the Anglo-Saxon kings were at the head of an organisation. Once the head was cut off (or shot through the eye), the body fell into other hands.

The same approach was followed in ecclesiastical matters as in civil ones, with the Anglo-Saxon Church more akin to the Roman style of governance, centralising rather than splitting fissiparously. This was decided officially in AD 663 at the synod of Whitby, which was a confrontation between the Celtic and the Roman systems of church government.

How this relates again to land use and land ownership, even into recent times, is another question still. One major cause of the Irish Gaelic failure to amass capital was the division of farms into ever smaller and therefore less profitable units. What a man inherited was, and could only be, poverty. This disastrous course was followed as late as the 1920s, by the first governments of the Irish Free State.

* * *

Anyone who spends time in study of these churches and churchmen is likely to fall in love with the subject and the qualities of the people, the buildings and the sites they encounter. Like their Neolithic forbears these churchmen showed a great sensitivity to the placing of buildings and monuments in the landscape; their buildings, from the beehive cell to the little chapel, partake of this sensitivity through their sense of detail, and within the cells and chapels and scriptoria the same relations of large to small obtain as on the manuscript page or the enamelled brooch. We intuit from them and through them human communities that remained at the simple human level of extended families; we seem to touch a bedrock of fellow-feeling and a lack of pretension. Their sites are created and discovered places and, to reiterate, not to be in a place is to be nowhere and to be nowhere is to be nothing.

* * *

And so it was that one windless evening we anchored our boat against the rocky strand of the Garvellach Islands and sculled in across the fronds of kelp which rose up under the oars like a blackish pasta. A peregrine wheeled over us, screaming, as we crunched on the gravel.

A group of beehive cells fitting snugly into a dell of rocks a few feet from the tide's edge, clustered together like the eggs of a giant stone bird. Within they were perfectly crafted, with an ovoid space formed of flat corbelled stones laid immaculately on top of another. This ovoid was wonderfully snug and shapely and completely dry; on the outer side the stonework was rougher and I imagine that they had once had a layer of sods and earth. Perhaps within they might have had a plaster or smooth daub finish, painted richly. Around, there was a low stone wall, a carved slab and what might once have been an orchard enclosure.

We went in search of water and found it in a third cell a few yards away. There a fountain gushed from a carved fissure in the rock, falling into a carved container; but when you tried to enter you had to crouch and in crouching you made pitch darkness for yourself. The water had to be found, like grace, by its sound and its savour.

> Brendan built, Columcille
> occupied the egg of stone,
> cut out the stairs and sill.
>
> Who drinks here, kneels.
> Descend to lean
> at the cold cistern
>
> and in darkness
> lap.

Notes

1   D. Jones (1952) *The anathemata: fragments of an attempted writing*, London: Faber and Faber, Part 2.

2   T. Traherne (D. Buresh, ed.) (2002) *Waking up in heaven: a contemporary edition of* Centuries of meditation, Spencervill, MD: Hesed Press, 3.23.

3   M. Richter (1999) *Ireland and her neighbours in the seventh century*, Dublin: Four Courts Press, p. 12.

4   There is a discussion of this in J. Creighton (2000) *Coins and power in late Iron Age Britain*, Cambridge: Cambridge University Press, especially in Chapter 6, which I have found useful.

5   It should be recalled that according to Caesar's *Commentaries* the pre-Christian 'druids' maintained their learning and religion without the aid of writing and that written records are relatively recent invention.

6   Lowe, E.A. (1969, 2nd ed.) *Handwriting: our medieval legacy*, Rome: Edizioni di Storia e Letteratura., p. 12.

7   See W.D. Simpson (1935) *The Celtic Church in Scotland: a study of its penetration lines and art relationships*, Aberdeen: University Press, p. 51.

8   The best introduction to this obscure and difficult period I have found is H.M. Chadwick (1949) *Early Scotland: the Picts, the Scots and the Welsh of southern Scotland*, Cambridge: Cambridge University Press.

9   There is a twelfth-century *Life of Kentigern*, written by Jocelyn, a monk from Furness Abbey,

which definitely describes these Icelandic settlers as followers of Kentigern. Like all such 'lives' it is full of miraculous events, but what is important is not the fanciful details but the accumulating concordance with similar accounts, which together bring out a definite and plausible account of the early Celtic Church.

10   S. Ross (1993) *The Stewart dynasty*, Nairn: Thomas and Lochar.

11   Simpson, *op. cit.*

12   J. Barker (2008) *The tournament in England, 1100–1400*, Woodbridge: Boydell.

13   L. de Paor (1993) *St Patrick's world: the Christian culture of Ireland's apostolic age*, Dublin: Four Courts Press, Chapter 15. Other writers, however, give other dates, some as early as AD 389. J.A. Duke (1937) *History of the Church of Scotland to the Reformation*, Edinburgh: Oliver and Boyd gives Dumbarton as Patrick's most likely birthplace.

14   L. and J. Laing (1990) *Celtic Britain and Ireland, AD 200–800: the myth of the Dark Ages*, Dublin: Irish Academic Press; S. Oppenheimer (2006) *The origins of the British: a genetic detective story*, London: Constable.

15   Simpson, *op. cit.*, pp. 77 and 89.

16   A remark ascribed to St Columba by his biographer Adamnan. Note his Welsh-sounding name.

17   For a comprehensive assessment of naval power in this obscure epoch, see J. Haywood (1991) *Dark Age naval power: a reassessment of Frankish and Anglo-Saxon seafaring activity*, London: Routledge.

18   N.A.M. Rodger (1997) *The safeguard of the sea: a naval history of Britain 660–1649*, London: Penguin Books, p. 6 *et seq.* What Rodger does not argue here is the degree to which arrangements such as the ship levies were not so much the requirement of a monarchy as formative of the state in its earliest days. It was creating a bureaucracy.

19   Strathclyde once again. I attribute the importance of Strathclyde in the story of the early church to its very peripheral and critically insecure position as the furthest outpost of Roman order. There is nothing like extremity for concentrating the mind. It was (like Deheubarth) the meeting point of several cultural spheres.

20   A.W. Wade-Evans (1934) *Welsh Christian origins*, Oxford: Alden Press.

21   Oppenheimer, *op. cit.*

22   We know about Samson from a 'life' written around 610 by a Breton monk who had himself visited Ynys Byr, Llanilltud and places in Cornwall, in search of material for his writing 'from what I found current among most holy and thoroughly competent men … gathering a few things from many' (see Wade-Evans *op. cit.*, p. 206 *et seq.*). The reconnection to Brittany was fostered by a remigration of some Britons back to the Bretons at this time to escape the general mayhem.

23   There is a 'life' of Illtud — A.W. Wade-Evans (tr.) (1944) *Vitae sanctorum Britanniae et genealogiae*, Cardiff: University of Wales Press Board — but this is, to say the least, improbable.

24   According to tradition, this quarrel began with a dispute over who should be allowed to copy a manuscript that Finnian of Moville had brought to Ireland from Rome. Columba sneakily

made a copy at night. When ordered to surrender it by Diarmuid, Columba refused. Blood was spilt and one thing led to another. A serious battle resulted in 3,000 dead, the O'Donnells being given aid by no less a figure than the Archangel Michael. A synod of bishops held Columba responsible for starting this fracas; he was, briefly, excommunicated. The book in question is a psaltery, now in the archives of the Royal Irish Academy, Dublin. It is known as the *Cattach* or the *Battler*.

25 The author recalls reefing in hurriedly and watching the catamaran that passed through the sound before us lose its keel on a midstream reef. Columba would have had no keel; his nippy craft was well adapted to this kind of constricted navigation but was hard to guide in open waters by sail.

26 Chadwick, *op. cit.*, p. xxii.

27 Simpson, *op. cit.*, p. 76.

28 An excellent starting point for all this material is provided in R. Butter and D.C. Lyons (1999, 2nd ed.) *Kilmartin: Scotland's richest prehistoric landscape: an introduction and guide*, Lochgilphead: Kilmartin House Trust.

29 M. Richter (1999) *Ireland and her neighbours in the seventh century*, Dublin: Four Courts Press, p. 51.

30 I am mainly following the account of these questions given in S.M. Foster (1996) *Picts, Gaels and Scots: early historic Scotland*, London: Batsford, backed up in Chadwick, *op. cit.*, Richter, *op. cit.*, F.J. Byrne (1973, repr. 2001) *Irish kings and high kings*, Dublin: Four Courts Press and W.C. Dickinson (A.A.M. Duncan, rev. and ed.) (1977, 3rd ed.) *Scotland from the earliest times to 1603*, Oxford: Clarendon Press. They and all the other writers agree on the difficulty of forming any clear picture of just what was happening at the top end of the Irish Sea in the fifth and sixth centuries.

31 D. Broun (1999) *The Irish identity of the kingdom of the Scots in the twelfth and thirteenth centuries*, Woodbridge: Boydell Press, p. 9.

32 See Chapter 7.

33 Compare this with 'Serbo-Croat', which to non-speakers is one tongue but to the native-born is at least four—Serbian, Croatian, Bosnian and Montenegrin.

34 Laing and Laing, *op. cit.*

35 Oppenheimer, *op. cit.*

36 L. Hull (2005) *The castles and bishops' palaces of Pembrokeshire*, Little Logaston: Logaston Press, p. 1.

37 These matters are discussed extensively in S. Bassett (ed.) (1989) *The origins of Anglo-Saxon kingdoms*, London: Leicester University Press, especially Chapter 1, to which I am directly indebted here, though it does not discuss the centralisation question.

FIVE
Re Innse Gall

> Tall men array the fleet, which swiftly holds its course on the sea's bare surface; no hand
> lacks a trim war-spear … They have a straight stern-wind behind them … their dappled
> sails are bulging, foam rises to the vessel's side.
> — 'The tryst of a fleet against Castle Sween'[1]

This fortress was probably founded by a Viking chief, Sweyn of Denmark, whose family
name was later Gaelicised to Mac Suibhne. They ruled most of Lorne and Kintyre in the
twelfth century but picked the wrong side in the Wars of Independence. 'The tryst of a
fleet against Castle Sween' is a Gaelic verse recounting an unsuccessful attempt by the
Mac Suibhne clan to recover their property. The manuscript is in the *Book of the Dean
of Lismore*, a multilingual anthology of the sixteenth century.

The graveyard at Craignish further up the coast of Lorne contains several grave slabs
in the uniquely barbaric style of the Innse Gall as it persisted into the fourteenth century.

The Isle of Man, at the centre of these tumults, was at different times known as
Monapia, Mevania, Eudopia (surely a copyist's error), Ynys Manaw, Oileán Mhanainn,
Eamhain, Falga, Eilean Mhannain, Ellan Vannin, Maun, Mann, Mannin and finally,

Illustration 1. Castle
Sween among the
lochs and islands of
Lorne—an ungainly
block of magpie-
coloured stone coated
with bluish lichen, like
a seacliff under a
white sky.

around 1600, the Isle of Man. Ellan Vannin, in fact, gives us an excellent point from which to conduct a circumspectus of the Vikings in the Irish Sea and their transformation into the lords of the Isles.

Illustration 2.
Gravestone, Craignish.

***

The monks who wrote the *Cronica Regum Mannie et Insularum* (*Chronicles of the Kings of Man and the Isles*) were in no doubt of their importance; the text begins with a swift tour of the Viking world which establishes the importance of Man and its kings to north-western Europe, tracing the rulership of Ynys Manaw back to Cnut, son of Svein, not to mention St Olaf, Magnus of Norway, Harald Hardrada, Sigurd of Northumbria and Edward the Confessor — in fact, almost anyone who was anyone in the Saxon and Viking world. And that misses out the Gaelic and Cymric chieftains of yore.[2]

Ellan Vannin first figures on the ground of this story as a locus of the Clyde-Carlingford culture of stone monuments, raths and chambered graves. Neolithic and Bronze-Age sites are as frequent as in Antrim and Kintyre and new ones are still being studied. One of the finest of all chambered graves stands atop a hill south of Ramsey. Cashtal yn Ard consists of a half circle of tall slates, a portico, and through it a passage, now open, with the remains of five distinct chambers.

All along the western coast are creeks, inlets and natural harbours. Visible from all points of the compass, the Isle of Man was very well placed to be a sort of clearing house for whatever was in circulation up, down and across the Irish Sea — people, flints, metals, slaves, beliefs, diseases and languages.[3]

From the various elements that comprise the Manx language linguists have concluded that the earlier tongue of the inhabitants was a P-Celtic, which was later replaced by a Q-Celtic. Broderick suggests that this change took place as late as AD 500, which places the change in the disturbances that followed the recoil of the Roman armies.[4] We are entitled to imagine a warlord from Uladh or Mide arriving in his galleys and establishing a forward base from which to raid the fertile plains of Rheged, and bullying the Brittonic-speaking peasantry into changing their speech-ways.

Though the cultural connections with Éire and Cymru were strong, the political connections established by the Vikings were largely northward towards the Hebrides into what was termed the Sudreyar (Skye, Mull, Islay and Jura) as opposed to the Nordreyar (the northern islands of the Outer Hebrides, Orkney and Shetland). Thus Manx is considered to have developed in parallel with Scottish Gaelic rather than with Irish. All trace of spoken Norsk has vanished but the place names are a spicy mixture of Gaelic and Norse. In this respect Man is similar to the island of Lewis, a mixed language zone where up to 70 per cent of the place names are Gaelic translations of Norse. I have already surmised that there was an Irish-Sea *patois* or trading language; Manx might, in fact, be the relict of it, though as a distinct language it seems to have developed quite late (in the thirteenth century, according to some scholars).

It may be that Manx came to be defined as a separate language only when it was translated and written down. In 1610, the Welsh-speaking bishop of Sodor and Man, John Phillips, had the *Book of common prayer* translated into Manx in what was essentially a Welsh style of spelling. Later, other religious books were translated into Manx by Bishop Thomas Wilson, who used a spelling much closer to the English, which has remained in use although it is ungainly. In 1764 the Society for the Propagation of Christian Knowledge reported that the majority of the population spoke no English, so they commissioned a translation of the Bible. In the next century Manx went into slow decline, which tends to happen to many local languages when their use is challenged by a more advantageous metropolitan tongue. In recent years Manx has become a much-studied test case for what is now called lugubriously, and prematurely, 'language death'.

This is premature because in the past 15 years there has been a revival of Manx consciousness that has extended into the names of streets and signposts, as part of a heritage movement ambiguously connected to the tourist industry and the growth of a much more genuine interest in Manx-language courses and clubs. The longer-term validity of this revival remains to be tested. As I shall observe later, these older languages seem to have become like King Arthur — not so much dead as sleeping.

***

On Ellan Vannin, which they called Maun or Mann, the Vikings created the norm for sea-going expansion — the seizure of an offshore island or peninsula from which to move to the mainland and to which one might retreat when the going got tough. This practice was later taken up by the British Empire. Bombay was a barren sandbank before it became Mumbai, Singapore a pirate-infested swamp and Hong Kong a worthless archipelago of rocks. Consider that Atlantic chain of Gibraltar, St Helena, Ascension and the Falklands. The most recent of empires is contrived upon islands too, only these float, Laputa-like, and can be moved around the globe.

In 798 the *Annals of Ulster* noted that 'Gentiles burned Inispadraig, broke the shrine of St Mochonne and took the spoils of the sea between Eire and Alba.' Historians always assume this 'Inispadraig' to have been a small foundation on the Skerries, north of Dublin Bay, and some have suggested Lambay Island, but it might easily have been the Isle of St Patrick in Peel Bay, where there had been, for at least a hundred years, a Patrician foundation.[5] This one was large enough to be worth robbing, secure enough to form a base for further operations and perfectly placed to interdict all sea-going north of Anglesey. It then contained at least two buildings, several monkish cells and a round tower from which it is possible to see the coasts of Ulster, Galloway and the whole northern sweep of the Irish Sea at a turn of the head. It subsequently acquired a cathedral, a fortress, a palace and a barracks: within an extensive curtain wall these parts all curiously collaged into one another.

***

Illustration 3.
Peel Castle.

Illustrations 4 and 5.
Peel Castle.

I got there some 1,207 years later, by ferry and bicycle, after a night crossing from Belfast during which I was thrown about and jolted from one breaker's crest to another, in an empty ship, like a pea in a pan. Douglas Harbour at three in the morning. A miserable road over the island in pouring rain and bitter cold. The day before the mountain roads had been blocked by snow — and this was the end of April. That night there was snow along the hedge bottoms and sleet froze my hands. Halfway across I squatted for an hour in a concrete bus shelter before the cold and damp drove me out. At length, in a wretched dawn, I came over a hill and free-wheeled into the steep narrow streets of Peel.

I spent the next two nights at the municipal camping ground, which turned out to be a windswept field at the top of the town. My little tent was buffeted and the ground every morning was wet with rain. It was remarkably cold, with flurries of sleet mixed in with the rain, and there was snow lying on the tops of the hills. Whenever I could I went down into the town out of this weather. I discovered a pleasant little local-history museum and a couple of good bars. Peel Castle also provided nooks where sunshine warmed the stones and I could sit to make some notes.

Beside the castle a deep inlet cuts into the coast lined with small warehouses and building yards. Peel was, for many years in the last century, a centre for the fishing-boat-building industry. These builders traditionally regarded their product as related to Cornish boat designs and designated then 'nobbies', 'dandies', 'yawls' and 'luggers'. I made a list of some of them:

Angelic Bell, 15 tons, nobby, 1911, for M. O'Neill of Tralee.
Beaver, 14 tons, dandy, 1865, for D. Logan of Glasgow.
Bonnie Maggie, 20 tons, lugger, 1901, for Irish Govt in Galway.

Of 150 similar boats, 18 were registered at Skibbereen, 20 at Tralee, 12 at Galway, 19 at Dublin, 8 at Belfast and 17 in the Isle of Man, with others at Westport, Liverpool, Glasgow, Whitehaven, Sligo, Greenock and London. (All except ten were for Ireland or the Isle of Man.) Much the largest was a 95-ton schooner registered to a William Thomas of Peel. It is clear that between 1865 and 1914 this was a notable place.

* * *

Inis Pádraig, St Patrick's Isle, Peel Castle, began to be inhabited quite late, around 600 BC. Excavation has shown up a collection of circular huts. Among a small number of objects found were loom weights, which suggests a settled farming community, and a number of dead fleas. These were the earliest human fleas so far found in the Islands and their successors will have fed upon Celtic maidens, Viking warriors, Norman warlords, Scottish and English soldiers and Tudor grandees before paying attention to a myriad and polyglot gang of smugglers and pirates. It may be that even today their descendants are at feast somewhere in the crofts of Man.

One of the huts was nine metres across — a substantial structure that had been used as a granary or store of some kind. This has suggested to the archaeologists that Inis Pádraig, before it became an ecclesiastical centre, had been a chieftain's stronghold.[6]

Further excavation within the cathedral precinct uncovered a cemetery with 327 identifiable burial sites; the most notable and grand was that of an adult woman. She had been interred in the Scandinavian pagan style, with her goods about her. The most notable was a long iron cooking spit, but she had also silver-handled knives, tailor's shears, a comb, needles, beads and the remnants of a feather pillow, together with fertility talismans and a spectacular necklace of amber, jet and polished fossils. These were the accoutrements of a great lady.

The excavators deduced from this and other graves that they were dealing with a well-established Viking/Manx settlement begun in the ninth century, when Vikings had begun to intermarry and convert to Christianity. There is a collection of Norse gravestones in the churchyard at Maughold Head at the north-eastern tip of the island. This ancient church site, founded from Whithorn in the days of St Ninian, lies below a Bronze-Age fort and contains a cross carved with Norwegian Urnes-style decoration and another carved with a warship.

This same glyph can be found on graves, seals, slabs and documents from all over the Hebrides, indicating the ubiquity of the longships. It becomes the insignium of the *re* Innse Gall — the lords of the Isles. An inscription reads, 'Hedin set this cross to the memory of his daughter Hlif: Arni carved these runes.'

Left: Illustration 6. Gravestone at Maughold (in a style similar to the Urnes style of Norway). Right: Figure 1. Carved warship at Maughold.

***

And who, I am asking myself, was Hlif? Everyone who has lost a child will be asking that and imagining the mourning parent and his discussion with the stonemason Arni. Was she a child or a grown woman? I imagine her fair and probably tall because, being a Viking's daughter, she would have to be, wouldn't she? But then she may have been little and dark-eyed and dainty. And I imagine Hedin recalling her and remembering how she returned to him at unexpected moments, now as a toddler and now the grown woman with her own children. The dead have no age. In the minds of parents, lost children wax and wane, appear and reappear in different guises. Sometimes you may meet them in the street, striding towards you, not recognising, or later, in the distance or across a crowd. Or even — and this is a moment of terror — feel them in your arms or leaning on your shoulder. Hail, Hedin. Hedin, hail. The wind beats down. I stand on the pedal to make the vertical move forward.

***

Gwyn Jones allows us three main sources of information about these new arrivals, who were not, as we have noted, entirely unknown to the Inland Sea: archaeology, coinage and the written records.[7] The difficulty lies in correlating them. The archaeological record is always liable to revision — often drastic — when a new discovery is made (it is this that entitles archaeology to be called a science). Coins offer a window through which to survey the politics of the period but, being valuable and long-lived, they travel far and pass through many hands, thereby changing in historical significance. Written records, where fact is concerned, are notoriously unreliable. 'Only a few,' writes Jones, 'deserve a full confidence, most demand caution, and many a bleak distrust.'[8] But fact is by no means the main point of written records; what they can provide are explanations as imagined by their authors. They also provide good stories; to make your way through the successive sagas of Iceland is a long read full of vivid incidents.

The main disadvantage of written records for all periods is that only certain matters are ever recorded. They were, for early days, the doings of rulers and matters ecclesiastical: the records give a peculiar bias to what we can know by their means. The normal day-to-day occupation of trade, to take one major example, is barely touched upon; yet at a time of extraordinary violence (as portrayed in written annals) substantial towns arose all round the Irish Sea, based upon a substantial trade. The two stories do not fit very easily with one another. Another question persists through this story that began in previous chapters: are we dealing with a population of settlers or with passing brigands? The annals do not help us very much.

The view taken here is that already broached: that the population as a whole remained genetically stable and that the successive convulsions were cultural events rather than population changes. Languages, practices, techniques and implements travel more easily than populations. We are all, in north-west Europe, much the same. Oppenheimer has shown that the population of the Irish-Sea coasts was already, from Neolithic times, of partial Scandinavian origins. Warrior aristocracies impose themselves easily on peasants and, as between one warlord and another, the differences are less striking than the similarities. That phase of incursion and settlement that we call the Viking Age had been preceded by many previous phases that have passed unrecorded. Moreover, the records of these events were kept in the mode of a 'heroic age' of war-chiefs and their followers who would, in accordance with the nature of their existence, stress differences rather than deeper similarities.

The evidence of dialects and place names is that large parts of what is now Cumbria and Galloway and south Lancashire were quite heavily settled by people of Scandinavian origin — enough to affect their accent to this day. The characteristic place-name endings of -by (as in Allonby or Kirby) or -ey (as in Ramsey and Anglesey) are scattered all along the coasts without regard for detectable genetic 'clusters' because, to make matters more complicated, the Danish Vikings who swarmed into northern and eastern England and up into the Irish Sea from the south and east turn out to be genetically identical to the Anglo-Saxons, making quantitative estimates of respective populations very uncertain. Indeed, considered in the light of genetics, the distinction between Vikings and Anglo-Saxons scarcely exists. Moreover (and this is the important matter) chromosomes tell us nothing about the really interesting issues. What made a Viking was his ship, his axe, his armoured jerkin and his methods. Viking was not a genetic category and was scarcely an ethnicity. It was a way of life.

Place names, however, point towards one interesting feature. Those Viking place names that occur in the Irish and Welsh quadrants of the Irish Sea are mainly coastal, whereas those in England are often well inland. This indicates that the Scandinavian warriors who first invaded the Isle of Man found the eastward coasts open to settlement, whereas the westward Irish and the southward Welsh coasts could not be penetrated so easily. The logical conclusion would be that the P-Celtic- and Q-Celtic-speaking populations of those parts, by maintaining their tribal or clannish society, also maintained a degree of military and political coherence, which had been lost in those parts of the Islands that had been extensively romanised.

What does appear certain is that traces of the specific Norse genetic markers in contemporary Ireland are few and far between. Where the Irish coasts are concerned we are dealing with small coastal settlements. These settlements, when they survived, grew into trading ports that included all kinds of persons. Those that did not succeed faded quickly away.

A typical example is the site of Annagassan on the Irish east coast, south of Dundalk. There are traces of a stockade and huts and a river mouth serves as an excellent small harbour. But a few miles further south is the city of Dublin which, founded by a Viking war-band at much the same time (*c.* AD 850) was, within 50 years, a major centre of trade and industry. Another 'failed' site was probably Hoylake on the Wirral. Finds of jewellery and other items along the shore suggest that there was once a considerable beach-based market there, but no town developed.[9] Perhaps there were similar beach markets at Strangford and Carlingford and Ulrecksfjord (now called Larne). I suspect that under the streets of Preston lies some relic, since Ribblesdale was used by Viking travellers on their way to York from Dublin. One at least left a great hoard of silver coins and bracelets behind him.

Illustration 7. Annagassan, County Louth, an anchorage a few miles south of Dundalk. On the high bank above the bridge are the (vague) remains of a Viking earthwork. Looking down from the rampart we see into the deep pool that marks the estuary of the little River Glyde. It is first mentioned in 823 and last mentioned in 923, but was not in continuous use. The river bends round the high ground, providing defence on three sides.

* * *

Piratical use of Mann was quickly succeeded by permanent habitation. A group of houses excavated north of Ramsey and adjacent to a sheltered anchorage 'appear to represent a wintering base used successively during the transitional period between raiding and permanent settlement'.[10] A number of farmsteads have also been excavated, some of which show clearly that the newcomers had taken over the sites of previous farms or were sharing them; round indigenous huts stand side by side with boat-shaped Norse halls. There is a deal of scholarly disputation about the actual numbers of immigrant Vikings involved and to what degree they ruled over the local P-Celtic and Q-Celtic speakers or coexisted with them more or less peaceably. But however it may have happened, by 850, Ellan Vannin, placed astride the sea-ways, had become the hub of Viking power in the Irish Sea.

When, around 900, the Vikings began to adopt Christian beliefs, we find several examples of undoubted Norse names coupled with Gaelic names and vice versa. Thus the first man to bear the Gaelic title of lord of the Isles (Toiseach Innse Gall — 'lord of the foreigners' islands') was a Godfrey MacFergus, who was a chief in Ulster and who died in 853. We even encounter a man named MacHaakon.[11] The great Hebridean chieftain, Somerled, was one of these naturalised Gaelic Norsemen. (Somerled or Somarlidi or Somhairle first comes to notice as the *regulus* of Kintyre in 1140, but by the 1160s he ruled the area from Man to Lewis. He met his death in 1164 attempting an invasion of central Scotland.) From his first name we may surmise that Njal Thorgeirsson, whose death is the key event in the saga that bears his name, had an Ulster parent or grandparent.

On the evidence of some very humble dwellings it seems likely that the Norse settlers and occupiers on Mann were by no means all part of a military caste or a band of mercenaries, but very ordinary Norwegian peasants who in time became part of the indigenous population. Irish-language sources depict this mixed population as a recognised group — the Gall-Gaedhils or foreigner Gaels. They also differentiated between 'black' Vikings (Dubh Gall), who were Norse, and the Danish, who were 'white' (Fionn Gall) — hence Douglas, the place of the black Vikings, and the name Fingal. Monkish sources often referred to them all as Gentiles because they persecuted the children of Israel (themselves).

When Viking rule was withdrawn in the thirteenth century the Norse language went with it and Q-Celtic asserted itself for the next 300 years. There is still more scholarly argument about the degree to which the renaming of sites took place and the degree to which the revived Manx was the same as the earlier version, and what all this may or may not imply. It involves some very technical disputation which has to be left aside for our purposes.

Some at least of the new inhabitants took to burying their wealth in difficult times; up to 20 hoards of silver coins and jewellery have been found on Man. The largest portion of the coinage is that minted in Dublin and York by Norsemen for trading purposes in the tenth century and later, and there are also Anglo-Saxon coins and the silver rings and bracelets that were used as currency all over the Norse world. There is, further, a class of coins known as Hiberno-Manx, which were minted in Mann, probably in Peel Castle itself — an indication of the island's political importance in the eleventh and twelfth centuries.[12]

Very little is written of Norse activities in Mann for the first 200 years; it is glimpsed through a few sentences in Icelandic tales or fragments in Irish and Welsh annals. But during the tenth and eleventh centuries, great *jarls* of Orkney and bishops of Trondhejm ruled the roost, along with Icelandic brigands. Magnus Bare-Legs, the Norwegian king, made Inis Pádraig his base of operations for a season before meeting his death in Ireland. He appears to have been one of the builders of Peel Castle, since he compelled the Vikings of Galloway to supply him with tree trunks in order to build a stockade, traces of which were found by the archaelogists below the cathedral ruins. He also built a fort on what became the site of Rothesay Castle.

The present diocese of Sodor and Man is one of the last remaining organisational traces of the Viking world of the Innse Gall, for its boundaries once shadowed those of the twelfth-century kingdom of Man and the Isles. The other, of course, is the Tynwald, which as a parliament of Man was created on the Norse model and which continues some functions inherited from the tenth century into the twenty-first. Manxmen like to claim this as the oldest parliament in the world, but it is better to think of it as a legislative council. Its claim to parliamentary sovereignty was always interrupted by larger matters — kings of Norway, Scotland and England took small account of the Manxmen.

Illustration 8. Tynwald Hill.

The Norsk-Viking occupation of Man had, of course, consequences for the Gaelic, Anglian and Cymric coasts opposite. Scandinavian settlements extended into the shores of the Solway Firth, with village names like Torthorwald and Allonby, as well as along the banks of the Mersey. It is well recognised that the accent of the Solway contains many Norwegian sounds. But as to written details, there is virtually none and there is little in the way of archaeology. We know also that most of what is now Galloway was ruled by a Scotto-Norse dynasty. We have no definite idea if the Solway region was a dependency of Man and ruled from there, or even what 'ruled' meant under the circumstances of the day.

Wendy Davies has listed a series of questions with which anyone trying to make sense of the sea coasts has to deal. She is concerned with patterns of power in early Wales[13] but her observations apply over all the time and space I am trying to comprehend. What did 'to rule' mean in early times? What did it mean to have power and be powerful? How do these terms square with those of other epochs? How far are they consistent with one another?

> An all purpose 'lord' and 'lordship' ... are liberally scattered (in most studies) without any attempt to spell out, let alone question, the user's assumption about the meanings of the terms; indeed, their use suggests analogies with political systems elsewhere in medieval Europe although any clarification of the nature and limits of the analogy is strikingly absent ... So, too, we find words like 'overkingship' and 'overlordship' tossed about with no attempt to investigate the nature of the dependence implied ... Nor the relationship between 'overperson' and 'underperson' ... in what circumstances did military victory have subsequent political implications? (We cannot assume that it always had any.) Was a victory only significant if settlers filled in behind it?[14]

After a torrent of such questions she moves on to more detailed but no less significant problems: what was implied by early Welsh words such as *gwlad* ('country') or *tud* ('population group/area')? Were these, and their equivalents on other parts of the coasts, real administrative units? If so, did they, together, constitute political units? How far did the writers of annals, using Latin, project onto their own times the late-Roman terms they had to use? And so forth. These are questions general to the whole area and epoch under discussion and apply as much to Dalriada as to Anglesey. (Davies's first chapter is a wonderful example of the way in which the practised academic can wither the reckless amateur.)

Viking raids on the Welsh coast began around AD 850; Rhodri Mawr, the most impressive of the ninth-century rulers of north Wales (whatever his title of *rhi*, or king, actually meant), defeated and killed the leader of a Viking fleet off Anglesey in 856. Dillon and Chadwick portray Rhodri as 'aiming at a united British nation and an ultimate conquest of the Saxons' but he was as much a victim of the Norsemen as any of the Saxon rulers he fought against.[15] The arriving Vikings probably regarded him as indistinguishable from the Saxon petty kings they had already encountered.

The first 'ravaging' of Mon is recorded in 877. The most likely immediate source of this expedition was a combination of forces from Dublin and Mann. Rhodri Mawr was forced to flee to Ireland. The first full-scale Viking 'invasion' of Mon seems to have been in 902 when one Ingimund, expelled from Dublin, occupied parts of the island. From there he moved on to what is now the Flintshire coast and the Wirral, where he settled or permitted other Norse to settle. There were additional raids up and down the Welsh coast — on Holyhead (in 961), in Tywyn (in 963) and in other places. AD 988 was a very bad year, with at least five military expeditions doing damage. St David's was looted four times. The Manx *Cronica* recounts how Magnus Bare-Legs also went to Anglesey from Man in 1098 'and subjected the island to his rule'.[16] There were also expeditions by Danish war-bands who arrived through a war-torn Mercia or by sea and the Severn. There was some Viking settlement on the Welsh coast and upon Anglesey (which now has, of course, as Onguls-ey, a Viking name). In *Njal's Saga* we learn of at least one settlement large enough to be described as a town, in Wales, whither Kol Thorsteinsson flees and is pursued and killed in revenge for the murder of Njal.[17]

Around the banks of contemporary Wales Viking place names are common for coastal features. The islands of Skomer, Skokholm, Ramsey and Grassholm off St David's Head are typical examples; Fishguard — the fort of the fishes — is beyond doubt a Norse name. And a number (though not a great number) of graves and silver hoards have been discovered that are certainly Scandinavian in character. These were all grouped around the Menai Strait, reflecting the Viking strategy of controlling significant waterways.

How far it can be said that there were Scandinavian 'rulers' in north Wales is another matter. They certainly collected tribute, but to what degree this was in the form of an administered tax or mere 'squeeze' remains uncertain. In 989 the Welsh leader Maredudd certainly collected tribute for a Viking gang. An important part of these winnings was, in fact, slaves to be sold in Dublin. The sons of one Harold of Man were heavily involved in struggles for the possession of Anglesey and were the effective rulers of Gwynedd for some years around 980. One of them had the title (according to Gaelic annals) of *re* Innse Gall. There was also a period in which the rulers of Dublin and/or Man, Gaelic or Viking, could claim to be legitimate rulers in or of Wales, but this was a claim that could scarcely be enforced. A hint of Viking rule appears in the fragmentary *Jomsvikinga Saga*, in which the chief Palnatoki appoints someone called Bjorn the Welshman to hold his kingdom while he goes off to ravage Scotland and Ireland.

The Dublin–Man axis was the most effective combination of powers in the whole area and when the Vikings of Man and Dublin worked together they ruled everyone else. Among the Dublin Vikings we have to include the Norsk and Dansk inhabitants of Wexford and Waterford. The Gaelic rulers of Leinster were frequently part of this axis. Cheshire and Merseyside were also, simultaneously, a zone of conflict between Vikings and armies from Mercia.

Mercia was that Anglo-Saxon-speaking kingdom that appeared in the seventh century across much of midland Englelond. By AD 757 it was being ruled by the famous Offa (d. 796) of the eponymous dyke — the earthwork that runs from the Flintshire coast to the mouth of the Severn. Whether this was built to keep the Welsh in or the Vikings out is not easy to say, but its construction has been described as an

Figure 2. Offa's Dyke, the Black Pig's Dyke and Hadrian's Wall: the three internal frontiers of the Islands were already largely in place in AD 700, when Offa of Mercia was dividing Wales from England. The Black Pig's Dyke, however, is not continuous and was the work of several groups carried out over several centuries.

undertaking comparable in scale and efficiency to that of the Pyramids of Egypt. It is probable that Offa got the idea from Hadrian, further north. Chester, Mercian since 615, was taken by Vikings in 863 and reoccupied by a Mercian force in 907. At the same time Mercian armies were invading north Wales (in 796, 816, 823, 878, 881, 942 and 967). Norsemen regularly hired themselves out to local Welsh rulers as mercenaries against the Mercians, just as Gaelic raiders and dissident Mercians employed Viking fleets to transport themselves back and forth. A further layer of complications was added by the Dansk occupation of large stretches of northern and eastern England and their attacks upon Mercia. Welsh and Mercian military forces combined to drive them back on at least one occasion. Danish fleets sailed into the Irish Sea from the south and it becomes difficult to tell who was doing what to whom. Norse Vikings clashed with their Danish cousins in a sea battle in Carlingford Lough; Mercian kings began to employ Norman mercenaries (who were, of course, Viking settlers from northern France) to defend their southern marches against attacks from Wales and Ireland. However, Viking ambitions (insofar as the Vikings had sufficient unity to have ambitions) were checked in 937 at the battle of Brunanburh. In this fight a Viking army, aided by Scots (though perhaps this means Irish) was routed and driven back to their ships. Where this encounter took place is a matter of dispute, but one serious candidate is the village of Bromsborough between Runcorn and Birkenhead, on the Wirral:

> There the Norsemen's chief
> Was put to flight, and driven by dire need
> with a small retinue to seek his ship …
> they left behind them corpses for the dark
> black-coated raven, horny-beaked, to enjoy
> and for the eagle, white-backed and dun-coated,
> the greedy war-hawk, and that grey wild beast
> the forest wolf.[18]

The battle was a significant event in the unification of the Anglo-Saxon kingdoms and the creation of England as a single political entity.

For a number of years after the battle of Brunanburh the principal power in the Irish Sea was the Anglo-Saxon royal fleet of Edgar (959–75). One sign of this was a custom of yearly mobilisation, during which the fleet would sail round Wales, from Bristol to Chester, 'showing the flag' and raiding Dublin when occasion offered. At Chester a ritual was enacted after Edgar's coronation in which the respective rulers of north and south Wales, Man, Dublin, Strathclyde and Galloway rowed Edgar up and down the River Dee, while he, with an imperial gesture, took the helm. By this submission the several rulers seemed to have accepted Edgar as a high king of some kind with lordship over the Irish-Sea area. But in the next reign — of Aethelred (the Unready) — Anglo-Saxon power had to be diverted to deal with new threats from continental Vikings, and sea power returned to the Vikings of Man and Dublin.

Large-scale raids into or through Wales, either by land from Mercia or across the sea, were endemic to the times. In 1049 a combined army of Danish Vikings and Welsh ravaged the Welsh Marches; this was repeated in 1053 by an exiled Mercian noble named Aelfgar, who had put together an army of Wexford (Dansk) Vikings in alliance with a Welsh 'prince'. This army sacked and burned the (Norman-built) frontier town of Hereford, coming upriver in longships. When the Normans attempted to carve out Anglesey for themselves they came up against Magnus Bare-Legs, the king of Norway, who put them to flight and killed Hugo, the earl of Chester. The Norman expedition into Ireland in the next century is merely another chapter in the same nasty story.

The political history of the Irish-Sea coasts during the tenth and eleventh centuries was so chaotic that the mind, reading of it, begins to sink. But life cannot have been uniformly violent because evidence from pottery and coin hoards suggests a plentiful Chester–Dublin trade from around 975. This was the period in which Dublin, Wexford and Waterford and their trading partners in Man, Chester, Bristol and smaller ports (probably including Carlisle and Ayr) became, under Norse sponsorship, a considerable market that traded to continental Europe and north Africa as well as to Norway and Sweden. The presence of this trade is evidence of normality apparently at odds with military facts. We have to remind ourselves again that the military forces were not, in fact, very large, because large armies were very hard to sustain in the circumstances of the times. We often seem to be dealing with groups of special forces — skilled, even professional, warriors engaged in limited operations for very highly defined purposes.

And what was being traded? Imports included, inevitably, wine from French and Spanish ports, but also: iron (as ingots or as ready-made goods and weapons) from Scandinavia: the occasional exotic cargo of silk or spices from north Africa; luxuries such as furs and amber from the Baltic and pottery from Mercia; and staples such as salt and dried fish. There is also abundant evidence that Dublin, especially, was a major slave market through which captives from all over the Islands were passed on. A set of iron manacles from this period have been found in Anglesey. A cliff path beside Waterford Bay is known to this day as '*bóthar na mná gorm*' — 'the road of the black women' — though this probably refers to the slavery of late-medieval times.

Exports were, without much doubt (but also with little quantitative evidence) the products of cattle: hides, tallow, salt beef, butter, horn and vellum; there were also sheepskins and wool. Metals included copper from Anglesey and gold from the Wicklow Mountains and Snowdonia. There was also a trade in hunting dogs and possibly horses. We also know that there was a shipbuilding industry in the Irish Sea; at least one of the Viking ships recovered in Denmark was built of Irish wood. But any estimate of the nature or extent of Irish-Sea trading has to be based on archaeology and coinage, not written records.

We think of Viking ships as exemplified in the ultra-lean longships, but trade had to be carried in plumper vessels such as the *knarr*, which had a hold and some decking, along the lines of the Frisian cog. These were quite capable of carrying horses, as the Bayeux Tapestry shows us. When Alfred the Great of Saxon England started to build a fleet to put off the Viking raids (in 896) he devised large vessels that were neither 'on the Frisian nor the Danish pattern', but one devised by himself.[19]

It was not until the extent and richness of Viking trade and industry was exposed by archaeological digging in, mainly, York and Dublin that it could become a real topic to investigate. (This in turn depended largely upon urban development, first in York in the 1960s and then in Dublin some 15 years later.) There was little record of this trade because bargains, accounts and trade agreements were not the sort of material that got written down: there was no permanent bureaucracy and no customs officers.

Moreover, to muddy the waters further, the distinction we make between trade and warfare is a modern one. To what degree did it hold good for the Vikings and their victims? We can make an analogy between the Viking methods of trade promotion around the Irish Sea and those of the European powers and the United States with respect to China and Japan. The Chinese emperors were forced to cede small territories and admit traders at the mouth of the cannon. Campaigns were waged to enforce the trade in opium; cities were sacked and burnt to gain access to their markets. An American war fleet arrived in Yokohama to insist that Japan enter into a trade agreement, which, not surprisingly, it did. The Viking manner of doing business likewise extended across a scale which, at one extreme, involved ravaging, went by way of demanding money with menaces to offering protection, to demanding trade on favourable terms, and concluded in an equalising 'cash and carry'.

The several Viking settlements were enabled in their trading enterprise by the enthusiastic adoption of coinage; coins on the Roman model were minted in Dublin, Man and York and immensely facilitated trade by freeing the circulation of wealth from barter in actual goods. Where coins were absent, rings and bracelets of silver were a recognised form of portable wealth, particularly favoured in the Nordreyar (the islands of Orkney and Shetland). With coinage came, we may suppose, exchange rates of a primitive kind and perhaps even forms of banking (though this is pure surmise).

Trade for the north-west of Europe came, by these means, to be centred upon Dublin. One writer goes so far as to assert that 'Even before the large scale excavations in recent years, there is suffcient evidence for Dublin to have been regarded as the most important Viking settlement in western Europe outside Scandinavia.'[20] And there are good geographical reasons why this should be so. The Dublin area was, from time immemorial, the focal point of a series of prehistoric trackways across Ireland from north, south and west (roughly corresponding to the main motorways of today); it had ready access to the cattle- and horse-raising pastures of eastern/central Ireland and to the mineral deposits of the Wicklow Mountains. It was mutually advantageous for the local population to have a market for their agricultural surplus and the city probably played a role in stimulating that surplus. It had a good harbour facing Cymru and Englelond and Dublin Bay was well positioned on the north–south line to serve both the Nordreyar and Scandinavia, as well as Normandy, Gascony and Galicia. Why it never became a town before the arrival of the Norsemen is part of the wider question of Gaelic society.

We can say the same for the other smaller trading ports of Wexford, Waterford and Cork. Each one of these gives immediate access to the sea and into the land by way of good rivers. Each one appears (subject to further excavation) to have been planned around lane-like streets with adjacent cottage-like houses, which were usually end-on to the streets and surrounded by fences. This is a pattern still to be seen in Scandinavia. There is evidence that these plots existed for a very long time — centuries in some cases — which strongly suggests legal forms of permanence and town government. In Dublin quarters of the town were set aside for particular trades — for cobblers, amberworkers, smiths and metalworkers, woodcarvers and so forth. Boatbuilders and merchants were located on the quays and beaches. The town as a whole would be enclosed on the landward side by a defensive embankment topped with a wall of wooden stakes, which would later be replaced by a gated structure made partly of stone. (When the Normans came up against the inhabitants of Wexford, the Vikings retired behind what definitely sounds like a stone structure of some height and permanence, not a stockade.) A number of building types have been identified and the general term 'Hiberno-Norse' has come into accepted usage.[21]

The Hiberno-Norse towns were a feature new to Ireland. Centres had built up around several inland ecclesiastical sites. Armagh, for example, had quarters clustered around the cathedral/monastery of St Patrick and its allied institutions. These settlements both served and protected the church. Such centres in turn generated elements of government, regulations and laws and the courts to enforce them. But whether or not we should describe these gatherings as towns has been a matter of debate.

One school has followed a line of argument propounded by D.A. Binchy:

> the idea of a town, with a corporate personality distinct from that of the ruler, was quite foreign to the Gaelic mind until the Scandinavians set up their 'cities' in Dublin, Limerick, Waterford and elsewhere. Slowly, indeed unwillingly, the Irish followed their example: but though a few monastic settlements eventually grew into towns, all the larger urban centres are of Norse provenance. It would be difficult to exaggerate the formidable impact of these prosperous trading stations, with their local and overseas markets, their cash and credit sales, upon the primitive economy of their Irish neighbours.[22]

This argument reinforces the assumption that Gaelic society was innately and deeply conservative in nature, a continuant of the Bronze Age in essentials, and it neglects the connections the church and secular society had established with continental Europe, with its many cities, during the pre-Viking years. It neglects, also, the already existing export and import trade. It forms in Ireland part of a retrospective nationalism, of 'saints and scholars' in a lost, rural and 'Celtic' golden age. But a counter-argument replies that the clerical and monastic centres around the Irish Sea, be they Irish or Welsh, were already (if not exactly incorporated towns) town-like in scale, variety of population and wealth — and, we should add, staying power. Though repeatedly raided and burnt, the seventh-century centres like Armagh, St David's, Cashel, Caernarfon and Kildare are still with us.

There was also sufficient civil government and accumulated capital in Gaelic Ireland to support the building and maintenance of public works, such as the immense wooden bridge across the Shannon at Clonmacnoise (dated 804) which was over 150 metres long and wide enough for herds of cattle to cross.[23] That Rhodri Mawr could put together ships and defeat a Viking army at sea (whatever the scale of the engagement) demonstrates an unrecognised competence in boatbuilding and seamanship. We have reliable reports of other large Gaelic or Cymric fleets. In Dalriada, as noted, there was a well-established system for the maintenance of a navy.

Crop-raising, too, developed all around the Irish-Sea coasts in the ninth and tenth centuries, releasing the population from its dependence on cattle. Grain encourages permanence in human affairs and long-term investment in drainage and such inventions as watermills and windmills. A number of very early watermills have been excavated in recent years, the most ingenious being one at the monastery of Nendrum on Strangford Lough. It was powered by tidal cisterns which, filled at high tide, were slowly let out as the tide went down to allow continuous use.

There seem to have been no good economic or technical reasons why the lands that became in time Ireland and Wales should not have developed into cohesive and administered states the equal of the Anglo-Saxon kingdoms of Mercia, Wessex and Northumbria and the growing kingdom of Scotland, complete with towns.

The reasons, in effect, have to be internal: the conceptual structure could not generate a strong enough political structure. Loyalties and identities remained rooted in the local, the clannish and the personal. The notion of large-scale ethnicity, and consequently of a nation, remained weak. These issues are comprehensively discussed by Kristian Kristiansen in his 1998 book *Europe before history*.[24] His concern is the historical generation of the early forms of the state out of the tribal conditions of the Bronze Age, but when we are dealing with the politics of the Irish Sea we seem to be dealing with the same problem, constantly repeated — the generation of an organising centre. The idea of a high king, an *ard rí* or *gwledig*, existed but was nearly always conceived in ritual or symbolic terms. It was not, or could only become in certain rare conditions, an instrumental concept. We have the strong impression of a society that was stuck in an earlier form, which always put it at a disadvantage beside Roman, Anglian or Norman methods of government.

The certain rare conditions included obvious external menace, such as was provided by the Vikings. Looking at the career and evident ambitions of Brian Boroimhe (d. 1014) we are seeing just such an attempt at statehood of an early kind, spurred on by the need to cope with menace. Having managed to wrest the control of the high kingship of Éire from the traditional holders, the Uí Néill, by 1002 Brian and his clan and affiliates were attempting to put together an instrumental high kingship, which was to have included revenue from customs, regular taxes and coinage. His proto-state was evidently modelled upon the example of Charlemagne and, as such, he bears an interesting comparison with Alfred the Great in Wessex.

The famous battle of Clontarf, on Good Friday 1014, is one of these confused and confusing encounters that illustrate very well the intermingling of interests and rivalries between groups and the effective absence of nations and states in spite of Brian. It has been claimed as a victory of the Irish over the Danes, and has entered into the retrospective legends of nationalism as the defeat of the proud invader. And it is certainly the case that the *ard rí* had put together a large and effective coalition. The other army was also a coalition — of Dublin Vikings, Gaels in opposition to Brian's centralising project (particularly from Leinster) and interloping war-bands from Orkney and Iceland (who were Norse rather than Danish). The Isle of Man was represented on both sides, as a base for Brodir (who figures in the Icelandic saga of Njal) and for another Viking chief called Ospak, who aligned himself with Brian. The Viking side also included Brian's Viking wife Kormlod (Gormlaith in Irish, who had been previously the wife of the Uí Néill warlord Mael Seachlain); she was now promising herself to Brodir and simultaneously to Sigurd of Orkney, and with her a claim to Dublin and the lands adjacent and its taxable revenues. *Njal's Saga*, which describes the participation of the Icelanders in this battle, depicts Kormlod as 'utterly wicked' and Brian as 'the noblest of all kings'.[25]

After a fearful struggle nominal victory went to the Irish side, but only with the death of Brian, his sons and many of his closest men. This effectively put an end to the proto-state. The Vikings were not in any sense driven out, nor were their towns or trading posts abandoned. On the other hand, the defeat of their confederacy signalled that any Viking attempt to overrun Ireland *in toto* was vain. In this respect Clontarf was not unlike the similar battle at Brunanburh 77 years earlier — it marked the limit of Viking power. Man seems to have become attached to Uí Néill interests for the next few decades, with the death of Brodir. For the following century control of the Irish Sea alternated between different rulers of Man, Dublin, Leinster, England and Norway.

From an Icelandic/Orkney point of view (and for the moment we can admit these northerly islands into the Irish Sea) the battle was an end point of the blood feuds initiated by the burning of Njal Thorgeirsson in his own hall and the conversion of Iceland to Christianity (around 1000).[26] Brodir, as one of the burners, met his death in a manner remarkable even for those times — his intestines were wound around an oak tree while he was yet living.

In Irish popular memory the Dansk remained terrible for many years after. During the battle of the Boyne, when the Irish troops recognised a Danish regiment drawing up to face them, it is reported that they cried out, 'Oh lord in heaven! That is Danish men! God save us!'

***

After three days of camping in the wind and rain the charm of Peel had worn thin. Man is interesting and indeed delightful, but out of season it is an awkward place for the solitary traveller. Campsites and hostels are mainly closed and the numerous bed-and-breakfast houses (where I longed to find a shower and a warm fire) were out of business. In a sort of desperation I decided to move on. At least in cycling I would keep warm.

The north-easterly coast of the island is bleak — the long shingled shore is bereft of harbours and holds few trees. A steady wind was blowing down from the North Channel and my cycle, well loaded with camping gear, cameras, wet clothes and notebooks, was heavy. It seemed a long ride and it was getting dark when I came into Ramsey along the road known to bikers as the Sulby Straight. This length of road is commonly but erroneously believed by the Manx to be a Roman road. Roman or not, I was glad to find it because it put the wind on my back. Just before Ramsey I pulled into a field gate for a snack and to reorganise myself. A large field sloped up to a wood and a high crest of hills. The map was marked 'battle'.

***

The Isle of Man was taken back under Norse rule decisively with the arrival of Godred Crovan and his fleet in 1079.

Not a lot is securely known about this man, save that he had been one of the few Viking chiefs to escape the defeat of Norwegian armies by King Harold of England at Stamford Bridge in 1066. He is described in the *Cronica* as the son of Harald the Black of Islay and is said to have lived on Man for some time. Other sources say he came from Iceland and had the backing of the Norwegian king. Whoever he was, he was able to put a large fleet together. The *Cronica* describes how he had made two unsuccessful attempts to invade and conquer Man, and now, at the third attempt:

> he gathered a massive force and came by night to the harbour which is called Ramsey, and three hundred men he hid in a wood which was on the sloping brow of the mountain called Sky Hill. At dawn the Manxmen formed up in battle order and after a charge joined battle with Godred. When the battle was raging vehemently, the three hundred men rose from their place of hiding at their rear and began to weaken the resistance of the Manxmen, and compelled them to flee … Now when the tide had filled the riverbed at Ramsey and the enemy were pressing constantly from the other side, those who were left begged Godred with pitiful cries to spare them.[27]

In 1079 the River Sulby was probably a wide estuary, now represented by a residual lake. I imagine the battle was fought across the line of the road, with the Manxmen driven backward. Godred acted with unusual humanity and spared the Manxmen:

> on condition that none of them should at any time lay claim to any part of the land for himself by right of inheritance. Whence it has come to pass that up until the present day the entire island is the property of the king alone, and that all its dues belong to him … Then Godred subjected to his rule Dublin and a great part of Leinster, also he tamed the Scots [i.e. the Irish?] that no one who built a ship or boat dared use more than three iron nails.[28]

The stipulation about iron nails suggests that this was a conventional criterion to limit the length and strength of boats.

Godred figures in Manx popular history as 'King Orry'. He and his successors ruled the islands, ports and headlands from Leinster to the Hebrides. His main achievement, retrospectively, was to align himself northward by marrying his granddaughter to Somerled, the ruler of Argyll and the Hebrides. Thus the Isle of Man was drawn into a realm increasingly Scottish, but not before Magnus Bare-Legs, the king of Norway, visited him with a huge fleet and reasserted Norse hegemony over the whole domain by traditional methods of terrorism and rapine. Magnus entered into an agreement with Malcolm of Alba — that is, of eastern and central Scotland — that he should have control over all lands that could be sailed around. It is said that he included Kintyre in this realm by having himself carried across the isthmus at Tarbert in a skiff.

Godred Crovan's sons ruled Man, one after another, with violent interruptions, until the last of them, Olaf, remembered by Manx chroniclers as wise and good, ruled for 40 years before dying at the hands of his own family (in 1152). He had been too good and too wise for too long. It was his daughter, Ragnhild, who married the Hebridean Somerled, who having risen from *regulus* of Kintyre was now styling himself Rex Insularum. He was then on his way to controlling the whole of the western seaboard of Scotland. Somerled and Olaf's son entered into an agreement to split the kingdom of the islands between them.

In the meantime, successive Scottish kings had begun to consolidate their realm by the Norman strategy of granting lands to their followers in return for feudal entailments and loyalties. These new fiefs, which were positioned so as to act as buffer zones between the lawless west and the more or less orderly central lowlands, brought a new principle of government into Scottish and Hibernian affairs. Local chiefs were no longer independent rulers of the own lands but dependent on higher powers for their legitimacy. Most of these were Anglo-Normans from the north of England or directly from the continent, who had aided the Scottish kings and now received their rewards; others were brought in directly as mercenaries. Some of these were Flemish and had been used by Malcolm IV to force the clansmen of Moray into obedience; others had been used to suppress one Fergus of Galloway (who also liked to style himself king; he was not to be allowed such impudence).

This was a process that had begun in 1070, when Malcolm III had married an Anglo-Hungarian princess, Margaret. All their sons were brought up in England or France and learnt, along with European culture, a new art of war and government.

Between the Scotto-Norse lordships of the western seaboard and Man and this modern concept of the organised state, no lasting agreement was possible, for they were mutually and radically antithetical. The one had to exterminate the other. This came to a head in 1164 when a combined force from Dublin, Man, Kintyre and the islands, headed by Somerled, sailed up the Clyde in 160 galleys and sacked the infant town of Glasgow. Then a battle took place near Renfrew, at which:

> in the first cleft of battle the baleful leader fell.
> Wounded by a spear, slain by the sword, Somerled died.[29]

This location was no accident: Renfrew had been designated by the Scottish king as the central point in a ring of feudal fiefs held by his Anglo-Norman warlords to defend central Scotland from the likes of Somerled.

Clydeside was also a centre of Viking settlement, to judge from the existence of gravestones in Govan, Glasgow and on Bute.

* * *

Ramsey, which I entered a little while later, was equally devoid of any accommodation that I could afford. The campsite was closed down. It continued to blow. I was thoroughly miserable and also hungry. A bar on the seafront was warm and friendly and I could have stayed there a long time slaking a large thirst, but outside it was almost dark. Moreover, alcohol and the cycle do not mix well. At least in a car, though you may miss the road and slaughter those on foot, you are not likely to fall over. A sober horse is wiser than a drunken rider and on your own two feet you will usually manage to get where you want to be, if indirectly. But the cycle is a very narrow support indeed. So I took to the saddle again and cautiously set off up a long road out of the town. I had noted that there was an outdoor-activity centre some four miles further on, along the way to Maughold Head. It might include a bunkhouse.

And to my relief it did, and I had a sociable evening with the staff, a stove to cook on, a bed and a shower full of hot water and a long blissful sleep. And then an early morning, riding towards the easterly summit of Maughold Head, with its ancient cemetery, its collection of ancient tombstones and still more ancient hilltop fort. I wanted to pay my respects to Hedin.

***

The history of the lords of the Isles is one of obscure battles and murderous bloody rivalries. These were lands on the very edge, the periphery of the periphery, and the doings of their rulers were usually recorded by 'landlubbers' whose notions of geography away from the centres of Britain were very hazy. Giraldus Cambrensis (Gerald of Wales), who chronicled the Norman invasion of Ireland and wrote a topography of Ireland around 1200, was particularly bald on matters one might have expected him to know with more detail: 'Among the smaller islands there is one of fair size that is now called the Isle of Man ... they say that it is equidistant from the North of Ireland and Britain.'[30] As late as 1380, John of Fordun, in a history of Scotland written to assert the new kingdom's ancient origins, could only write of:

> many islands both great and small at the back of Scotia, between it and Ireland, separated from the Orkneys by a great intervening firth ... the above mentioned islands, as well as many others, lie scattered about in the sea ... and some of these, to the north-west, look out upon the boundless ocean; whence it is believed that the inhabited world is bounded by this region of Scotia.[31]

But, putting ourselves back into their shoes, the kings of Man and their like were in no sense peripheral. They were their own centre, since within the sphere of the Irish Sea and the Hebrides they had geographical and military supremacy. And on the basis of their fine castles and stone carvings they had a definite cultural character. There is a splendid family of fortresses that extends from Dunvegan in Skye to Peel in Man, which for size and grandeur bespeaks a certain magnificence of mind and ambition.

The last of these fearsome grandees was Godred's descendant Ragnhald (otherwise Reginald) who became king of Man in 1188. He secured his rule by a pact of mutual support with John de Courcy, the Norman conqueror of Ulster; de Courcy married Affreca, Ragnhald's sister, to seal this bargain and Ragnhald sent 100 galleys at de Courcy's request. He also secured for himself the support of King John of England, who gave him land and anchorage at the mouth of Carlingford Lough. He conducted raids of plunder into Ireland. Such was his energy and renown that the *Orkneyinga Saga* described him as 'the greatest fighting man in all the western lands. For three whole years he had lived aboard longships and not spent a single night under a sooty roof.' An Irish poem from around 1220 observed this same man from a less advantageous position:

> you are the man of the speckled ships
> unlucky the strand to which you will come.

On Ragnhald's death Man became increasingly drawn into territorial jostling between successive kings of Norway, England and Scotland.

Accordingly, in 1263, King Haakon Haakonsson prepared a huge fleet in Bergen, claimed by annalists of the day to be the largest ever to cross the North Sea. Its object was to settle the question of who was to rule the Irish Sea. It gathered off Skye in August of that year but did not receive the whole-hearted welcome Haakon had expected. Only the then-king of Man, Magnus, and a few malcontents rallied to the Norwegian cause.

The fleet then moved south and based itself upon the island of Gigha, while an offshoot, largely composed of Manxmen, invaded Bute once more. (Their main exploit was to capture Rothesay Castle yet again.) Another branch of the fleet was sent north up Loch Long, from where they carried their ships over the narrow portage at Tarbert, occupied Loch Lomond and made a foray by land towards Stirling. The main fleet was now in Lamlash Bay, Arran (a notable anchorage for the control of the North Channel, used in later years by the Royal Navy and as an assembly point for transatlantic convoys). This campaign of steady encroachment came to an ignominious conclusion at the start of October, when the main battle fleet of the Norwegians was grouped around the Cumbrae Islands. Bad weather drove some of the Norse ships aground and the Vikings, setting out to recover them, were involved in a series of minor battles up and down the shoreline near Largs, in which they came off worse. After this, it being late in the season and the fleet having failed to get a good winter anchorage, Haakon withdrew back to Lamlash, then to Gigha; then he left the Irish Sea forever.

The battle of Largs was subsequently portrayed by Scottish annalists as a great victory, on a par with the battle of Clontarf 200 years earlier. This was manifestly not the case, for Haakon sailed home again in good order (only to die in Orkney in December). But for the Irish-Sea regions it was decisive, for Magnus of Man, who had been of material assistance to his Norwegian overlord, now had to pay homage to the king of Scotland and to provide ten galleys to fight the Norwegians if they ever came again. When Magnus died the next year, Alexander of Scotland assumed the throne himself. Those Hebridean chiefs who had sided with Haakon were reduced to the condition of desperados. Some of them were hanged and others were so heavily fined they might have as well have been. Others, adroitly and permanently, changed allegiance.

The kings of Scotland and Norway made a treaty in Perth (on 2 July 1266) in which the Norwegian king disclaimed any further interest in Man and the Sudreyar for himself and his heirs forever. The Scots were to pay Norway 4,000 marks and 100 marks a year thereafter. Man, it concluded, 'shall be subject to the laws and customs of Scotland and be judged and dealt with according to them henceforth'.[32] And that was the end of the kingdom of Man. From then on, Ellan Vannin became a football for the kings of Scotland and England to kick about and the Vikings took no more part in the affairs of the Irish Sea. Whereas there had previously been three royal realms claiming the Islands, there were now two, Scotland and England. Ireland, of course, was still a geographical term without consistent political substance.

***

For lack of other evidence the story of Man must mainly be one of war. But there was a more peaceful way of arriving at the same place, which can (just) be traced through the various bishoprics and other matters clerical.

The case of the diocese of Sodor and Man makes the point. This first appears in records around 1079, in connection with the arrival of Godred Crovan. For almost a century this diocese included Man and most of the islands as far north as Skye and it looked to the archbishopric of York for its validity. Then in 1153 we find it transferred to the archbishopric of Trondhejm. This was, we may presume, part of the attempts by Norwegian kings to reintegrate the lordship of the Isles into the Scandinavian world. But it was clearly not successful because some bishops of Sodor and Man continued to look back to York or Durham or Dublin for consecration, these higher authorities being sought, presumably, as part of the power politics of the Irish Sea.

In 1134 Olaf of Man granted the monks of Furness Abbey in Cumbria the privilege of electing the bishop of Sodor and Man, his aim being to preserve the church in Man 'entire under its own bishop, rather than rendered desolate under strangers, and as it were mercenaries, who seek their own and not the Lord's advantage'.[33]

Macdonald comments:

> It is possible that Olaf was erecting Man and the Isles into a single diocese along territorial lines, effectively substituting a territorial diocesan organisation for an earlier monastic and tribal one.[34]

Olaf's other notable act was to grant land to Furness Abbey to establish a new monastery at Rushen, as part of a wider move visible in both Scotland and Ireland towards more regular styles of church government. A king of Man would, we imagine, be happy to be playing off Scots and Norwegians against one another by linking himself more closely to English institutions. Olaf's eventual successor, Ragnhald, went a stage further in 1219 by entering into an agreement with the papacy itself, stipulating that Man should become a tributary state and perform fealty for the same. For this security Ragnhald paid only 12 marks a year. In Ireland, the men of Man established a long-lasting connection with the Norman rulers of Ulster and it was monks from Rushen who established two early Cistercian monasteries, at Grey Abbey and Inch in County Down.

This consolidation of both diocese and kingdom was cemented further with the building of a cathedral of St German at Peel within the ancient fort. Thus the later kings of Man were trying to found their domain on something more durable than military muscle by linking themselves securely to the wider European feudal and religious structure, be it through England, Scotland or the papacy itself. It is evident that John de Courcy, in conquering Ulster, had long-term intentions in mind. His political and military planning was paralleled by ecclesiastical manoeuvres. The abbeys that he and his wife founded were all staffed by monks from Cumbrian abbeys. Their architectures all show features in common with one another and with the St German's Cathedral on Peel Island. The days of Gaelic rule and the Celtic Church were coming to an end.

The new monastic foundations associated with Norman feudalism were generally of the Cistercian order, owing ecclesiastical allegiance and discipline strictly to continental Europe. Nothing more different from the autonomous Celtic monasteries can be imagined. However, owing to its geopolitical location within the Islands, Ellan Vannin remained a bone in the throat for all concerned for the coming centuries. It remains to this day a constitutional oddity.

A brief photo essay

Illustration 9. Furness Abbey, the leading abbey of Cumbria, whose extensions and daughter houses were in both Man and Ulster. Founded in 1123 by a count of Blois, it was taken over by the Cistercian order in 1147 and swiftly rose to be one of the wealthiest abbeys in all England, with extensive land holdings (especially in Man), and a huge investment in the iron trade.

Illustration 10. Grey Abbey, County Down, founded by Affreca in 1139. In marrying Affreca John de Courcy was departing from custom. All the other major Norman warlords took Gaelic Irish wives but Affreca was Affreca Godredsdottir. Affreca had brought in Cistercian monks from Holm Cultra in Cumbria, just as her new husband was importing Benedictine clergy from St Bee's in Cumbria and Cistercians from Furness Abbey.

Illustration 11. Inch Abbey, founded c. 1180 on an older site by John de Courcy in collaboration with Furness Abbey. An elegant little building, superior in finesse to Grey Abbey. A very beautiful site outside Downpatrick.

Illustration 12. Rushen Abbey, Isle of Man, founded in 1134 by Olaf of Man for the monks of Furness Abbey. With Furness it became part of the Cistercian order in 1147. It was here that the *Cronica* was compiled.

Notes

1   From 'The tryst of a fleet against Castle Sween', a Gaelic poem of about 1310, cited in R.A. Macdonald (1997) *The kingdom of the Isles: Scotland's western seaboard*, c. *1100–c. 1336*, East Linton: Tuckwell Press.

2   G. Broderick (ed. and tr.) (1979, repr. 2004) *Chronicles of the Kings of Man and the Isles*, Douglas: Manx Museum and National Trust. The chronicle was compiled by the monks of Rushen Abbey, the main Cistercian foundation on the island.

3   The annals make reference at several points to something they call the 'yellow plague'. No one knows what this was, but it sounds bad.

4   G. Broderick (1999) *Language death in the Isle of Man: an investigation into the decline and extinction of Manx Gaelic as a community language in the Isle of Man*, Tübingen: Niemeyer.

5   The attribution to Patrick is legendary. According to it, St Patrick put one of his converts, chained and locked, into a boat and pushed him adrift with orders to found a monastery wherever he landed. Then he threw away the key. The monk came ashore some time later on the Isle of Man, where he was kindly entertained with a fish supper. The key was in the fish's stomach. In fact, Inis Pádraig is visible from County Down, so there is a sort of plausibility about the story.

6   See D. Freke (1995) *The Peel Castle dig*, Douglas: Friends of Peel Castle for the Friends of Manx National Heritage.

7   G. Jones (1968) *A history of the Vikings*, Oxford: Oxford University Press.

8   *Ibid.*, p. 9.

9   Of course, like much of the Wirral, it may have been washed away. There was a great harbour, the Hoyle Lake, in the Dee Estuary in earlier times.

10 M. Cubbon (1983) 'The archaeology of the Vikings in the Isle of Man' in C. Fell, P. Foote, J.G. Campbell and R. Thomson (eds), *The Viking age in the Isle of Man: select papers from the ninth Viking Congress, Isle of Man, 4–14 July 1981*, London: Viking Society for Northern Research, p. 13.

11 See G. Fellows-Jensen (1983) 'Scandinavian settlement in the Isle of Man and north-west England' in Fell *et al.* (eds), *op. cit.*, pp. 38–51.

12 Cubbon, *op. cit.*, p. 22.

13 W. Davies (1990) *Patterns of power in early Wales*, Oxford: Clarendon Press.

14 *Ibid.*, Chapter 1.

15 M. Dillon and N. Chadwick (1972, 2nd ed.) *The Celtic realms*, London: Weidenfeld and Nicholson, p. 115.

16 Broderick (1979), *op. cit.*

17 M. Magnusson and H. Pálsson (eds and trs) (1960) *Njal's Saga*, London: Penguin Books.

18 'The battle of Brunanburh' in R. Hamer (tr.) (1970) *A choice of Anglo-Saxon verse*, London: Faber and Faber. There is also a rambunctious version by Tennyson.

19 See N.A.M. Rodger (1997) *The safeguard of the sea: a naval history of Britain 660–1649*, London: Penguin Books, Chapter 1 for a detailed discussion of ship types.

20 A.E. Christensen (1989) 'Vikings in the Irish Sea' in M. McCaughan and J. Appleby (eds), *The Irish Sea: aspects of maritime history*, Belfast: Institute of Irish Studies, Queen's University, pp. 13–21.

21 See P.F. Wallace (2001) 'Ireland's Viking towns' in A.C. Larsen (ed.), *The Vikings in Ireland*, Roskilde: Viking Ship Museum, pp. 37–51.

22 D.A. Binchy (1962) 'The passing of the old order' in B. Ó Cuív (ed.), *Proceedings of the International Congress of Celtic Studies held in Dublin 6–10 July 1959*, Dublin: Dublin Institute for Advanced Studies, pp. 119–32.

23 F. Moore (1996) 'Ireland's oldest bridge—at Clonmacnoise', *Archaeology Ireland* **10** (4) (winter), pp. 24–7.

24 K. Kristiansen (1998) *Europe before history*, Cambridge: Cambridge University Press.

25 Magnusson and Pálsson, *op. cit.*

26 The background to this is supplied in *ibid.*

27 Broderick (1979), *op. cit.*

28 *Ibid.*

29 *Ibid.*

30 Giraldus Cambrensis (A.B. Scott and F.X. Martin, eds and trs) (1978) *Expugnatio Hibernica:*

the conquest of Ireland, Dublin: Royal Irish Academy.

[31] John of Fordun (d. *c.* 1384) attempted to write a complete history of Scotland in several books. While his work undoubtedly contains a good deal of legendary material, it provided a starting point and basis for much later history.

[32] Broderick (1979), *op. cit.*

[33] From the *Carmen de Morte Somerledi,* a thirteenth-century monkish epic in Latin.

[34] Macdonald, *op. cit.,* p. 215.

SIX
The view from Carnsore: looking for Strongbow

The banks of the sea south of Arklow consist mainly of low crumbling cliffs of boulder clay which are easily loosened and swept away by tides and storms; the resulting banks of shingle and sandbars accumulate around the mouths of the Slaney and other rivers, forming half-enclosed estuaries, lagoons and lakes of brackish water. These stretches of liquid blend almost imperceptibly into great reed beds and green levels intersected with sheughs set here and there with low hills. Rocky intrusions form little headlands at Greenore, Carnsore and Crossfarnoge and islets such as the Tuskar Rock with its lighthouse, the Saltees and the Keeraghs. Inland is an undulating plain of sandy soil with pleasant woods and townlands. It is best explored by bicycle — there are no hills, the roads are narrow and route-finding is intricate.

Being the nearest part of Ireland to continental Europe, this area has been most visited. Perhaps it was the very first point reached as the post-glacial waters receded. There is evidence of early settlement wherever you go in this corner, with standing stones, enclosures, promontory forts and all manner of prehistoric relics. On the very tip of Carnsore Point, amidst a grove of giant steel wind turbines, will be found the well-preserved but untended fragment of an early church, which we have already visited — the gable with a little Romanesque window, an enclosure, the remnants of a house or byre and a pattern of fields about it. The gleaming blades hollow the air above.

Other religious sites abound — old churches buried in ivy and a holy well in every third field. But it was a place vexed with intruders and local disputes and there are as many fortifications, moats, mottes, and castles as there are churches. In fact, there are military relics from every age, including our own. Going backward in time we pass the concrete gun-embrasures above Rosslare Harbour (which only the quick-eyed visitor will notice), encounter a Martello tower on Baginbun Point, discover the formidable fortress of Duncannon, built by Elizabeth I to guard the entrance of Waterford from the Spanish, and wander through a countryside scattered with medieval tower houses of every description, size and state of preservation.

I made my base in a campsite at My Lady's Isle, near Carnsore Point, not far from a convenience store and a pub that sold decent meals every evening. There was a well-tended old pilgrimage site, a lake, green lawns and shady trees. The name of the place suggests that it was once much closer to the sea. There is, indeed, a large area of salt marsh just to the south, a long lagoon and several smaller lakes. It is a *paysage* for wading birds.

The weather was clear, bright and warm and the summer still fresh. The lanes were hedged with honeysuckle and hawthorn blossoms.

* * *

The Norman conquest of Ireland was a major political event for all the peoples of the Irish Sea because it began the incorporation of the late Q-Celtic, Gaelic world into European political culture. This was in parallel with a similar expansion of Norman skills and power into Scotland (although that was peaceable, at the invitation of the new monarch, David I (d. 1153), who brought Norman ways with him at his accession). It was also preceded by the Norman conquest of Pembrokeshire and the annexation of that area as an almost independent territory by successive earls of Pembroke. This three-pronged intervention into the affairs of the Irish Sea involved, not surprisingly, a huge clash of mental orientation — a great jolt such as happens when two very different senses of reality come into conflict.

I have been avoiding extensive theoretical discussion but I don't think we can understand this aspect of the Irish Sea and the history of its coasts without engaging to some degree with the theory of states and their emergence out of earlier organisations based on the tribe or kin group and its chiefdom.[1]

The people who lived in Ireland comprised a network of clans, each clan being divided into subsections called septs. The population was stratified into a large range of occupations, roles and different forms of status, ruled by warrior elites. The lowest were slaves and bonded servants. There was a dominant language — Q-Celtic — overlaid upon a plethora of local tongues and dialects. What in general the people lacked was any centralised and supra-individual concept of authority more inclusive than kindred, which would enable them to form states. In consequence, successful rulers could exact tribute but not collect taxes; they could demand, receive and accept arms and men, but not maintain an army. Nor was there any lasting coinage. Wealth was usually in goods — either staples such as cattle, textiles or metals, or prestige goods such as goldwork, precious objects or rings. In matters of justice there could be no permanent system of courts, even though legal practices, norms and codes had some commonalty across different groups. There was, moreover, no automatic right of succession, so the next ruler after the death of an older one was not always obvious and often disputed. The role of *ard rí* or high king was very largely ritualistic and honorific, though such a man might from time to time act as arbitrator in disputes and enjoy a measure of power. The existence of a permanent church made no difference to this decentred state of affairs because the Celtic-speaking churches had similar organisational principles. There is a lot in this with which we can have empathy, living in an almost entirely administered society that seems to leave little room for spontaneity or improvisation. It is hardly surprising that romantic people seek to romanticise it further.

The coming of the Normans into the Irish Sea was a serious attempt to change this method of governance, since they brought with them both a new method of war-making and a new method of governing, each reinforcing the other.

However, before the Norman military incursion there had already been a considerable ecclesiastical 'invasion' in the form of the monasteries of the Cistercian order. This was not Norman but it was quite definitely continental and organised upon hierarchical principles, with strong lines of authority. It was the discipline of the Cistercian order that recommended itself to the reforming bishop of Down, known in English as St Malachy and in Irish as Maelmhadhog O'Morgair. With the organisational reforms came a return of the Roman liturgy and, effectively, the undoing of the Celtic Church. With the agreement of the local ruler, who provided both land and building materials, a Cistercian abbey was founded at Mellifont, north of Drogheda, in 1142. This was inhabited by a group of followers of Malachy, who had been trained in Clairvaux by St Bernard, and a number of French monks. The building was designed upon early Gothic rather than Romanesque lines and took time to build. Construction was not complete until 1157. The completion ceremony was a grand event attended, it is reported, by 17 bishops, as well as the high king and numerous chiefs and local kings.

By the time of the Norman incursion into Leinster (in 1169) Mellifont Abbey had begot seven daughter houses and two granddaughter houses. In another 20 years there were 18 foundations and finally 22 abbeys owed affiliation to the original. Mellifont (the name suggests a fountain of honey) had become a major force in the church affairs of pre-Norman Ireland — a beachhead for a new form of organisation. Nor was it the only Cistercian mother house in the land. It was followed by Greyabbey in County Down, independently founded by the new Norman ruler of Ulster and his Manx wife, and another ten in different areas. John de Courcy had already re-established the much older monastery of Inch at Downpatrick along Cistercian lines and staffed it with monks from monasteries in England by 1180. This was paralleled by the spread of Cistercian foundations on the other side of the water, often linked. Thus Tintern Abbey in Monmouthshire begat a daughter house called Tintern near Waterford and Furness Abbey in Cumbria gave birth to Rushen on Man. Greyabbey was founded by Affreca, the sister of Ragnhald, the ruler of Man, to celebrate her marriage to John de Courcy. Cistercian organisation was thus linked to Norman military and political power from the very start.

There may be a chicken/egg problem here. Did the Cistercian system beget the Norman version of feudalism or imitate it? It is pertinent to point out here that not only were the Cistercians organisationally modern, but they also initiated advances in agriculture, milling and manufacture. The prosperity of Norman Ireland and its ecclesiastical counterpart were inextricably linked. The organisation of the Cistercian order mirrors the feudal and economic structure of secular life that the Normans were to introduce into Ireland.

***

William the Conqueror had claimed and won the Anglo-Saxon kingdom and its state with remarkable speed and ease. This was partly because, unlike Ireland, it really was a kingdom, with a degree of central state authority and government. Take the head and the body followed. William's success encouraged him to give away Wales to anyone that had the nerve and strength to seize upon it, though there the same conditions of centralised authority did not apply. Several of his knights and henchmen availed themselves of this opportunity under the feudal system of holding land while acknowledging William's overlordship. Because Anglo-Saxon kings had laid notional claim to the rest of the main island, William (as effective inheritor of the claim) could properly give away lands he did not actually control. However, there being no central authority in Wales, each part had to be taken separately. Accordingly, Norman adventurers had taken over stretches of central and southern Wales and established themselves there with some success. However, in the north of Wales they had met with less fortune and had been ousted from Gwynedd and Mon with Viking help after only a few years.

Pembrokeshire was, however, efficiently conquered by the formidable Arnulf de Montgomery, who established himself at Pembroke in 1093 and surrounded his territory with a ring of lesser fortresses controlled by his followers (several of whom were Flemish). This put them in a state of permanent rivalry with the ruling Welsh dynasties of Deheubarth, which had been a greater Pembrokeshire, comprising most of Cardigan and other territories. Border wars and rebellions became the norm. Indeed, the enormous number of forts and castles in the far west of Wales attests to the violent opposition with which the incomers were faced. Arnulf, however, was given to rebellion himself and in 1101, after an attempt to overthrow Henry I, he was banished. Pembrokeshire then became, for many years, a direct royal dominion. Henry encouraged settlers from Devon, Somerset and Flanders, as well as his Flemish mercenaries, and began to turn earthworks and stockades into stone castles.

Matters in Scotland were handled much more peaceably. A number of other Norman (and also Flemish) knights were invited by David I of Scotland to serve under him and were given estates in reward, which they held in the feudal manner by paying homage to the king as their overlord. This effectively separated them from the indigenous chieftains and provided the Scottish kings with an independent loyal power. These formed a definite social/military caste, spreading a feudal network over the older kinship-based forms of rule. Some historians have referred to this process, which included a tacit acknowledgment of the submission of the Scottish crown to the rulers of England, as the Norman conquest of Scotland. This Norman Scotland extended to the east from Lothian to Moray across the borderlands into Galloway, but not into the highlands and islands. Their most westerly Irish-Sea fortress was at Rothesay on Bute.

The Norman conquest of England was not completed by William but by his son. In 1092 Caerluel was still a Saxon town, ruled over by the earls of Northumberland. It seems to have become a very depleted place, alternately Scottish or Saxon and most of the time neither with any certainty. William Rufus put a stop to this by marching an army there, throwing out the Northumbrians, rebuilding the castle and planting the locality with farmers and their wives from southern England. This is, so far as I have been able to find out, the first instance of a deliberate plantation of a population in these islands so as to create an enclave of people loyal to the crown at a strategic site. The precedent was to be followed by Scottish monarchs in the Hebrides and English and British monarchs in Ireland, and subsequently at strategic sites all around the globe. A number of these implants were Flemish stonemasons who came to work at building Carlisle Castle and remained. Their names are recorded. One Botchardus left his name to the hamlet of Botcherby. (The suffix -by suggests that the local language was still heavily under Norse influence.) Local tradition has it that some of the newcomers were transplanted from Hampshire when the king cleared his serfs out of the New Forest to make way for deer. He also created a brand-new deerpark for himself to the south of Carlisle and set about organising the district into a defensive zone against the Scots, with baronies and subdependent castles.

Thus Norman power and the feudal system encroached on Ireland from both ends of the Sea.

**

Meanwhile, in Ireland …

This book is not a linear history, but there are times when the hound of storytelling should be let off the leash, and this may be one.

We are lucky in that there are two complementary and fairly reliable sources for the Norman intervention in Gaelic affairs — *Expugnatio Hibernica: the Conquest of Ireland* by Giraldus Cambrensis,[2] a vivid prose narrative in Latin written around 1190, and *The Song of Dermot and the Earl*, a Norman/French *chanson de geste* from slightly later. The main difference between the two accounts (apart from the distinctions of the two genres) is that Giraldus is seeking to put his own family, the Fitzgeralds, in the thick of things, always taking a leading part, and he despises Dermot of Leinster, whereas the poet of the *Song* is more disposed towards the earl, Richard FitzGilbert de Clare (known best by his sobriquet Strongbow) and he calls the infamous Diarmuid MacMurchada '*le gentil reis*'.

Dermot (to use the Norman spelling) was the irascible and violent ruler of Leinster who, having engaged in one feud too many, was expelled by a coalition of his neighbours arranged by the *ard rí*; he fled to Wales in 1167. From there he went to Aquitaine, seeking help from Henry II, king of England and half of France. Henry also had claims on Wales and Scotland and seems to have had slight sense of being English. He was not strictly speaking a Norman either, but an Angevin. Henry had his own plans for Ireland and already had some kind of charter from the pope giving him leave to take possession of the land and reform the state of the church in Ireland.[3] In return for an oath of fealty (the first stage in the process of feudal submission) Henry granted Dermot leave to recruit 'English, Normans, Welsh and Scots' in an expedition to recover his lands. In retrospect this was a foolhardy bargain for an Irish chief to have made but, as Orpen writes, 'exceptional patriotism and exceptional wisdom are not to be looked for in banished princes'.[4]

Basing himself in Bristol — a town with many trading connections across the Irish Sea — Dermot cast about to gather himself an army. This was a good time and place to find desperados, for the Norman absorption of Deheubarth had been checked by its present ruler, Rhys ap Gruffydd, who had bundled several Norman warlords out of their new castles. Typical among these were members of the Fitzgerald family. They and others had sided with the losing party in the civil wars between the Normans Stephen and Matilda. Among these was Strongbow, whose family had come down in the world and who was regarded with suspicion by Henry II. There was another group — Flemish settlers who had been brought in as mercenary soldiers. They had their own castle, too, near Haverfordwest, from which they were expelled at least twice in this period, and wanted it back, or at least its equivalent elsewhere. There was a large reservoir of discontented men.

An agreement was made between Dermot and Strongbow that the Norman should assist Dermot in the retaking of Leinster, in return for which he would have Dermot's daughter Aoife (Eve) as wife and inherit the kingdom on Dermot's demise. The former ruler of Leinster was free to bestow his daughter as he pleased (and he did so, liberally) but he was not free to give Leinster away, since it was not his to give. He was merely its former ruler and, anyway, the land belonged to the people of Leinster at large under clan custom, its ruling families and chiefs governing it for the communal good. Nor could this land title be inherited, for it was not owned in that way. There was no automatic rule of primogeniture and therefore no obvious succession. This is a classic instance of the clash of political cultures and their definitions of political legitimacy. Dermot was stepping outside the norms of Gaelic legitimacy (see below). He was, in fact, playing a typical Norman card — giving away other people's land to third parties, provided they conquered it for themselves, in his name.

Moreover, it was not by any means the first interaction between Normans and Gaels; Arnulf de Montgomery, who had ruled Pembrokeshire, had formed an alliance with Muirchertach O'Brian, who controlled the fleets of Dublin and Waterford, to further rebellion against Henry I, who had no effective power in the Irish Sea. His rebellion came to nothing, but further north the Normans were thrown out of Anglesey by a combination of Welshmen, Dubliners and the Viking fleet of Magnus Bare-Legs in a campaign in which Hugo, the Norman earl of Chester, lost his life. Dermot and Strongbow knew what was possible and the risks involved. Theirs was a typical Irish-Sea enterprise.

A preliminary expedition was got ready in Pembroke and a Norman force, organised largely by the Fitzgerald contingent, landed at Bannow, a town that no longer exists, between Waterford and Wexford. This is now an out-of-the way location, but an intelligent choice because it provided a large bay and a defensible island as a rear base.

This force was composed, according to Giraldus, of 'Angli' (that is, Normans coming mainly from England), 'Normanni' (that is, Normans coming directly from France) and 'nostri' (our people — Normans mainly from Wales, many of whom had intermarried with Welsh leading families).[5] It is notable that Giraldus's 'nostri' were, in point of fact, largely related to one another. The whole enterprise was in large measure the undertaking of an extended family. The force of archers was recruited locally in south Wales. There was also a squadron of Flemings who came as independent freebooters.[6] Some of the population, still loyal to Dermot, met them and joined forces against the city of Wexford (which, of course, was a Viking settlement, largely of Dansk origin).[7] According to Giraldus:

> the people of the city came out, about two thousand strong, hitherto unvanquished and with great faith in their long-standing good fortune … But when they saw the lines of troops drawn up in an unfamiliar manner, and the squadrons of knights resplendent with breastplates, swords and helmets all gleaming, they immediately turned back and withdrew inside the walls.

After a short siege the city was taken and awarded to the Fitzgerald cousins, according to an agreement Dermot had made with them behind Strongbow's back. Strongbow's nephew, who was there to keep an eye on his uncle's interests, was awarded another stretch of land. Once again, Dermot was notionally within his rights to award a city, which was anyway a Viking city, but the *tuath*, the clan lands, were not his to give away. Giraldus also notes the different military tactics — the squadrons and lines. Gaelic and Viking armies of the period were generally 'hosts' that came and attacked *en masse*, with personal duels an important part of the proceedings. The Fitzgeralds had probably drawn up their forces in the proper Norman manner — with a mixture of mounted and foot archers, a line of foot soldiers and heavy cavalry on the wings. It was this combination that, a hundred years earlier, had overcome the Saxon shield wall and was, in the twelfth century, invincible provided there was open ground. Moreover, they did not burn or loot the town, as was the local custom, but fortified it as a base for further campaigns.

One success was followed by others until Dermot had conquered back most of the south-eastern corner of the island. This alarmed the other rulers, who once again gathered in a confederation against him; Ruairi O'Connor, the last high king of Ireland, declared that 'this man, himself our enemy, has brought in a race most hostile to ours, a race that has long been eager to rule us all alike'. What did Ruairi O'Connor mean by this? He seems to have thought of the Normans as being English; or had he divined the ultimate outcome of Cistercian modernity? However, he organised to some effect.

Dermot and the Normans were driven back on the defensive. A pattern of warfare emerged in which the Gaelic troops kept wherever possible to woodlands and small-scale, close-order conflict, from which the Normans would try to lure them into open ground and there defeat them. This was a pattern of battle that persisted into Tudor times and even later.

Strongbow now came in person with a large force. His advance guard took over a promontory fort at Baginbun Point, where they distinguished themselves by throwing their prisoners off the high cliffs. Earl Richard himself disembarked shortly after with a force something like five times the size of any other in the field, for it contained 200 knights. Waterford was quickly taken, 'large numbers of citizens being slaughtered in the streets'. Several chiefs with Viking names were executed or imprisoned 'and there too, Dermot's daughter Eva was lawfully wed to the earl … then all joined forces and turned their standards toward Dublin'.

The marriage of Aoife to Strongbow has been seen as a turning point in Irish history — the acceptance of the proud invader by which feminine Ireland is compelled to submit to the masculine aggression of England. So, at least, it was painted by Daniel Maclise in his huge and theatrical painting now hanging in the National Gallery, Dublin. At their feet bards and maidens lament amid bodies and broken harps; the city blazes in the background. At the centre of the canvas we can see Strongbow's mailed fist gleaming in the light, though his face remains in an ominous shadow.

As we have seen, however, this is a simplification of something much more interesting. It was Viking Ireland that was taking the brunt of the Norman onslaught and Dermot's mixed army can scarcely be called English. Gaelic annalists of the time referred to the invaders as 'foreigners', which was largely correct, and sometimes as 'Saxons', which was certainly incorrect (except perhaps in the case of some foot soldiers). For the annalists, the terms 'Saxon' and later 'English' become shorthand for anyone from the other side of the Irish Sea. It seems clear that the annalists did not understand what or who had hit them. Welsh annalists, with more experience, described the Normans as 'the French'.

The Norsemen were driven out of Dublin in a campaign of exemplary speed and violence: 'the greater part of them, led by Askulv, went on board ship, taking their most precious belongings, and sailed off to the northern isles'. They probably went to the Isle of Man because, when the united forces of the Irish chiefs tried to drive the Norman army out of Dublin, they were helped by a sea blockade organised by the

Figures 1 and 2. 'The marriage of Eva and Strongbow' by Daniel Maclise, with enlargement of detail. We might note that Maclise, though here functioning as a visual ideologist of Irish nationalism, was at the same time a member of the editorial board of the *Journal of Design and Manufactures* — that is, he was at the very heart of English industrial ideology (reproduced courtesy of the National Gallery of Ireland).

Viking rulers of Man. This attempt met with ignominious failure. Richard Strongbow ruled in Dublin.

It was now that Henry II made his appearance, with 500 knights and many mounted and foot archers arriving in 400 ships off Waterford. This was a stupendous force for the times, which also included engineers, prefabricated wooden castles and luxurious tents. There is some evidence that Ruairi O'Connor, the high king, feared Strongbow more than he understood Henry and was happy to oblige with ships to cover the invasion fleet. It is also likely that Henry suspected Strongbow of trying to create an independent kingdom for himself and so appeared in overwhelming power. But that commander, astutely surrendering all the conquered lands into Henry's hands, was appointed governor of all Ireland in 1173. Shortly after this Henry gave his son John the title of Rex Hiberniae. The feudal chain that notionally was to unify Ireland with England for the next 800 years was now in place.

The Gaelic chiefs then came to swear feudal loyalty and to be reconfirmed in their 'rights'. Ruairi O'Connor was, in Henry's name, set to rule over all that part of Ireland not then in Norman hands and given the impossible job of collecting tribute for the Angevin king — a task for which the office of high king was never intended and which Ruairi never carried out.

Henry was careful not to appear as a conqueror but as a just intermediary between the rapacious warlords and the native population. Then he set about reorganising south-eastern and central Ireland along Norman lines. The king retained for the royal power the cities of Dublin and Waterford, much of the east coast and the area approximately covered by the modern county of Dublin — the Pale. The rest — as much as the Fitzgeralds, de Burghs and de Lacys could appropriate — became lordships owing fealty to Henry and his successors. Leinster was then set on its course to become what Irish people today often regard as the 'most English' part of their country (though to an English eye Leinster rather resembles Normandy). A simple trawl through the place names of County Wexford shows some very mixed origins — from the pure Norse of Hagansgate to a hill called Danescastle to a Tottenham Green. A recent study by Billy Colfer (2002) sets out the complex layers of new and older authority and lordship that helped to create the distinct landscape patterns of Leinster.[8]

Dublin itself was confirmed by charter as a Norman borough subordinate to Bristol and merchants from there had extensive rights of trade. The city once again became the polyglot and culturally mixed trading centre of the Irish Sea. A roll of names shows the range of its new citizens, which includes 37 from Cardiff, 29 from Worcester, 28 from Gloucester and smaller numbers from other towns along the Welsh Marches. (Many of these were Norman in origin.) In addition, there were 27 from London, 14 Cornishmen, 11 Flemish and 6 French. Glasgow, Dumfries, Edinburgh and Carlisle also appear on this list as well as 56 names from the new

Norman settlements and fiefs in Ireland. Scandinavian and Irish names are few.[9]

However, it would be wrong to regard this as the subjugation of one people by another. It was in all important respects an enterprise similar to the Norman conquest of the Anglo-Saxon kingdom, and what one historian has written of that applies just as well to the later Norman conquest of Ireland:

> To view the Conquest in terms of national struggle ... places a great strain on the available data. It is difficult to see any national solidarity in the motley band of Norman, Breton, French and Angevin adventurers who accompanied William (or Strongbow). Little more can be discerned on the English (or Irish) side ... neither of the opponents had any extensive popular support, and national feeling only became apparent at a much later date.[10]

Just so with Strongbow's invasion, with the addition that it was partly a Welsh enterprise. As such it was almost routine. In the previous century, as noted in the last chapter, combined armies of Vikings and Welsh ravaged and raided repeatedly, crossing the Irish Sea in both directions. The Vikings of Dublin or Wexford would hire out their fleet, at a price, to any discontented lordling with ambition and a full purse; Dermot was merely following precedent. The main difference between raids and invasions was that the aim of the first was to seize loot and the aim of the second was to seize land. In neither case was there a considerable movement of population, any more than there had been in the original Norman invasion of England.

There may have been one notable exception — the town of Bannow, which developed around the harbour where Dermot's force had landed. It seems to me likely, in the absence of evidence either way, that this was established as a distinctly Norman settlement for security purposes. In time it acquired full civic status, along with Kilkenny and Ross, with nine named streets and a substantial church. But the coast of Wexford is very unreliable and, much like the east coast of England, is given to swallowing fields, houses, villages and even towns and to closing up harbours. This happened to Bannow in the fifteenth century. Nothing of it now remains but the ruins of the church and a mound, which, when excavated, proved to be a midden full of cattle bones.

***

And this was where I arrived around noon on a hot July day, cruising down a long slope to turn at last onto a sandy foreshore. To the right was an expanse of salty turf and mud-flats from which rose a substantial mound; this, I supposed, must be the midden. To the left, sand dunes and gorse, and ahead a low hill which seemed from a distance to have been crowned with an earthwork of some description. There was a farm and some holiday cottages but no sign of any town. Before long, up a farm road, I discovered a substantial ruin — the nave of a large church surrounded by a high cemetery wall. It had vestiges of the Gothic manner of building so I supposed it to have been at least thirteenth rather than twelfth century. I had at least expected the outlines of a house or two. There was nothing else remaining and only a few yards away was a broad sandy beach. It was a perfect, warm windless day with a bright sun beating down on the sand; a family party was enjoying the low waves that came rhythmically up the strand. There were a pair of lively dogs, skylarks and pungent gorse. I found myself a corner of turf and stretched out.

Bannow is in the medieval records as a substantial town. Some of the buildings were to be seen in the eighteenth century, ruined but still above ground. A chimney is on record. It even returned two members to the Dublin parliament as late as the Reform Acts, though by then it was as empty as Old Sarum. From the character of the site, beside a substantial harbour and backed by an island/fort, I imagine it to have been a Viking settlement on a par with Wexford, if smaller.

(Among the curiosities that research delivers was a tale which, reading like a first draft of an Irish *Ivanhoe*, portrayed Bannow as a city with an assembly hall, shop windows and a population of noble warriors and doe-eyed maidens, all prepared to defend Ireland to the death. The reader is led around the events of 1169, which conclude when the lovers, a Norman soldier civilised by Eva, the virtuous Irish maiden, plight their troth in the convent garden only to perish in a combined hurricane and sandstorm as the 5,000-year-old city of Bannow perishes with them.)[11]

Looking at the lie of the coast between Bannow Bay and Wexford, the erosion and shifting of successive shingle bars and lagoons would seem to be a continuous process. The town may well have lain on such a bar which, like Hilbre on the Wirral, was shifted back into its own harbour. The church would then have been on the landward side of the town.

***

Giraldus has been criticised by Irish scholars for his apparent contempt for the indigenous population and their manners. They are reproached for living like beasts among the beasts, for living rudely in the woods, for being consistent only in their inconsistency and loyal only to their chronic treachery. But these reproaches are largely the figures of speech and rhetorical tropes that were the standard censures used by late-classical authors against barbarians whose conquest the authors were called on to justify. They were repeated, almost word for word, by Tudor apologists for English expansion, such as John Derricke in his *Image of Irelande* (1581); the prints that accompany this text give the 'savage kerns' the features and shaggy appearance of satyrs and wild green men.[12] The reform of the old Celtic Church (or rather, its submission to Roman practice) was the ostensible aim of Henry II and his bishops so to blacken Gaelic society as a whole as 'barbarous' may be seen as standard imperial propaganda. But the real bone of contention at the time was that consistency and loyalty went by very different definitions within the several cultures of the Irish Sea. Feudal customs demanded strict consistency, a well-defined chain of command and authority and a strong sense of reciprocal duty, which went hand in hand with a different concept of land ownership and inheritance. There was no automatic law of primogeniture in the Celtic-speaking lands, though it was essential to the Norman concept of legal ownership. Tribal customs on either side of the Irish Sea (and, for that matter, Anglo-Saxon customs until they were overwhelmed by William of Normandy) had a more relaxed chain of command, depending more on honour than on duty, and a relatively decentralised polity. (Within the Islands, however, Anglo-Saxon England was by far the most unitary realm.) Gaelic land ownership, as we have seen, was notionally common to all the clan: there was no equivalent in Norman law and custom. Two deeply antithetical concepts of social life were in conflict here.

MacMurchada has been despised by older Irish historians and their more nationalist readers as the traitor who brought in the English. But there is a counter-argument put by Francis Byrne — that the king of Leinster, seeing the chronic weakness of the Gaelic polity, had conceived an alternative. He would gain power and institute a fully fledged feudal system for himself, much as the Scottish kings were doing at the same time:

> Diarmait's readiness to overthrow Irish law in order to win Strongbow's support — thereby ignoring the claims of his sons and agnatic kinsmen — can only be explained on the hypothesis that he was aiming at total innovation. By setting himself up as a feudal king and reserving the monarchy for his own dynasty he could well afford to infeudate his faithful Norman allies.[13]

If we mediate between the two we are likely to find the late clan society of Éire a good deal more sympathetic to our tastes. I, at least, find little appeal in the Norman manners. On the other hand, Giraldus's ascription of savagery to the indigenous population is supported by the behaviour of Dermot, who, on receiving the severed head of one enemy (along with sacks full of other heads) gnawed upon it. The ritual blinding and maiming of rivals (on the grounds that only a whole man could be a ruler) was a practice followed by Ruairi O'Connor, the high king, to discipline his rebellious son, who had called in Norman knights to spoil Connaught out of hatred for his father. The father put out the eyes of the son. One earlier historian describes these events as an arid desert of human misery. With hindsight and distance we might admire the kin-based culture of Gaelic Éire; up close we might reasonably opt for Norman terrorism.

Norman organisation is best revealed in its military character. The mounted knight depended for his power on both technical and social developments. The use of the heavy horse and the stirrup enabled him to carry a long spear, to wear protective armour and to stand in the saddle wielding a long heavy sword. This was an unbeatable combination — the twelfth-century equivalent of the tank. But to get a knight into the field equipped cap-a-pie required a team of squire, groom, artificer, stable staff and more, a long organisational tail which could only be administered on hierarchical lines. The heavy horse or destrier was a very large specially bred animal that had to be very well fed to be kept at full fitness. He demanded oats, peas, beans and fresh clover or he would not charge. So the Norman army demanded and created an agricultural surplus and the means to deliver it with a commissariat in which the horses were probably better fed than the infantry. The Norman/Welsh archers used the powerful Welsh longbow, which had long-distance force and a quick rate of fire, in disciplined volleys; it demanded high-level skill and continual practice.[14] Archery developed as a trade, which in turn developed social patterns, hierarchies of skill and coordinated organisation.

Illustration 1. The evolution of a form. The Norman castle grew out of the simple motte-and-bailey formation: a) the mound that today forms a pretty centrepiece to the village of Katesbridge.

Illustration 1. b) The small-scale castle of Clough (now in stone, with an earthen rampart).

Illustration 1. c) The large-scale architecture of Greencastle, which guards the entry to Carlingford Lough.

But the mobile troops fought and advanced in tandem with a system of fixed fortified positions, typically the motte-and-bailey form of castle, in which a walled enclosure abutted onto a raised redoubt. These could begin as temporary timber-and-earth structures, to be replaced with stone later, but their invariable purpose was to permit a small number of soldiers to terrify a large number of civilians by means of their well-stabled cavalry. By 1200, large tracts of Ireland (and nearly all of England and Wales and the eastern slice of Scotland) were controlled from a succession of such fixed points. These ranged from enormous structures of keep and curtain wall, like the brutal mass of Greencastle, which guarded the entrance to Carlingford Lough, to the platoon-sized outpost that now makes a pretty centrepiece to the village of Katesbridge in County Down.

This system of combined static positional control with open, rapid and heavyweight attack enabled the Normans to be, while numerically small, militarily supreme; and it created a society while serving it. The war-making capacity of the Normans structured their social life, which in turn was affirmed by war. Strongbow's army was, in effect, a state in the making.

The peaceful correlative of military organisation was the creation of excise dues and taxes paid in coins, not in kind, charters of incorporation, royal warrants recorded in writing and something of a bureaucracy. The idea that the Celtic-speaking societies of the Irish Sea could have imagined, ordered and executed such a project as the *Domesday Book* is inconceivable. However, the creation of the book supposes an already existing system of records. In this respect Strongbow's invasion of Ireland was a modernising project, while in other respects it was a typical piece of warlordism.

No sooner were the Normans established than Dermot died — 'before,' as Byrne concludes, 'he could ride the tiger he had mounted'.[15]

* * *

From Dublin the Norman conquest moved north. John de Courcy, with a remarkably small force of 22 knights and 300 foot soldiers, rode north to occupy the ecclesiastical centre of Downpatrick. He set out not from Dublin but from Howth; before he left he had to fight his way through a Norse army of some size who had, perhaps, come over from Man to see what they could do. In Downpatrick he encountered a papal legate, the Cardinal Vivian, who was *en route* for Dublin by way of the Isle of Man as part of the proposed reform of church affairs in Ireland. The cardinal suggested peace, but in the midst of discussions the local ruler arrived with a large army. Giraldus writes that there was a hard battle, but a native annalist says that the native forces 'retreated without striking a blow when they saw the Englishmen with their horses in full battledress'. De Courcy (who, of course, was a French-speaking scion of a Viking and scarcely English) then went on to subdue all of Ulster to the east of the River Bann.

The only part of the Irish eastern coast not under Norman control was the hinterland of Dundalk, including the notorious Moyry Pass, where the north–south passage was very vulnerable, and the wild shores of Antrim. Indeed, the Irish Sea was now on its way to becoming a Norman lake, since they were ensconced on its shore in most directions. By 1180 a long sequence of castles stretched from Wexford to the north, namely Dublin (c. 1175), Trim (1175), Drogheda (c. 1175), Greencastle (1180), Dundrum (c. 1180), Killyleagh (1180) and Carrickfergus (c. 1180). Each of these had its satellite strongholds and tower houses located at significant fords and anchorages. Rushen Castle on the Isle of Man was under construction as part of its ruler's Normanising policy.

John de Courcy was a man of immense energy and aggression; he was well known for getting down from his horse and fighting alongside his men in the thick of the fray. Giraldus admired him, and wrote that:

> after the many conflicts of a long war, and severe struggles on every side, being raised by his victories to the summit of power, he erected castles throughout Ulster in suitable places and established in it a most firm peace, not without the greatest labour and privation and many perils.

De Courcy did not enjoy his firm peace for very long and he was not saved by his marriage to Affreca, the sister of Ragnhald, the Viking ruler of Man, nor by his long-term alliance with the rulers of Galloway, who supplied him with troops. Despite a fleet of Manx ships sent to his aid, he was displaced by the de Lacy family in 1205. The de Lacys, to consolidate their links back across the sea, built a substantial castle at the mouth of Carlingford Lough, opposite Greencastle, and fortified the little town of Carlingford.

Meanwhile, a Scotto-Norman feudal system was coming into being. Landless men, younger sons and malcontents took up offers of employment from David I of Scotland. Perhaps most notable of all was Walter FitzAlan. His family had been among William the Conqueror's early contingent and had been rewarded by a large slice of the Welsh borderlands. But Walter, as the third son, had poor prospects at home; he took the chance of becoming King David's steward in 1136 and so initiated the Stewart dynasty. Other knights took similar offers. The de Brus family was moved to Annandale and became the Bruces; they and the followers of Hugh de Moreville ruled most of the border country on King David's behalf.

***

The character of the tiger is known by the nature of its lair. The progress of the Normans around the Irish Sea and into the adjoining lands is best illustrated by a survey of their castles. These Normans were, of course, as the years went by, directed by Angevin and then Plantagenet kings but the feudal type of castle and of government by way of castle that persisted was undoubtedly Norman in origin.

As we have already noted, the usual practice of the Normans was to build what they called a motte and bailey — a mound of earth and rocks surmounted by a stockade and surrounded with a ditch. These were frequently on the site of much more ancient existing structures. Mottes were then progressively turned into stone castles with keeps and curtain walls with subsidiary towers, which might enclose small towns or settlements — such as at Conwy.

Most of the Norman outposts along the coasts are of the Conwy kind — fortifications presiding over useful harbours, surrounded by or enclosing small settlements. They were built over two main periods. The first period was that of the immediate post-conquest decades, when William gave over as much of Wales as he could to his henchmen as their private lands (provided they could win them). In Wales, those with a bearing upon the Irish Sea include the huge fortress of Pembroke, which was built over a long stretch of years, though begun in 1093. It was from here that Strongbow sailed. Harri Tewdwr, the future Henry VII, was also born here, so it is a point where English, Welsh and Irish stories intersect. It had a real military purpose right into the civil-war period, for it was the main embarkation port for expeditions into and from Ireland. Indeed, it has strategic importance down to this day as a major oil terminal and naval base.

The most prominent of all Welsh coastal castles are not, strictly speaking, Norman at all, but form part of the same sequence of architectural types and embody, in a more advanced form, the feudal state of the twelfth century. They are by some distance the most remarkable buildings created beside and along the Irish Sea and very much part of its coastal history. I mean the series of fortresses that Edward I of England created along the edges of north Wales to suppress the population and any attempt at a polity independent of England. Each one defended or enclosed a small town of dependent settlers (mostly English) and each one was adjacent to a harbour, which meant that it could be supplied by sea and could thereby remain independent of the lands it was designed to dominate. All were begun in between 1277 and 1293 and were built speedily by a corps of engineers and masons under the charge of a remarkable military architect called James of St George. There is a good deal of technical evidence to suggest that he had learned his castle-building trade in the holy land, where stone castles first became great architecture. Defensive refinements found in, for example, the Krak des Chevaliers in Syria reappear in Harlech. These castles were in part financed by dues from the Dublin trade, which Edward was able to claim by virtue of his overlordship, and each is enmeshed with the use of Ireland as a base from which to support attempts upon England. Each was a place where any failed attempt to rule in England might come to grief; Richard II on his forlorn return from Ireland had to surrender to Henry Bolingbroke's army at Flint. Each had to be taken by the parliamentary army in the course of the English Civil War, when they were held by royalist forces.

The sequence forms a litany: Flint (begun 1277), Conwy (begun 1283), Caernarfon (begun 1283), Harlech (begun 1283), Criccieth and Beaumaris (begun 1293). These mirror across the sea the earlier sequence of more primitive fortresses. Up in the far north, Rothesay Castle completes this circular tour. In the midst of it all we have the Manx stronghold of Castle Rushen, which is one of the finest of all castles of its kind, despite the changes and adaptations of the centuries.

Travelling clockwise around the Irish Sea provided a very good introduction to the art of fortification, from the crudest promontory fort to the apexes of military architecture; and I began to amass for myself a dossier, some of the fruits of which follow.

The castles of the Irish Sea

Hugh de Lacy was Henry II's right-hand man and he was placed north of Dublin, at Trim, to secure the Pale for the king. There he built an immense fortification and administrative centre, of which the huge keep is merely a fragment. It also included a small river port that gave access to the sea by way of Drogheda. De Lacy settled many of his vassals and retainers in smaller castles roundabout, giving him and his descendants great power.

Further north, Drogheda Castle (another of Hugh de Lacy's creations), is on the site of a much older mound. It has been largely incorporated into the town's fabric. It was extensively altered in 1808, when it became part of the series of Martello towers built with the intention of repelling Napoleon. Drogheda is another example of the purpose-built fortified port the Normans favoured.

The castle at Carlingford was probably built for the de Lacys, but no one seems to be certain. It is often called King John's Castle because that monarch stayed there for three days. In its protection a considerable medieval town developed, with city walls and fortified tower houses. The entire ensemble is picturesque in the extreme, with views of the Mountains of Mourne and of the Cooley Peninsula. Hugh O'Neill attempted to capture it at one point in his wars with Lord Deputy Mountjoy; it also changed hands between royalist and parliamentary forces. Its last serious use was as a hospital and supply base for William of Orange in the campaigns leading up to the battle of the Boyne.

Hugh de Lacy was also responsible for Greencastle at the entry to Carlingford Lough, another solid rectangular keep, but it has become so decayed and been so knocked about that it is hard for the amateur visitor (such as I) to make a lot of sense of what remains. It is also incorporated into a farmyard. During the period

Illustration 2. Trim Castle, 1175–1205, built for Hugh de Lacy.

Illustration 3. Carlingford Castle, c. 1200, probably built for Hugh de Lacy.

1280–1310 it was the favourite resort of Edward de Burgh, who married off his daughter to the Bruce family over the water in Scotland. This did not prevent Edward Bruce from capturing and sacking the castle in 1316 as part of the War of the Irish Sea. It was further battered by parliamentary forces in the English Civil War.

Further north still we come to Dundrum Castle, which was originally created by John de Courcy on more ancient foundation (the Gaelic name means 'the fort on the ridge'. De Courcy, however, did not enjoy it for long, since de Lacy chased him out in 1204. The de Lacys built it up in stone, more or less as it is today.

Dundrum is a small, almost miniature castle, now hidden in trees above the town. It had several changes of fortune and overlordship, with parts added and subtracted. In 1642 it was captured by the Magennis family in the course of the English Civil War but taken back shortly afterwards by parliamentary forces, who pulled down much of the wall in 1652.

The little town of Dundrum was once a significant small port but is now largely silted up.

Illustration 4.
Dundrum Castle
(1177).

Further north again, beside Strangford Lough, is another of John de Courcy's fortresses — Killyleagh Castle. This became the stronghold of the Hamilton family, who played a great part in the Scottish settlement of Ulster (and are still in residence). In the middle of the nineteenth century they employed Charles Lanyon to remodel it into a French *château*. Lanyon, fresh from completing Scrabo Tower, did an excellent job; the result (if it now seems eccentric) has a fine air, especially when seen from the road to the north and west of the town. The original structure still remains beneath the overcoat of heavily modelled stucco placed upon it by Lanyon. This remodelling was not in the least eccentric in 1850 — it was the standard ploy of modern taste.

The last military use of this castle was in the 1920s, when the Hamilton family fought a gun battle across the courtyard with the IRA.

Illustration 6.
Carrickfergus Castle
(*c.* 1180).

Illustration 7.
Rothesay Castle,
Isle Of Bute (1220).

John de Courcy's lasting monument, and the best-preserved medieval fortress in Ireland, is Carrickfergus Castle. It became the main military establishment in the north and the centre of government. It had, of course, its full share of violence, principally in 1315–16, when it was besieged by Edward Bruce in the War of the Irish Sea; it is said that the garrison became so hungry that they ate a number of their prisoners. It became the principal base for English soldiers during the plantation of Ulster. In 1760 it was sacked and damaged by a French fleet and in 1798 the waters of Belfast Lough saw a battle with an American ship commanded by John Paul Jones. It remained a piece of coastal defence until 1945 (in the woods on the far side of the lough is an immense cannon, large enough to sink any visiting battleship). Of course, it is now a heritage attraction, with dummy plastic Normans looking out from the mended battlements.

Rothesay Castle is a splendid drum of stone that was, considered from the military point of view, a failure. Alan, high steward to the king of Scotland and founder of the Stewart dynasty, had it built. It was completed by his son Walter just in time for Uspak the Viking to knock it down in 1230, after a three-day assault in which the assailants hacked down the stonework with their axes. The circular form of the walls made it impossible to bring enfilading fire to bear upon them. Details can be found in the *Saga of Haakon Haakonsson.* The Stewarts built it up again, only for Haakon IV, with an army of Vikings and Manxmen, to perform the same trick a second time (in 1263). During the Scottish Wars of Independence it was captured by Robert the Bruce in 1311 and lost again to an English force in 1334. John of Islay, the last of the *re* Innse Gall, took it in 1462 and it fell again to Henry VIII's 'rough wooing' in 1544. Rothesay Castle was finally made redundant by the Clan Campbell in 1685. In consequence of this chequered history it was constantly repaired and modernised and became a very popular west-coast headquarters for successive Scottish monarchs (nearly all of them Stewarts). It was originally on the seashore, surrounded by a salt-water moat, but today it is situated right in the middle of Rothesay town. The moat is now full of fresh water, graced with nesting swans.

***

Galloway is largely devoid of truly Norman castles because it remained, through the Anglo-Norman centuries, a largely Gaelic domain controlled by a succession of independent princelings and Scotto-Norse brigands. David I and subsequent Scottish monarchs managed to isolate Galloway from the rest of southern Scotland by settling Norman knights along the intervening marches, the most notable family being that of Robert Bruce. These knights built their own fortresses, of which the most prominent is Doon Castle, whose octagonal keep was lifted up and moved in an act of piety to save it from the rising, dammed waters of Loch Doon.

The large motte at Innermessan, strategically placed across the isthmus at Stranraer, giving access north into the Firth of Clyde and south into the Solway Firth, seems not to have been studied or excavated at all. In its present state (see Chapter 3) it looks to be a early Norman earthen motte that never quite became a stone castle, built probably on a much older site.

There are substantial tower houses and small forts all over the region, of which the finest is Maclellan's Castle in Kirkcudbright. A real curiosity is the triangular Caerlaverock Castle on the Solway flatlands between Dumfries and Annan. This figures largely in the border wars of Edward I and Robert Bruce and was subject to several sieges, destructions and rebuildings. It usually belonged to the Maxwell family, an astute gang of survivors who would take a pension from anyone.

I had every intention of taking good photographs of Carlisle Castle, but arrived there in continuous drenching rain and abandoned the task. It is, of course, an impressive pile of red sandstone, first begun by William II and continued by several monarchs and commanders in subsequent centuries. But by the time you have driven or cycled round the Solway floods, in conditions that would have dismayed Noah, you don't feel like taking yet another shot, but make towards the nearest 'Vacancies' sign.

Similar excuses must be given on behalf of Lancaster Castle, another very old structure built, like Carlisle, upon a Roman base. It was started around 1090 by one Roger of Poitou, a relation of William the Conqueror, and had many additions. However, in its function as a prison and a law court it has had much more recent work interwoven with the older, so that it has lost its Norman feel more or less completely. This is best revealed in the plan rather than the elevation, which retains the authentic character.

Indeed, to reconnect with the progress of military architecture we must pass along the Irish-Sea coast as far as Chester and take the shore road along the Dee as far as Flint.

The castles built for Edward I in his conquest of Wales are the creations of Master James of St George, his chief engineer. It is my view that they comprise collectively the finest and most innovative building programme of the Islands, their sinister function notwithstanding. Each is superbly adapted to its particular site and each bodies forth a distinctly articulated sense of mass and void. Master James came from the Savoy region and appears to have learnt his craft in the holy land, building castles for Crusaders and with French/Swiss lordlings. His whole family made castle-building their trade and their hand has been spotted in some French *châteaux*. We can see this hand not only in the defensive ingenuity of the structures but also in their spatial organisation.

Flint dispenses with the motte-and-bailey plan normal to castles derived from the Norman type. It is wholly original, so far as I can tell. It isolates three huge block-like cylindrical towers, creating three keeps within the one curtain wall. The sea and quays

Illustration 8. Flint Castle (built by Master James of St George for Edward I, from 1277).

come right up into the centre of the ensemble, rendering it secure against starvation tactics when under siege. This harbour is now silted up.

This was the castle where Richard II surrendered to Bolingbroke; we are to imagine Richard descending into the base court from the north-west tower (Illustration 8) and kneeling in the central yard. But this is only part of the castle. In front of it, to the left of the photograph, is the broad outer ward, separately walled and moated and bridged. Perhaps this was the base court ('where kings grow base/To come at traitors' calls, and do them grace').[16] So was Richard imprisoned in the donjon or great tower, looking over the wall at Bolingbroke on the causeway below?

The interior of the donjon or great tower contains an atrium-like space, with broad inner galleries and deep vaulted passageways. This entire enterprise, which required a workforce of 1,500 men, also included building a small fortified town or *bastide*, thus creating an economic as well as military base for the proposed subduing of the Welsh.

The next Edwardian castle, built again by Master James, is a day's march further west, at Rhuddlan.

Built at the same time as Flint, Rhuddlan required an even larger workforce. The river had to be deepened and straightened to give easy access to the sea three miles away — a huge undertaking in the thirteenth century. A port access is fitted under the west wall of the castle.

Illustration 9. Rhuddlan Castle gatehouse, and the remains of the outer walls (built by Master James for Edward I, from 1277).

Illustration 10. Conwy Castle (built by Master James for Edward I, from 1283).

This is a more conventional keep-and-curtain-wall concentric design, but diamond-shaped in plan, with two huge cylindrical towers at each apex, forming gatehouses. The upper two-thirds of the walls are in white limestone with red sandstone below. A lot of the sandstone has been quarried away and can be found gracing nearby manor houses. This polychrome approach to the walls can also be found at Caernarfon and it may have been reinforced by painted details and limewash, making each castle brightly coloured rather than grimly grey.

It was here, in 1284, that the Statute of Rhuddlan was enacted, bringing all Welsh law under the principles of English common law and dividing the principality into counties — a founding moment for the British state.

The patched and smoke-blackened profile of Conwy stands over foreshore litter and a castellated railway embankment — a complicated linear structure with two large wards or courtyards that extend further to become the town walls. There are altogether eight large cylindrical towers, which make an imposing sight as you approach the town, and further towers along the walls. Conwy is the best example of a French-style *bastide* to be found in the Islands. Edward populated it largely with men and women from south Lancashire.

Master James's crowning achievement, successfully combining the military with the state-symbolic functions of its place and purpose, was Caernarfon Castle.

Illustration 11. Caernarfon Castle (built by Master James for Edward I, from 1283).

Though it appears fantastic and romantic in style — a sort of neo-medieval fantasy conceived while still in the middle ages — it is formidable in the extreme. There is not an inch of dead ground at the foot of its walls from which any attack could be launched unharassed. If, by some chance, attackers had got through the five or six gates of the main entrance and got themselves into the elongated and angular inner ward, they would have been in yet worse peril because (surrounded by no fewer than nine substantial towers) they were in a killing ground without hope of shelter. Then, if by slender chance and suicidal bravery they had got a foothold on the walls, they would have had to fight their way around all nine of the towers, each a small keep of its own and each full of ingenious arrow loops, murder holes and reversed spirals. Each of these towers was also capable of providing covering fire to all of its neighbours — an object lesson in static defence.

In symbolic terms, this was the castle as pure swank. As ornate and fanciful as a book of hours in its appearance, the building was a royal palace *de luxe*, designed with staged ceremonials in mind. The visual ideology of Edward's court was full of neo-Roman references (Edward was claimed as a second Justinian for his law-making) and these associations are made solid in the polychrome walls, which refer to the vast walls of Byzantium. We should probably assume the appearance of resplendent banners and painted walls such as also graced contemporary cathedrals. The Roman camp at Segontium nearby was the assumed headquarters of Macsen Gwledig, or Maximus, the 'Welsh emperor of Rome' and his Welsh wife, Helen (see Chapter 3). Edward also appropriated to himself all the regalia of the Welsh high kings in much the same manner as he seized upon the Scottish Stone of Scone — symbolically foreclosing on any possible reinvention of those separate kingdoms.

The more one learns about Edward and his *modus operandi* the greater and more foresighted and terrible he seems to have been, with a ruthless and obsessive eye for detail.

Architectural historians debate the origins of the notable little fortress known as Criccieth Castle. It looks at first as if built by an apprentice of Master James but the impressive gatehouse towers are not cylindrical but D sectioned, a feature often found in Welsh stone castles built in imitation of English ones. I shall not try to sort out that particular problem. It has a wonderful situation, looking out over the bay towards Harlech, and affords perhaps the finest of such views in Britain.

Harlech Castle represents the building as killing ground. It is the most sinister building in all the Islands. You can open up the chapel floor to kill people in the passageways below.

It is a sublime building, terrifying and beautiful in equal proportions. Separated from the main mass of the hillside by a deep quarried cleft, it could only be attacked from the east, on which side there are portcullises, drawbridges, murder holes and every contrivance of harm. It endured three long sieges in different wars and could only be captured by closing off the sea access to a landing dock below the western cliff.

Illustration 12.
Criccieth Castle
(thirteenth century).

Illustration 13. Harlech
Castle (built by Master
James for Edward I,
1283–9).

Master James was Harlech Castle's first governor (constable). The living quarters, arranged around a small deeply set courtyard within, appear to have been comfortable.

The *ne plus ultra* of all symmetrical, concentric castles is Beaumaris, with up to 16 lines of defence and many independently fortified inner towers. It is the Platonic idea of Castle, in which the spirit of symmetry communes with the spirit of murder. These later castles, developed out of the motte and bailey, look forward to the insanely complicated geometries of the sixteenth century and the cannon-proof monsters of Vauban and the Maginot line.

Illustration 14. Beaumaris Castle (begun by Master James for Edward I). This castle was probably planned in 1283 but not begun until 1295, when it employed a workforce of 2,500 men. It was never completed.

Subsequently Master James went with Edward to Scotland and probably assisted at the siege of Stirling Castle and other occasions of brutish power. He is also known to have had a hand in designing Aberystwyth Castle (along the lines of Rhuddlan but now almost wholly ruined) and Builth Castle.[17]

Cilgerran Castle is the latest of the several forts that had been built at this spot — the furthest point that can be reached by sea-going craft up the River Teifi.

I found it almost by accident in the course of an endless cycle ride down the coast of Ceredigion on a very hot, windless day. Almost desperate for a drink, I slumped down in a pretty village and there it was — a compact mass, with three tough-looking towers, on a remarkable site with cliffs falling away below it into the river.

The Marshall family were virtual kings of Ceredigion and Leinster for a hundred years, building not only castles but also a great octagonal lighthouse on Hook Head near Waterford.

Illustration 15.
Cilgerran Castle (built
for William Marshall
the Younger, from
1225).

* * *

The plan was that I should conclude this clockwise odyssey by arriving in Pembroke
and its castle. But, I must admit, I was too tired and I had other calls on my time,
other fish to fry and other books to finish. This is like going to Rome and not seeing
the Vatican, because Pembroke Castle, its first stage built for the Montgomerys and its
second for William Marshall and the successive earls of Pembroke, is a sort of
Himalayan giant among castles. The whole of Harlech could fit into its main ward and
still leave room for a scaffold.

But I never promised myself, let alone any readers, the comforts of completion.

I think of my climbing companion of many years who, for the very last peak on
his list of Munros, chose an absurdly remote summit that required the better part of
a long snowy day before we even saw it. Having found it and waded up it in thigh-
deep snow, we arrived on the last slope. He made the decision then and there to go no
further lest he could find no other object worth so intense an effort. Very cool. And
in that spirit I have declined to visit Pembroke.

However, before leaving the castles of the Irish Sea entirely, it seems important to
visit Ellan Vannin again and look over Rushen Castle.

Illustration 16. Rushen Castle (see also Chapter 5).

Rushen Castle is much altered and developed from a small cubic keep probably built around 1200 by King Magnus — the last independent Manx king — on a site previously used by Magnus of Norway. Internally it was altered a number of times, having been extensively wrecked (or 'slighted') by Robert Bruce in 1311. It has also been adapted into a prison and part of the government offices of Man and further adapted to withstand cannon fire in the civil-war period. As a result it is a structure of intricate character and fine proportions whose interior does not quite seem to fit into its exterior.

It stands right in the town square of Castletown, with harbours all around it, as well as houses of distinction.

Notes

[1]   Fortunately this has been done for us in K. Kristiansen (1998) *Europe before history*, Cambridge: Cambridge University Press, which is lucid, balanced and relevant. See also T.W. Moody and F.X. Martin (eds) (1967, repr. 2001) *The course of Irish history*, Cork: Mercier Press, Chapter 3.

[2]   All quotations are from Giraldus Cambrensis (A.B. Scott and F.X. Martin, eds and trs) (1978) *Expugnatio Hibernica: the Conquest of Ireland*, Dublin: Royal Irish Academy. See also G.H. Orpen (1911, repr. 1968, vol. 1) *Ireland under the Normans, 1169–1216*, Oxford: Clarendon Press.

3   It has been asserted that this charter either never existed or was a forgery; it can no longer be traced. True or false, it was a typical feudal stratagem for maintaining the chain of authority. For discussion of this issue, see Orpen, *op. cit.*, Chapter 9.

4   *Ibid.*, p. 83.

5   Giraldus was himself a relative of Nesta, the Welsh princess who contrived to have children by several Norman husbands as well as by Henry II himself. The presence of Normans in the Welsh Marches preceded the Norman conquest of the Anglo-Saxon kingdom; Herefordshire had become something like an Norman colony by 1050, tasked (by Anglo-Saxon kings) with the defence of the western borders of Mercia. See L.H. Nelson (1966) *The Normans in south Wales, 1070–1171*, Austin: University of Texas Press, especially Chapter 1.

6   The presence of Flemings in part derives from King Stephen's use of them as mercenaries in his wars with Matilda; Henry had packed them off to Pembrokeshire. Their leader in Ireland was one Maurice de Prendergast, a man who was quite happy to change sides if paid well enough. The Flemings spoke a 'low Dutch' very close to then-current English and traces of their speech are still to be found in parts of County Wexford. See Orpen, *op. cit.*, pp. 397–8, and Nelson, *op. cit.* I have also noticed some very Flemish names in the telephone book. Flemings from Pembrokeshire also engaged in military adventures in Scotland and were employed by Scottish kings to control border areas.

7   The local support was organised by one of Dermot's illegitimate sons. This capable young man was later sacrificed by his father in a hostage deal.

8   See B. Colfer (2002) *Arrogant trespass: Anglo-Norman Wexford, 1169–1400*, Enniscorthy: Duffry Press. A wonderfully detailed piece of work, with an account of Viking Wexford. And see also T.B. Barry (1987) *The archaeology of medieval Ireland*, London: Methuen.

9   Orpen, *op. cit.*, p. 271.

10 Nelson, *op. cit.*, pp. 22–3.

11 P.R. Hanrahan (1866) *Eva, or the buried city of Bannow*, London: Hanrahan. This is a curiosity, for it seems to take the chronology of the *Lebor Gabála Érenn* for fact, though it was first published in 1866 (and then in 1932 and then again in 1960 by John English and Co. of Wexford).

12 The best summary of this civility/barbarity argument that I have come across is by R.R. Davies (2000) *The first English empire: power and identities in the British Isles, 1093–1343*, Oxford: Oxford University Press, Chapter 5.

13 F.J. Byrne (1973, repr. 2001) *Irish kings and high kings*, Dublin: Four Courts Press, p. 274.

14 Buried archers can always be identified by the great development of their right shoulders. They were full-time professional troops.

15 Byrne, *op. cit.*

16 William Shakespeare, *Richard II*.

17 L. Hull (2005) *The castles and bishops' palaces of Pembrokeshire*, Little Logaston: Logaston Press.

SEVEN
Sitting on the roundabout watching all the trucks roll by

The Belfast–Dublin road crosses the present border at a broad defile that goes by several names: the Moyry Pass, Bealach an Mhaighre, the Gap of the North and, more recently, 'Apache Pass'. The use of the word 'pass' in Ireland does not necessarily indicate a mountain pass; it just as often means a way through forests. The Moyry Pass, though, is both thickly wooded and surrounded by hills, satisfying both conditions. Nor does it go directly, for the road goes south down a narrow valley known as Ravensdale and the railway goes a broader way two kilometres west by way of the townland of Faughart. The land in between and to either side is rocky and mostly forested or covered in a thick scrub of gorse. To the north, nearer Newry, the valley bottoms are very marshy. The hills between, if not high, are steep. It was always regarded as difficult country, being an undrained wilderness with deep bogs until the eighteenth century.

Both ways of the pass converge on the broad flat plain immediately north of Dundalk. Here there is a new roundabout which (at the time of writing) is the present terminus of the M1, a place where five roads meet. I am sitting on this broad hillock looking towards the town and Dublin. Straight ahead of me the old road goes southward between walls and little houses and some untidy trees. To my left a new road crosses reclaimed land and Dundalk racecourse; it finds a new bridge into an industrial zone. Dundalk Bay with its extensive mud-flats is visible. Immediately behind me (to the north) the road passes a clump of substantial trees on a mound, some pleasant parkland and the road leading towards Ragnhald's old anchorage at Carlingford. Over to my right is the last mile of the new motorway, coming up from Dublin and continuing behind my shoulder into Ravensdale through a wilderness of churned earth, where colossal machines are busy tearing open the hillsides. By the time this book is in print the road will have reached the outskirts of Newry.

Through these churns and trenches threads the road to Faughart. In former times this was the old road to the north, which wound its way through hills and bogs between Slieve Gullion and the Carlingford Mountains. This was once thick forest and every valley was a bog. It is still wet country, which every rain turns into a sponge, though it is now arrayed in white cottages and prosperous farms.

And, persisting in the idea of locating each chapter on a site and a real place, I have lain on my back to think. And it seems to me, with my head in the vetches, that a

Illustration 1. The roundabout on the Dundalk–Newry road.

roundabout is a good image for the Irish Sea, with its many exits and entrances and its giddying motion.

It was through these hills that John de Courcy and his 300 men rode in 1177 to seize and conquer the north. And it was through these hills in 1315 that Edward Bruce and his army of Scots and gallóglaigh rode to invade southern Ireland, and it was these hills to which they retreated in 1318, only to perish at Faughart. Through them a Tudor army fought, trench by trench, in mud and rain. Here also came the troops of Europe, across the same fords and causeways, towards the ill-fated River Boyne.

During the writing of this book these hills and lanes, these bogs and forests, have been subject to intense electronic scrutiny from a series of listening posts supplied by helicopter.

As an innocent cyclist passing from Dublin to Belfast many years ago I just happened to be panting away through south Armagh when, coming round a corner, I was confronted by a purely medieval structure, built of sheet steel and wire mesh covered in spikes and antennae. It seemed to take up acres of ground. And while I gazed there rose from within it a large helicopter carrying what looked like an elephant's shopping bag. Following the contours of the drumlins the machine and its burden whisked away at what looked like reckless speed, dodging the trees. In the conditions that then obtained in south Armagh, the forces of the crown had reverted to the basic Norman model.

This roundabout is a place where the fate of nations has been fought over. With that in mind I have decided to split what was to have been a single chapter into two parts and in the second set off south on the rocky road to Dublin.

Illustration 2. Police post in Crossmaglen, south Armagh—the modern equivalent of the motte and bailey (reproduced with permission of Jonathan Olley).

***

Part one

It is here, give or take a mile or so, that the great encounters of *Táin Bó Cuailnge* took place. At the risk of boring my Irish readers I will describe this for the sake of the rest.

In this legendary war the armies of Connacht were led by the redoubtable Queen Medb (Maeve) and they came off worse in an encounter with the warrior Cuchulainn, the 'Hound of Ulster'. The *Táin* resembles a version of the *Iliad* in which Cuchulainn plays the part of the man-slaying Achilles and the part of Helen is played by a prodigious bull that the men of Connacht and their allies are seeking to capture from the men of Ulster. If the *Iliad* is a story of adultery raised to an epic, then the *Táin* is cattle-rustling on a Homeric scale. But just as the *Iliad* is clearly about a great deal more, so the *Táin* has a great deal to say about ethnic and clan rivalries in the Bronze Age. If we knew how to decipher it more completely it might even tell us something pertinent about more recent history.

Medb is the most vivid character in the whole poem because she is a fully realised human being. Randy and sarcastic and a terror to men, you might easily meet her in a Dundalk bar tonight. Cuchulainn, on the other hand, has superhuman attributes and is described in fantastic terms; his deeds are always prodigious.[1] His one-man Thermopylae is a rearguard action to close the Gap of the North while King Conchobar of Ulster and his army celebrate a religious festival during which they must not fight.

The main encounter takes place across a ford. With single-minded ferocity the Hound slaughters the warriors that come against him, one after another, until confronted by his childhood friend and blood brother, Ferdia. Their confrontation, fatal to both, has a tragic force that lifts the story out of its primeval terror, and in Thomas Kinsella's translation Cuchulainn's lament over his friend goes like this:

> It was all play, all sport
> until Ferdia came to the ford.
> Misery! A pillar of gold
> I have levelled in the ford,
> the bull of the tribe-herd
> braver than any man
>
> All play, all sport
> until Ferdia came to the ford.
> I thought beloved Ferdia
> would live forever after me
> — yesterday, a mountain side;
> today, nothing but a shade.[2]

Irish scholars and poets who can encounter the story in its original speak of it in the same breath as Homer and it is easy to see why. Both epics seem to originate in similar societies with shared values of intense loyalties, territorial imperatives and an intermingling of the sacred and the secular.[3] Individual prowess is (almost) everything. But the differences are telling.

At the heart of the *Iliad*, as Achilles prepares to go out against Hector in the climactic battle, the poet gives his hearers a still centre to the whirlwind of blood and ambition into which he has plunged them. We see, upon Achilles's heaven-made shield, a vision of peace and civic fulfilment:

> … two cities, noble scenes:
> weddings in one, and noble feasts, and brides led out
> through town by torchlight from their chambers

amid chorales, amid the young men turning
round and round in dances: flutes and harps
among them, keeping up a tune … the town elders
sat in a ring, on chairs of polished stone …
— Homer, *The Iliad*

This urban, idealised and ennobled normality is a counterpoise to the furious
action of the Trojan War and it is wholly lacking in the world of the *Táin*. What we
are seeing there is glimpse of a pre-urban 'barbarian' culture and, as the translator
remarks, 'It is possible that the kind of culture the *Táin* describes may have lasted in
Ireland up to the introduction of Christianity in the fifth century.'[4]

The *Táin* was taken up by Irish nationalism as an epic of resistance:

What comes out of the mountain
Where men first shed their blood?
Who thought Cuchulain till it seemed
he stood where they had stood?
—W.B. Yeats, *The death of Cuchulain*

When Oliver Sheppard made a monument to the rebels of 1916, he made it as a
Cuchulainn/Christ figure in the form of a *pietà*. But, conversely and knowingly, the
Ulster loyalists of 1980 painted across a wall at what they term 'Freedom Corner' in
east Belfast an image of the same *pietà*, with the slogan 'Cuchulainn, Defender of
Ulster, Then and Now'. The obscurity of a legend acts like an obsidian mirror in
which every faction can see its darkened face.[5]

There has been scholarly dispute about exactly where this fight took place and which
ford precisely was the one. Two rivers and several large streams converge on the muddy
shores of Dundalk Bay and they are backed by wooded hills and crags; all provide
possible sites. On the basis of place names an itinerary has been constructed which will
take the walker or cyclist all over the rocky hills of Carlingford. Faughart (Fochert)
figures prominently, as do Ravensdale and the shore of Dundalk Bay. But that is to miss
the main point, for epics, though grounded in the specific, to be epics must depart from
the circumstantial and seek the universal landscapes of pass, ford, gap, gate or bridge.
The Hound of Ulster is in company with Leonidas and Roland and Horatius.

Then out spake brave Horatius,
the Captain of the Gate.
'To every man upon this earth
Death cometh soon or late.
And how can man die better

Than facing fearful odds
For the ashes of his fathers
And the temples of his gods'?
— T.B. Macaulay, 'Horatius', from *Lays of ancient Rome*

Following this gloss on Irish geography a little further you are invited to drive north from Dublin until, some miles before you reach Dundalk, you get a long view of the border hills. Along this prolonged ridge of raised ground runs a line of outposts that dates back to the Bronze Age. It culminates in a discontinuous earthwork known as the Black Pig's Dyke, which protected Ulster from the rest of Ireland — or the rest of Ireland from Ulster. The dyke, which hereabout is known as the Dane's Cast, comes down to the Bealach near Camlough and can be seen north of Newry above the line of the Newry Canal and on further sides in Armagh and points west. The dyke is usually dated to around AD 200 and may represent a final frontier constructed by the Cruithin clans of Uladh against northward attacks by the Gaels. Or it may be a millennium older; or it may be a trick of the light. Nor is it impossible that Cuchulainn's rearguard action is an epitome of retreats consequent upon shifts of power within Éire at that time. But that is mere conjecture.[6]

***

Just how Edward Bruce came to be a king of Ireland for a few months before coming to grief fields away from where I am now sitting is a complicated story of which an outline is required.

The lack of a common history for the Islands taken as a whole means that we cannot assume that basic stories such as these are part of the common equipment. Yet the debacle that overcame Edward Bruce's army was a significant moment in the process by which the nations of the Islands took their present form.

Until around AD 900 monkish chroniclers (writing in Latin) made no clear distinction between the Scots and the Irish. Both were Scotti. All Q-Celtic speakers acknowledged one another as a network of kinsmen speaking approximately the same languages and adhering to a common religious and monastic tradition. Across the North Channel the great Clan Donald possessed islands and peninsulas and never worried whether they were Scottish or Irish. This idea never quite vanished from medieval poetry and annals but was progressively thinned out by the different direction the two realms took. Social organisation at the clan level on both sides was similar but this never amounted to political solidarity. Nor could it, for the character of Gaelic society prevented the solidification of institutions into a state just as much as the sparse population and difficult countryside and extended coastline, which united people by sea and emphasised their differences by land.

G.W.S. Barrow has made it clear that in several key respects the thirteenth-century Scottish state was positively anti-Gaelic in that it had withdrawn itself from the western seaboard and adopted feudal methods of government. Its political structure was similar to that of European kingdoms in general. Succession was by primogeniture. There was a developed administration with permanent officers, marshals and an exchequer that issued a coinage; there were the beginnings of a shire system and of local government by officials loyal to the crown. Most of these men were of Norman origin. Q-Celtic as the common tongue was being steadily pushed into the highland regions (and Galloway) by Scots and Inglis and French. The capital sites were now urban (Perth, Stirling and Edinburgh); that there should be administrative capitals is itself most un-Celtic. Iona had long ceased to function as a symbolic site of high importance, St Columba having been replaced by St Andrew and St Brigid by St Margaret, the hallowed Anglo-Hungarian wife of Malcolm Canmore. The state was a North-Sea power, with extensive political and trading links to Norway, Denmark, northern Germany and Flanders, with whom it engaged in diplomacy and treaties as an equal.[7]

As we have already noted, the Scottish state from its beginning sought reliance upon forces that had little to do with Gaelic kin or clan. The kingdom of Scotland was surrounded with a zone of Norman baronies between itself and the western isles and Ireland and England. These were a force supporting the feudal monarchy, independent of the clans and Gaelic culture. To repeat, some scholars have written of a Norman conquest of Scotland taking place alongside that of England and Ireland, with the important difference that the conquest was not an invasion, nor a violent seizure, but a peaceful, even bureaucratic, process enmeshed with the establishment of the state and national kingship.

Among the several Norman knights in south-western Scotland was one Robert de Brus. He had served Henry I of England (receiving lands in north Yorkshire for that service, as well as in Tottenham, north of London) and then he served David I of Scotland, who settled him in Annandale, north of the Solway, across the lands now traversed by the A74. Here his task was to stand guard between the heartlands of the Scottish kingdom and the 'unruly' (from the feudal point of view, of course) Gaelic-speaking chiefs of Galloway.

The Bruce family was a characteristic node in the network of feudal lordships that ringed the Irish Sea. Colm McNamee writes:

> This francophone aristocratic culture is generally labelled Anglo-Norman, in recognition of its eleventh century origin in the Norman conquests. By the fourteenth century, this aristocracy had almost nothing to do with Normandy, but the anachronistic term is tolerated as it serves to distinguish the broadly similar English, Anglo-Scottish and Anglo-Irish culture from the distinctive aristocratic cultures of Gaelic Scotland and Ireland and Wales.[8]

This net was knotted together by marriages — across the North Channel with the de Burgh family, which had succeeded John de Courcy and the de Lacys as the earls of Ulster and in turn was linked with the Stewart family, who were neighbours of the Bruces in Strathclyde, along with other smaller families such as the de Boyvilles of Kelburn. This formed part of an array of family alliances and lordships extending across Ireland and southern Scotland and into the Welsh Marches, which was always partly independent of the kingdoms to which they nominally belonged. A full history of the interlinking marriages and alliances, at any level below the most scholarly, has yet to be written because the nineteenth-century notion of history as the history of distinct nations (which still largely prevails) gets in the way of our seeing what was actually going on.

The largest family of all was that which came to be called Stewart or Stuart (Scottish or French spelling confusingly optional). Beginning as the FitzAlans, by diligent service to successive kings the Stewarts had become hereditary stewards and counsellors who sat at the king's right knee.

From their original base in Renfrew and Paisley their feudal lands, or fiefs, extended into the highlands and islands of the west. They had six stone castles, including the prodigious keep of Rothesay.[9] The Bruce family was hardly less powerful, for it had lands in Ulster and Robert, the eldest son of the family, was married to a de Burgh daughter. There were also the Comyns, Balliols, Douglases and Murrays. Each had its own corps of retainers and subdependent knights and lordlings. Among the Stewart 'family' was a formerly Welsh contingent they had brought with them at the start, named Wallace. These followers formed a secondary layer of Scotto-Norman sheriffs, landowners, bishops and military personnel below the grandees, bound to them by feudal vows and oaths. This was a sub-system of government not unlike a clan system *sui generis*. Indeed, by 1300 these families very nearly constituted the Scottish state in and by themselves, independent of royal power.

The Norman lordships in Ireland were particularly independent, since English kings were not kings in or of Ireland (except in the Pale) but feudal overlords. The process of naturalisation by intermarriage begun when Strongbow had married Aoife continued when de Courcy married Affreca, the sister of the king of Man. It was well advanced by 1300. The Stewarts, for example, had married the descendants of the fearsome Somerled, whom they had defeated and killed at Renfrew a hundred years before. Intermarriage was reinforced by the custom of fostering, in which one family would look after the children of another.

Each knot in the net had its own resources of income from lands, rents and taxes and could call upon an armed retinue of soldiers and upon temporary forms of military service. Each feudal magnate was in turn required from time to time to supply their forces and wealth to the earldoms and monarchies of England and Scotland. Church organisations followed a similar pattern and often coincided with the same families. These families promoted, mainly through the Cistercian order, a monastic system that comprised both religious discipline and economic expansion. The connecting lordships and baronies served politically and militarily as a 'crumple-zone' between the two monarchies of Scotland and England and between them and the westerly Gaeltacht of the Atlantic seaboards.

Linguistically, the lordships around the Irish Sea were extremely diverse. Latin was the official language of law and government, though the polite functions of language were carried out in Norman French. The everyday language at all levels of society depended on location — it could be English, an antique form of French, Scots English, Scots Gaelic, Irish Gaelic, Welsh, Manx or whatever local variants existed, such as the Norse English of the Solway and remnants of local P-Celtic in Cumbria. The degree to which Pictish (whatever that might have been) continued to be spoken remains unclear. Considerable literatures flourished in Welsh and Gaelic; the literature of Norman French was part of the wider culture of western Europe and contiguous with it; English was about to develop as a literary language, as was Scots. In the ports of Dublin, Chester and Bristol we may assume a richer mixture still and there were enclaves of Flemish and the Scandinavian languages. To participate in this network at the level of a cleric or a skilled travelling craftsman required some sophistication, such as inheres in any multilingual society, since a skill in several languages is a skill also in several ways of thinking and seeing the world. The educated nobility of Anglo/Scotto-Norman and Gaelic notables travelled widely; many Scottish lawyers were trained in Bologna and one of the Bruce family became a famous scholar at Oxford.

At a distance this seems to have been a dynamic and remarkably stable society and a method of government that balanced local peculiarities with central requirements rather well, though up close it often resembles a basket full of iron crabs, each clambering over one another. It was possible to be the servant of two masters and the great Scotto-Norman families found themselves pulled apart by simultaneous allegiances to the respective monarchs of Scotland and England. This had a bearing on how the Scottish War of Independence worked its way. Norman families in Ireland were becoming steadily more Hibernicised, without losing formal allegiance across the water. You did not lightly break an oath of fealty, and not only because might you forfeit your lands. To break an oath was to unpick the net that held all order in place.[10]

The Scottish feudal lords had a great interest in good order because they did homage for their landholdings to two kings on both sides of the Anglo-Scottish border. Robin Frame, in his 1990 book *Political development of the British Isles 1100–1400*, has counted them up and reckons that 9 out of 13 Scottish earls had holdings in England and 9 out of 22 English earls had a similar concern for the lasting peace of Scotland.[11] It was also quite common for these magnates to have lands in France or Flanders and to take French wives from the nobility of France, of which they were a semi-detached part. This was a situation that encouraged the *status quo* and a state of affairs that had lasted without serious interruption for 200 or more years.

Just why this mutually satisfying arrangement should have disintegrated depends on how we wish to explain human affairs. It could be that Edward I of England was power hungry; his continental ambitions had been frustrated so he turned on the Welsh and, having subdued them, it was Scotland's turn. Or it could be down to an agricultural decline, contingent upon many factors, which was setting in, so great lords had to expand to maintain their state. Alternatively, it is possible that feudalism provoked periodic war as a systematic requirement for its existence, or that brave-hearted Scotland was being oppressed by the wicked English and had to find its freedom; or, simply, that human beings must prey upon others, like monsters of the deep.

Happily, this is not a problem I feel a need to solve. But I do feel a need to understand why the road from Newry south to Dundalk should play such a role in my travels and my reading and why it was, and is, a strategic node.

***

English monarchs had, since Anglo-Saxon times, claimed a right of overlordship over the whole island of Britain. This was a right that was not enforceable; it was merely a convenient fiction, just in case. It proved convenient indeed when there was a crisis of succession in the Scottish monarchy (in the autumn of 1290) and Edward I was invited to arbitrate between the different parties. This was a common feudal practice but on this occasion it was like asking the hungry wolf to choose between succulent lambs. Edward, seeing a chance to turn a convenient fiction into fact, demanded that Scottish lords acknowledge him formally as their overlord and deliver up all royal castles into his keeping, just to show they meant it. He then adjudicated the dispute in favour of a member of the Comyn faction — a decision that provoked a palace coup in Edinburgh and a revolt of the other factions. The Bruce family and many others took Edward's side in the brief ensuing war.[12]

When a new government for Scotland was put in place, Robert Bruce expected to be made king in return for service given. Edward is reported to have replied, 'Have I nothing better to do than win kingdoms for you?' and scooped the pool into his own pocket. He appointed himself the sole monarch of Scotland and in sign of this carried off the Stone of Destiny, on which all Scottish kings since the days of Dalriada had stood to be anointed.[13] This symbolically foreclosed on even the possibility of an independent Scottish kingdom. The war started again, taking on the character of a national patriotic struggle. (Perhaps the idea of a patriotic struggle was an outcome of the war as much as a cause.)

Edward's army, created to fight wars in France and to subdue the unfortunate Welsh, was a formidable organisation but was very expensive to maintain and difficult to provide for. The heavy cavalry horses that were used to deliver the main shock of battle had to be fed and the great siege engine known as the Warwolf (which was used to demolish Stirling Castle), as well as the prefabricated bridges, the portable stockades and all impedimenta, had to be brought in by sea. Every town and village in England was to provide its quota of men and weapons, its sacks of grain and packs of arrows.

Though the bulk of this material went by the North-Sea route of Newcastle and Berwick, the army had a secondary supply route up the Irish-Sea coasts from Chester to Carlisle or Ayr. The Isle of Man became an important staging point for provisions, for levied and mercenary forces from Wales and Ireland, and for patrolling the seas — so it had to be fortified. The North Channel had to be controlled by a specially commanded fleet which by 1301 numbered 74 vessels, 46 of which came from Irish ports. This was the first time an English royal fleet had operated in Hebridean waters and the success of the campaigns very largely depended on the capacity to supply Edward's army by sea, since land transports were so bad. The inlet of Skinburness, near Silloth on the Solway Firth, became Edward's principal western staging post for the next few years. From here assaults into Galloway, Bute and central Scotland were launched. In 1303 a fleet of 173 ships, commanded by the earl of Ulster, sailed from Dublin, Drogheda and Dundalk up the Firth of Clyde and captured Rothesay. The Scottish War of Independence, also known as the Wars of the Bruces, had become the War of the Irish Sea.

***

By 1306 Robert Bruce had staged a swift and bloody coup and got himself made King Robert I. Edward of England swiftly saw to it that two of the Bruce brothers were executed and their sister hung in a cage over the walls of Roxburgh Castle. Bruce's forces were soon annihilated; he was derided as the 'summer king' and fled the country, hotly pursued by his rivals and by Edward's armies. His wife made a bolt for Norway but was captured and imprisoned.

Robert, with his brother Edward, spent his exile in the Hebrides and probably Ireland in the same way exiled princes usually spend their time — plotting. Legend has it that he spent time observing the habits of spiders on Rathlin Island, but this seems unlikely since Rathlin and indeed all the islands were being closely watched by Edward's fleet, commanded by one Hugh Bisset, an Ulster-Scotto-Norman who was, in fact, ruler of Rathlin and a slice of the Antrim coast. However, since the Bisset family frequently changed sides, we cannot be sure. The Bruces certainly developed a close concord with the MacDonalds of Kintyre and the MacRuaridhs of Skye, who were both possessed of land, provisions, galleys and gold, not to mention mercenary soldiers in plenty.

To be a mercenary soldier was a well-recognised way of life for the men of the Hebrides. The 'gallowglass' was a familiar figure along the Irish-Sea coasts. The

English term derives from the Gaelic *gall* — foreigner (with a sense of a Viking foreignness) and *óglaigh* — fighting men. By the eleventh century the term was used for a well-established system whereby a chieftain could maintain an armed retinue, which was either kept up at his own expense or billeted on his people. In time, bands of *gallóglaigh* acquired or were granted farmlands in payment and so became permanent Scottish features in Irish medieval society. The Clan Donald is prominently featured in the few records that exist and it seems that most gallowglasses had their origins in Islay, Jura and Kintyre, for which Ireland was in no sense foreign parts. Much of Antrim, in particular, was Clan-Donald land.

Figure 1. Two gallowglasses and their retinue: drawing by A. Dürer (1521).

The gallowglass was to medieval Britain as the Swiss mercenary was to medieval Europe. It was an arrangement entirely of its own kind, which enabled small armies to be raised very quickly and kept in the field for as long as they were paid and provisioned. They were highly mobile, arriving and departing in rowed galleys on the Viking model; their ships were well adapted to the confined waters of the Hebrides and the North Channel but were at a disadvantage when faced on the high seas by the high-sided, plump cogs that were generally preferred for North-Sea conditions and for trade.

By 1307 the Bruces were ready to try again, backed by a coalition army from the Hebrides. Edward I conducted a counter-operation from his sick bed at Lanercost

Priory near Carlisle and we owe our detailed knowledge of these events to the annals written there. Bruce came back to a hostile reception; within a few weeks he was once again in hiding from the English. However, at this juncture (1307) Edward died and the throne was taken by Edward II, a man wholly unable to rise to the task facing him.

* * *

Here we can pause to look at Edward, dying in his tent on the bleak flats of Solway, near the last stones of Hadrian's Wall, just long enough to notice that under his rule the extent, depth and permanence of anglicisation of the Islands seemed to reach a high tide — so much so that leading historians have referred to a 'first English empire'. In population, wealth and European scope, England now greatly exceeded the rest of the Islands combined, but under the conditions of medieval society and its land communications that did not give an automatic advantage in war.[14]

But almost before this fearsome old man had gone cold, the extent, depth and permanence of English rule was very severely challenged. Within a year, Bruce grew from being a man on the run for his life to the successful leader of a guerrilla army, then to an effective general commanding men from most parts of Scotland, in touch with merchants and suppliers in Flanders and north Germany and conducting a political campaign with the Scottish lords and in Europe to sustain his claim on the Scottish kingship. His brother Edward Bruce was laying waste to Galloway and preparing to attack over the border into Northumbria.

Robert Bruce, whom we shall now call Robert I, was still some way from leading a united Scotland, however; in 1309 he was fighting the MacDougalls of Argyll and driving them over the water into Ireland. Ireland, in fact, became a place of refuge for the enemies and rivals of the two Bruce brothers. Anti-Bruce forces in south-west Scotland were being supplied from Ireland and the earl of Ulster (Robert's father-in-law) was preparing a sizeable army against him. It was planned that this force, with many ships, should assemble in Dublin and be joined by a further 45 ships from Bristol and Devon. Promises of large rewards were made to island chiefs like the MacSweens and MacDougalls if they would aid the expedition. But, as with most of Edward II's ventures, it came to nothing and the force was diverted to secure the Isle of Man. In fact, the Scots were back in Man two years later, destroying Rushen Castle and chasing English forces back into their boats.

Many of the king's men were Welsh and insisted on going home once their 40 days' service was up, and Edward was constantly harassed by lack of seaborne supplies for his cavalry. To make matters worse his own lords in parliament had called in royal debts and were refusing to provision him. Ships that were promised to bring new men and munitions from Ireland under the command of the MacDougall leader, John of Argyll, failed to arrive. The king was reduced to demanding a levy from the wretched

Northumbrians and, at length, having now spent the better part of a year doing nothing, he went back to London, leaving his captains to do the best they could in the situation — which was to arrange local truces and pay off troublemakers. By 1313 large parts of northern England were paying taxes and protection money northward into Robert's pocket and the English garrisons in Edinburgh, Perth, Dumfries, Berwick and Carlisle were under siege. Trade had sunk almost to zero and the harvest was failing yet again. There is evidence that bad weather was afflicting English markets more than Scottish, which anyway relied more on cattle than corn; and cattle were easily replenished by an expedition south. Figures collected by Colm McNamee and other scholars tell a dismal story: rental incomes from the Penrith district dropped off catastrophically after 1314 and did not begin to recover until 1326. The export trade from Newcastle virtually ceased but imports of food supplies increased dramatically, since the army was being supplied by sea from Flanders, paid for (on credit) by a Genoese banker merchant named Antonio Pessagno. There is always someone who does well out of wars and Antonio Pessagno figures as a prince of profiteers.

King Edward now made a last and fateful attempt to recover the English position in Scotland: he pawned off his revenues from Gascony to the pope and raised a huge loan from Pessagno. One very large army was to be assembled at Newcastle and Berwick and another in Ireland, to be led by John MacDougall of Argyll at sea and by the earl of Ulster on land. In all, Edward II was leading about 20,000 men, all very well equipped and provisioned by Pessagno, who was also providing ships for both the North-Sea and Irish-Sea fleets. As is well known, and to the great glee of Scotsmen ever since, this army went down in total ruin on the 23 and 24 June 1314, just outside Stirling (as one born in England I can scarcely bring myself to write 'Bannockburn' without wincing).

The weather now took a decisive hand in human affairs. The River Thames had frozen in 1310 and fairs and bonfires were held on its ice; farmers were unable to feed their beasts through the winter months so they ate their own capital. The years became known in Flanders as 'the great dying'. In 1315 an invading French army drowned in the Flanders mud, and we have to imagine the smaller wars of the north Britons as being conducted by men wretched with hunger and cold. The Viking settlements in Greenland died out.

The Scots were now in the ascendancy and in the next years were raiding down as far south as Yorkshire. Their usual practice was to go south down the east coast and return north up the west with flocks of cattle, and there was nothing local barons could do about it. Robert now began to give English estates away to Scottish lords in the true feudal fashion — if they could take them. One of the very few obstacles on his way to the general conquest of northern England was Carlisle, intermittently besieged and nearly always surrounded. Scottish armies were still lightweight organisations all through this period and they were rarely able to undertake with success the heavyweight task of reducing a walled town or major castle. Carlisle was being supplied by sea from Ireland, by way of Dundalk and Skinburness, and could not be starved out. It was under these conditions that the Bruce brothers opened a second front in Ireland.

They justified this invasion in an open letter carried by their emissaries, thus:

> To all the kings of Ireland, to the prelates and clergy, and to all the inhabitants of Ireland, his friends … Whereas we and you and our people and your people, free since ancient times, share the same national ancestry and are urged to come together more eagerly and joyfully in friendship by a common language and by common custom, we have sent over to you our beloved kinsmen, the bearers of this letter, to negotiate with you in our name about permanently strengthening and maintaining inviolate the special friendship between us and you, so that with God's will our nation may be able to recover her ancient liberty. Whatever our envoys or one of them may on our behalf conclude with you in this matter we shall ratify and uphold in the future.[15]

The issue to decide is the degree to which this proposed alliance was mere propaganda or something more substantial.

It is difficult to believe that the Bruce brothers truly imagined that such a project was feasible in military and political terms; they had extensive experience of Irish affairs and Robert was himself a local lord in Ulster. But if you had spent a year or more drumming up support among the several lords of the Isles (who were as close to Irish ways as to Scottish), relying on them for your safety and putting yourselves forward as rulers, not of Ireland but of a larger Gaeltacht, then you would have need of such an argument and to feel that it was, at the very least, plausible. There is a further possibility: that Robert and his brother had actually conceived of a means of constructing a large-scale alliance against English ambitions. There is some evidence that they hoped to involve the Welsh, whose soldiery was a major part of the Edwardian forces.[16]

A Scottish army of gallowglasses and Bruce retainers disembarked, unopposed, at Larne on 25 May 1315, where the Bruce family held Olderfleet Castle at the mouth of the lough. This was cleverly timed, since the earl of Ulster was away in Connacht attempting to settle a dispute among the clans. Edward Bruce was joined by a group of northern chieftains, notably Domhnall O'Neill, the ruler of Tír Eoghain. Finding no one to oppose him, he and his army set off south towards Dublin. They were attacked by local forces in the Moyry Pass; they scattered them and, marching past this roundabout, set Dundalk ablaze. Since Dundalk was being used to supply the English garrison in Carlisle, this was only to be expected and it was, presumably, a war aim. However, to judge from the general conduct of this army, it was also done, as they say in Ulster, just for badness. To add to their glory the Scottish troops massacred all the monks they could find.

This was the first time that a modern army had waged war in Ireland since the days of Strongbow and it met with little opposition. There followed several smaller battles that the experienced Scots won without difficulty but shortage of supplies and lack of local support made it impossible for them to exploit these successes. They lacked the resources to besiege Dublin.

The earl of Ulster now returned from Connacht with a large force. The Scots withdrew back into Ulster, where they had at least some friends.

There followed campaigns in which different Gaelic factions in Ulster sided now with the Scots and now with the earl, without any apparent plan or strategy, until most of the earl's men were besieged in Carrickfergus Castle and himself defeated and sent wandering to no effect around Connacht. Edward and his invading army, still undefeated, took up where they left off, on the road to Dublin. It was on 1 May 1316 at Dundalk (or possibly at Faughart or at Armagh on the way there or by the roadside at Kilsaggart, just below what is now Moyry Castle) that Edward had himself crowned 'king of Ireland'. There is some vagueness about the whole event. It impressed very few since there was not, nor had there ever been, a king of Ireland in the feudal sense of a single ruler of a united realm. How far this was pure personal ambition and how far a part of a broader strategy it is now impossible to say. He had the support of Domhnall O'Neill but no one else. There was certainly no general rising of enthusiastic Irish to welcome him. There was a substantial clash between Normans and Gaelic chiefdoms all over the west at this time, culminating in battles, but so far as I can tell no historian ancient or modern has suggested that there ever was any kind of sustained joint effort between the Gaelic Irish and the Scottish populations.

It was now that the great famine of 1315–18 passed over from England into Ireland. Crops failed in the field and cattle were struck down with murrains; the weather was unusually cold and wet. The Scots could not besiege Dublin, nor any other strong place, and the Anglo-Norman/Irish Gaelic forces had rallied themselves into a semblance of order. Edward was forced to march circuitously, looking for provisions and minor victories. By February his men were starving. A chronicler reported:

> The Scots suffered from such famine that many of them died of hunger, and on account of this, they secretly marched toward Fore in Meath. On the Sunday following, they were so weakened, both from hunger and from exhaustion, that many of them began to die.[17]

The Scottish army, depleted and bedraggled, marched back to Ulster through a starving and wasted land. Edward's only military success in this period was the capture of Carrickfergus Castle, where the garrison had been reduced to chewing on leather and, if one account is to be believed, on their Scottish prisoners as well. It is possible that Robert I himself was present to take the surrender of this important redoubt. At all events, taking advantage of English incompetence in Northumbria, he joined his brother for a while with reinforcements.

While these events were taking place on land, at sea there was a series of expeditions and confrontations between the English and the Scots. To support his Irish-Sea fleet, Edward II sent ships from Bristol and even the Channel ports and tried (without much success) to bring in Genoese galleys. John of Argyll may well have hoped to use these ships to support a bid to reconquer his own lands in western Scotland. But, as it turned out, the Scots continued the offensive by sea as well as land. Not only did they freely move men and supplies across the North Channel, but their main captain, one Thomas Dun, also sailed into Lough Neagh in support of Edward Bruce's retreating army. The same Dun moved south in September and raided Holyhead, capturing a fully laden cargo vessel and terrifying the English settlers along the north-Wales coast. It is possible that he may have been acting, or hoping to act, in collusion with Welsh sympathisers.

Viewed from this roundabout, the still centre of the whirling world, I would like to know more about Dun. From this distance he seems like a throwback to Viking times, happy to venture up rivers, accustomed to combined operations by land and sea and appearing suddenly in unexpected places. His ships were lean birlinns based upon the Viking longships. Dun appears in English reports as a 'cruel pirate' who committed 'great depredations' and had 'a great navy' — Magnus Bare-Legs come again. When one of Edward II's most capable servants crossed to Dublin to stiffen up resistance, he came with a large bodyguard because 'robbers on the sea between the lands of England, Wales and Ireland are doing much mischief and daily perpetrate evil'. Ships from Dublin and Drogheda were commandeered by the royal captains to pursue Dun, who was held to be lurking between Ulster and Scotland. Dun's base is likely to have been Carlingford Lough, whose narrow entrance is guarded by Greencastle and other forts. Greencastle was in the possession of Edward Bruce. His name suggests he may have come from County Down where he would have been known as Tomás an Dúin — Thomas of Down. However, his reputation around the Irish Sea is perhaps an indication of the fear he inspired rather than any substantial threat. According to some reports he only had four ships.

Thomas Dun was not the only bold commando; an English flotilla made a night attack upon the Scots, besieging Carrickfergus, and carried off their tents and equipment and 40 of their lives.

The Scottish army went south again in 1317. Once again they took the road to Dublin, past our roundabout, and once again steered away from the protracted difficulty of undertaking a siege of the capital city. Perhaps also they had heard the news that 1,000 Genoese mercenaries, very well equipped, were ready to arrive in Dublin (although it seems they never came). Edward II of England had been busy on the diplomatic front as well: as part of the loan negotiations with the pope he managed to have the vacant bishoprics of Cashel and Dublin filled with his nominees and the followers of Edward Bruce excommunicated. None of these measures affected the war situation; it remained the case that the Gaelic chiefs sided with the Scots only in a sporadic and opportunistic manner. No one took any notice of Edward's claim to kingship.

Again, it is difficult to make much sense of the Bruce campaigns during the spring and summer except as a wander in search of provisions. Had they captured Wexford they might have posed a very serious threat to King Edward's position, but they arrived instead outside Limerick in the opposite direction. They were not able to besiege Limerick for lack of means and, when they were attacked by a local chief, they retreated again and once more found themselves hungry in Meath (a bad district for Scotsmen), where many died and many almost died of hunger and fatigue. Edward Bruce took what was left of his army back to Ulster, at a serious disadvantage.

The sea war continued, with the city of Bristol providing 20 ships, Winchelsea and the Cinque Ports another 17, and seven other ports a ship each 'to destroy Thomas *le mariner* who is infesting the sea towards the west with a crew of Scots, doing great damage to trade coming towards England'. In this naval force was the medieval equivalent of a dreadnought, a 140-oar galley (to compare with the typical 26-oar vessel). This was, presumably, a Genoese craft on hire to the English crown.

Fate and the executioner's axe caught up with Thomas Dun on 2 July 1317, when he was defeated in a sea battle, location unknown. Before his death he revealed, or was compelled to reveal, that another Scottish attempt on the Isle of Man was being prepared, as well as an invasion of Anglesey. The Isle of Man was indeed recaptured by the Scots in early 1318, but the invasion of Anglesey never took place.

Such was the condition of hunger into which everyone was plunged that, during the winter of 1317 to 1318, no campaign could be made that has survived into the records. But by October of that year, after a good harvest, Edward Bruce went to war again. With him went the MacDonalds and MacRuaridhs of the western isles, with their gallowglass army, and a scattering of Ulster Anglo-Normans, but the Gaelic chiefs seem to have held apart once again. An Anglo-Norman force from Dublin and Meath met up with them one mile behind and slightly to my right as I sit on the roundabout at Faughart. Edward, according to the *Chronicle of Lanercost*, was marching ahead, with three divisions, well spaced out. Accordingly:

> the first was done with before the second came up, and the second before the third, with which Edward was marching, could render any aid. Thus the third column was routed, just as the two preceding ones had been. Edward fell at the same time and was beheaded after death; his body divided into four quarters, which were sent to the four chief quarters of Ireland.[18]

With him died the chiefs of the MacDonald and MacRuairidh clans.[19] So ended the War of the Irish Sea.

***

The re-established monarchy of Scotland returned to its former orientation, overlooking the North Sea. Flemish, German and Baltic trade was much more profitable, and we learn that Scottish sailors cruised the Newfoundland Banks in search of cod and were tasked with the suppression of Icelandic pirates. Thereafter no Scottish king (until the union of the two crowns) ever showed much interest in Ireland, with exception of affairs around the North Channel. There, far from following the Bruces' notion of a Gaelic nation struggling to find its liberty, successive kings of Scotland did all they could to weaken and destroy Gaelic society in the western highlands and Hebrides. James IV in particular conducted a war against remnants of the lords of the Isles, building a fleet especially to that end in purpose-built shipyards at Dumbarton and arming them with heavy guns. In this respect the Scottish kingdom defined itself as being as much anti-Gaelic as anti-English. James IV is often reckoned as the last king of Scotland to speak any Gaelic.

Along the east coast of Ireland the extent of English royal rule appeared to be unaltered. The Pale remained intact, as did English control of Wexford and Waterford and Cork. But the character of Anglo-Norman Ireland changed. It had been demonstrated that the Fitzgeralds and the great earldoms of Ormond, Kildare and Desmond were a deal less almighty than they seemed. At the edges of Norman rule, in Munster and Connacht and the north-central parts of the plain, their rule was fraying away, or becoming increasingly Irish in spite of itself. Ulster was confirmed in its singularity (there seems to have been no map drawn of Ulster until the sixteenth century). Reciprocally (although it lies beyond the scope of this book), there was a general revival in the energy and confidence of Irish Gaelic society, which now began to diverge still further from Gaelic Scotland.

The English regions of Ireland were without doubt very heavily afflicted by the Black Death, which arrived in 1348 and continued in a reduced form for the next three decades. Gaelic society, being almost wholly rural and very largely outdoor, suffered less, though the detail of respective losses has disappeared.

However, the invasion of Ireland by the Bruce brothers, and the assumption of kingship and common interest that went with it, raises important issues that touch on that existential question with which this book began — what is it to live and die on these shores? As we have seen, the military and political enterprise was wholly misconceived and, for total lack of Gaeltacht solidarity and adverse objective conditions, went down in hunger and blood. But the idea of a cultural identity is another matter. The success of national warfare had produced a Scottish national sentiment, which defined itself over and against a corresponding English national idea. This entailed the insertion of nationality into the medieval and feudal cauldron of the Irish Sea. This was an idea which, for the Islands considered as a whole, was created by the Scots. The Scottish feudal state had generated a distinctive concept which both supported and overrode the feudal concept of kingship; this was the Community of the Realm.[20]

When the Scottish monarchy was in suspense, when the succession was uncertain or disputed, the usual practice was to defer to 'guardians' — lord protectors whose task was to ensure the continuity of the state. It was the guardians who had appealed to Edward I to settle the succession in 1290. They ruled not in the name of monarchy but for the Community of the Realm. This was not a formal body and still less a parliament: it was an idea of common interest between the nobility and smaller gentry of the land. It was to this community that the monarch was answerable. By the time of the *Declaration of Arbroath* in 1320 this had solidified into a doctrine saying that the Community of the Realm could legitimately oust a king who failed in his duties. The declaration (which was in fact a part of the diplomatic offensive the Scots were waging to establish their hard-won independence clearly all over Europe) both affirmed Robert I as the rightful and necessary monarch in the true line of succession, but added:

> Yet if he should give up what he has begun, and agree to make us and our kingdom subject to the king of England or the English, we should exert ourselves at once to drive him out as our enemy and a subverter of his own rights and ours, and make some other man who was well able to defend us our king …[21]

The authorship of this document is unknown, but it was written by someone or some group that had been intimately involved in the complicated politics surrounding the Wars of Independence. It comes from the centre of that Community of the Realm from which Scottish monarchs now derived their legitimacy. Barrow writes:

> Although it was official and served the purposes of the Scots king and his government, the *Declaration of Arbroath* was indisputably national and not merely governmental.[22]

Neither is it a feudal document. It makes the oaths of fealty provisional and renders the monarch subordinate, in the last resort, to a secular, collective and abstract concept. Indeed, it is constitutional in a very profound sense, since it reconstitutes the basis of the state on national, even ethnic, grounds and not upon feudal vassalage.

We should not think of the declaration as being a 'democratic' document but, rather as Magna Carta opened a door through which one could glimpse a rule of law, so the *Declaration of Arbroath* suggests the prospect of a written constitution far beyond feudalism. Considered retrospectively, we can interpret it as a development of the Gaelic/Welsh idea of the *tuath* or *tud*, the land that is the collective inheritance of its inhabitants, not the estate of the great lord, and something much more than an administrative unit. There may be a hypothesis here that would argue that the declaration represents a coming together of a Gaelic tradition with contemporary Norman practice, a nation-defining idea. Considered prospectively, the Community of the Realm is essentially a cultural idea, imaginative in character, which invites us to reimagine the basis of society and thus the basis of the single person. While not democratic as such, it contains the seed of a democracy within which 'A man's a man for a' that', and of a sovereignty of the people.

***

Nations, however, bring with them the idea of 'the people'. Here we are dealing with relations between cultural identity and political legitimacy and how the one can guarantee the other.

Early European nations and peoples (the two, of course were not by any means the same: their unity had to be manufactured) were frequently defined in reference to biblical chronology. Edward Gibbon, in the first volume of his *Decline and fall of the Roman Empire*, put the matter as follows:

> The last century abounded with antiquarians of profound learning and easy faith, who, by the dim light of legends and traditions, of conjectures and etymologies, conducted the great-grandchildren of Noah from the Tower of Babel to the extremities of the globe.[23]

This 'ethnic theology',[24] as it has been called, first appeared as far back as the *Lebor Gabála Érenn*, with its attempt to square Gaelic legendary material with biblical chronology, and persisted well into the nineteenth century.[25] Echoes of it persist even into the present time. The question with these stories is not, 'Are they true?' but 'What work are they being asked to do?' I think the answer is fairly clear: their task was (in current jargon) the construction of identity. The *Lebor Gabála* amalgamated all kinds of different events and peoples into a single story and set them on their way. In so doing it invented, for the purposes of the eleventh century, a plausible conceptual unity for Gaelic society in Ireland, which was easily transported into Scotland to form part of the early underpinning of the Scottish kingdom. So when Robert and Edward Bruce put out their letter to the Irish chiefs and great men, their argument was based on a shared notion.[26] But to define a separate nation of Scots, an ancient people that was not dependent on an Irish prototype had to be called into existence.

This foundation story entailed a flight from Egypt and a roundabout journey of settlements by way of Spain and Ireland, undertaken by a Lady Scota, who was a daughter of a pharaoh, and her Greek husband and their descendants. It even included an encounter with Julius Caesar. This was compiled some time after the *Declaration of Arbroath* and it served the purpose of founding the struggling kingdom of the Scots upon the most ancient precedents. This tale was backed up by a much more historical and secular military epic, *The Bruce*, written for Robert II by John Barbour in the 1370s, which in turn begat a number of 'chronicles' and 'ancient histories'. Webster writes that 'This "national literature" marks a crucial stage in the articulation of a Scottish national identity.'[27]

Edward I and his court were simultaneously and reciprocally engaged in a similar search for 'origins' that would justify English hegemony over the islands as a whole and found it upon a story of comparable antiquity that was not dependent upon Norman claims. The difficulty here was to reconcile two very different kinds of story. There was the sober, non-magical account (if misleading and misled) that told of the coming of the Anglo-Saxons into England as given by the Venerable Bede, and there was the legendary material within which King Arthur sits embedded like a jewel in the mud. A great deal of this Arthurian material is late classical, written in Latin by the likes of Nennius (a notoriously muddy annalist). The rest of it is in early Welsh and is unmistakably P-Celtic and epic in character, though transformed by Norman authors such as Geoffrey of Monmouth to assimilate the classical world and early Christianity in complicated and obscure ways (mud muddied).

Edward's theft of the Stone of Scone and his earlier appropriation of Welsh regalia and titles (of which the most obvious was the creation of a prince of Wales) are to be seen as a symbolic appropriation of both Scottish and Welsh foundation stories. Thus the narratives of the Islands were being brought together into a form that would be distinctly English — in effect, writing an ancient England into the general record of the Islands.

Edward's aim was wholly imperial. From both the Arthurian and the Saxon strands he could extract a claim to imperial suzerainty, if not outright kingship. But one cannot direct the outcomes of an idea; a strong idea will run wild. Just as the English king's prolonged campaigns *against* the Scots provoked an outpouring of national feeling *among* the Scots, so the triumphs and failures of the wars in Scotland, Ireland and Wales brought about an equal and opposite reaction in England. Just when Angleterre became England is a rather whimsical question, but Edward himself, his son and grandson all used Anglo-Saxon names and habitually spoke in English rather than Norman French. By the 1360s English had become the predominant language of law and of parliament. The degree to which this new English consciousness was popular, rather than a directly constructed and directed consensus, is a difficult and obscure matter.

It becomes clear that the War of the Irish Sea was fought in an arena in which concepts of national identity were beginning to form — to condense, as it were, out of the clouds of supposition and pseudohistory into recognisably national foundation stories.

**

Part two: taking the road south

The Gap of the North figures twice more in a military aspect, each time moving the idea of nations forward into new fields.

When Elizabeth I recalled the earl of Essex from Ireland, where he had failed to subdue the great O'Neill, she appointed in his place Charles Blount, later known to history as Mountjoy. O'Neill's nine-year campaign against the English crown was sustained with skill, not only in the field but also in the commissariat. His were not clan hostings but semi-professional troops, stiffened with Scottish mercenaries and trained by Spanish and other 'advisors'. They conducted campaigns over a period of years, rather than the months or weeks of any previous force in the Gaeltacht. The challenge to the royal arms and exchequer was immense but it had to be undertaken to ensure that Ireland could not become a Spanish base for operations against and into England.

But the O'Neill forces faced the question every insurgent army comes to face: at what moment would they be ready to pass from a strategy of harassment to the fully offensive action that alone could give them a lasting victory?

This was only partly a military problem; its heart was political.[28] What were the long-term goals of the rebellion and could they be enforced over the rest of the country? The O'Neill rebellion was asymmetric — not only in military strategy but also in conceptual structure. O'Neill and his allies could not rely on a genuine national consciousness to sustain them. They remained poised between the Gaelic world of kindred and clan and the early modern notion of the state. When the rebel forces moved outside their core territory, local support had to be negotiated and was always liable to break down. The crown forces, on the other hand, had a very clear aim — that of subduing any insurgency that could threaten metropolitan England. In the circumstances, the warfare was extremely nasty. Something of the horror is caught in a contemporary publication, Derricke's *Image of Irelande* (1581) (see Figures 2, 3 and 4).

Mountjoy had devised a strategy of reducing the O'Neill core territory by surrounding it with military bases that could be supplied by sea or by secure inland routes and 'squeezing'. It was to forward the squeezing strategy that the lord deputy moved out of the Pale and set off to force a passage from Dundalk into Newry and so into central Ulster and Tyrone — the core of the core.

It was near this roundabout that the two armies met on 20 September 1600. O'Neill had built barricades across the pass at several points by felling trees and interweaving cut branches; this was a military device known as 'plashing', which made the use of cavalry impossible. He had dug trenches that were particularly deep and wide and crowned with stakes and thorn bushes. It was pouring with rain. Contemporary reports seem to come from a seventeenth-century Passchendaele.

Figure 2. A detachment of crown troops return to their base after a search-and-destroy mission, led by three officers carrying severed heads.

Figures 3 and 4. Derricke's wide-screen woodcuts function as a storyboard account of the exploits of the general Sir Henry Sidney. Each part of the sequence of images is accompanied by a brief verse. On the left: 'There creepes out of Saint Filcher's denn, a pack of mates/both hurtful to the English pale and noysome to the state.' On the right they burn a farm (an Irish farm). 'They spoil and burn and beare away, and to the woodes return'.[29]

After establishing his camp somewhere around the townland of Faughart, the lord deputy wrote his report back to the Privy Council:

October 8th 1600

The extremity of the weather hath been such almost ever since we sat down in this place … as if we had no enemy in our way, we could hardly have passed for the rising of the waters. In the mean-time few days have passed without more or less fight. At our first encamping we fought almost two hours for our lodging and our wood, and at length beat the rebels out of sight, killing one of the O'Neales, a principal man among them, and divers others. Of ours some four or five were killed and as many hurt; only one of Sir Robert Lovell's brethren, of any name, shot through the face, but likely to recover.

The 25th, because they should not conceive that their trenches (which are indeed the greatest and strongest works that ever they made, and in a place of most advantage for them) were the cause of our stay, we drew up to their trenches, beat them out of the first, brought away some victuals of theirs and hurt 120, as I hear out of their own camp. Of our men some seven slain and some 30 hurt.

The 2nd of October, being the fairest day we had till that time, I, the Lord Deputy, was determined to have made a strict muster, and to that end had set a guard upon the gates of Dundalk, lest any should come from there … the rebels came, horse and foot, close to our camp … We fell out presently upon them, beat them to their trenches, forced their trenches, won them, and possessed them as long as we listed to keep them; and at length our men being commanded off, made a very gallant and orderly retreat.

We lost in this fight, one of the greatest skirmishes in this kingdom, about twenty men and some seven score hurt …

On Sunday the 5th we drew forth again towards them, and in a very resolute charge that they gave to Sir Charles Percie's regiment, both in front and on both sides at once, they were gallantly repulsed … In this service Sir Robert Lovell was shot through the body dead. Of the rebels, many were killed and hurt.

By these and other daily skirmishes, our companies grow weak and unserviceable; but especially we find a decay in our shot, for supply whereof we have sent unto the Council at Dublin …

Since my coming to this camp, where we have been almost 20 days, there hath been weather scant fair enough to write in our tents … Our tents are often blown down and at this instant it doth rain into mine, so that I can scant write.[30]

This small-scale but brutish skirmishing continued and it took the lord deputy and his men another week before they reached Newry. Reading between the lines, it was a bloody business that only just succeeded. Subsequently, Mountjoy built a fort to secure control of the pass, and when he came that way again he took his forces around by the coastal route to Carlingford. It was another three years before O'Neill was ultimately (and finally) defeated outside Kinsale, prematurely attempting a battle in the open field in even worse weather.

**

The great advantage of reaching 65 is that in Ireland you get a free rail pass, and to do a great deal of my groundwork I have been combining the rail and the two wheels to good effect. I take the Dublin train from Belfast and arrive in Dundalk by mid-morning. A bright cold winter day. Not much wind. Perfect cycling weather.

Dundalk deserves a little book of its own, done in a scholarly way, because although it lacks beauty it is full of interesting corners and has a mixed and violent history. There are buildings of every quality and kind from each one of the last ten centuries.

Cycle northward on the Belfast road and cross the river; after about half a mile you find a signpost leading to an 'old graveyard'. Do not go this way or you will get lost in the changes wrought by motorway construction. Instead, go back right and find the roundabout already described. Take your life in your hands and cycle around it to the road for Faughart. This is pleasant enough and still level. After another half mile go under the railway and come to the Faughart junction and signpost indicating 'old graveyard'. It is so bent and twisted it is now impossible to tell which way it points. Twisting signposts is a rural sport in parts of Ireland. Ask a gang of three road workers who are resting on their shovels. They speak an unknown language. 'Polski?' you ask. 'Litvan?' 'Nem tudok magyarul. Ruski,' they reply. Ireland, having been for 200 years a relentless exporter of population, has now become a considerable importer. There is a Polish delicatessen in the streets of Dundalk.

My guess is that the site of Edward Bruce's demise took place close by here on the south-facing slope above the village school, but there is nothing to mark it. We ought to think of this as being mostly scrub and woodland in the fourteenth century and not the undulating pasture that it is today.

Continue north on what I surmise is an eighteenth-century road line to the top of a small hill; a fine old house lies derelict and a signpost points up another hill. This, though not long, is hard and it takes you to the rounded top of Faughart Hill. Here a very old and ruined church stands in a clump of yew and ivy surrounded by graves from every century and of every family in the land.

There is also what is, without doubt, the foundation of a round tower and an enclosed well, reached by steep steps and roofed in a corbel. Fragments of clothing hang on the bushes nearby for an offering. On the other side of the road is a very well-preserved motte and bailey. The top of the motte is paved with river stones and it contains the fragment of a small building.

The view from the Hill of Faughart is remarkable — southward as far as Howth and the Skerries and westward clear across County Louth into the midlands. It now

Illustration 3.
Graveyard on the Hill
of Faughart.

seems to me likely that this hilltop was the site of Mountjoy's camp; it has its own
water supply and in 1601 it was probably above the treeline.

Another mile and a half away, across a shallow bowl of fields, there is a marked
shoulder on the hillside and a rocky outcrop called Claret Rock. Here and down the
slopes beneath is the likely site of O'Neill's trenches. I searched for them without
success, though there are a number of sunken boreens and heavily sodded walls and
along the shoulder of Claret Rock there are hollows and hummocks. But only a
detailed survey would find anything. However, as you come over the brow of the hill
and look due north towards Newry, you can see a remarkable stone tower and
fragments of a wall. This is what remains of the small castle built by Mountjoy to
secure the pass in 1602. From a distance it looks like a typical tower house, but closer
up and within there is nothing domestic about it. The corners are rounded and
embrasured with small gun ports to permit a 360-degree arc of fire across the hillside.
It is a very early example of a redoubt specially built for defensive small-arms fire. It is
the equivalent of the concrete pill-box.

From Moyry Castle you can look north and take in, at a glance, not only the old
frontier of Ulster (which is a real and natural feature of the land) but also the curious
and arbitrary frontier of Northern Ireland, which is based essentially on the voting
registers of 1921. The remains of six British-army listening posts could be seen on

hilltops between here and Newry, steel equivalents of the castle rose, until very recently, on Cloghogue Mountain and at Forkhill. Radio and telephone masts overlooked Cuchulainn's ford.

Illustration 4. Moyry Castle, near Faughart.

Where the old Dundalk to Newry track ran in 1601 is not clear. Records speak of a 'causey' or causeway made from laying faggots of reeds and twigs over the bog but the land has now been extensively drained and tidied into an intricate prettiness. It probably ran up towards the townland of Jonesborough. Nor is Moyry Castle the only fortification. There is an old cashel nearby and four miles further north is the townland of Meigh, where you can find beside the road a stretch of embankment and ditch that marks the end of a section of the Black Pig's Dyke.

What we can also find, if we look around, are blockhouses and machine-gun posts built in the 1940s to defend Northern Ireland against any possible German assault through the Free State. The most prominent one is at Scarva where the dyke (here known as the Dane's Cast, though it has nothing whatever to do with any Danes) follows a hill crest along the eastern rim of the shallow boggy valley known as the Glynn Bog.

Illustration 5.
Blockhouse at Scarva.

***

The ill-fated River Boyne: travelling south

The Moyry Pass was also the conduit for the last major land engagement in the Islands: the battle of the Boyne. Since this is a point of major significance in the political history of the Islands it is worth spending some time on the site of it. Get on your cycle again and head off south on the long road to Dublin. Think of this road as the axle of Ireland — and therefore of the United Kingdom.

Until recently it was a poor sort of road, built (like most of the major roads in Ireland) along the model of the British-army roads in India. It had a narrow hard carriageway in the centre and broad hard (often, in fact, soft) shoulders to either side. To overtake you had to nudge the car in front into this gravelly shoulder. These were not good conditions in which to cycle and, until the building of the motorway, it was usually safer and more pleasant to cycle the back roads or to cut across to the more westerly N2 road at Ardee. There is now a fine motorway, beautifully landscaped and engineered, perhaps the finest stretch of such road in all the Islands. But it is not available to you, so you must either go beside the coast on the old road (still perilous) or follow your former track by Ardee. This involves several wearisome hills, for the land north of the Boyne is high and rolling.

***

James Stuart may have been chased ignominiously out of London in 1688, but he was back in Ireland the next year, arriving at Kinsale in March 1689. Here he could put himself at the head of a loyal army, supported by the French, and call an Irish parliament. That gathering, once called, promptly declared itself independent of any parliament of England and for the very first time asserted the sovereignty of the 'King, Lords and Commons of Ireland', making no mention of England or Scotland. This was a crucial moment of Irish (rather than Gaelic) political consciousness, for it was delivered in constitutional terms comprehensible in European society, deliberately making a schism between Ireland and England and breaking up the Magna Britannia that James's father had initiated. This was by no means to James's liking, but he had to agree to a series of decrees that made the new parliament independent of that in London. In a more enlightened move, the Irish parliament also made all religions equal under the law, but the political effect of this was nullified in the next moment by a demand that the Cromwellian land settlements be declared invalid. James had other ideas, being wholly concerned with getting back to London.

During 1689 both sides were attempting to establish their respective military positions. William sent a squadron which famously relieved the siege of Derry and his general, the duke of Schomberg, made a landing of 20,000 troops and captured Carrickfergus. The retreating Stuart troops broke down bridges and burnt Newry but failed to defend the Moyry Pass.

When Williamite forces started a movement south towards Dublin it came to a halt at Dundalk for lack of supplies.[31] Incompetence and graft were, as always, the order of the day, and there was a shortage of vessels to bring munitions and food across the Irish Sea. Supply by land was as ever very difficult and the advantage of Dundalk was that it had a decent harbour. William was, in effect, reversing the strategy of Edward I, but simply did not have enough ships at his command.

The Williamite army, unable to go forward or back, set up camp just north of Dundalk, probably on the very roundabout where I have been lying, and here they stayed from September until November, hungry, wet and dysenteric, suffering also from typhus and pneumonia. There were 5,674 deaths, most among the newly levied English recruits. Another source, taking in the number of men who, invalided out by ship to England, died on the way, gives a figure of about 7,000. However, the Stuart forces encamped a few miles away at Ardee were in no better shape. Neither seems to have been capable of attacking the other, but William had gained an important initiative. The mere presence of William's troops in Dundalk prevented his foes from using the port and pre-empted any seizure of the pass.

Another possible site for William's camp is the present cemetery half a mile further into town; it is on a low rise and is conveniently nearer to the river crossing. Short of digging up the former citizens of Dundalk there seems to be no way of determining one way or another. Neither site was very good, being too close to marshy ground and too close to the town for good discipline. The behaviour of the Williamite troops was in general bad: the Ulster Protestants were said to have plundered the Catholics, the unpaid English supposedly stole from anybody, while the Danes were compared to the Tartars.

The misery of the place required the bulk of the Protestant forces to retire back into Ulster. James's army, in no better condition, also retired, leaving Dundalk a no-man's land. William of Orange and his commanders used the time of winter inactivity to requisition a small fleet of coal ships from Whitehaven in Cumbria and to enter into a contract with suppliers from his native Holland to institute proper field kitchens and regular issues of decent food for his men. He engaged with Isaac Pereira of the Hague for bread and biscuits and his men, who had hitherto been badly fed, now wanted for nothing. As with Signor Pessagno of Genoa, there is always a good grocer somewhere at the back of a successful army.

William's principal captain was the duke of Schomberg, a French Huguenot general of great experience. He was later blamed for excessive caution, but his death, leading his men across the river, would have been thought reckless in a man half his age. He was 84 years old.

When warm dry weather came around again William gathered his men at Blaris, south of Belfast, and again prepared to move south. James's *avant garde* got quickly off the mark but, in spite of a spirited defence of the Moyry Pass in which the Williamite forces came off much the worse, James retreated, first to Ardee and then to Drogheda.

Once again the Dublin road saw traffic. The Williamite army took the road by way of Ardee, along which I am presently cycling through pleasant fields and beside large woods, and on 10 July 1690 (today's calendar) arrived on the steep northern bank of the River Boyne, four miles upstream from the bridge from which the town of Drogheda takes its name. William's general headquarters were at Mellifont Abbey; James's were at the village of Donore, directly across the valley.

The centre of Ireland is full of lakes and bogs, which in the seventeenth century were much less constrained than they are today; they provided for large broad rivers with large broad tributary streams running through broad marshy valleys. The Boyne is no exception; it is an obstacle. Today it is controlled by weirs, canals and enclosing levees, but it is still formidable. One would hesitate to ford it, even on horseback. In 1690 it was probably shallower but bordered by extensive swampy meadows and, near the sea, by tidal mud.

William and Schomberg drew up the troops along the high crest of the northern bank and at its foot, at an outcrop of rocks and a ford (now deep, but probably shallower then). This ford is at the foot of a narrow valley descending from the plateau above, now called King William's Glen, and led across to the little village of Oldbridge. James, opposite, set out his men across a broad sloping hillside now crowned with a monument.

Illustration 6. Mellifont Abbey. William of Orange made his general headquarters here, before the battle of the Boyne. The ruins are of the first Cistercian abbey in Ireland (see Chapter 6) but by then it had been largely knocked down and quarried to make a substantial manor house.

Illustration 7. The ford at Oldbridge. The Williamite forces crossed here. We should imagine the River Boyne wider and shallower. The far bank is now contained by the Boyne Canal, which runs through the wood; the houses of Oldbridge were beyond the trees, which were probably not there in 1690—at least, no mention of them was made in accounts of the battle. The new Boyne Bridge is on the skyline, and the little nineteenth-century bridge to Oldbridge is just out of shot to the right. The Williamite guns were positioned at this point.

They were not equal armies. James had at his command some 25,000 men, of whom 6,000 were seasoned French troops. Most of his Irish troops were inexperienced. The Williamite forces comprised a mixed corps of Dutch soldiers with his personal regiment of guards, over 7,000 Danes, a Huguenot regiment, a further corps of German soldiers, Protestant Ulstermen[32] and several regiments of English troops. In total there were 35,000 men. The military experience of the men, officers and commanders on the northern bank was very great. They also had with them about 50 cannon under the command of the duke of Schomberg's son. Some of these were siege guns but 36 were light field artillery. James had only 20 cannon at the most and his supplies of ammunition and even basic weaponry were short.

Nevertheless, to hold his enemies at the river should not have been impossible and the armchair general may reasonably think that James's men could and should have done better than they did. That they failed was not the fault of the men on the ground but of the generalship. William's staff expected a hard fight and considered ways of avoiding it.

The 11 July was spent in bringing up the full force, positioning artillery and digging trenches. James fortified several houses opposite the ford, while William and his staff rode up and down the lines encouraging the troops. An artillery duel ensued, which forced some of William's men back from the banks of the river and which nearly brought the proceedings to a premature end, for William (in the thick of things as always) took a glancing blow on the shoulder from a cannonball; he fought the next day with his right arm in a sling.

James's commanders, realising how badly they were outnumbered, planned to retreat, but left it too late and as a result were dithering when dawn came up. James's personal baggage was already on the Dublin road, but the men knew this only by rumour.

The morning of 12 July was very misty, which prevented the Stuart forces from seeing what was happening; the large right wing of the Williamite army started to move westward towards Slane and then south-westward across the valley, passing beside the great prehistoric passage graves of Newgrange and Dowth, with the aim of fording the river and outflanking James. This had been anticipated and James (or rather his staff, since James did not direct his troops in detail) had positioned the French contingent with that in mind. But as the mist cleared they mistook the flanking move for the advance of the whole army. They then made the fatal mistake — moving all possible reserves and all artillery westward, so reducing the relatively untrained battalions at the Oldbridge ford and dividing the force.

At 9.30 a.m. it was low tide and the Oldbridge ford was at its shallowest. At 10.15 a.m. the Dutch regiment, the Blue Guards, started to cross, holding their muskets over their heads, up to their chests in water, and keeping time to their band (it was playing that jaunty and taunting air 'Lillibulero', played by Orange bands ever since). Getting out of the river and onto the bank was another matter; the guards took 150 casualties before they were able to drive the Jacobite regiments out of Oldbridge. Here they paused and other troops were ordered over to join them.

At this stage the battle might have been decided, for a violent cavalry charge led by James's son, the duke of Berwick, forced the Blue Guards to form squares for their defence and (on the third attempt) drove through them and reached the riverbank again. The duke of Schomberg was now leading the Huguenot and Danish troops across and the battle became furious. It was in the midst of this, with William's troops staggering back from yet another charge, that Schomberg, rallying the men in person, was cut down and shot through the neck. He had gone forward with his own Huguenot troops, who were being beaten back in disarray, and cried, 'Come on, messieurs, there are your persecutors!'

William then seized the moment by commanding another assault across the river, about a mile further downstream — beside the pillar of today's bridge. The tide was now rising and many men had to swim; William's own horse became dangerously stuck in the mud. This crossing was undoubtedly in a bad place and it was nearly a disaster — Jacobite soldiers on the steep hill immediately above the Williamites had the position of advantage. But heavy and accurate field-gun and musket volleys drove them off. Before long, in the face of repeated attack, the largely Danish force was across, with cavalry; for the first time William's forces could reply adequately to the cavalry charges that had made their direct assault so difficult and bloody. They now began to advance

Illustration 8. The new bridge across the Boyne. Halfway between a tuning fork and a giant harp, this handsome structure now carries the M1 motorway; William of Orange and his men had to wade and swim the river under fire from the wooded hill to the right. This photograph was taken from the point where William's horse got stuck in the mud. The river, of course, was wider and shallower in 1690 and it would be a reckless commander who would lead his men across in such conditions today.

on the Jacobite forces upstream, who were still fighting furiously with the Williamite army that was still wading across the river. King James's forces, finding themselves increasingly outnumbered, began to retreat up the slope towards the village of Dunore.

The cause of King James was now in a very poor state, for half of his army and all his cannon were away to the west trying to stave off encounter with the right wing of William's force, which had now crossed over the river in its entirety and was gathering itself to move forward. The French commander, fearing that his lines of retreat would be cut, remained entirely on the defensive. Thus, half of the Jacobites never saw action, while the other half was now hopelessly outnumbered and being beaten. William himself, holding his sword in his left hand, led the assault on the Jacobite rearguard, with hand-to-hand fighting in the lanes of Donore. William took one bullet through his cap; another bullet took off the heel of his boot.

By midday the Jacobite army was in full retreat through the narrow roads towards Duleek, detachments colliding with one another and mistaking each other for the enemy. James had been led away by his staff and was galloping ignominiously away to Dublin. A Captain Stevens climbed onto the high banks of the roadway to look for his men:

> I thought the calamity had not been so general 'til viewing the hills about us I perceived them covered with soldiers of several regiments all scattered like sheep flying before the wolf.[33]

In fact, King James's troops kept their heads rather better than that account suggests and the French troops, hitherto unengaged, fought a rearguard action at Duleek. The Williamite right wing got stuck in a bog and was unable to close the gap through which the defeated Jacobites were streaming. But their comprehensive defeat was undeniable.

Three days later James, suffering from nosebleeds and 'in a manner stunned', left for France aboard a Breton privateer.

***

In the despair of defeat, James and his commanders blamed his Irish regiments for running away. This was manifestly an excuse for their own bad generalship. As the duke of Berwick said of the French commander Lauzun, 'he had quite forgotten all his military knowledge if he ever possessed any'. But that is too convenient an explanation, because underlying the defeat of the Jacobite army lay a dilemma — the different parts of that army were fighting with different war aims. It would have taken a commander of great ability to hold them all together.

James had one aim only — to get back to London and regain the throne. He was surrounded by his own men, who shared this aim and had little interest in Irish matters (in fact, they excluded Irish advisors and despised them). James was dependent on King Louis XIV of France for money, munitions and a third of his force, but Louis was engaged in a much larger European conflict in which Ireland was only a very small part. It was in the French interest to avoid catastrophic defeat and to embroil the Orange army in a protracted and wasteful campaign. Whether or not, in avoiding contact with the enemy, Lauzun was following secret orders to keep his force intact we cannot know, but the effect was identical.[34] At the same time, the Irish component of the Jacobite army (about two-thirds) was fighting on behalf of the new Irish parliament and was itself a mixed body, consisting of 'Old' English Catholics and not-so-old English who, on the losing side of the English Civil War, had lost out under the Cromwellian settlement.[35] Their main war aim was the swift restitution of their lands and religion and that meant a likely separation of the English crown from the Irish crown. The terms in which their case was put were English and constitutional in language and character, but the degree to which this should be called 'national' is a matter for debate. It was certainly not English, nor even British, and not quite Irish either.

Within this there was a definite Gaelic element as represented by Sir Neil O'Neil and other officers with similar names.[36] O'Neil fiercely defended the crossing below Slane, with 500 men against 10,000, until he was killed. Another locally raised regiment was left with 30 men standing out of the 480 who began the fight. Taken all in all, the Irish contingent that took the brunt of the fighting and that continued the Jacobite struggle for another year fought well and bravely. Their interests were by no means the same as James's, and the Stuart's unwillingness to engage with those interests was the sign of his fundamental lack of concern for Irish affairs. He deserved to lose. Indeed, there is something contemptible and incompetent about his conduct and that of his party.

Within the Williamite army, composed of even more parts, the Enniskillen regiment was the oddity — the least professional and the least controllable. The extreme aggressiveness of the Ulstermen, which all commentators noticed, was the product of their insecurity. They already displayed an intense attachment to the crown and to their settler interests, which still plays its part in politics today.

But what is referred to in Irish as the *Cogadh an Dá Rí* was for Catholic Ireland a total disaster, for the rest of Europe was a part of a much larger picture. It was an action to curb the expansion of French and Catholic absolutist monarchical ambitions and, only in second place, to maintain Protestantism. European wars had entered into the affairs of the Irish Sea. The island beyond Britain had become part of Europe.

***

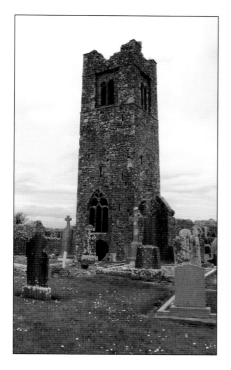

Left: Illustration 9. Tower on the Hill of Slane.
Right: Illustration 10. The bat-winged dragon at Slane.

In time I reached the battle site by way of Slane and Mellifont Abbey. The Hill of Slane, famous in history as the site of the St Patrick's great challenge to paganism, holds, in addition to a tower and a roofless nave, several smallish ruined halls. In one of these a dragon can be found, carved into the wall. This appeared to my eyes as a Welsh dragon (indeed, it is possible to see across to Wales on some lucky days). A similar beast can be seen on the church within the walls of Caer Gybi.

From here I went by country ways and, with night coming on, I slept in a wood beyond the village. Waking to a cold but hungry dawn I took the valley road above the river and so found the burial mounds of Dowth and Newgrange. Newgrange is so extensively restored that it almost amounts to a facsimile, but Dowth still has something of the wild about it, with cave-like adits and great carved kerbstones all around the foot. Here I found myself back in touch with Carnanmore.

When William's troops marched past the mound on their way to outflank those of James, it was probably almost hidden in hazel-scrub and gorse and probably not noticed by anyone. When William's troops marched past the grave mounds, did they, like Napoleon's troops beside the pyramids, reflect on the thousands of years of history that were looking down on them?

**

Illustration 11. The mound at Dowth. Dowth seems a good place to end this chapter, because (if I follow my own arguments, the Boyne-Valley complex of Neolithic tombs was, in its heyday, a site for the Irish Sea rather than for Ireland. From the central plains of Ireland it would take two or three days to reach Newgrange, Dowth or Knowth; it would take one and half days from Mon.

Illustration 12. Unlike Newgrange, the mound at Dowth contains several small tomb passages rather than one large one.

When I first began this book the Moyry Pass was widely known (in the north) as 'Apache Pass' and Dundalk as 'El Paso'. South Armagh was 'bandit country'. Driving northward home to Belfast on the day that Sinn Féin has agreed to participate in the police and judicial system of the United Kingdom, I salute, passing over the little stream that marks the border, a family named Hanna, blown to pieces at this place.

For a' that and for a' that,
It's coming yet, for a' that,
That man to man, the warld o'er,
Shall brothers be for a' that.
— Robert Burns, 'A man's a man for a' that'

Notes

[1]   He is able to change shape in a horrid fashion when in battle fury. Commentators on the *Táin* are usually at a loss with this phenomenon. But we should interpret the transformations as if they were Picasso's drawings, in which a weeping woman turns into a tangle of lines and profiles that perfectly catch the sensation of hysterical distress felt from within. If you were engaged in slaughtering hundreds of your bitter enemies, you too might feel that your eyes were bulging out of your head and your skull splitting open.

[2]   T. Kinsella (tr.) (L. le Brocquy, illust.) (1979) *The Táin*, Oxford: Oxford University Press, pp. 204–05.

[3]   There is a survey of the problems of linking the *Táin* to real events in J.P. Mallory (ed.) (1992) *Aspects of the Táin*, Belfast: December Press.

[4]   Kinsella, *op. cit.*, p. ix. See also Mallory, *op. cit.* for this problem. There are serious anachronisms in the existing text. However, these need to be balanced against the real-life interpretation of the events as analysed by Ewa Sadowska in a remarkable article (E. Sadowska (1997) 'Horses led by a mare: martial aspects of the *Táin bó Cuailnge*', *Emania* **16**, pp. 5–44). Sadowska, by taking the military aspect of the story very seriously, brings out a range of fresh meanings which are highly credible. The *Táin* was, she concludes, much more than 'a mere cattle-raid'. It was, in effect, an all-Ireland invasion of the province which aimed 'to reassert the political dominance of Connacht over Ulster'. If we then set it in the context of a 'Gaelic' expansion at the expense of the Pictish Cruithin the overall meaning of the epic is much expanded.

[5]   Why 'obsidian', which I wrote without thinking? It was an unconscious reference to John Dee, Elizabeth I's magus and propagandist of empire. He possessed such a mirror of volcanic glass, probably of Aztec origins, in which he could see the shape of things to come. I will let it stand.

[6]   See also the discussions of this in Mallory, *op. cit.* and Sadowska, *op. cit.*

[7]   G.W.S. Barrow (1988, 3rd ed.) *Robert Bruce and the community of the realm of Scotland*, Edinburgh: Edinburgh University Press, Chapter 1.

[8]   C. McNamee (1997) *The Wars of the Bruces: Scotland, England and Ireland, 1306–1328*, East Linton: Tuckwell Press, p. 5.

[9]   A good popular account of the Stewarts and their history is provided in S. Ross (1993) *The Stewart dynasty*, Nairn: Thomas and Lochar.

[10] A great deal of relevant material will be found in K.J. Stringer (ed.) (1985) *Essays on the nobility of medieval Scotland*, Edinburgh: John Donald.

[11] *Ibid.*, pp. 59–60; R. Frame (1990) *Political development of the British Isles 1100–1400*, Oxford: Oxford University Press.

[12] Needless to say, it was a deal more complicated than that. Barrow (*op. cit.*) gives a blow-by-blow account of the proceedings, which reads like a Mafia chronicle. In the midst of this Edward had contrived that the Manxmen should invite him to take over their island, which strongly suggests that the king of England was acting with cunning aforethought and had laid plans.

[13] The difference between coronation rituals is not a small matter: English monarchs from Saxon times sat in a chair and were presented with an orb and sceptre, indicating the globe and the power of rule (abstractly conceived and symbolically carried out). Scottish kings, in what seems to have been a survival of the archaic practice, stood on a real piece of Scotland to be sworn in and proclaimed, placing their foot in a carved footprint in a physical gesture. By taking the stone away, Edward was denying the existence of a separate Scottish monarchy. He put the stone under his own throne in Westminster and there it stayed for the next 700 years. A fascinating account of these matters is to be found in E. Fitzpatrick (2004) *Royal inauguration in Gaelic Ireland* c. *1100–1600; a cultural landscape study*, Woodbridge: Boydell Press.

[14] See R.R. Davies (2000) *The first English empire: power and identities in the British Isles, 1093–1343*, Oxford: Oxford University Press.

[15] Barrow, *op. cit.*, p. 314.

[16] McNamee, *op. cit.*, p. 192.

[17] *Ibid.*, p. 179.

[18] H. Maxwell (ed.) (1908) *The Chronicle of Lanercost*, Glasgow: J. Maclehose and Sons.

[19] According to a Dundalk story, Edward was killed by a juggler who threw an iron ball at his head. In another account he was killed in personal combat with one John Malpas of Drogheda.

[20] The best discussion of the formation of Scottish national identity that I have yet encountered is in B. Webster (1997) *Medieval Scotland: the making of an identity*, London: Macmillan Press.

[21] Quoted in Barrow, *op. cit.*, and other works.

[22] Barrow, *op. cit.*, p. 306.

[23] E. Gibbon (1789) *The decline and fall of the Roman Empire*, London: G. Kearsley.

[24] I am especially indebted to C. Kidd (1999) *British identities before nationalism*, Cambridge: Cambridge University Press.

[25] Ethnic theology took a long time to die. As already noted, the Milesian story of Irish origins was still believed in the 1860s and an English parallel lies within William Blake's writings.

[26] Some very tortuous scholarship was employed to fit the Stuart dynasty into this continuous history by transforming it into a tradition of royal legitimacy. Unfortunately for those

engaged in this task, the Stuart dynasty, from James IV to James VI, was attempting to extirpate the Gaelic society this ideology supported.

27 Webster, *op. cit.*, p. 102.

28 The problem was well understood later by Mao Tse-Tung and by General Giap of Vietnam. If the military course of the Tudor Wars in Ireland is clarified by comparing them to the anti-colonial wars in Indochina it becomes much easier to see the working out of O'Neill's eventual defeat. By moving out of his core territory, O'Neill could no longer play the part of the fish in the water; he was now on dry land.

29 John Derricke, *Image of Irelande, with a discouerie of woodkarne* (London, 1581).

30 J.S. Brewer and W. Bullen (eds) (1869) *Calendar of the Carew manuscripts preserved in the Archiepiscopal Library at Lambeth, vol. 3: 1589–1600*, London, Longmans Green, pp. 464–6. Anyone who has camped in Ireland will know the score.

31 See J. Childs (1996) 'The Williamite Wars, 1689–1691' in T. Bartlett and K. Jeffrey (eds), *A military history of Ireland*, Cambridge: Cambridge University Press, Chapter 9 and also P.B. Ellis (1976) *The Boyne water: the battle of the Boyne, 1690*, London: Hamish Hamilton.

32 The men of Enniskillen, who had waged a successful guerrilla war on James's men for the past two years, were especially wild: 'they could not bear to be given orders, but kept saying that they were no good if they were not allowed to act as they pleased' (Ellis, *op. cit.*, p. 36).

33 *Ibid.*, p. 114. This is the best source of contemporary accounts. Another contemporary says that the oncoming victors 'shot them like hares among the corn'. On the other hand, they lived to fight again, so clearly the Irish troops were not utterly dispersed.

34 In the nature of things we should assume that mixed motives and incapacity played a very large part. Boulger quotes French sources to the effect that Lauzon and his staff ran away contemptibly. See D.C. Boulger (1911) *The battle of the Boyne*, London: Martin Secker.

35 The 'Old' English of 1690 were not the same as the 'Old' English of 1590. We note that of the two Irish regiments that were at Oldbridge to oppose the crossing of the ford, one was commanded by a Clanrickarde, whose forebear (possibly grandfather) had led the attack at Kinsale in 1603.

36 Of the 83 officers' names recorded in the fleet that took James to Kinsale in 1689, 23 appear to be Gaelic Irish names (Boulger, *op. cit.*, pp. 57–8).

EIGHT
Circumspectus from a column

Part one

> He who would England win
> must with Ireland begin.
> — Old verse

In the early hours of 8 March 1966 the population of north Dublin was awoken by an explosion and the rumble of tumbling masonry. The flash and roar woke people six miles away in Clontarf and echoed right across the whole city. When glass had stopped

Figure 1. From *Belfast Telegraph*, 9 March 1966. The view outside the General Post Office in O'Connell Street.

falling out of the windows, the people ran into the street and found that Nelson and the column on which he stood over O'Connell Street — universally known as 'the pillar' — had been shortened by a third. The admiral himself was in fragments.

The Nelson monument had been raised by public subscription at the behest of the aldermen and merchants of Dublin in 1809. It was designed by Francis Johnston of Armagh, with an effigy of the great man carved by Thomas Kirk RHA of Cork. The Iberian trade, very important to Dublin, had been destroyed by the Napoleonic Wars and anyone who brought them nearer to an end deserved the city's thanks. The pillar had been 134 feet high, 20 feet of which had been the statuary, and 168 steps within it gave access to a platform that afforded a wonderful view of the city — and a leap for disappointed lovers. This is the station I have taken up from which to view the Irish Sea in its naval aspect.

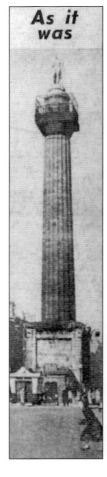

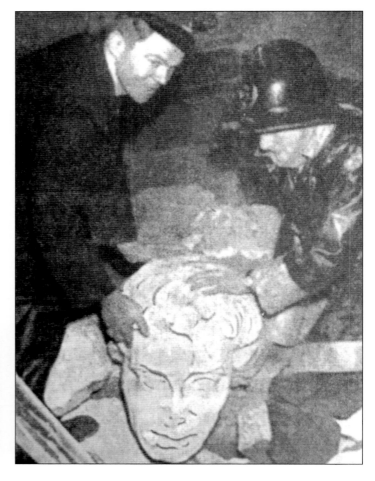

Figures 2 and 3. The column as it was, and Nelson's head rescued. Note: he seems to have both eyes.

The pillar was not universally admired: why, it was asked, should contemporary Irishmen and women tolerate a monument to a one-eyed English adulterer? And its presence outside the General Post Office was obviously questionable after the battles of 1916. It was also an intrusive, huge presence in a otherwise shapely public space.

In 1966 it was blown up. The usual suspects were rounded up, questioned and released. They denied everything, of course. The following week the Irish army felled the remaining stump and broke still more windows, though nothing like as many as recorded in popular imagination. Compensation worth £120,000 went to the shopkeepers and hoteliers of O'Connell Street. Some weeks later the statue's head was offered for sale in a London antique shop, the dealer having purchased it (he said) from seven students of the National School of Art and Design who had found it in the street, but a rival head was being displayed in a south-Dublin bar at the same time. What happened subsequently to either head is not known to this writer; instead he imagines the one in Dublin and the other in London, winking with one good eye each across the Irish Sea.

Viewed from the top of the pillar, looking east or west, the Irish Sea is resolved into a problem of naval and military strategy. How can it be controlled?

***

This question is part of a larger one posed in all the major parts of northern and western Europe in the later fifteenth century. Where, in effect, were the operational boundaries of the kingdoms that had begun, in their several and complicated ways, to resolve themselves into nations with organised states that inhabited defined territories? How precise could or should frontiers be? Was a frontier a line or a zone? Where did France begin and end? Was Spain one, two or three countries? How did the Hapsburg lands hang together? Where, in particular, were the boundaries of island states such as England and Scotland to be drawn?

The operational boundary of island states extends as far as their ships can reach to enforce their will. In the sixteenth century this rarely extended far beyond the shoreline and the sea was an intrinsically lawless zone. To bring it under the rule of the state meant to expand the state across the ocean.

The last years of the fifteenth century also mark a sudden expansion of maritime capacity in trade and exploration, related, in chicken/egg fashion, to the improvement of navigation, cartography and shipbuilding. The most significant decade was the last ten years of the fifteenth century, during which the first expedition of Christopher Columbus reached the West Indies (1492), John Cabot of Bristol (formerly Giovanni Caboto of Genoa) landed in Nova Scotia (1498) and Vasco da Gama attained India (1498). Most significantly of all, the Portuguese crown showed itself capable of sailing a fleet of 20 vessels for thousands of miles to inflict itself upon the rulers of Calicut

(1503). If this could be done across two oceans it could surely be done across the Bay of Biscay or the English Channel.

The unification of Spain and its later annexation of Portugal (in 1580) and the addition of varied Hapsburg lands created a prodigious state that was then, thanks to the improvement of warships, directly adjacent to the Islands. The consequence of these global enterprises upon the peoples of the Irish Sea were very deep, for they compelled the English and Scottish states to extend their operational boundaries to include all possible entries into the inland sea and greatly to extend their defensive scope. For this a naval effort was required. New classes and kinds of vessels were needed, with the organisation to support them.

As a general class of ship, the rowed galley, large or small, was the preferred vessel for enclosed or narrow waters and for amphibious assault. Genoese and Venetian shipbuilders had learnt to build very large ones, with forward-mounted guns. James IV of Scotland had learned from this and used large cannon called basilisks, permanently mounted forward on galleys, to batter the lords of the Isles into submission; he had a royal shipbuilding yard at Dumbarton, another at Leith and a gun foundry at Edinburgh to supply them. His naval tactics were built around the use of big guns. There was nothing equivalent to this in England and Rodger argues that it was this that marked 'the real end of medieval naval warfare in northern waters.'[1] Since Scottish kings had to fight on two seas as well as on the Arctic Ocean they developed two fleets, one based upon the Firth of Forth and the other at Tarbert in Kintyre.

***

While writing those sentences above the image came into my head, drawn from some book on shipbuilding, of a combined fish and ship hull, drawn in the early sixteenth century by a shipwright whose name, at this moment, I cannot remember. But it contains, in a few lines and a little wash, almost everything that needs to be or can be said about the design of objects that must cut through fluids and about the relationship between artefacts and nature. The image was drawn to explain the advances in design that made sea warfare so much more effective and deadly in the new century.

And at the same time, such are the tricks of the wandering mind, that another image has slipped between me and my studies. A popular picture of Bad King John, who shamed the throne that he sat on:

> Not a penny, not a straw
> cared this monarch for the law.
> Promises he daily broke,
> none could trust a word he spoke.

And there is the monarch himself, twirling his drooping moustaches as he postures across the page. The book it appeared in was, beyond doubt, *Kings and queens* by Eleanor and Herbert Farjeon, and the illustrations – very bold and colourful and funny – by another lady.[2] Looking about in catalogues and the like I find out this artist was Rosalind Thornycroft, though that is not the name I half remember. This Rosalind may well have been a lady who figured in the life of D.H. Lawrence as the model for Lady Chatterley. There was, as I recall, something rather louche about the whole production, but as a small boy I loved it extravagantly; indeed, if I had a copy now I am certain I would remember every page of it. But every catalogue note I have so far come across refers to a later edition illustrated by Robin Jacques. And why, in the middle of a disquisition on naval artillery, should I remember such childish matters? It is the Muse, speaking to me obliquely, as she always speaks.

And what is she telling me as I press down and forward? She is reminding me of the importance of popular histories in the human life.

During the first decade of the sixteenth century James IV began a shipbuilding programme with very large craft, vessels up to and including 1,000 tons. One of these, the *Michael*, carried 24 heavy guns mounted broadside and three basilisks, two forward and one aft. The basilisk was, as its name suggests, a frightful weapon that was fired at point-blank range with multiple projectiles and stunning detonation. Its only possible use was in full sea battle, where it was terrifying. With craft like these the Scottish king could extend his operational boundaries as far as Denmark and the Grand Banks of Newfoundland. There was, in fact, a naval agreement between Scotland and Denmark and the cities of the Hanseatic League, which was primarily aimed against England, though its main activity was in suppressing piracy and guarding the fishing fleets as far as Iceland and beyond. The trade in salt cod was of immense importance for the north-European diet in the winter months and it had to be controlled and protected.

In this way Scottish navigators and shipwrights, civil and military, gained much more experience in oceanic navigation and had the edge on Henry VIII and his vaunted Royal Navy. In the intermittent warfare of 1511–24 between France and England, the Scottish fleet played a part, bombarding Carrickfergus and sending a fleet to fight in Breton waters. Nor was Henry VIII capable of preventing a French fleet from sailing up the Irish Sea in 1522 and landing an army of 3,000 men at Kirkcudbright. This feat was repeated in 1545, demonstrating the slenderness of England's control of its own back door and 'private entry'.

All this was sufficient to alert the government of England to the necessity of controlling access to the Irish Sea. Since the Irish Sea was the highroad by which the Tudor dynasty made its way to power in the first place, one might have expected that they had come to this conclusion earlier. Their technical response to the problem was the design of the 'race-built' warships of the later sixteenth century, which combined lean lines with deep draught, high manoeuvrability and efficient, swiftly loaded cannon embedded in the body of the ship. The ship became, in effect, a weapons platform rather than a container of fighting men.

***

There had been many advance warnings of this necessity. French warships had sailed into Cardigan Bay to help Welsh princes fight off Edward I's campaigns against them. Genoese galleys had been brought to the aid of Edward II in the War of the Irish Sea and Genoese pirates frequently made life miserable for the merchants of south-west England. (One of these raiders, Giovanni Doria, had his name transferred to the John Dory, an ugly fish to be found in Cornish waters.) But the most significant event was probably the invasion of Harri Tewdwr, who landed a force of French and Irish mercenaries at Milford Haven in 1485 and went forward to Bosworth Field, where he defeated and killed Richard III.[3] He knew from his own experience how very vulnerable an English ruler might be to an attack through the Irish Sea.

Successive attempts to displace Henry VII by Yorkist claimants of the throne came from Ireland, where the Anglo-Norman lords were Yorkist to a man. In 1487 Lambert Simnel was crowned King Edward IV of England in Dublin and, supported by the Council of Ireland, took an army consisting mainly of a corps of German mercenaries, backed up by regiments of Irish gallowglasses, over into Lancashire. The lord chancellor of Ireland, Thomas Fitzgerald, was the foremost of the many Irish nobles who died in the battle that ensued (at Stoke Field in 1488). Far from home, the Germans went down to the last man in defence of the impostor.

Twelve years later, another claimant, Perkin Warbeck, was put forward at Cork and proclaimed as one of the Yorkist princes who had died in the Tower of London. To suppress this trouble, Henry Tudor sent an army back in the other direction. Warbeck — a curious figure of obscure origin who had been taken up by the Irish lords as a convenient stick with which to threaten Henry — then attempted an invasion of Cornwall. He ended on the gallows.[4] These comings and goings demonstrated to holders of the English crown the importance of ensuring their Irish subjects (as they termed them) remained loyal or at least docile. They came to see that, in the conditions of warfare created by naval advance, the domination of Ireland was a geopolitical necessity for the continued existence of their state. The realisation by continental powers that Ireland existed as 'the island beyond Britain' had suggested a new strategy against England.

***

A long-term strategic requirement of both English and Scottish kingdoms, bearing in mind the longer reach of military expeditions from continental Europe, was a regularisation and modernisation of their western edges, both of the feudal lords of the marches and of the Gaeltacht chiefdoms. The next piece of historical business, so to speak, was to bring the old Norman lordships and the inhabitants of the Gaeltacht into regular subjecthood. Henry VIII's first step was to declare himself king rather than merely feudal overlord of Ireland (in 1541).

He tried four principal means of modernising the Gaeltacht. The first was a policy of 'surrender and regrant', whereby the Gaelic chiefs were willingly to give up their present status, recognise the royal powers and in return be granted a feudal title and the rights and lands that went with it, accepting the king's authority and agreeing as part of his government to keep the peace. This seemed to be an intelligent offer that had something to give to both sides and a number of great chieftains accepted it. The head of the O'Neills, for example, became the earl of Tyrone. However, the assumption of an earlship or lordship on feudal terms, which included primogeniture and vassalage, was not likely to be acceptable to all the lesser chiefs, who were accustomed to jockeying and often fighting for the main place. The O'Neills in particular were very fractious with one another. It was only in the 1580s that the policy of surrender and regrant began to work with any success.

Related to this was the practice of replacing the Gaelic *tuath* (or the Welsh *tud*) with the Anglo-Saxon concept of the shire — regridding the land according to administrative boundaries that ignored feudal fiefdoms and even more absolutely overrode clan territories or kinship boundaries. Shiring was a principle of state management that went flat against the Gaelic way of seeing the land, and it was bitterly and violently resisted whenever the chance came.[5]

The third way was plantation — the imposition of a new population to settle, enclose and develop particular areas. The effect of this policy depended very much on where you were. Along the coasts of Ulster the population was constantly being modified by incoming Scots and outgoing Irishmen, because the distinction between them was slight; indeed, it hardly existed, since (for example) the Clan Donald extended across both sides of the North Channel. This had been the case throughout human history. But to introduce English farmers and tradesmen into the central plains of Ireland, as was done in large numbers in 1557, was to drive native men and women off land that had been theirs for millennia. The unwritten purpose of plantation and enclosure was to break up the clan system by destroying its spatial coordinates, which were a matter of custom and practice developed over thousands of years, and replacing them by new forms of space division. With this went other regulations such as weights and measures. Enclosure, coming in with James's plantations in Ulster, was an imposition of the new space of the early modern state over the space of the clan. Everything subsequently required boundaries and borders defined, measured, marked and policed. There is no more certain way to create lasting hatred than this, and the consequences do indeed flow down to the present day. Nevertheless, planting and subsequent enclosure was followed with enthusiasm by both Scottish and English kingdoms. To this day, the idea of common land and right of way scarcely exists in Ireland.

The last way was by naked force: those who resisted were to be killed. Since the first three ways met with small success, recourse to extreme violence became a matter of routine. The usual method was to interpret any resistance as rebellion, which entailed forfeiture of life and the loss of all estates to the crown. The crown would then hand on the rights of those estates to whoever had the power to take possession of them, using what means he may. Extension of the state was thus placed in private and rapacious hands.

> Let it be understood that we are not here concerned with the problem of evil. We are concerned with the problem of history as history, of the evil that is bound up not with man's condition but with his behaviour towards others. We would wish to know, for example, how it would be possible to tolerate, and to justify, the sufferings and annihilation of so many peoples who suffered and were annihilated for the simple reason that their geographical situation set them in the pathway of history, that they were neighbours of empires in a state of permanent expansion.[6]

Human beings, as ethical agents, require justification before they do wicked deeds, but the state has only one possible ethic, which is to perpetuate itself. In this it resembles the crocodile, who knows only crocodile law.

In Ireland it had been the custom to allow the Anglo-Norman lords to conduct their own affairs but once the decision to 'normalise' the Gaeltacht had been taken the crown had to extend its direct rule beyond the Pale, and so it came into conflict with the 'Old' English. Not surprisingly, a series of rebellions took place, Anglo-Norman and Gaelic. All came to nothing:

> It was easy for the king to out-manoeuvre the Irish nobility, as Ireland was a jungle of inter-sept and inter-racial rivalries. The lords of this jungle were unable to set aside their feuds in favour of combined action against the king. Their inability to present a common front also made it impossible for them to exploit either Habsburg or Valois against England. Their lack of political sophistication allowed the crown to isolate them one after another, and the outcome of their revolts was only to secure more firmly royal control of Ireland.[7]

To extend our view from Nelson's pillar, or from Nelson's column, we have to extend the boundaries of our Irish Sea northward into the western islands and westward to Dingle and Kinsale and Bantry Bay; southward too into Breton and Spanish waters, to make brief situation reports.

***

Rathlin, 1573

In the 1550s Rathlin had become an island fortress and supply base for different sections of Clan Donald, for whom it was conveniently placed between their Irish and their Scottish lands. It was against Rathlin that the earl of Essex sent out an expedition in 1573, with the aim of cutting off the bands of *gallóglaigh* that all his opponents employed. Essex had cajoled Elizabeth I into appointing him governor of Ulster, a title invented especially for the occasion. However, he seems to have had no coherent plan of action since he attacked both the O'Neills and the Clan Donald simultaneously when those two were already at war with one another. His intention, however, was to attempt a plantation and thereby to enrich himself. In August 1575 he had the Irish chieftain of the Clan Donald, Sorley Buy Macdonnell, driven back into the north-eastern corner of the Antrim Glens, around Ballycastle.

Sorley Buy had prudently moved his clan's non-combatants and supplies over the water to Rathlin and was awaiting an attack by land. Instead, it came by water, commanded by Francis Drake and John Norris, very suddenly. They seized the castle, killing all of its garrison, and then set about killing 400 women and their children, followed by 300 cattle, 3,000 sheep and 300 brood mares; they also burnt the 11 vessels they had surprised at anchor and stole tons of supplies. Sorley and his men had to stand on the shore and watch this horror unfold.

The mission was conducted by captains well known to Queen Elizabeth,[8] but they were not part of a royal force. It was Tudor practice to 'privatise' this violence, on license to whoever could offer to suppress rebels at least cost to the crown. Essex had put together his own army, equipped it from his own purse with six cannon, 150 muskets and 200 archers. He was paying his own troops (when he could) so he was under great financial pressure to succeed.

The ferry from Ballycastle has to butt its way across the boisterous current that runs around Fair Head towards the Atlantic. Off its southern end is a notorious tidal whirlpool and towards the Scottish shore lies a foul coast of underwater reefs. The island is mainly low lying and composed of the usual Antrim mixture of chalk and basalt, which gives it a pied appearance. It contains a good sheltered anchorage on the south side, which now supports a street of holiday houses, a bar, a little museum and quayside huts. Today the human inhabitants are outnumbered by the seals, which congregate along the shingle of Mill Bay a mile or so from the landing. These creatures lie in the sun, fanning their faces, snorting and mewing to one another in lazy companionship. You may, if you are quiet, approach them across the fields. If you are slow and patient and take on their air of somnolence you can come with a few yards. They are without fear, but circumspect.

We sat together for two hours, watching and whispering. Their peace flowed into our spirits and still remains there, to drink in recollection.

The sacking of Rathlin is cited because such an egregious wickedness could only be justified on strategic grounds. In fact, the entire Gaeltacht was subject to numerous predatory attacks of this land-grabbing kind under cover of legality and pacification. The policy almost equally dismayed the Anglo-Norman population: while Essex was laying Antrim waste Sir Thomas Smith, another courtier, was planting the Ards Peninsula. In this case it was an Anglo-Norman as well as native Irish peasantry that was being forced to move to make way for (in this case) English farmers. Thomas Smith claimed to be colonising Ireland after the Roman and the Norman fashion, in order to bring civilised behaviour to a barbarous people; he has been claimed as an early theorist of colonialism. Actually, he was repeating the odious rhetoric of 'civilisers' before and ever since.

A similar policy was pursued by James VI a little later. In 1597 the Scottish parliament, with prompting from James, passed an act requiring all chiefs and landholders in the Hebrides and adjacent highlands to produce valid title deeds or forfeit their territory. Such documents were not part of Gaelic legality and few had them; this was, of course, the very idea. The political aim was to cut down the remnants of the lordship of the Isles and to curb the powers of certain great clans, notably the (Catholic) Clan Donald, who, as we have seen, sat astride the North Channel, respecting no formal division of countries or states. The economic aim was to collect rents and taxes and to create a modern economy by founding burghs and importing 'civilised' lowlanders who would be loyal to the crown rather than the clan. The highlands would then be shired.

Since James VI had no army to speak of, and was averse to risk, he gave the task to others. The marquis of Huntly was offered all the northern isles except Skye and Lewis on condition that he massacred the inhabitants. He declined — not, it seems, out of humanity, but because he could not afford it. A commercial company known as the Fife Adventurers then obtained (that is, bought) the rights to the island of Lewis, but when they tried to enforce them they were driven off by an alliance of local chiefs. The head office of this vile association (which was comprised of the leading men of Fife and St Andrew's) sold on the rights to the Clan Mackenzie, who in turn engaged in a colonial war of their own, taking over and, in effect, conquering Lewis. There followed a period of clan warfare all through the highlands and islands, in which the Campbells and Gordons, with the Mackenzies, became imperialists within their own country. James, for his part, designated the Clan MacGregor as an 'unhappie and detestable race' who were to be 'extirpat and ruttit out' and employed other clans in a policy we might now call genocidal.

In the southern islands and Kintyre this infamous method was promoted by the Campbells to take advantage of the several branches of Clan Donald, which they did in a violent campaign supported by royal ships and heavy artillery, with mercenaries. Lowlanders from Ayr were transported over into Kintyre where, in 1597, the burgh of Campbeltown was established. Southern Kintyre, in effect, became a plantation of Scots within Scotland. Thus this crucial headland was made loyal to the crown (see Chapter 2).

***

Smerwick, 1579

Smerwick Bay, at the tip of the Dingle Peninsula, is the most western and most sheltered anchorage in the long, foul coast of south-western Ireland. It is a point which every boat must pass and its strategic importance is indicated by its Viking name.

In both 1559 and 1569 the remnants of the Fitzgerald rebels had approached Philip II of Spain with an offer of an Irish crown if he would help them against Elizabeth of England. They claimed that a rebel confederacy existed and that their aims were purely religious. Of course, no such all-Irish unity existed nor ever had, nor was there much sign of Catholic revolt against the alien Protestant bastard she-despot. But this did not deter the leaders (who do not seem to have had a firm grasp of reality).

An unofficial force of Spanish troops led by a dissident 'Old' English noble, Sir James Fitzmaurice Fitzgerald, arrived in the bay late in 1578 and ousted a small garrison. This expedition was timed to coincide with another, largely imagined, uprising throughout Munster. The aims of the participants were mixed. From the 'Old' English point of view it was an attempt to restore their former position; from a religious perspective it was a response to the excommunication of Elizabeth the heretic and a move in the Counter-Reformation; from the Spanish point of view it was a warning to the English crown of what might develop if it continued to support the Dutch rebellion. Insofar as there was any native Irish response it was the killing of Fitzmaurice in a skirmish with the locals.

The first battalion was reinforced the following year by another, again privately financed; it had a contingent of Italian mercenaries consisting of 600 men and arms for another 5,000. This was a serious force. They occupied a fort beside the bay and prepared to wait for the expected uprising. Instead they met the *Revenge*, with 50 guns and 250 men, and ten other warships under the command of Sir William Winter. The *Revenge* was among the first of the 'race-built' galleons commissioned by Elizabeth and, in design, speed, weight of armament and rate of fire, probably exceeded any other vessel then afloat. In shipbuilding terms it effected a synthesis of the lean and the plump and was a new kind of weapons platform of exceptional effectiveness. It is a measure of the government's concern that this dreadnought was sent into action in so remote an anchorage. A sketch of 1580 shows this fleet firing upon Smerwick Castle.

The invaders surrendered and were massacred; and the territories of Kerry and south Limerick were then devastated to such a degree that according to Edmund Spenser 'a most populous and plentiful country [was] suddenly made void of man and beast'.[9]

The extreme ferocity of English arms in Ireland may be explained, though not excused, by the extreme insecurity of the crown. Spain, by the annexation of Portugal (in 1580) at a stroke doubled its already very great naval power and there was a real likelihood of an invasion mounted simultaneously from Spain, the low countries, Brittany and even Scotland, which had, briefly, a pro-Catholic government. In the face of this the government in London was beginning to perceive the world in paranoid terms. The inlets and bays of south-western Ireland became the forward defence zone of the kingdom as the Anglo-Spanish Wars began, and the Irish Sea was the essential link in communications. Rodger makes it clear that the new designs developed in the royal dockyards were purely military in character and this distinguished them from the bulk of the Spanish fleet, which was composed of adapted merchant vessels and transports.[10]

***

Waterford Bay, 1588

As a consequence to the perceived and imminent threat of a Spanish fleet an old promontory fort outside Waterford, which had existed since the Bronze Age, was taken over and replaced by a piece of *avant-garde* military engineering, Duncannon Fort. The purpose of this was to safeguard the principal supply port for the Tudor army in southern Ireland, reached directly from Bristol or Pembroke. To the landward side the fort offers only modest defences but the size of the gunports on the seaward side suggests it housed very large guns. Charles Fort at the inlet to Kinsale Harbour is a similar, though later, structure.

A plan for Duncannon was first made in 1551, but work did not begin until 1587 and it was not completed until 1590. Fortifications were being built on the other side of the river and around Waterford town at the same time.

The first maps of Ireland are all associated with this period. A pencil sketch of the whole island done in 1558, with annotations in the hand of Elizabeth's chief secretary, William Cecil, looks as if it was hastily drawn in a Privy-Council meeting as part of a briefing to ministers. Another from the same year is a more formal affair, marking all the forts around Bantry Bay. Yet another, from 1587, has fathom soundings from Cork to Dingle added in notes. Cork and its harbour were fortified during this period and the plans still exist in the Office of State Papers, as does a map of the southern coast from Cork to Waterford, annotated in Cecil's hand with the names of leading Gaelic families. This is worth comparing with another annotated map, this time of southern Lancashire, in which Cecil or his secretaries marked the seats of prominent Catholic families. In time Ireland became the best-mapped land in Europe, thanks to English military surveyors. But Abraham Ortelius's *Theatrum orbis terrarum*, published in Antwerp in 1593, shows most of Ulster as empty wasteland.[11]

Duncannon Fort was subsequently fought over during the English Civil War; it was besieged by successive parliamentary forces for five years because it hindered access to Waterford Harbour. Cromwell himself was one of the besieging commanders. Later a Martello tower was built at Baginbun Point to guard the coast, this time against Napoleon.

Illustration 1.
Duncannon Fort.

The long headland known as the Hook, which extends south-eastward from Waterford Bay, is a coastal zone full of historical interest. It contains, among other maritime curiosities, the lighthouse of Hook, built in 1247 and still working. It was to Baginbun Point on the eastern shore of the Hook that Strongbow's vanguard arrived and it was at Passage East, directly opposite Duncannon, that Strongbow himself disembarked. There is an old church founded by the Knights Templar, several small castles and an early Cistercian Abbey, a daughter church of Tintern Abbey on the Wye (and also called Tintern).[12]

***

Western approaches, 1585–1601

Had the first Armada (which was actually the second to be prepared, the first having been burnt before it left port) been a more modest affair and more intelligently planned it might have landed a large army in southern Ireland or Cornwall, but it went its disastrous course. The English riposte to the Armada (led by the old team of Drake and Norris) burnt a few ships but cost a great deal; it was necessary to repeat this expense several times in the next few years as the war was increasingly fought out in the western approaches, in Ulster and in Brittany.[13] There were also expeditions to Galicia, well remembered by the locals but, it seems, forgotten by the English.

In the centre of the Irish Sea, Peel Castle was extensively refortified and Elizabeth took the government of Man directly into her own hands, installing a military governor and building forts. She warned the governor in May 1593 to expect a Spanish invasion of Ireland. The main action, however, was in Ulster.

The Nine Years' War of the O'Neills and the O'Donnells was the last autonomous effort of the Gaeltacht in Ireland to maintain itself. Hugh O'Neill, as we have seen already, called on Spanish officers to train and arm his men, and 'Red' Hugh O'Donnell could rely upon a stream of Scottish gallowglasses. His mother, Inneen Dubh, was a scion of the Clan Donald who had no interest at all in steady encroachment of state power. Between them the two Hughs were able to put together a political alliance and a large guerrilla army, supported by a supply chain with proper administration. This was far beyond what the Gaelic lords had ever been able to create before and it usually proved more than capable of dealing with English crown forces, which continued to be starved of good men and munitions. The defeat of the army of Sir Henry Bagenal at the Yellow Ford near Armagh (1598) is one of those debacles, like the retreat from Kandahar or the battle of New Orleans, of which little is heard in English popular history.

Exactly what the strategic aims of the O'Neill rebellion were remains unclear. Perhaps they never extended far beyond a policy of 'what we have we hold'. But such a policy was certain to lead into irreconcilable conflict with the expansionism of the Tudor state and the rapacity of the 'New' English. Hugh O'Neill, through his emissaries abroad, was liable to make vague offers of kingships of Ireland to susceptible princes and talk of restoring the 'true faith'. This was well known to English agents in Spain and Italy and had to be prevented at any cost.[14] The destruction of the two Hughs became a prime aim of Elizabeth's government.

In the midst of this a second (or was it third?) Armada sailed from El Ferrol in December 1596. This was absurdly late in the season for sixteenth-century warships; up to 40 were lost and 3,000 men were drowned, without sight of the enemy. In reprisal an Anglo-Dutch fleet sailed to Cadiz and sank 57 more.

It was mainly in return for this assault that Philip decided to give direct aid to the Gaelic rebellion. O'Neill and O'Donnell wanted the Spanish force to land at Galway or, if the wind compelled them, to sail right through the North Channel and into Carlingford Lough. The Hapsburg Archduke Albert was to be made king of a Catholic Ireland and his wife Isabella (Philip's daughter) was to be made queen of a Catholic England. The rebels collected supplies and munitions in expectation but, once again, the Spanish fleet chose to risk the equinoctial gales of October 1597 and was utterly wrecked on the Galician coast. 32 major ships were lost along with, once more, thousands of men.

This third (or fourth) Armada was accompanied by a fourth (or fifth) of 136 ships, which planned simultaneously to occupy southern Ireland and Falmouth. It too was driven back by storms, with further losses. The fruitless expense drove the Spanish government, for all its gold and silver, into bankruptcy.

It was not until the autumn of 1600 that the Spanish government, now under the much less vigorous management of Philip III and his chief minister, the duke of Lerma, could summon up the funds and fire to try again.

The expeditionary force of 1601 qualifies as the final (fifth or sixth) Armada. Characteristically, it set out late in the year (from Lisbon on 3 September) and arrived, storm tossed and scattered, off Kinsale. It had set out with 33 ships and 4,500 fighting men. Only 3,400 men disembarked, the others having been scattered up and down the coast or having returned to Spain, unable to make landfall. Nor did the inhabitants of Munster, Gaelic or 'Old' English, offer the expected support. Moreover, the Spanish were about as far from the O'Neills and O'Donnells as they could be in Ireland. Lacking the strength to do anything more, the Spaniards occupied the town and prepared to be besieged.

The campaign leading up to the battle of Kinsale has been written about many times and lies beyond our detailed interest. Briefly, the English lord deputy, Mountjoy, arrived with a force of similar size and in due course besieged the Spanish, with trenches, redoubts and artillery. The English forces were, however, too few to take the risk of storming the town and settled down, in very bad conditions of snow, rain, mud and cold to do what they could. Both sides began to starve and the English to die of exposure. The Spanish ships had to leave for lack of provisions and because their captains did not trust their crews (many of whom were English prisoners who had to be locked into their quarters when not actually working the ships). An English warship then sailed into Kinsale Harbour and punished the invaders. To make the Spanish situation worse, the Catholic clergy in Ireland were urging their flock to stay loyal to the crown, which they did. So much for the Counter-Reformation, they might have complained.

We do not have space, either, to describe the remarkable march of O'Neill and O'Donnell with their men across Ireland at a rate of 30 and sometimes 40 miles a day, in snow and rain, outwitting their pursuers. This is one of history's great exploits of guerrilla warfare. Transposing these events into modern terms, the Gaelic forces were in the classic guerrilla dilemma. They could not win without turning themselves into a real army; in moving south they came out of their core region and into territory where they lacked the immediate local support which is the absolute precondition of guerrilla victory.

The arrival of more Spanish troops at Castlehaven, some miles down the coast, made the English predicament more difficult still, since now the besiegers were becoming the besieged. They were dying in their dozens of cold and hunger. Mountjoy, seeing the approach of O'Neill's patrols, is reported to have said, 'This kingdom is lost today.'

However, the Gaelic leaders went down in total defeat on Christmas Day 1601 (old calendar). The planned-for juncture with the Spanish force never took place; the guerrilla army collapsed when faced in the open field by professional troops, however hungry; a cavalry charge by horses almost too weak to gallop led to panic and hundreds of deaths in a brief hour.

Within weeks Hugh O'Donnell had fled to Spain, never to return, and the Spanish commander had accepted easy terms and sailed away. Before the next year was out Elizabeth had died and her successor had become king of a new polity of Great Britain, comprising all the islands. By 1607 Hugh O'Neill had abandoned all hope of maintaining his minimal position, keeping the ancestral lands intact, and had also left for Spain. This gave King James the legal excuse for taking most of Ulster into his hands and distributing it to Scottish and English planters and 'undertakers'.

From being the last redoubt of Gaelic power in the Islands Ulster went forward to become the advance base of the Protestant and united Magna Britannia, whose internal unity and communication was guaranteed by control of the inland sea.

But this was merely the start of it.

Horrible confusion, 1642

The Scottish settlers in Ulster were Presbyterian to a man and woman. King Charles, in his wisdom, determined that they and all Scotland should abjure their covenant and sent his deputy in Ireland, Thomas Wentworth, to enforce his will. A force of 1500 men arrived in Carrickfergus, while another force engaged in Scotland in what became known as the Bishop's Wars. These were small enough affairs but they broke the back of the royal exchequer. Charles was forced to recall a parliament; that was his undoing. Magna Britannia fell into several kinds of pieces.

By 1642, when civil war was comprehensively engaged, the several causes and factions overlapped all around the Irish Sea. An Irish Catholic army, led by later members of the O'Neill family and heavily backed by papal money and munitions, was fighting a Presbyterian Scottish army up and down Ulster. Sectarian atrocities had become commonplace and much exaggerated by propaganda. Charles was negotiating with the Irish rebels to get them to help him expel parliamentary authorities from Dublin, with a view to using Ireland as a base from which to supply his armies in England and Scotland. The several castles of north Wales came back into military history and each one had to be captured by parliamentary forces in order to deny Charles a safe landing for his reinforcements. Ellan Vannin became, once again, a bone in the parliamentary throat. It was garrisoned and refortified on behalf of the king by the earl of Stanley, who created yet another string of batteries, watchtowers and earthworks. Rushen Castle remained royalist to the bitter end, until taken in the course of a local coup. Down to the south, facing France and Spain, the royal 'navy' — a force of 30 ships of different sizes and kinds — was commanded by Prince Rupert to harass the parliamentarians. A combined Scottish and parliamentary fleet ranged through the North Channel and right up into the Hebrides to prevent royalist forces in Ireland making contact with Gaelic dissidents in the highlands and suppressing pro-Stuart chieftains. At different times Scottish armies were fighting the English along the east coast of Ireland and in Lancashire. The boldest single campaign of the war was conducted across the Irish Sea — by Cromwell, who by 1650 had subdued Ireland to the parliamentary will.

In doing so he had to besiege and capture Drogheda. The event was so appalling in an Irish context that the massacre of the opposing troops, normal by the violent conventions of the time, was magnified in rumour into a general massacre of the entire population. In today's prissy language, there was extensive collateral damage. How much was done and how many were killed remains (at present) uncertain; there is a discernible tendency in some recent scholarship to reduce the figures. That this figure grew and grew in rumour and is still widely believed to have included most of the city may stem from the nature of the fighting. First of all there was the sheer scale of conflict. Cromwell's force was by some measure the largest that had ever waged war in Ireland. What made it more appalling was that this was the first occasion when an early modern army had fought in the streets of an Irish city, with all the firepower, casualties and mayhem that entailed. Cannon were used in the streets and buildings full of fighting men were set on fire. That this horror was also visited on the people of Wexford some time later strongly suggests that the campaign was for terror rather than for military advantage.

With Ireland subdued, parliament was ready to settle accounts with the Scots — which it did, promptly.

Viewed with a Nelsonian eye from the top of his pillar in O'Connell Street, the Civil War was not an English affair at all, but most emphatically pan-British, fought in, around and across the inland sea. Irish historians do not reckon this a civil war and instead have designated it the War of the Three Kingdoms.

***

After the Boyne, 1690

As we have already seen, the long road to Dublin town was the focus of a campaign by land and sea to drive away the last of the Stuart kings. In the course of the preparations to bring his army south, William of Orange brought a fleet into the Irish Sea and a contingent of it raided Dublin Harbour to good effect. This was led by a bold young officer named Cloudesley Shovell who, when appointed admiral, managed to wreck his entire fleet on the shoals of Scilly.

After the comprehensive defeat of James II at the battle of the Boyne, the Irish adherents of the Jacobite cause withdrew to Limerick and the far west. The Irish Jacobites, who now entirely despised their king, put up a spirited and largely successful defence of Limerick town, but the French troops, under the command of the hapless General Lauzon, were at Galway waiting for a fleet to pick them up and take them home.

***

Bantry Bay, 1796

The French returned to Ireland in December 1796 in support of risings, imaginary, planned and actual, by the United Irishmen. The aim of this attempt was made clear in the French admiral's instructions, as issued by the revolutionary directorate:

> to restore to a people ripe for revolution the independence and liberty for which it clamours. Ireland has groaned under the hateful yoke of England for centuries.

We can admire the spirited rhetoric of the revolution, repeated by fronts for national liberation ever since, but the degree to which a political entity called Ireland had existed before then is a case to be argued. We might, I think, more closely compare this situation with that of the liberation of Algeria, in which the nation of Algeria was largely the creation of the colonial power against which the Front de Libération Nationale was fighting. The nation state of Ireland came into conceptual being only with the parliament convened by James Stuart in 1689 and it was still a long way from being actualised.

The advantages to France of an invasion of Ireland were obvious: England, without Ireland, would be deprived of much of her naval power. One might have supposed that the Royal Navy would have had better intelligence and force than to allow 17 large warships and a flock of transports carrying 14,500 men and a huge amount of weaponry even to approach the shore of Bantry Bay. And one might have thought the French admiral would have advised his government against the time of year. (No continental admiral, French or Spanish, ever seems to have understood what a bad idea it was to have sailing ships rocking about off the Atlantic coast of Ireland in the middle of winter.) As it was, less than half the storm-scattered fleet actually arrived, and that part was limply led. They had left by the first week of January but the Royal Navy even then failed to catch them on the return. The main cruising station for the channel fleet from now on was to be off Brest in Brittany, to prevent any large French or Spanish force approaching southern Ireland, either directly, by sailing down-channel, or by way of Spain. This resulted in major sea battles at Camperdown and Cape St Vincent, both in 1797, which were repeated the next year with a sea battle off the Donegal coast and a small landing at Killala, County Mayo.

General Humbert's little Franco-Irish army successfully got ashore and won a first battle against a larger British force, but found it had nowhere to go and insufficient support from the population at large. After wandering across Counties Mayo and Sligo it surrendered itself, hungry but unbeaten, at Ballinamuck, which is (with due apologies to its inhabitants) on the road to nowhere. The engagement off Tory Island ended in total defeat for the French squadron and the capture of Wolfe Tone, who had been the principal coordinator of the United Irishmen in these attempts. Tone cheated the hangman with his own knife.

Land-based risings in Ulster and Leinster enjoyed a brief success and suffered a swift collapse for reasons much debated by the historians of Ireland. The Anglo-Scottish government now took the inevitable step (from the column's point of view, that is) and brought about the Act of Union.

This did not, of course, end the strategic problem, which was still the amalgamation of the Gaeltacht. An Act of Union supposes an Ireland that was now generally conceived as a distinct nation and state of a kind that could unite with another; it was not simply a territory to be absorbed. Reciprocally, the title of United Irishmen stood for something substantial, worth winning for its own sake. The question of what it means to live and die along these shores had acquired a more definite meaning. Thus the Tudor couplet, 'He who would England win/must with Ireland begin' came to be replaced by the slogan, 'England's difficulty is Ireland's opportunity.'

***

Western approaches, 1805

Napoleon, taking over where the French Revolution left off, had a similar idea in 1804, with an army of 15,000 men assembled at Brest.

At this moment the admiral 'of immortal memory' steps down (voluntarily) from his pillar and becomes an actor in the events. The naval comings and goings prior to the battle of Trafalgar were all predicated on the assumption that the French/Spanish fleets were positioning themselves for a simultaneous assault into southern England and/or southern Ireland. Nelson's reports to the admiralty make this absolutely clear. His colleague, Collingwood, was more definite still:

> I have always had an idea that Ireland alone was the object they have in view, and still believe that to be their ultimate destination ... the real mark and butt of all their operations.[15]

After Trafalgar the Irish Sea became a British lake until a new stage of sea warfare changed the rules of the game. It was therefore absolutely appropriate that the merchants of Dublin should set Horatio Nelson firmly on his pillar, and just as appropriate that others should cause him to fall off it in so spectacular and noisy a fashion.

And this tale, as we shall see, is still not over. As I write the British government is debating the renewal of the Trident submarine fleet based upon the Firth of Clyde.

***

Part two

> Whether we like it or not, the crux of international politics is war.
> — Patrick O'Sullivan

Geography has been described as 'the study of the distribution of phenomena on the earth's surface'.[16] These phenomena are both physical and cultural — mountains, deserts and seas are experienced in relationships with farmland, cities and trade routes, languages and beliefs. The distribution is a matter of the topology and geometry of surfaces — a study of shapes. This explains why:

> visualisation is the specifically geographic mode of thought and the map is the geographic mode of record. By comparing maps of different kinds of phenomena we interlock our visualised generalisations ... Correlating shapes is the geographical mode of research.[17]

When we use geographical study to help explain human affairs or changes in the environment we do so in the tense of the 'historical present' because our aim is 'to restore imaginatively the dynamic system of some past moment of time'. This requires a trained imaginative aptitude and, as Mackinder puts it:

> that power of seeing vast masses of detail in orderly relationship and proportion which distinguishes the ideal geographer and the ideal historian; the one in regard to space and in the other with regard to time, and both as they exist on this earth's surface.[18]

Mackinder calls this a 'school of concrete philosophy.'

The concept of geopolitics — the study of the distribution of the phenomena of power on the surface of the globe — cannot be other than a contested field because the language of description employed has consequences. Ideas of domination, race, 'manifest destiny' and *lebensraum* are embedded in its discourse, to which has been added recently the odious notion of 'ethnic cleansing'. To read the classics of geopolitics requires the capacity to suspend revulsion. But the condition of living, armed and conscious, within a world of global trade and environment absolutely demands that we take geopolitical understandings seriously and form concepts that enable us to live together. As Mackinder himself wrote (in 1928), 'More than ever will it be necessary that the next generation should contain men and women with a trained power of geographical imagination.'[19]

Mackinder's central thesis, elaborated when Britain was engaged in an intense naval rivalry with Germany, was of a recurring conflict between land power and sea power. The application of this basic notion coincides very well with the view from Nelson's pillar, all the more so because Mackinder perceived that a long period of dominance by sea (he called it the Columbian epoch) was coming to an end. As early as 1890 he had written that 'it may be that the balance of geographical advantages has already inclined against England, and that she is maintaining her position by inertia'.[20]

This sense of declining advantage underlay the desperate quality of British naval dispositions in the great wars of the twentieth century, to which was added the novel conditions of submarine and air warfare and the extreme importance that attended the control of the western approaches. Until 1914 British defence strategy was what it always had been — aimed at preventing anyone at all from controlling the narrow seas and keeping open access to the oceans. Open access had become ever more important for the maintenance of food supplies and industrial raw materials. But submarines were not susceptible to surface attack and at first there was no adequate defence against them. In September 1916 three German submarines sank 30 merchant vessels in a week off Beachy Head, despite being pursued by 670 armed patrol craft. A fleet of over 400 small armed craft was assembled at Cork but could do little. Before long the German fleet possessed longer-range submarines that could sail right around the north of Scotland and attack North-Atlantic shipping. To counter entry into the inland sea, the North Channel was closed to all except supervised traffic and a barrage of mines lain from Scotland to Norway. The German naval war aim was, by way of incessant submarine attack, to sap and if possible to destroy Britain's war economy. In the first half of 1917 almost two million tons of shipping and 977 ships were sunk. Such a rate of loss prompted a letter from the American naval commander to the American ambassador:

> It remains a fact that at present the enemy is succeeding and we are failing. Ships are being sunk faster than they can be replaced by the building facilities of the world. This simply means that the enemy is winning the war. There is no mystery about that.[21]

Around the same time, President Wilson described the British admiralty as being 'helpless to the point of panic'.[22]

In May 1917 a convoy system was instituted, employing as assembly points such ancient anchorages as Lamlash Bay to the north and Milford Haven and Cork to the south. But what did most to save Allied shipping was the arrival of US destroyers in Cork and a high level of cooperation between American and British captains. This was augmented by the arrival of US reconnaissance aircraft to be based at points in the south and west of Ireland and at Londonderry in the north. Three US battleships with supporting craft took up station in Berehaven in the far west. In 1918 there were 36 US vessels in Cork Harbour, compared to 11 British. It was on these beginnings that the continuing dependence of the British state upon US power was instituted. It has not changed since.

At the very same time, the Irish Republican Brotherhood was in close contact with American supporters and with the German Foreign Office, who had also perceived that England's difficulty was Ireland's opportunity. The failure of the insurrection of Easter 1916 was seen by many despairing Irish nationalists as yet another debacle, but it took place in a deeply altered context.

***

The second round of the great European civil war, beginning in 1939, followed a similar pattern, but on this occasion Great Britain was without naval facilities in southern Ireland. This followed the partition of 1921 and the perception of Irish nationalism that Ireland was indivisible:

> No claim to separation from Ireland can be substantiated by any section of the Irish people; it can only be made by a foreign colony, alien to the soil, deriving its authority from an external source and basing its claim upon force. And no such claim can, or ever will be, entertained by the Irish people.[23]

Sloan describes this assertion as a 'key geographical falsehood' based upon the demonstrably false belief that because Ireland is an island (a single geographical unit) it must therefore necessarily form a single political unit. This was refuted by the refusal of many or most people in the northern quarter of the island to participate in any such deterministic and exclusive concept of an Irish state. It remains the key tenet of republican nationalism, however hedged about with qualifications, and it remains unfeasible to the present day. The crucial dilemma recurred time and time again in the negotiations surrounding the Anglo-Irish Treaty of 1921: the eventual agreement, which led in time to loss of use of the treaty ports, breached the defensive field.

This forced a new view of reality on the successors of Nelson. In 1941 the command of the western approaches passed from Plymouth (facing the world) to Liverpool (enclosed within the inland sea). At the same time, defence became increasing aerial and finally electronic and submarine, basing itself upon Clydeside.

This is not an argument for or against partition, unionism, exclusivity or nationalism, but it indicates the impossibility of agreement between essentialist ideals of nationality and strategic geography, in which Ireland (as the 'island beyond Britain') was and always would be an integral part of the defensive field of the British state. This impossibility would last as long as Britain looked to Atlantic trade for survival. It does so no longer. It is a singular fact that of all the scholarly studies of the Northern-Ireland conflict of the past 40 years, not one devotes more than a page to a study of this geopolitical reality — yet it underlies all dealings. The willingness of the British state to rethink this problem dates from the signing of the Single European Act in 1986.

Notes

[1]   N.A.M. Rodger (1997) *The safeguard of the sea: a naval history of Britain 660–1649*, London: Penguin Books, p. 168 *et seq.*

[2]   E. and H. Farjeon (1953) *Kings and queens*, Philadelphia: Lippincott.

[3]   The Tudor dynasty was Welsh in rather more than name. They first appear as owning land along the north-Welsh coast and making an accommodation with Edward I. They were among the Welsh magnates who sent troops to help Edward's campaigns in Scotland. During the 1370s and later they were royal bailiffs in Anglesey. Owain Tudor became a household manager for Henry V's queen Katharine (the French princess portrayed so amusingly by Shakespeare). It is reported that Owain's family could speak no English. After Henry's death he married Katharine. His two sons became counsellors of Henry VI and, as the earls of Pembroke and Richmond, were major players in the Wars of the Roses. Jasper Tudor built up Pembroke Castle into a major naval fortress against the Yorkist faction in Ireland. When his nephew Henry invaded Yorkist England he was greeted by Welsh

supporters as a Welsh monarch who would revive Welsh fortunes, and he carried the red-dragon standard at Bosworth. Close family servants continued to speak Welsh for the next hundred years. Elizabeth Tudor was brought up by a Welsh-speaking nurse, Blanche Parry, whose Welsh cousin Thomas Parry became Elizabeth's business manager and 'fixer'. Elizabeth herself almost certainly spoke Welsh with her family servants. The Tudor family appearance was (for those who want to make anything of it), notably 'Celtic', with red hair and pale skin. The standard work on the origins of the Tudor dynasty appears to be A.R. Griffiths and R.S. Thomas (1987) *The making of the Tudor dynasty*, Gloucester: Sutton.

4   See I. Arthurson (1994) *The Perkin Warbeck conspiracy, 1491–1499*, Stroud: Sutton.

5   Against this resistance one has to point out that the counties of Ireland, Wales and Scotland as established (finally) in the 1600s have endured. They must have corresponded to something real and geographical for this to be so. The English shire system is, of course, of greater antiquity still and has proved very resistant to change. Counties thought abolished have tended to reappear; new amalgamations have withered.

6   M. Eliade (1954) *The myth of the eternal return, or Cosmos and history*, Princeton, NJ: Princeton University Press, p. 150.

7   J.S. Silke (1970, repr. 2000) *Kinsale: the Spanish intervention in Ireland at the end of the Elizabethan Wars*, Dublin: Four Courts Press.

8   Norris was one of the sons of Lady Norris, the 'dear Crow' of Elizabeth's private letters.

9   E. Spenser (1849) 'A view of the state of Ireland' in *The works of Edmund Spenser: with observations of his life and writings*, London: H. Washborne, p. 510.

10   Rodger, *op. cit.*

11   These notes on maps are indebted to M. Swift (1999) *Historical maps of Ireland*, London: Parkgate Books and S. Duffy (ed.) (1997) *An atlas of Irish history*, Dublin: Gill and Macmillan.

12   The district has been beautifully studied and pictured in B. Colfer (2004) *The Hook Peninsula: County Wexford*, Cork: Cork University Press.

13   The Brittany campaign is a feature of the story that is not well known; the Spanish fleet seized harbours to use as a staging post for supplies up and down the channel and as a base for attacks on southern England. After a violent little war they were driven out by an English army led by the same John Norris.

14   A full account of O'Neill's diplomacy is found in Silke, *op. cit.*, Chapter 5.

15   Lord Collingwood to Lord Nelson, 21 July 1805, from C.C. Collingwood (1828) *A selection from the public and private correspondence of Vice-Admiral Lord Collingwood: interspersed with memoirs of his life*, London: Ridgway, pp. 107–08; see also G.R. Sloan (1997) *The geopolitics of Anglo-Irish relations in the twentieth century*, London: Leicester University Press, p. 110 *et seq.*

16   H.J. Mackinder (1928) 'The content of philosophical geography' in *The proceedings of the International Geographical Congress, Cambridge, July*, Cambridge: Cambridge University Press.

17 *Ibid.*

18 *Ibid.*

19 *Ibid.*

20 For discussion, see G. Parker (1985) *Western geopolitical thought in the twentieth century,* London: Croom Helm, p. 19. A very useful book. (Mackinder's use of 'England' rather than 'Britain' is revealing.) Reading through Mackinder's later writings, they seem like a profound and deeply thought projection into subsequent history and, though often mistaken in detail, the *longue durée* view they develop is proving true.

21 US Admiral Sims to US Ambassador, 25 June 1917, National Archives, Washington DC, cited in Sloan, *op. cit.,* p. 145.

22 See Sloan, *op. cit.,* for a detailed analysis of this situation.

23 P.S. O'Hegarty (1919) *Ulster: a brief statement,* Dublin: Maunsel, cited in Sloan, *op. cit.,* p. 166.

NINE
Intermezzo: all at sea

Part one

> The limits of my language are the limits of my world.
> — Ludwig Wittgenstein

From pitch, through rat, to oyster. These are the colours off the bow, through which the packet is emerging into day. Howth is a dark bulging and darkness behind, but in front is pearl for dawn and brown, navy and russet for shoulders crouched against the gunwale. Holystoned teak for the deck, tar for the sheets and a salty sewer air from the outgoing tide. The boat smells of many people in a little room, of a stove being raked for the day and of coal. Every now and then a burst of metallic steam and heated iron though the sails bangs in the uncertain breeze that comes just before dawn.

They have pressed themselves down low out of the wind.

Her cloak is a greyish blue with a round bonnet hood and she looks out of it with a weary lack of expectation, seeing only within herself, backward. He has a heavy loden coat buttoned tightly up to the neck and a dark slouch hat that shadows his scowling and resentful face. Their right hands are clasped. His left is stuffed protectively within the fold of his coat but hers, just visible, holds tiny fingers. There is a little child in there, cocooned against her bosom.

At a time when the world is being resettled, when more are on the move than at any time for millennia, when whole populations have been decamping from countryside to town (yet again), and when exile, flight, docks and departure lounges are the common locations of humankind, I think again of my maternal grandfather and his parents.

Seeking to escape the miserable conditions of the west, they left Mayo in the 1870s and settled in West Yorkshire, arriving by way of Liverpool and unknown points between. The census of 1881 identifies a Peter Brett, aged 34, a tailor, of Leeds Old Road, Heckmondwike, his wife Mary and the children, the first three of whom were born in Ireland. My grandfather, however, was born in Heckmondwike along with four more children. In a later census, George Brett (then perhaps 14) was recorded as a wool worker, but his two elder brothers were respectively a coal miner and a tailor. His big sister Ann was a wool weaver. The four little girls are all listed as 'scholars'. Peter Brett, as a tailor, was not one of the huddled masses of folk memory, not a refugee from famine or absolute poverty, but a skilled man, possibly of some education. This he may have passed forward to his children. At all events, and in ways unknown to me, George acquired an idiosyncratic and wide education and in time became a figure in local labour politics, as a man who could organise the Irish vote. Despite being vehemently anti-clerical in private life he maintained for his own pleasure and political work an Irish identity (to use a current phrase) which he treated with irony. His children always regarded themselves as English. (But their father was Irish.)

***

This chapter is premised on the growth of colossal technology and titanic enterprises at the service of global trade. Its general focus will be the shipbuilding that took place around the Irish Sea and the canals that expanded it. The interconnections between the several sites involved permit me to treat this enterprise as a single entity existing in a single place — a family of interdependent leviathans with a homeland sea in common.

These huge undertakings were integral to the project we usually call modernisation and are, thereby, enmeshed with the larger existential enquiry that I am sporadically trying to follow — what it means to live and die along these shores. For modernity, being a time-based notion, never stands still; it is not a condition but a process in perpetual motion that eats up its own past and continually redetermines the experience of those who undergo it. It is characterised by the absence of norms:

> Modernity can and will no longer borrow the criteria by which it takes its orientation from the models supplied by another epoch; *it has to create its normativity out of itself.*[1]

This was as true in 1870 as it was in the years 1000 and 2000. The recurrent overthrowing of the norms of settled life, which is the inward content of every historical change, have common consequences. But, of course, in this case we are dealing with that particular spasm of modernisation which, more than anything else, formed contemporary life. I mean by this the shock of primary industrialisation. The shock and immiseration which this uprooting entails comprises not only physical difficulty but also a more lasting psychic dislocation. It acts as a vast caesura, severing one kind of past — ancient, customary and, in retrospect, unchanging — from the conditions of the present. Industry enforces upon its workforce a distinct and articulated sense of time and a discipline of mind significantly distinct from rural occupation. I think it cannot be stressed too strongly that, within the numerous benefits of modernisation, which include freedom from expected pain and freedom from accustomed hunger, is the experience of a wound inflicted. There are no willing peasants, but neither are there willing migrants. The sense that you have been driven out, by malevolence or mere circumstance, leaves a lasting scar, which in migrant communities which have not flourished may last for centuries and flourish in its own terms as ethnic trauma.

The wound is felt in all aspects of customary life, from diet to language, because it is exactly the customs of men and women that are both the object and subject of change. But perhaps it is the loss of language that most marks the patients of these actions in its passing.

**

I have no recollection of my grandfather showing any interest in the speech of his parents, which must, without a shadow of doubt, have included a deal of Irish. This had wholly vanished from his own speech, but there were expressions and rhythms in his English that I now recognise as, in a very general sense, Irish, without his having any clear Irish accent. He enjoyed loquacity in himself and others as a display of character. He was not shy of speaking in public, nor of singing, which he did in a tuneful light tenor voice. His repertoire was chiefly of music-hall songs learnt in youth

Illustration 1.
George Brett.

and other more formal parlour songs by Thomas Moore and others. To these he added an English repertoire, such as Charles Dibdin's 'Tom Bowling', which he could perform very affectingly.

All these entertaining aspects of his character were perceived by himself and his family as representing something Irish, refracted into present time by irony. He knew he was playing a part, but one that was also something authentic. Some years ago my brother unearthed a Dictaphone recording of his voice and we heard the words of an elderly man confronted with a recorder for the first time in his life. He chooses his words very precisely and speaks slowly and carefully in a light, dry voice. I, hearing that voice again for the first time since childhood, was surprised at its self-control. This was not quite the funny, genial grandfather I remembered. This was a voice that he had formed for public occasions, for council meetings and committee rooms. There was a slight strangled tension in the throat. I now think that what I was hearing in his voice and witnessing in his carefully modified sociability was the persistence into a later generation of earlier language loss. I have heard this before in the throat of those who have to pretend to something. And it has often seemed to me, writing this book, that I am perpetuating this pretension, this claim, as an act of piety towards my forebears.

***

Broderick, in his study of the Manx language and 'language death' which I have already cited, lists the multiple interactions that must take place as a language 'decays' and finally 'dies' (or seems to die).[2] This distinguishes between the different categories within which the phenomenon can be studied and the different stages through which a language passes on its way to 'death'. Thus under 'external setting' we must note the salient historical conditions such as invasions and the impositions of foreign rule, and having to use another language for legal purposes. Successive historical conditions induce successive negative attitudes towards the threatened language.

The imposition of a foreign language for legal purposes can be caught on the wing in the several proclamations of Scottish and English rulers who attempted to enforce their ways of speech upon the late-medieval Gaeltacht. The outstanding example of this is contained in Henry VIII's Acts of Union (1536) between his Welsh and English kingdoms, which paid close attention to the issue of the language of the newly unified state. Persistence in speaking Welsh was identified as a source of discord and even as subversive:

> Because that the people of the same Dominion have and do daily use a Speech nothing like, nor consonant to the natural Mother Tongue used within this Realm, some rude and ignorant people have made Distinction and Diversity between the King's Subjects

of this Realm and his subjects of the same Dominion and Principality of Wales, whereby great Discord, Variance, Debate, Division, Murmur and Sedition hath grown between his said subjects.[3]

It followed that the use of Welsh in official matters was, in effect, banished from the law courts of the land, making it impossible for the monoglot Welsh speaker to hold office. An English-speaking Welsh educated class was specially fostered by the grammar schools that were founded in the Tudor period all over Wales. The result of this, foreseen and planned, was that ambitious young Welshmen came to develop a degree of negative attitude towards the Welsh language, or saved it for domestic use, which easily shaded off into the realm of children and servants. (We note that the Tudor family staff were Welsh speakers, even in Elizabeth's day. Elizabeth's nurse, and later librarian, Blanche Parry, was a Welsh speaker, as was Thomas Parry, her kinsman, Elizabeth's business manager and 'fixer' in the first years of her reign. Presumably Elizabeth herself spoke some Welsh, though I do not think it is listed among her known linguistic accomplishments.)

The legal use of the phrase 'natural Mother Tongue' directs us towards the gender considerations of language and language learning — indeed, towards the most profound existential entailment of this kind of language legislation. Mothers, grandmothers and nurses, as the 'transmission belt' of customs, have always carried languages forward and so we should see legislation of this kind as being gender directed. The effect of the grammar-school curriculum, reinforced by boarding pupils away from the family, always was and still is to break up linguistic continuity. This remains the primary function of that style of teaching known in England as a public-school education. Linguistic and other patterns of authority are displaced from the family and the kin onto the new institution and the institutions behind them. It is a stage in the creation and constant renewal of a new class with new language habits, loyal not to kin but to the guiding institutions.

Broderick's list concludes the category of 'external setting' with a bald 'decision to abandon Manx'.[4] He delivers a summary description of what was and is an extremely drawn-out and complicated process, full of distress and misunderstanding. We can witness it daily today in the families of Urdu-speaking and other immigrants, within which language use is a nexus of deep conflict between generations and genders because it touches on every facet of life and culture.

Nationalist historians have commented at length on Henry's legislation of 1536 and later and describe it as cultural imperialism. This is so obvious as to say nothing. And I wonder what the Picts might have said about the enforcement of Gaelic. However, a more dispassionate approach points out that Welsh gentry were already voting with their tongues, and bilingualism was widespread, even normal, among the educated. The Tudor assimilation of Wales into England was not seriously nor steadfastly opposed, partly because the Welsh saw the Tudors, with some truth, as Welsh. Conversely, English speakers in England viewed Welsh speakers with a mixture of condescension, humour and contempt, but not as seriously threatening. (The key document for this is *Henry IV, Part 1*, in which Shakespeare demonstrates all three.)

The same was not true of Gaelic Ireland, to which Henry attempted to apply the same sort of legislation. The terms in which the 1537 acts 'for English Order, Habit and Language' are framed for Irish use are noticeably more aggressive:

> There is nothing which doth more conteyne and keep many of his Subjects of the said Land in a certain savage and wild kinde and manner of living, than the diversities that is betwixt them in Tongue, Language, Order and Habit.[5]

Ireland was, in imagination and in fact, a serious threat to the Tudor polity and the wording above seems to imply that the 'diversities' were as much within Gaelic as between Gaelic and English.

Just when and by what steps the government of Scotland came to be conducted in Scots/English is not clear. There was certainly a sixteenth-century dispute as to what they should be calling the language of the court. To some it was 'Scots', to others 'Inglis'. Gavin Douglas is credited as the first Scot to refer to his language as Scots as opposed to Inglis or to the Scots Gaelic that was still widely used (depending on where you were living and who you were). What is more significant is that Scottish writers and law drafters (writing in Scots/Inglis) began, in the fifteenth century, to refer to Scots Gaelic as Irish and to describe its use as a mark of barbarity. This was little to do directly with the supposed influence of English because the use of Inglis was being directly sanctioned by the Bruce kings as part of their national project. John Barbour, writing his epic account of the Wars of Independence around 1360, used an amazingly direct and passionate Inglis that I have no difficulty in following. It is easier than Chaucer to read but, of course, much harder to read aloud without affectation, because the stresses do not fall where expected and the rhyme and assonance schemes are sometimes hard to grasp.

For the non-technical student such as myself, the distinction between the read language and the spoken language is much more than formal. Speaking is a performative act that involves the body and the breath. That is to say, in the terms I have been using, it is lived rather than known. Not having much fluency with the sound of Scots I find that I have to read passages several times over in order to get the swing of it. And that swing, that inner impulsion or kinetic, is at the heart of each language. I incline towards the non-technical distinction — that the *spoken* Inglis of the fourteenth century is a different language from English, but that its conventions of script, typography and lineation, and the practice of silent *reading*, render the two tongues increasingly more similar (though not, of course, identical).

Durkacz argues that the Scottish attempt to extirpate Gaelic was bound up with religious reformation and the kind of education that was deemed suitable for the new dispensation. One aim of the setting up of parochial schools in 1616 was:

> that the vulgar Inglishe toung be universally plantit, and the Irishe language, whilk is one of the cheif and principall causis of the continewance of barbarity and incivilite amongis the inhabitants of the Ilis and Heylandis, may be abolisheit and removeit.[6]

Against this we remind ourselves that James IV, a hundred years earlier and prior to the Reformation, was the last Scottish king to have spoken Gaelic and that his military campaigns against the lords of the Isles were continued by James VI as part of the general extension of metropolitan rule also clearly visible south of the border. The written instruments of metropolitan rule were conceived and published in Inglis (of which the *Declaration of Arbroath* is the most obvious and probably best written). This predates the Reformation. Also, Henry VIII's legislation in Wales and Ireland also (just) predates the English Reformation and the use of English in the liturgy. Both the religious reformation and edicts on language must be seen, in Henry's case, as the marrow of his larger project — the extension of royal and state power.

In addition, it seems to this writer that the claims of linguistic nationalists seriously overestimate the power of states to enter the larynges of their subjects and they perceive these attempts at regulation as being more ruthlessly applied than in fact they ever could be. They repeat (with suspicious alacrity) many folktales and myths of the suppression of popular speech. A short but telling summary of this pseudohistorical grudge has been made for us by Malcolm Chapman, who analyses the claims of:

> many writers who have persuaded themselves, and attempted to persuade others, that the decline of the Celtic languages has been due to the systematic persecution and oppression of those who spoke them.[7]

He cites as a particular example the hoary old tale about Hebridean children who spoke a single word of Gaelic being ritually thrashed at the end of the day; he then shows that this is the product of the systematic repetition of a single piece of hearsay. The same story was being repeated in the Isle of Man quite independently a hundred years later.[8]

Similar tales are told everywhere, all around the world. They are the equivalent of the stories that are repeated during or after every war, which alter mainly by means of the available technology of atrocity. (Thus the premature babies in Kuwaiti hospitals were said to have had their life-support systems vandalised by the brutish Iraqi troops; in another era they would merely have been impaled.) But as Durkacz shows, the decline of languages is slow, multi-causal, very complicated and includes, as a major factor, the enthusiasm of speakers to lose one language in order to gain another for their obvious advantage. This is rational, unsentimental behaviour and to be commended; regret and nostalgia are for others to enjoy.[9]

I take my great grandfather, braced against the gunwale of the Liverpool ferry, to be one of these mobile individuals. He may very well have taken the 'decision to abandon Irish' out of canny self-interest, without regret.

However, there is a difference between what actually happens and how it is remembered. These are not actual contradictions but discontinuities of explanation, which occur when different modes of experience and cognition deal with the same matter. They do not translate directly. What is fact in these circumstances is not as clear as it should be because the different accounts use different languages of description. In the language of positive fact we can decide meaningfully that no, or few, or many Hebridean dominies thrashed their Gaelic-speaking pupils; in the language of memory (which centres upon symbolic rather than factual experience) it felt like a universal thrashing, as does any compulsory education. The purpose of an education system is to alter people, whether they like it or not. However, people can and do resist. Successive Irish ministers of education have been frustrated in their demand for compulsory Irish by the obtuse refusal of their fellow countrymen to learn it or, having learned, to remember or speak it. In the 2002 Irish census I understand that some 42 per cent of the population claimed to be able to speak some Irish, but this is hardly borne out by actual practice. This, however, says less than it seems to because it is undoubtedly the case that there is a revival of Irish as a language of literature, with a body of poetry being written that is not neo-traditional, but authentically contemporary and vigorous.[10] Moreover, the use of Irish has once again acquired, in the north, a political dimension.

Many years ago, during periods of residence in Hungary, I became steadily more and more aware that although Russian was taught as a major and compulsory part of the school curriculum, very few people either could or would speak it. Instead, a modest level of German and English was commonly understood, though hardly taught at all in early schooling. The issue here is that of compulsion. Men and women will happily abandon one language for another if it is in their interests and done freely and relegate the first language to what they take to be lesser or more intimate purposes, but they will resist, stubbornly and intelligently, attempts to enforce a language on them. And it is natural that this should be so, since if (as the philosopher avers) the limits of your language are the limits of your world, then it is another world that is being enforced upon you. Every language and, to a degree, every idiom or dialect is a unique way of construing reality. It is knowable reality that is being altered as speech is altered.

And this is still the case. A woman in her middle years, recalling her schooldays, still remembers the stress of having to lose her Cockney accent and only separates that particular stress from the wider dislocation of having to learn to negotiate changing class and status with difficulty. Both involved kinds and degrees of bullying and the stress remains in the throat as a tightness and an anxious concern with vocabulary. With this went the demand to extirpate regional accents, which was very strong in early twentieth-century English schools, as part of what was then perceived to be modernisation (the so-called 'BBC accent' was partly a consequence of the available recording and broadcasting equipment). One consequence of 'correctness' is to make many educated contemporary English men and women sound as it they had learnt English as a foreign language. And how many of them can sing?

In another and more scholarly book it would be valuable to compare the altering fate of Gaelic with that of Welsh. When as a child I spent summer holidays in Lleyn or beside St David's Head I always understood the use of Welsh to be a quaint survival — that it was, in a real sense, something dying. No one could think that today, when Welsh has, for whatever reasons, made a great recovery. One now hears, lying by the side of the road or buying provisions in a village shop or supermarket, the language used by everyone at every age — not universally, but commonly and un-self-consciously.

When a defunct language is recovered (as with Manx) it is usually as part of a largely spurious claim to identity. What is called by some people 'identity politics' seems to this author to be largely (though not always) an inauthentic claim to difference in the face of real growing similarity. This is what it is to be modernised — to be forever inventing pasts.[11] But we cannot see into the future and it is possible that, within time, Manx will pass beyond the merely self-conscious and *voulu* condition within which it presently lives to gain a measure of customary use in some sections of life, for some authentic purposes.

What, in the terms of this book, we need to understand is the persistence, the stubborn and successful persistence, of the older languages of the Islands in the face of the claims of English to advantage, status and *force majeure*. These languages are not dead, nor dying, nor yet sleeping, like Arthur within his mountain. They are, in fact, waking up — slightly dazed, it may be, but manifestly alive.

Our speech is an echo chamber that perpetuates and propagates vibrations with such pertinacity that we no longer recognise the sounds from which it sprang. The sounds of contemporary spoken English vibrate with myriad origins and myriad decays, and with the pain of loss.

**

Part two: The Titanic Quarter: a view from the Dargan Alps

In their haste to present Belfast to the world as a desirable venue for tourism, loft living and light industry, now freed from the blight of civil conflict and fit to take its place beside the other cities of Europe, the corporation of Belfast has designated the former site of its great shipyards as the Titanic Quarter. The city authorities have an unhappy habit of naming significant sites and historic objects after people or objects that came to a bad end. The two great mobile cranes that once prowled up and down Queen's Island are universally known as Samson and Goliath. The city airport, which also occupies reclaimed, foggy land, is now named after a notorious drunkard because (say the wits) it is always blocked.

The quarter is, in fact, a former island created around 1840 by the mud dug out of the River Lagan in an exercise of deepening and straightening. The island was first called Dargan's Island, after William Dargan, a great digger of holes and channels and later of railways. The island was first used as a pleasure ground for the citizens, with exhibits and amusements of several kinds, improving and otherwise. It then became, in an effort of public dignification, the Queen's Island. Finally, owing to its position outside the centre of town, it became a space for unlimited industrial expansion.

All that remains of that industry today is a few vast sheds and an immense hole in the ground, like an inverted ziggurat. This is the Titanic dock, womb of great liners. There is also a mountain range of scrap iron, sometimes referred to as the Dargan Alps. This cordillera of decay consists of cut-outs, blanks and sawn-off ends from ships of all kinds, from drilling rigs, from bridges and from every kind of steel fabrication, now rendered into small-size chunks and steadily dissolving into ochreous rubble. It is a melancholy zone whose emblem is the rusty bucket.

Illustration 2. The Dargan Alps.

Illustration 3.
The Titanic dock.

But prior to this decay was the decay of the canal system that once fed these docks, these basins and these channels. Dargan's digging, which brought the ships of the ocean directly into the streets of Belfast and built up his eponymous island, was one with another enterprise. This one connected Belfast Lough southward with the fjord of Carlingford Lough and westward into the freshwater plains of Lough Neagh and finally into the Shannon. These works need to be considered together with the basins and the docks, since all are extensions of the waterways and the enlargement of the Irish Sea. They also provide good cycling paths.

***

A scheme for a Newry–Lough Neagh canal was first conceived by General Monck in 1641, who was well acquainted with the low countries and the Dutch way of working with water. However, the plan lapsed for many years until revived by a group of landowners with a view to exporting coal from Dungannon to Dublin. A survey was made in 1703 but it was not until 1742 that the canal began to function. The original designer of the undertaking was a Richard Castles or Cassells, a Huguenot architect refugee who set out the initial plans and started work in 1731. The work was completed by Thomas Steers, who had earlier been engaged in dock construction in Liverpool and, like most of these civil engineers, had learnt his trade as an army officer.

Once in operation the canal quickly acquired, and encouraged, further functions. Linen mills around Lisburn and in the lower valley of the Bann supplied many cargoes. Substantial warehouses in country farmyards suggest the development of a grain trade.

One scholar has written:

> It is hard to think of another part of Ireland where the course of economic change can be tracked with such clarity from so early a date or where the changes wrought were so dramatic.[12]

An early industrial corridor began to develop, but for this expansion to work well the outlet to the sea had to be deepened and canalised further downstream to Warrenpoint. Docks were built in the middle of Newry. Pleasure and passenger boats began to cruise the waters of the canal. This in turn helped Newry to become a flourishing little passenger port with regular sailings to Glasgow and Liverpool; passengers could take ship again as they landed and sail up the canal as far as Portadown.

A route had been already prepared for them in post-glacial times, when a vast outflow, running south from what was the precursor of Lough Neagh, had gouged a channel southward into Carlingford Lough. When the river departed, turned north and became the Bann it left a long marshy defile known as the Glynn Bog. In wet weather there is still a more or less continual flood from Portadown to Newry, which in the days before drainage was an effective frontier. On the eastern shore, as you cycle southward towards Newry, you pass long traces of the Dane's Cast, an Iron-Age fortified line that once defended this easterly half of Ulster from all the rest. This dyke has nothing whatever to do with any Danes, but seems to come from those times of conflict when Gaelic-speaking war-bands may have been pushing those 'proto-Celts', the Picts or Cruithin, northward into Scotland — if they ever did.

***

The sea expands: a photo-essay

Travelling inland from the sea, the canal reaches the centre of the town in a series of substantial basins. The first, the Albert Dock, was in time built large enough to take passenger steamers for Glasgow and Liverpool, and the inner basins can easily take two substantial canal boats side by side. To judge by the size of the inland locks along the canal, these boats cannot have been large, but according to some reports they were seaworthy enough to pass from inland waterways directly to the saltways and so continued south to Dublin without offloading.

Illustration 4. The Albert Dock, Newry. Today a sequence of substantial warehouses is being replaced by hotels and malls, but some fine buildings remain.

Illustration 5. The last of the warehouses of Newry.

Illustration 6. The gateway to the compound, Newry, with spinning wheel and regalia.

Illustration 7. The Newry Canal at Jerretspass.

From being a small but effective port and market, Newry has declined to being a frontier town with an economy heavily dependent on changing rates of tolls and taxes. At present its prosperity counts on large quantities of goods going south of the border, purchased by day-trippers coming up from the republic to take advantage of lower prices; but this can change in a moment. All significant seaborne traffic now goes through the container terminal of Warrenpoint, five miles away at the head of Carlingford Lough. No trace now remains of the coal trade for which the canal was built and, just beyond the centre of the town, a handsome stone gateway in the middle of a housing estate is all that is left of a large compound that once housed the linen hall and, like a cantonment of the Raj, a barracks.

Beyond the limits of the town the canal is now merely picturesque. The towpath provides a cycle track that wanders past willow-fringed pools and lock-keepers' cottages. There are couth abutments of granite, old flumes and leats, and some shapely stone bridges. Here and there are large grain warehouses from the early nineteenth century.

You can follow this pleasant way as far as Belfast by taking the Lagan Canal towpath from Lough Neagh eastward into the outskirts of the town, where river and channel together touch sea level in a quiet reach.

Illustration 8. Canal and river: Lagan Meadows, Belfast.

***

The early success of the Newry Canal encouraged the building of the Lagan Canal, from Belfast to Lough Neagh, for much the same purposes. Work began on this waterway in 1756, though with 42 locks the undertaking was slow and costly. Both these labours preceded the famous Bridgewater Canal (opened in 1763) by several years. The hydrology of Ireland lends itself to travel by water, for large rivers connect and reconnect with large lakes and there is never any shortage of supply. Much later, a further canal wound through what are now the borderlands of Monaghan to join the River Shannon. Just before the Newry Canal, the Mersey and Irwell Navigation was opened (in 1730) to connect Liverpool to Manchester. In this way the Irish Sea began to extend itself into the central plains of both Ireland and England, bringing with it a distinctive architecture and a grandiose style of civil engineering.

Ambitious schemes to connect Dublin and the Irish Sea with the River Shannon were under discussion as early as 1715, but adequate finance could not be raised privately and so the task of commissioning the work fell to a government office. Work finally began in 1757. The slow completion of these plans, in the form of the Grand Canal and the rival Royal Canal further north, was an epic of burst banks and lawsuits.[13] However, by 1786 there was a cut right through to the River Barrow in the westerly direction, thence towards Waterford on the south coast and back easterly to a custom-made dock area at Ringsend, Dublin, large enough to hold 150 vessels, and to a similar dock area on the northern bank of the Liffey, served by the Royal Canal. The connection with the Shannon was ready to take cargoes in 1805. Goods could now pass, with little interruption, from Limerick to London and back from the North Sea to the Atlantic, over land.

Illustration 9. The Royal Canal as it is today. I went to scout out the point at which the canal debouches into the Liffey, not far from the great Custom-House building. Alas, I could only find it at the bottom of a deep hole, being either fed or drained by pipes and pumps. It is in the process of disappearing under yet another inner-city development.

Illustration 10. The Grand Canal, however, provides an enjoyable swathe of greenery and still water as it cuts its useless way through the city, south of the river.

The early trade of the canal system consisted mainly of building materials such as bricks, slates, lime and turf into Dublin, and of horse dung and imported goods outward. A subsidiary function was to supply Dublin with water. However, foodstuffs and particularly grain goods became a major cargo within a few years.

With this went an architecture of noble plainness, made of massive beams of laminated oak and, above all, brick reinforced with iron. What the canals (and later the railways) propagated was a uniform and industrially produced building material — the common standardised brick. It was not, of course, a material new to the Irish Sea but, until the advent of canal transport, brick manufacture was perforce local. It was a regular custom in districts such as London, Dublin and Belfast to build a house out of the clay dug up when its foundations were excavated, firing them more or less on the spot. But it was now possible to load a barge and to ballast a boat so that bricks, made to a common mould and fired to identical hardness, could be made in Stoke, to be used in Liverpool and beyond. The longer-term result of the standardisation of building was to make the uniformity of modern brickwork visible and hence, before very long, problematic. By 1850, the issue of uniform and identical production had begun to create an equal and opposite reaction in the form of a reconsideration of the handmade and local character. It is not too much to say that the issue of artistic brickwork became an issue between radical and conservative ideologies. In the meantime, a uniform building type had begun to imprint itself upon the grain of cities all around the Islands: the brick terrace which was the uniform and ubiquitous housing of the canal and railway companies set the pattern for the next 200 years.

The canals of central Ireland, centring on Dublin's docks, increased trade exponentially. In 1810 over 200,000 tons of food and building materials were moved into Dublin. Something of the scale of the canal business can be seen at Tullamore, which became an inland port, with basins, docks, granaries and warehouses on a maritime scale, set in a rural landscape.

***

The other export of central Ireland was its people. In times of mass migration from the country to the town, the passage boats that provided a convenient system of public transport before railways became the scenes of rioting and mass gatherings. In April 1834 one contractor, writing of the Royal Canal, described how his barge was boarded by an 'immense mob':

> Notwithstanding that the soldiers and police had their bayonets to the common people, they found their way thro' the lines formed and literally dashed their luggage down on the boat when little better than half raised in the lock, and leaped on board in numbers after it, they then forced the boat out of the lock.[14]

Such scenes were already commonplace before the migrations of the famine years.[15]

The very existence of a large workforce was a cause of rural instability. The Irish canals were held to ransom by wreckers who broke the locks in order to obtain more work in the mending of them. Rural secret societies compelled the canal contractors to pay protection money. The condition of the countryside became that of a developing nation in which development had to be secured by armed force while the population rushed in on the capital city, unstoppably.

The common people of central Ireland, having forced their way onto the canal boats, found their way before long beyond Dublin into Liverpool, where thousands of them became the labour force that enabled the expansion of the system that had brought them there in the first place, by enrolling in the armies of 'navigators' who were at that very time (1830s) expanding the Shannon into the Trent. The simultaneous outflow of population spread before long far beyond the confines of the Irish Sea. Indeed, from the perspective of trade and manufacture, the Mersey ports were in a Siamese relationship with Dublin. They shared the same life-support system and suffered the same insecurities. Looked at in a larger view, Dublin stood in relation to the hinterland of central Ireland as Liverpool to the English midlands; the Irish Sea was merely an adventitious interruption to the making of profits and the movement of goods. The extension on one side of the Irish Sea was a mirror image of that on the other side. The canal network centring on the two cities extended the effective boundaries of Irish-Sea trade to oceanic parameters.

***

An element in this was the progressive closure of the port facilities of Chester. The ancient Roman and medieval harbour had been well served by an extensive anchorage known as the Hoyle Lake, which provided safety for coastal vessels until the seventeenth century. What is now Hilbre Island was then part of a long spit of sand extending over towards the Welsh coast. But such is the nature of the coastline hereabouts, largely composed of dunes, that nothing is very stable. Birkenhead Docks are aligned along a former channel of the Mersey and the entire area has reconfigured itself several times.[16] Hilbre continued to be joined to the Wirral at least until 1575, as shown on a map of Cheshire of that date. The *Theatrum orbis terrarum* also shows it joined. Another atlas, published in 1636, shows Hilbre detached. The Hoyle Lake was no more. To save their port status the burghers of Chester put immense efforts into dredging and into clearing channels. Several sites along the shores of the Wirral were used for quays and warehouses, all going further and further downstream from the town, seeking the open water that was withdrawing itself. In some of the early maps the Wirral is drawn as an island with a channel connecting the two estuaries, along the line of the Shropshire Union Canal and the little River Gowy, but, while quite credible from the topology of the area, I think there is no actual evidence for it. The Isle of Wirral is one of those ghosts that enter the records whimsically and then gather substance as they are copied repeatedly. It persisted on Dutch charts into the eighteenth century.

Liverpool first comes to notice in 1206, when King John was preparing an army to go to Ireland. He took over a stretch of shoreline where a quay of some kind already existed and made it his supply base. It is quite possible that he chose Liverpool because he had a feud with the earl of Chester and needed a secure rear.[17] A small town grew up around the base, to which John gave a borough charter in 1209. Liverpool then became a military port for Edward I, who used it to supply his campaigns in north Wales. Vessels from Liverpool took timber to Caernarfon for use in the building of the castle. The *bastides* that he founded around the castles of Conwy, Caernarfon and Harlech, and later at Beaumaris, were largely peopled from south Lancashire.[18]

By 1565 the mayor of Liverpool was able to claim that 'Liverpole hath ever heretofore byn reputed and takyne for the best porte and herbar from Mylforthe to Scotland'. Nevertheless, the burghers of Liverpool were still playing second fiddle to Chester as late as 1600, when they complained to the Privy Council that they were still required to send their ships to Ireland by way of Hilbre. That year there were 64 vessels embarking troops and provisions in the Hoyle Lake for use against the O'Neill rebellion. It was not until 1626 that Chester was overtaken, as shown by the shipping returns taken in by the government. The old town had but 15 vessels to the 24 sailing out of Liverpool, and most of these were in fact sailing from other ports.

***

The new canal system led inevitably to the Mersey. The Shropshire Union Canal, though visiting Chester, opened to the sea at Ellesmere Port (in 1795). Here it met up with the greater English canals, notably the Trent and Mersey Canal, which was begun in 1776 and took more than ten years to complete. This crosses England from one side to another, as does the Leeds and Liverpool Canal, begun in 1770. These in turn connect and interconnect by way of locks, aqueducts, tunnels and even lifts and swinglocks, with scores of other smaller canals and deepened rivers, to make the unique industrial landscape of south Lancashire. The very first wet dock in the world was created on the Liverpool waterfront, designed in 1709 and completed in 1719, principally by Thomas Steers, who went on to complete the Newry Canal. This was a remarkable feat for the times, requiring deep piling in very soft mud. What was also created was an architectural world of docksides, inland ports and quays, of facilities, channels, reservoirs and underground workshops of a prodigious kind. The vast arches and tunnels in central Manchester and Leeds stand beside the Albert docks in Liverpool as the only buildings connected to the Irish Sea that can rival the castles of Edward I.

Illustration 11. Albert docks, Liverpool.

The tidal conditions of the Mersey encouraged, and in fact required, civil engineering on a heroic scale. The reach of tides was and is very great and the currents are fast. Until enclosed docks were built the loading and unloading of large vessels was difficult and even dangerous.

Construction on the Lancashire shore expanded in tandem with the expansion of the canals. Thus, from the original city dock of 1719, now vanished under streets, there was a succession of still-surviving docks, such as Coburg and Salthouse (both 1753), King's (1783), Queen's (1786) and Prince's (1821) and some six miles of continuous enclosed basins from Herculaneum (1864) in the south to Seaforth (1972) in the north. These were all linked like a chain by a continuous wide street and finally by an overhead railway. Each separate dock had its particular rail link. The resulting chaos of road, rail and water was, and still remains, astonishing in its complexity and ugliness.

It was into this tumult that Peter Brett, at the age of 33, with his wife, Mary, and three children, disembarked some time in 1879. In that year something like 15 per cent of the population of Liverpool had been born in Ireland and a very large Irish community had become well established. Most of this population had been born in Liverpool to the post-famine immigrants (who had seen the Irish-born population of the city rise to 22 per cent in 1851). A census of church attendance in the same year showed that 32.5 per cent of the population attended Catholic services, but a family tradition had it that Peter, like his son George, was vehemently anti-clerical, so he may not have been among them. A good number of these Irish immigrants were by no means the stereotypical Irish Catholic convivial crowd of popular English myth and joke culture, but vehement Orangemen (or, in my family's case, free thinkers) who had brought their anti-Catholicism with them and made it a notable part of local politics.[19] It would be my guess, although it is unsupported by evidence, that Peter Brett had family or friends preceding him in the West Riding of Yorkshire and, conceivably, a job already arranged, since Heckmondwike was a centre of the clothing industry and the heavy woollen trade and numerous Irish immigrants had already settled there.

***

It seems to have been Thomas Steers, in 1712, who was the first to suggest that a waterway could be constructed for sea-going vessels by combining the Mersey and the Irwell as far upstream as Manchester and that a further enlargement of rivers into Lancashire and Cheshire could be undertaken. This enterprise required an act of parliament, so it was not until 1734 that a ship could make the awkward journey through winding rivers and mudbanks as far as the Salford docks. This journey required eight locks and was usually travelled by a particular kind of barge known as a Mersey Flat — 12 feet across the beam but up to 60 feet in length, driven by a large and usually red sail. Though designed exactly to fit the lock sizes, Mersey Flats were still capable of coastal voyages. By 1826 this standard size had been much enlarged along with an enlarged lock size to an 18-foot beam. The whole enterprise was one that assumed the passage of sea-going vessels from the very start and, like Steers's plan for the Newry Canal, it presupposed a minimal handling time. We should perhaps honour Thomas Steers as a pioneer of the land-and-sea container trade. Nevertheless, the engineering was never quite up to the expectations of the design. Floods and awkward tides and winds could hold the traffic up for days, and for efficiency it was overtaken by the Bridgewater Canal from 1776.[20]

The real value of these or any waterways was that they avoided a reliance on the horse and cart across the miserable swamps and bogs of south Lancashire (the main Liverpool–Manchester road was known, until the 1960s, as 'the drain'). The two canals vied with one another for business and the consequent improvement turned the Mersey/Irwell/Weaver Estuary into a maze of channels and waterways, some crossing over others on aqueducts, while rivers were made to flow beneath them in culverts and siphons. A passenger could, by changing boats, go to almost anywhere in the region by water. George Head's *Home tour through the manufacturing districts of England in the summer of 1835* gives a vivid picture of a passage from 'continuous panoramas of cows, cottages and green fields into ... water as black as Styx and absolutely pestiferous from the gas and refuse of the manufacturers'.[21]

Both canals managed to survive the arrival of railways because the sheer quantity of bulk cargoes (of grain, cotton and flax), which were not dependent on time, ensured continuity of business. In the midst of the railway boom of the 1830s still larger aquatic schemes were proposed. These aimed at cutting out Liverpool altogether, making Manchester a true seaport. In 1825 one was planned to cross the Wirral and run into the Dee Estuary and would have accommodated 400-ton vessels capable of sailing the Atlantic. The backers of this scheme believed that it would soon pay for itself by saving dock dues otherwise payable in Liverpool. Not surprisingly, it ran into fierce opposition. In 1840, a far more practical scheme would have sailed up the Mersey River by a series of dams, lakes, weirs and connecting locks. This became the basis for several more rival schemes in the next decades, none of which passed political scrutiny. Among the cargoes of the period are listed potatoes from Ireland arriving on boats from Dublin, which sailed into Manchester and returned carrying coal.

By 1884 a scheme had evolved that envisaged a radical redesign of the estuary to provide a direct approach to Manchester, almost without locks, now to be named the Manchester Ship Canal. This was, as might be expected, opposed in parliament by the Liverpool Dock Board and other powerful interests — including the original canal's owners, who reckoned it would improve the asking price for their companies, which would have to be purchased to enable the final scheme to go ahead. At this point we leave the Irish Sea and enter the far more treacherous waters of parliamentary committees. The resultant ten-year struggle to raise the millions of pounds now required would have burst the blood vessels of a saint along with the banks and culverts.

Much of 1889 and 1890 was lost to floods and collapsing levees:

> the river … began to pour over the bank where a river bend had been cut off … the river, making its own course easier, at last poured into the cutting in such volume that it broke down the protecting bank across the canal and, sweeping down in an immense wave, carried away bridge after bridge, of course using the timbers of the first bridge as battering rams to destroy each succeeding erection.[22]

Nor did it get better the following year. Heavy snowfall, further floods and extreme difficulties were encountered when attempting to connect the Ship Canal to the Bridgewater — two total failures and consequent floods on the first two attempts. However, by 1892 ships were beginning to use the lowest sections where a depot, known as Saltport near Ellesmere, had come into being, shipping in timber from as far away as Mobile, Alabama on the Gulf of Mexico and exporting chemicals from the salt industries of Cheshire. Vessels of up to 4,700 tons were now able to avoid the Liverpool docks. The whole canal was open by 1894 and Manchester became one of the cities of the Irish Sea, linked to it by the largest waterway ever yet constructed (including the Suez Canal and those on the lower Rhine).

**

As Merseyside stood in relation to Dublin and central Ireland, so Clydeside stood in relation to Ulster and the highlands and Hebrides. In both cases it makes good sense to consider the great conurbations of Liverpool, Glasgow and Belfast not as being Scottish, English or Irish, but as the three great products of the Irish Sea, which were symbiotically linked by the joint enterprises of canals, ships and heavy industry. This was exactly the point made by Edward Carson when he called shipbuilding in Belfast, on the Clyde and on the Mersey 'one great undivided organisation'.

The great and undivided organisation had, in fact, begun early, when the Belfast Ballast Board, charged with promoting the use of Belfast as an oceanic port, invited William Ritchie of Saltcoats, near Ayr, to open a shipyard at the Auld Lime Kiln Dock (near the foot of what is now Limestone Road, Belfast) in 1791. The first significant cross-channel steamer was the *Rob Roy*, built by the great David Napier to run between Clyde and Lagan in 1818.

Dublin, of course, does not fit so easily into this pattern since it significantly predates the other three as a major port and never acquired the modernised shipbuilding interests that united the trio. But Carson's idea of the 'great undivided organisation', imagined in the furore of Home Rule for Ireland and Ulster's resistance to it, is also a first run at the academic concept of a socio-technological system, which is defined as a social organisation that has developed in interaction with a specific set of technological innovations. This idea, which first emerged in the writings of T.P. Hughes and a critical socially directed history of technology, deals with organisations of very great size that are dependent upon widespread use and immense capital investment.[23]

The socio-technological system that was formed by the combined canals, docks and shipyards of the Irish Sea was riveted together not by simple causation but by mutually reinforcing requirements and a common medium — water. The technical innovations that provided the starting point were all directed towards the control and overmastering of water, tides, currents, floods and weather.

* * *

Shipbuilding, when it came to the Mersey on any scale, was conducted mainly from the Wirral shore, using a succession of enclosed basins. The most significant of these were part of the Cammell Laird empire, which had been created by an amalgamation of Laird's iron foundry, built to exploit local ore deposits, and Charles Cammell's steel mill in Sheffield.

The first boats built by the Cammell Laird yard were steam paddlers for the Irish Inland Steam Navigation Company (from 1829), made to cruise or tug along the new canals and the old lakes of Ireland, but within two years similar or repeated designs of the same ships were to be found from the USA to Egypt, Turkey, China, Poland and Russia and on every river in Latin America. An important part of their trade was with the East India Company, for whom they built armed paddle steamers to patrol the Ganges, the Brahmaputra and the Irrawaddy Rivers. By 1838, the first screw vessel to cross the Atlantic was the *Robert F. Stockton*, and from 1852 most vessels were of screw propulsion.

Cammell Laird built whole fleets for any government that would pay for them — troop ships for the British government, what were called mortar ships (for infantry support) from 1855, and Zambezi gunboats for the Portuguese. A notable case was the *Alabama*, an iron warship for the Confederate forces in the US Civil War. To the *Alabama* we owe one of the great maritime work songs:

> When the *Alabama*'s keel was laid
> (Roll, *Alabama*, roll)
> It was laid in the yard of Jonathan Laird.
> (Oh roll, *Alabama*, roll!)

From the Mersey she sailed forth
(Roll, *Alabama*, roll)
To destroy the commerce of the north.
(Oh roll, *Alabama*, roll!)

The ill-fated *Alabama* was followed by torpedo boats and torpedo-boat destroyers. His majesty's government began commissioning battleships in 1894, submarines in 1915, landing crafts in 1940 and guided-missile cruisers in 1960.

These ships and yards were the sinews and muscles of global empires; the trade went by every kind of merchant vessel but one notices a long line of refrigerated ships for the United Fruit Company and similar concerns (from 1911), oil tankers (from 1945) and what were called nuclear-facility barges from 1966. One of the few shipbuilding archives to survive, the Cammell Laird Archive, is simultaneously a document of technology, of empire, of warfare and of global trade. Its last entry is for 1993, with the launch of HMS *Unicorn*, a nuclear submarine.

The last shard of this remarkable company can be found, suitably enough, running the naval dockyards at Gibraltar.

***

In Scotland, canals were built not to expand trade within the country by making the interior more accessible for heavy cargoes, but to make it possible to link different parts of the ocean. The Caledonian Canal was built to shorten the sea journey around Cape Wrath. The Crinan Canal made it possible to avoid equally unpleasant waters on the intricate and rocky Lorne coast; and the purpose of the Forth and Clyde Canal, which opened in 1775, was to link the North Sea with the Irish Sea through the narrow waist of central Scotland. It fed into the Clyde on the north shore, well south of Glasgow and the shipyards of Clydeside, and its initial purpose was to enable Scandinavian timber to reach the shipyards at Greenock.

The canal was designed and executed by James Smeaton, one of the most clever and daring civil engineers of his day, whose other great achievement was the completion of the Eddystone Lighthouse.

It was now a simple matter to float timber downstream to the timber ponds of Port Glasgow and thence downstream to Greenock. However, the change from building with wood to iron building and then to steel was immensely to the advantage of the upstream Clydeside yards, since both coal and iron were available more or less onsite in Lanarkshire. Iron ore could enter at one end of the Clyde Valley and completed ships could leave at the other. Another advantage was intellectual — the proximity of serious scientific research at the University of Glasgow and later at the Strathclyde Institute. This was linked directly into the engineering works of Glasgow, where colossal steam engines, generators and turbines were soon being created for the railways of the world. By 1802 the barges on the Forth and Clyde Canal were being towed by a steam-driven tug, the *Charlotte Dundas*, reckoned to be the first truly practical steamship.[24]

The upper Clyde could only become an extensive port and a mighty collection of shipyards when the original bed of the river had been deepened and its banks made permanent. This was achieved by James Golborne between 1768 and 1773. Transverse dredging so deepened the channel that the flow was self-scouring; from a typical depth of two feet in 1769 it had attained 21 feet a hundred years later, and this was at low tide. However, the channel, being well inland, was also narrow. To cram both offloading and shipbuilding into the available space required some ingenuity. Ships came to be launched sideways or diagonally into the river. For some six miles downstream from the city, quays and shipyards alternated.

The newly canalised river issued into the Firth of Clyde at the confluence of three deep sea-lochs — the Holy Loch, Loch Long and the Gare Loch, each facing a different way and providing for varying kinds of anchorage and now exploited by different classes of vessels, from super-tankers to nuclear submarines. The broad conclusion of the Clyde River opposite Greenock, known as the Tail of the Bank, is reckoned the safest, largest and most sheltered anchorage on Britain's west coast.

What finally provided for the success of the entire Clyde venture was the amalgamation of the seven old harbour boards of the eighteenth century from Greenock to Glasgow city into a single board (in 1858). In 1858, Glasgow was in fact perfectly placed to become what, in 1905, an American visitor was to describe as 'the most aggressively efficient city in Great Britain'. Well before this, the architectural profession had identified it as a city to be watched; in *The Builder* it was reported that, so far as modern technology was concerned, 'Glasgow ... is at the present time the most go-ahead city in Great Britain'.[25] The scale of Clydeside shipbuilding was indeed phenomenal. Most authorities reckon that in 1900 up to half the existing world tonnage, mercantile and naval, had been built and launched on Clydeside from a series of yards backed by complex industrial installations. Their presence transformed Glasgow and its satellite towns into a metropolis with a metropolitan architecture. The commercial and industrial buildings of nineteenth-century Glasgow are unmatched for their confidence, technical excellence and aggressive variety.[26]

The city disputed with Liverpool for the title of second city of the empire. The impression of titanic energy, which it shared with Chicago, was augmented by the very crowded character of its central area. A number of geographers have remarked on this, describing it as a city turned inside out:

> Glasgow never developed the symptoms of suburban sprawl typical of many other cities until well into the twentieth century, and remains an extraordinarily compact and

densely populated city … You took from your populous centre workmen to work away from the centre and you brought them back at night … as the city increased the works were sent out into the countryside and the population remained.[27]

This remarkable place was very well served by a public-transport system of tramways (electric after 1898) and a subway (effective from 1897). The works that were sent out to the countryside included, in addition to shipyards, which spread along the water meadows of both shores, factories for locomotives and other engines and every sort of textile, each in turn feeding upon and building up a host of smaller enterprises, especially those connected with the fitting-out trades. Many of these, though rooted in craft tradition, had developed high-speed and semi-industrialised production in order to keep up with the immense demand generated by the shipyards. It was among these subcontractors that the artistic phenomenon known as the Glasgow Style developed.

Art Nouveau was a marker of extreme modernity, which took different forms in the different cities of Europe and America. It provides a link between Glasgow and Belfast in the person of E.A. Taylor, the designer of interiors on land and sea. A number of houses and interiors in south Belfast, once built for leading figures in the shipbuilding and fitting-out trades, exhibit a sober version of the Glasgow Style, rather similar to what we have already noticed in Campbeltown. A case can be made for a distinct Irish-Sea school of adventurous domestic architecture, whose monuments spread from Glasgow, by way of the Firth of Clyde, across to Belfast and Liverpool by way of the Isle of Man, with a colony to be found around the head of Lake Windermere. Small but grand country mansions and townhouses by C.R. Mackintosh, M.H. Baillie-Scott, Edwin Lutyens, C.F. Voysey and Clough Williams-Ellis are to be found all through the area, precisely because the domestic culture of late-nineteenth-century shipbuilding was the most advanced, artistically and technically, of anything in the Islands at that time (and perhaps throughout Europe). It was here that the industrial and intellectual elite of north-British society was creating its own forms of modernity. It was here that some of the earliest kinds of architectural modernism were being invented and investigated along with modern lighting, services and hygiene. This is what Patrick Geddes, the geographer, described as the 'Neotechnic order' of electricity and cleanliness and light that would sweep away the 'Palaeotechnic order' of smoke, steam, gas and the iron foundry.[28]

**

In some respects Belfast was an unusual place in which to develop a very large industrial enterprise, far from sources of materials and fuels. However, in the 1830s it was still far easier and cheaper to move heavy goods by sea. In 1828 the Belfast paper the *Northern Whig* compared the 'extent, safety and despatch' of maritime trade with 'puny and contemptible' land-based communications.[29] The crucial factor was not distance from materials but the availability of skills; the very first iron ship to be built in Belfast was made by a firm much better known for making boilers for steam engines. The firm of Coates and Company, the leading supplier of steam engines in Ireland, launched the *Countess of Caledon* in 1838. From now on the building of wooden vessels, in which Belfast shipyards had been an important player, went into decline. While the *Countess* was being built William Dargan was straightening and deepening the River Lagan. Belfast's position halfway between the Mersey and the Clyde encouraged the mobility of labour and capital, and its relatively small size may have encouraged the interplay of expertise at home. Harland and Wolff (incorporated by 1858 on the basis of earlier manufacturers) rapidly rose to pre-eminence.[30]

There is no human activity that requires so many skills, sciences, trades, crafts and arts as the designing, building and fitting out of large vessels. Because, until 1914, the bulk of Harland and Wolff's orders were for passenger vessels (particularly for the White Star Line of Liverpool), the trade in luxury fittings and furniture expanded immensely during the latter part of the nineteenth century. Nor should we forget the equally prosperous, though smaller, yard of Workman Clark, which specialised in cargo vessels. The city became home to engine-builders, screwcasters and anchormakers to the entire industry. The Belfast Ropeworks, which made thousands of miles of cordage of every size, from hawsers to fishing lines, became the largest enterprise of its kind on the globe, supplying the oceans with ropes and string. This horizontal integration around the Irish Sea was matched with a vertical integration within the yards themselves, which was specially developed in Belfast. In 1911, *The Shipbuilder* drew attention to this vertical integration as follows:

> Unlike many shipbuilding firms, Messrs Harland and Wolff may be termed builders in the most complete sense of the word. As in the case of all vessels built by them, not only have they constructed the hull of the *Olympic* and the *Titanic*, but also their propelling machinery, while much of the outfit usually supplied by sub-contractors for ships built in other yards has been manufactured in their own works.[31]

Harland and Wolff was also renowned for technical originality, with a long length-to-beam ratio, stiff iron decks and high-powered turbine engines with double and triple screws (from 1905).[32] This enabled the yard to invent the first true passenger liners that could cruise the oceans. The *Oceanic*, launched in 1871, may be said to the originator of all the rest.

Belfast in 1900 was fast on the way to becoming a second, smaller, Glasgow. Apprenticeships and education in the technical trades grew apace. In a previous study of design education in Glasgow and the surrounding district I estimated that a total of 2,700 full- and part-time students were engaged in design studies of several kinds around 1900, to which we should add the 4,600 students of the Glasgow Technical College and other bodies, each providing a creative workforce in training. Belfast was proceeding in the same direction and along similar lines. Begun as part of the government-sponsored 'art-manufactures' schools, in 1849, the Belfast School of Art was reformed in 1870 with a committee that included Edward Harland, shipbuilder. It rapidly acquired a good reputation, though its actual curriculum, like that of the more famous Glasgow School, was always uncomfortably poised on a seesaw balancing the supposed 'needs of industry' with the demands of 'art culture'. By 1900 it was part of a much larger technical institute, with a similar mix of students, though it is merely speculation to decide just how many there were.[33]

One of the great frustrations the scholar must endure is the paucity of records; the records of the shipbuilding yards and the specialist designers and technicians that worked in them all around the Irish Sea were scrapped like so much rusty iron when the yards were closed from around 1970 onward. However, we can be confident that the directors, committee and board members and honorary secretaries of each and every industrial concern and allied institute in Belfast were Protestant almost to a man (I have found no female names and very few that one might identify as Irish/Catholic).

Illustration 12. Great iron bollards are among the remains of Belfast's days of glory.

Illustration 13. The two great cranes, known as Samson and Goliath, are still employed, now and again, to shift great sections of ship, since the main business of what is now called the Titanic Quarter is ship repair and stretching. (In stretching, a ship is cut in half and an additional section, already constructed, is stitched into it; the whole is then reassembled.)

The degree to which Catholic workers were excluded from certain key classes of work remains astonishing. A fitter in the shipyards was earning at rates comparable to the rest of the United Kingdom. At the same time the recruitment of unskilled workers into industry was organised so as to exclude those young people and children who were not already 'spoken for' by current employees. Thus, rural immigrants were, in considerable measure, selected against in the labour market.[34] There is a historiographical consequence to this: when Irish nationalist history began to be written in its twentieth-century form, and to enter into popular consciousness, its industrial aspect was systematically erased. The version of Irish history that then took root excluded Ireland's one great moment in modern history — when the Irish Sea became a site of world significance, with all that entails of good and ill. It also condemned Ulster — or, at least, what came to be known as Northern Ireland — to alien status. It was no longer part of the material with which national history had to deal. At the very same time, reciprocally, what came to be the south (the 'authentic' Ireland) had to take on a symbolically subordinate position, whatever might be the reality, because the country is always symbolically subordinate to the town.[35]

Ireland south of the border had to wait for the dawning of Geddes's Neotechnic order before it began to creep out from under its rural 'heritage' and its actual frustrating poverty. This in turn required a wholesale societal and ideological change.

Nor, in this connection, ought we forget the smaller city of Barrow-in-Furness, which has the distinction of being one of the few company towns of the Irish Sea (along with Port Sunlight). Though created mainly by iron founders from Newcastle — notably the firm of Vickers — it came to be largely inhabited from Ireland and, above all, from Belfast. This is symbolised by the town hall, which was created by W.H. Lynn, a colleague of Charles Lanyon and a notably romantic designer. His town hall (which survived the protracted process of civil commissioning with some difficulty) is a truly outstanding building for its function. The view in Illustration 14 is merely of the back door!

Illustration 14. The town hall, Barrow-in-Furness.

Barrow went on to become, through the agency of the Vickers yard, a major naval shipyard, producing submarines through two great wars. Their prowess in producing pressure vessels led to close involvement with nuclear-electricity generation. The shipyard area contains a vast shed sometimes claimed (incorrectly) to be the biggest shed in the world, constructed especially for these purposes.

Notes

[1]   J. Habermas (ed.) (1987) *The philosophical discourse of modernity: twelve lectures*, London: Polity Press, p. 7.

[2]   G. Broderick (1999) *Language death in the Isle of Man: an investigation into the decline and extinction of Manx Gaelic as a community language in the Isle of Man*, Tübingen: Niemeyer, p. 11. This book contains a very extensive and useful bibliography.

[3]   Printed in I. Bowen (1908) *Statutes of Wales*, London: Unwin, pp. 75–6.

[4]   Broderick, *op. cit.*, p. 11.

[5]   Cited in V.E. Durkacz (1983) *The decline of the Celtic languages: a study of linguistic and cultural conflict in Scotland, Wales and Ireland from the Reformation to the twentieth century*, Edinburgh: John Donald, p. 4.

[6]   *Ibid.*, p. 5. Compare this to the terms which were used of the MacDonalds of Kintyre as the 'fosteraris of all barbaritie' (see Chapter 2).

[7]   M. Chapman (1992) *The Celts: the construction of a myth*, London: St Martin's Press, p. 99 *et seq.*

[8]   Broderick, *op. cit.*, p. 22, note 16.

[9]   As part of the reading around this difficult and very technical topic I have found useful such books as J.R. Dow (ed.) (1991) *Language and ethnicity*, Philadelphia: Benjamins, and books in the *Politics of language* series edited by T. Crowley and T.J. Taylor for Routledge, London. Another invaluable volume is L. Burke, T. Crowley and A. Girvin (eds) (2000) *The Routledge language and cultural theory reader*, London: Routledge. It seems unlikely that one language has any real merit over and above another, though it is often alleged that 'French is very clear' or that 'some languages are harder to learn than others'. For a stimulating and funny discussion of these issues, see L. Bauer and P. Trudgill (eds) (1998) *Language myths*, London: Penguin Books.

[10] I am thinking of the work of Cathal O'Searcaigh and Nuala Ní Dhomhnaill.

[11] This is the main theme of my 1996 book *The construction of heritage*, Cork: Cork University Press.

[12] See B.M.S. Campbell (2003) 'Economic progress in the canal age' in D. Dickson and C. Ó Gráda (eds), *Refiguring Ireland: essays in honour of L.M. Cullen*, Dublin: Lilliput Press, p. 65.

[13] The most complete account is in D.R. Delany (1973) *The Grand Canal of Ireland*, Newtown Abbot: David and Charles.

[14] *Ibid.*

[15] See *ibid.*, Chapters 4 and 8.

[16] See J.H. Bird (1963) *The major seaports of the United Kingdom*, London: Hutchinson, Chapter 12.

[17] A comprehensive general history of Liverpool has recently been published: J. Belchem (ed.) (2006) *Liverpool 800: culture, character and history*, Liverpool: Liverpool University Press.

But see C.N. Parkinson (1952) *The rise of the port of Liverpool*, Liverpool: Liverpool University Press, Chapters 1 and 2. And see also other writings detailed in Belchem, *op. cit.*

18 Beaumaris subsequently became a significant little port of its own, as a clearing house for trade coming up the Irish Sea with wine and other continental goods. (This was the trade on which pirates such as Thomas Dun thrived.) Beaumaris was increasingly favoured by Chester merchants who wanted to keep in business as their town declined. In fact, most of what we know about Chester's trade from this period comes from the port records of Beaumaris. There are records of Breton ships bringing cargoes of wine as early as 1295. We know that by 1366 this trade was coming directly into the Mersey because Stephen Warde, a 'captain of Lyverpulle', laid a complaint before the courts that he had to pay duty on his cargo of Bordeaux wine first to Liverpool and then, as well, to the authorities in Chester. Customs duty, being a privilege of the crown and a main source of royal revenue, was organised on a regional basis and any trade into the Mersey/Dee area was deemed, for tax purposes, to come through Chester. This was greatly to the advantage of that city, whose burgesses clung like limpets to the status of 'port' long after the sea had departed. They even had an admiral.

19 There is a very good survey of these matters in Belchem, *op. cit.*

20 A contemporary newsletter called *The Ship Canal News*, as cited in Owen, *op. cit.*, p. 51.

21 G. Head (1836) *Home tour through the manufacturing districts of England in the summer of 1835*, London: Murray.

22 *The Ship Canal News.*

23 See especially T. Hughes (1987) 'The evolution of large technological systems' in W.E. Bijker, T.P. Hughes and T.J. Pinch (eds), *The social construction of technological systems: new directions in the sociology and history of technology*, Cambridge, MA: MIT Press, pp. 51–82.

24 The most concise summary of Clyde shipbuilding and its technical and intellectual infrastructure is probably in F.M. Walker (1996) 'The river Clyde: birthplace of an industry' in G. Jackson and D.M. Williams (eds), *Shipping, technology and imperialism: papers presented to the third British-Dutch Maritime History Conference*, Aldershot: Scolar Press.

25 *The Builder*, 14 April 1855.

26 See D. Brett (1992) *C.R. Mackintosh: the poetics of workmanship*, London: Reaktion Books, Chapter 2 for a short description, and many other authors.

27 See D. Daiches (1977) *Glasgow*, London: Deutsch, Chapter 12.

28 This is a significant theme in Brett (1992), *op. cit.* See P. Geddes (1949) *Cities in evolution*, London: Williams and Norgate, and P. Boardman (1978) *The worlds of Patrick Geddes: biologist, town planner, re-educator, peace-warrior*, London: Routledge and Kegan Paul.

29 *Northern Whig*, 27 March 1828.

30 A useful comparative account of the Lagan and Clyde shipbuilding industries and the growth of Harland and Wolff can be found in Jackson and Williams, *op. cit.*, especially Chapter 8, 'Lagan and Clyde shipbuilding' by M.S. Moss.

31 *The Shipbuilder* **6** (1911), p. 7, cited in L. Kennedy and P. Ollerenshaw (eds) (1985) *An economic history of Ulster, 1820–1939*, Manchester: Manchester University Press, p. 93.

32 *Ibid.* pp. 90–1. By these technical means the entire ship was turned into a rigid horizontal box girder capable of withstanding great stress and moving at high speed.

33 See Brett (1992), *op. cit.*, pp. 26–7; for Belfast I am indebted to research published in M. Catto (1994) *Art and design matters: exhibition catalogue*, Belfast: Ulster Museum and University of Ulster.

34 Kennedy and Ollerenshaw, *op. cit.*, pp. 153–4.

35 See Brett (1996), *op. cit.*, especially p. 5, for a general treatment of this theme.

TEN
By way of epilogue

Is there anywhere an attractive ferry-port? Rosslare is no worse than another, but on a cold December day the railway sidings, truck parks and pedestrian ways are without charm of any kind. You offload your cycle and wheel it awkwardly up and over the ramps and the bumps. You raise your eyes to a glacis of scrubs and bushes where, as you pass, you notice gun emplacements and obscure abutments of concrete disguised as rock, and then emerge upon a windy esplanade. You can't wait to get away. But there are further windy streets to negotiate, roundabouts crowded with tourist cars and trucks, and a bleak ring road that leads to a bleak trunk road which, as you follow it, is forever turning into the wind across a bleak sweep of salt-flats and marshland.

Like all such places, Rosslare, and Stranraer and Holyhead exist to be passed through. All are much alike. This shows in the architecture, which is always a dreary mixture of the commercial and the touristic. It shows also in the animal population, in the groups of stray dogs that hang about the quaysides and that follow the lonely pedestrian, in the dingy clowders of cats that inhabit doorways and alleys and in the disconsolate moping of the gulls.

As for the geography of the south-eastern nook of Ireland, it seems to be the wrong way around. It is akin to Holderness or Orford or even, for that matter, to the Frisian heathlands of north Holland. And Wexford, in the evening gloom, feels like a small East Anglian town, with its white walls and its restored elegance. Good on a warm summer's evening, less good right now. A long curving waterfront leads into a long rail platform; there are substantial warehouses such as we find in the older corners of Colchester. On a windy December afternoon I acquire a list of possible accommodations in the tourist office, which, when I find them, carry 'No Vacancy' signs. In the northerly quarters vacancy is being made manifest and the wind is carrying rain on the darkness. There is still an hour of daylight and the road beckons you forward. Cross the Slaney before the lamps are lit and cycle northward across fields and dusky heaths. This will be a rough night.

The impromptu bivouac in a corner of a cabbage field is a situation only too familiar, but it is something to make the best of. And there is a craft to it, which urges the traveller to excel himself, making comfort out of mud. The aim, as always, is to rise above circumstance. It does not matter that you are cold, but you must stay dry.

You have already realised that this is what you might expect at the day's end and have eaten well of stale pasties from the petrol-station grill; but you know, from many years of experience, that a hot drink will be necessary. So, wrapped up in a groundsheet that doubles back into something approximating to a tent, you take out the little stove and the emergency rations. Out comes the collection of film canisters containing tea and sugar, nested within the pan; out comes the water bottle and the spoon. Out comes the lighter and the tablet of solid fuel. Orange flame gives way to blue flame and the comforting mutter of the burner. Cold hands around a hot cup. One pannier bag forms a pillow and the other, now emptied, makes an adequate mattress. You are trying not to use the head torch so as to avoid drawing attention to yourself. Sleep comes quickly but does not last. Flurries of rain wake you and you curl up as small as you can and draw the sleeping bag over your head. You wait for the light.

How many early hours have you spent like this, dreaming, when dawn's left hand is in the sky, on decks and platforms, in dunes and woodlands, belayed to the rock on icy ledges, huddled on rakes and under boulders beside glacial torrents? Cooking one-handed as the light returns? Not moving more until you must?

***

My final northward journey coincided with the publication of a book by a noted historian. Roy Foster's *Luck and the Irish: a brief history of change* had accompanied me on the boat from Fishguard and was now in my saddlebag.[1] It addresses itself to the most recent history of Ireland, conceived as a reconceptualising of the state and the nation under the pressure of its belated modernity: 'There is a sense that we are experiencing history in a fast-forward mode.' The fast-forward mode as achieved by the laden cyclist lacks the impetus that Foster is suggesting, but I found myself reflecting on that notion as I continued on my way to Arklow in the weak morning sunshine. It was a way of distracting myself from the sensation of having missed breakfast.

The countryside of east Wexford is composed of undulating farmlands that border a long and rather uninteresting coast which, year by year, grows less as the waves take it around the corner towards the Atlantic. Inland, the country mounts slowly to some well-formed forested hills. All about are large to medium-sized farms. It was past these prosperous establishments that I made my way, without any hurry. The fast-forward mode is to be avoided when you have a long way to go. Keep it slow; keep it stately.

It was also, I reminded myself, an occasion to remember the historical principle which I had determined to follow, that of *longue durée*, of those 'underlying consistencies that bind communities together and the rhythms that moderate their development over long periods of time'.[2] This did not seem to fit well with Foster's persuasive theme. That theme was persuasive because it chimed with my experience of

Ireland. The fast-forward mode. A good part of my experience of the country was rooted in an older Ireland that had never failed to shock me: a world without public services of any quality, of quite remarkable and deep pockets of want and even indigence, of deeply ingrained chauvinism and self-pity. An ideology of MOPE — of the 'most oppressed people ever' — of everything negative, from which the present Ireland has had to be developed like an new photograph from an older plate.

I ask to be forgiven the use of personal anecdote, but the writer who addresses contemporary reality cannot hope to avoid it, however occluded by academic method it may appear from time to time.

In 1990 my wife exhibited a collection of her paintings and drawings at the Butler Gallery, Kilkenny, under the title 'De humani corporis fabrica'. The opening night coincided with a critical event in the 'procreation politics' of the republic — a nexus of extraordinary passion. A young woman, no more than a girl, had been made a ward of court to prevent her parents taking her to England to terminate an unplanned pregnancy. Our exhibition was opened by the Irish-language poet Nuala Ní Dhomnaill, who took the title of the work as her text. On the structure of the human body: its ownership and the claims of states and churches. Her brief speech, in a vehement mixture of both languages, made strong men weep tears of rage and shame. The women present largely confined themselves to commenting, 'Well, what the feck else did anyone expect of this country?' I felt myself to be living through someone else's moral and constitutional crisis and, ever since, I have privately interpreted the increasing secularisation of Irish life as a sustained campaign of revenge upon clerical and legal institutions that had disabled and impoverished and insulted the people. I became, in the watches of the night, subject to gales of ancestral indignation.

The degree to which an older conservative Catholicism has been discredited in the past 20 years or so can hardly be exaggerated. This is, of course, some way from the thoroughgoing and more or less unconsidered secularism of the rest of the Islands and it is not the same as a wholesale rejection of religious belief. But it is infused with a strain of contempt that includes a determination never to be fooled that way again. This extends even into the hearts of faithful believers.

Foster describes this as part of 'how the Catholics became protestants' ('with a small p') and writes that 'The notion of Catholicism as indivisible from Irish nationalism and even from Irish identity might be counted as one of the casualties of the last 30 years' cultural upheaval.'[3] He also ascribes a leading role in the upheaval to the women's movement. I am sure he is correct in this, not least because the Catholic Church had for so long attributed to women a retrograde function in society and the state, which could hardly fail to provoke a dialectical reversal.

Seen in the longue durée, however, sudden dialectical reverses are to be expected of societies in which the institutions are shaky or recent. Irish philosophical thought provides one excellent and highly relevant example — the conversion of John Toland (1670–1721) from a Catholic upbringing in Derry to a pioneering atheistical and materialist maturity. It is no accident that works like *Christianity not mysterious* have recently been re-edited and republished in Dublin.[4] They reassert a distinct and very radical strain in the practice of philosophy in Ireland. I use such roundabout phrases to avoid using essentialist notions such as 'Irish philosophy'. It is hardly useful to describe John Locke, Toland or even Berkeley as Irish philosophers, but to read them against an Irish landscape — linguistic or historical — offers another dimension of meaning. Irish conditions (rather like those of Poland) were a spur to thorough renovation and aggressive originality because they were frequently so bad. To think at all would be enough to make men and women rage.

Toland, who first used the term 'pantheism' to denote a belief in the undivided and absolute unity of everything, thus annihilating the distinction between God and his creation, seems to me a true progenitor of modern Romanticism, and thus of contemporary sensibility and morals. He paid bitterly for his daring and died a hack writer in poverty. Such are the thoughts provoked by cycling, constantly pressing down to move forward.

And what we see, as we cycle through what was hitherto an entirely agricultural landscape, are pockets of modern industry — parts of the new Ireland. Not just of the most modern food-processing and food-packing business, of which there are many signs, including the rapid passage of huge container trucks, but also of the electronics industries. Brightly coloured alloy sheds emerge from the soft greens and browns of pastureland; gleaming titanium canopies shelter cages of glass beside deeply hedged boreens.

The large question that Foster raises, without attempting a conclusive answer, is whether or not the so-called Celtic Tiger was the offspring of autonomous effort or a new version of the colonial condition, now provided by capital from the United States and other foreign parts, taking advantage of favourable conditions created by the European Union. He provides and discusses a number of alternative stories and starting gates, but he fails to address one significant topic that unavoidably emerges in the long run proposed here — the issue of energy sources. The westward shores of the Irish Sea are notably lacking in fossil fuels, without which industrial wealth has always proved impossible, leading to poverty in capital.

Following Patrick Geddes, the concept of technological orders enables us to conceive a three-stage pattern for human societies. In a Neotechnic world, human society depended upon the natural forces of wind, tides and currents and the principal source of heat energy was wood. These set limits on the scale and character of human endeavours, the possibilities of political control and the exercise of power. This was the world of most of this book, from which the peoples of the Irish Sea emerged at irregular intervals and different times at different places into what Geddes calls the Palaeotechnic order, which was fuelled and lit mainly by coal and later by oil. This produced the massive industrial enterprises of extraction and the grosser manufacturing processes based on iron and the steam engine. Undertakings tended to the colossal in both war and peace; the scale of human endeavour was increased in all realms, but notably in the political. This in turn is to be succeeded by a Neotechnical order, fuelled and lit by electricity (variously produced), therefore clean, and tending towards reduction in immediate size and scale. It remains to be decided the degree to which we may now find ourselves in this world, or the degree to which we remain uncomfortably stranded between the two or the three orders. Geddes's classification is not primarily based on historical time but on technological classification, which in turn implies cultural and political forms. If we consider it as being in one time direction (like the arrow's flight) we miss the most salient fact, which is that different orders coexist within the world as a whole and within the differing societies of the world. It depends on who we are, where we are living and what we are doing. Wind and weather determine how our days are passed the moment we go outdoors. This whole journey has revealed that to me, very starkly. Geology determines where we can find a dwelling place on this surface we call the earth. If we imagine otherwise we find ourselves imagining a world without contingency, a virtual existence. A no-place.

The geology and what we can call the geo-economics of the Irish-Sea zone (the disposition of physical resources across the surface of the globe) have tended towards the impoverishment of Ireland and the western isles. Lacking the physical resources for its own Palaeotechnical order, Ireland was compelled to — and still must — import its heat energy (and therefore its main capital investment) in the form of coal, gas and oil. It remains the fate of the whole island that it should always bear something of a colonial status from the moment that Palaeotechnical conditions began to supervene over Neotechnic. Just as in the past states justified themselves by their capacity to wage war, now they exist primarily to secure resources of energy, to which end they will employ any means whatsoever. The inability to command these resources significantly reduces the justification and significance of the state.

With the coming of Neotechnical society, different conditions begin to obtain. Ireland's fundamental technical status is changed. This I take to be the precondition of southern Ireland's recent prosperity. It skipped a stage. In a centreless net of electronic telecommunications and global investment patterns, 'peripheral' position has no meaning. I take this to be an undeniable good in principle and an advantage in practice.

(We leave aside the question of nuclear energy, which always requires immense capital investment and a degree of governmental control and security that was always missing in Northern Ireland. The republic's moves towards nuclear power, which was to have involved a reactor on Carnsore Point, now the home of wind turbines, was resisted by popular pressure and the then-current cheapness of oil. What happens in the future remains, of course, very obscure.)

It is certainly the case that the Republic of Ireland (unlike the north) has not had to carry with it into the twenty-first century the Palaeotechnical jetsam of the nineteenth. But the idea that the new post-industrial economy preserves an Irish political independence is something to question. The original aim of economic autonomy, on which the nationalist project depended, is blown to the winds. The whole of the island is dependent on open or hidden subsidies. In the north this comes in the form of direct subventions from Whitehall; in the south it comes in the formless flood of American capital investment supported (in the early years) by EU funds and preferential treatment. To climb out from under this warm blanket will be no easy task.

I write American investment because America is where, initially, the profits are received, but increasingly we have come to understand that all this profit is global in scope. Money has no nationality and investment follows global opportunity. Recent prosperity based on global investment was a will-o'-the-wisp ready to be blown out by the gales of commerce and long-term debt. Of all European nation states, the Republic of Ireland presently demands among the highest *per-capita* expenditure of energy and the highest *per-capita* expenditure on energy. The territory has become, for the first time since the plantations, an importer of population and has its own autonomous population growth.

How this will work out in the future remains to be seen. One rural accompaniment of this, visible all the way up the eastern coast, is the slash-and-burn attitude to land use and the growth everywhere of commercial development in the form of a once-and-once-only cash crops of houses.[5] At the time of writing, the Dublin hinterland is reckoned to have a population density similar to Los Angeles, without the road network or the cheap petrol to support it.

'Keep those wheels turning,' I told myself.

***

Arklow passed in blur of sleeplessness and low mists. It seemed a strange town — half a nineteenth-century seaside resort (now out of season) and half a country market being steadily displaced by modern retail chains. I picked up sandwiches from a seafront kiosk and a mug of sour tea to wash them down. I was now in that dour condition provoked by a night in a wet field and an insufficient breakfast. If the wind had been against me or the weather bad I think I would have looked for lodgings there and then, but it was still, just, dry. Beside the shores of Mizen Head I drowsed half an hour in my sleeping bag. Wicklow provided a solid meal and a pleasant interlude.

North of Wicklow I had hoped to follow a track beside the railway line that follows the coast upon ridges of shingle and sand dunes, but it was not obvious how to cross the river onto the spits (at least, I was too dozy to notice and had drifted into the control of my autopilot). Accordingly, the last ten miles of this day, to the outskirts of Greystones, was spent on a winding secondary road. Here a sole bed-and-breakfast establishment offered an early night in a warm bed.

In the morning it was raining steadily. This was my excuse to take the train for the last 30 miles into Dublin and another 20 beyond.

South Dublin ought to be attractive. Houses, estates, golf courses, parkland and the few remnants of countryside back onto the Wicklow Hills, which are variegated with forest and moorland, with uplands which are rounded and, where appropriate, spiky. There are fine close valleys thick with old woodland and, in the interstices of the road system, the remains of small villages and towns. The seashore is variable and picturesque. Some of this remains, but most is swamped and criss-crossed with housing development of the worst kind. Working-class settlements such as Tallaght are among the poorest and ugliest in western Europe; the expensive estates are moated by golf courses and contain some houses that are individually good but hemmed around with gruesome vulgarity. Shopping malls and motorway slip roads complete the chaos. None of these features, with the exception of some nameless, is bad in itself, but the cumulative effect is of waste, greed and ugliness.

It has grown from an already-existing mess, the lack of functioning public services. A notable recent analysis has concluded that:

> the multi directional, unguided sprawl of Irish housing cannot be serviced by a functional transportational system, as development has spread too widely and at too low a density ... Ireland's lack of viable alternative transport and accommodation models increases the pressure for new housing on farm land to a degree unimaginable in societies having advanced infrastructure networks and higher residential densities.[6]

The effect of this uncontrollable and prodigal development is progressively to increase dependence on imported petrol, following north-American models, using housing types derived from the south-east of England. This arises from attitudes to land and from legislation that in turn grows out of Ireland's miserable political history and lack of political self-analysis. The nationalist insistence, developed to a state ideology in the years of the Free State, handed on to the present century a spirit of extreme individualism which has stultified the growth of civic responsibility in the use of space and in planning legislation. The norm is that you can and should do whatever you like on your own land.

It might be useful in this connection to look again at the old Gaelic concept of the *tuath*, the clan territory, as a common good that did not belong to any individual but only and ultimately to the community as a whole, supervening over individual rights and ownership. Simultaneously, we might look at the Swiss/German idea of the

Gemeinde, which continues medieval usage into the present, inculcating a very strong sense of fitting into such matters as new building without in any way hazarding originality. Both of these act as brakes on the headlong chariot of greed.[7] But in today's conditions, social forethought is out of fashion.

Where Dublin and its hinterland are concerned, the particular conditions are the product of the unrivalled rascality of the governments of Charles Haughey and his cabal of colleagues, who comprised a regime of, by and for land developers. (Roy Foster devotes a chapter to this in his book, which would be comic were it not for the permanence of the results.) The consequence for the laden cyclist are severe. There is but one experience that may be worse than crossing Dublin by cycle, south to north, and that is the same journey in the opposite direction.

Fifteen years ago the small town of Balbriggan comprised only itself and not much more. It is now but the northerly limit of ribbon development. It has acquired a marina instead of a run-down fishing quay and a set of large 'portside' apartment blocks and commuter developments. Its friendly though ramshackle main street connects to the Belfast–Dublin motorway by a crowded slip road lined with new houses and retail parks. The old main road continues, of course, but it is depleted and unkempt. This, however, is the way I must go.

I pressed down and rolled forward; the winter afternoon was coming on.

***

The pedal plate connects to the pedal crank, the pedal crank connects to the chain wheel, the chain wheel connects to the sprocket wheel, the sprocket wheel connects to the back wheel and the back wheel connects to the main frame. Them wheels, them wheels, them round wheels. Them wheels going to go around. Now hear the word of the Lord!

***

By midday the wind had changed several points to the north-west and was blowing a steady rain before it. My new waterproofs were no longer waterproof. In the outskirts of Drogheda, sodden to the skin and cold, I pulled into a bar with a buffet and sat steaming over fish and chips. I had the sense that other people were looking sideways at me as if I were a dead cat in a ditch. Enough of this. The railway station was only a few hundred yards away. Give it up.

As you bring a book to a conclusion you progressively foreclose on choices you might have taken earlier. Looking out over the deep-cut harbour estuary of Drogheda I find myself regretting that I never took it sufficiently to mind that I should spend more time here. Drogheda is, in fact, among the best smaller cities of the Irish Sea, with a notable history. Beginning as a Norman creation, connected with the de Lacy reorganisation of County Meath and the building of the castle at Trim, Drogheda was a flourishing port and market and bridge (the *novus pons de* Drogheda) well downstream from the old ford of Oldbridge (of the battle site). It is perfectly possible that the river provided a handy way of reaching the great ceremonial sites around Newgrange well before the Normans, but the de Lacys created something like a fully planned colonists' town, with charters and rights on the Norman model by 1194. By 1200 it was a major port and the centre of the wine business for most of the Irish Sea, with many connections to Chester. It was also an important source of military provisions, with a shipbuilding industry. (There is an account of all this business by John Bradley in his work *The topography and layout of medieval Drogheda*).[8] Ships conducted trade with Iceland, the Baltic and Lisbon.

***

Now I remind myself I must stop my interest continually expanding and concentrate on getting home against the wind and rain. But it is not easy to abandon a long-cherished plan, and mine had been to complete the full circuit of the Irish Sea under my own power. Under my general rules of engagement I could take public transport to pass through the great conurbations and was to forgive myself the weaknesses of age by taking decent accommodation when it offered itself. My days of martyrdom are well over. But there was a principle to be observed: that of ending where you began. There was, I knew, a motel just on the outskirts of Newry, about three wet miles from the station, that there was a stopping train, that the weather forecast for the next day was for drier, colder weather, and the wind on my left shoulder.

And so it was that, shortly after eight on my last day, I turned the bars eastward onto the A25 and started to make my way through the hillocky landscape of south Down, with the morning sun in my eyes and a cold wind over my left shoulder, exactly as predicted. I was dry and clean and well fed, with about 60 miles to go. In my home country.

Following the general rule of taking secondary roads whenever feasible, I took a right turn onto the more southerly track that goes over high pasturelands, with fewer trees and much less traffic, through the aptly named village of Hilltown and then onto a long ridgeway that passes below the skyline of the Mountains of Mourne. It was the first time I had been that way since smashing up my knee on Ben Cruachan and being forced into retirement from mountains, but cycling had long ceased to be a substitute, for I had rediscovered, 60 years later, the boy's delight in speed — in the swooping curve downhill, in the last lung-burst at the hilltop's edge. The high rocky cockscomb of Slieve Bearnagh slid past me as I turned left towards Castlewellan, down the long straight towards the town and then, after a brief lunch of hot pasty (again), down the still more precipitous straight into Annsborough and up the long hill beyond, where the road is narrow and the traffic fast. At the ridge end came the view southward over Dundrum Bay towards the profile of Man and, closer to hand, the *druim* on which stands one of de Courcy's first castles, overlooking what had once been a deep harbour. Then, my lungs about to pop, I rode up beside the old Presbyterian church to the crossroad of Clough. In my home country.

The peninsula security of Lecale, which contains not only the old town of Downpatrick but also several ancient sites of different kinds, was maintained by a narrow passage between the medieval coastline of Dundrum Bay and an arm of Strangford Lough known as the Quoile River, which still runs up beside precincts of Downpatrick to link up with an area of fens and small loughs. Sea-going ships could come in from Strangford Lough as far as Inch Abbey, an old monastic foundation a mile to the west of the town. Dundrum Bay nowadays consists of a large open bight that runs from the holiday resort of Newcastle as far east as St John's Point and, within that shore, an inner harbour reached by a narrow passage and a series of tidal lagoons. High overgrown sand dunes form the barrier between land and sea and marsh. In Norman days, when John de Courcy arrived with his 22 knights and his 300 foot soldiers, the inner bay was less enclosed and Inch Abbey stood on an island in the intermediate swamp country, which had already been raided at least once by the notorious Viking chief Sitric Silkbeard. John de Courcy refounded this monastery on Cistercian lines in 1180 and had it staffed by monks from Furness Abbey in Cumbria. The district of Lecale seems to have become closely linked with the Isle of Man and Cumbria, through both ecclesiastical and political alliances.

De Courcy then went forward, like myself, to Downpatrick, which he made his headquarters for the next few months. In the twelfth century the town had been in existence for a good 500 years, since the days of Patrick.

Annals refer to Downpatrick as a town and even as a city, but what it really amounted to in 1169 is not certain. It was not a town in the sense of a political and legal entity, but it was a permanent settlement of some size, with at least one monastery and perhaps one or more churches. Today it has the compactness of a medieval town, with streets referred to as 'Irish' and 'English', and a 'Scotch quarter'. The substantial townhouses indicate a trade in corn from the fertile fields of Lecale. There are also old warehouses and coal quays, for the Quoile River continued to provide a useful port even into the twentieth century, before it was closed up with a dam. It is now a still and beautiful series of tree-fringed loughs, preserved for the use of wintering geese and a gang of resident swans. Herons strut among the reeds.

De Courcy built himself a small fort somewhere near the central crossroads, of which no obvious trace remains. He stayed there for a while, defeating clan armies sent against him and entering into agreements with Ragnhald, the king of Man, and with clan chiefs from Galloway. In the course of these negotiations de Courcy married

Affreca Godredsdottir, the sister of Ragnhald, who was simultaneously engaging in alliances with King John of England as part of his campaign to secure his own dynasty. (This Affreca is one of the very few female names to come down to us from this early period and it would be good to know more about her. She seems to have been a political figure in her own right. She was born in or around 1187 and her mother was a lady with the Gaelic name Fionnuala MacLochlainn.)

***

I passed through Downpatrick around midday and took the road to Strangford. A bright winter light illuminated the bare ash trees. Rooks were blown about the branches like scraps of charred paper.

Strangford village, on the west bank of the sound, is a shapely place, with a central green, a tower house and several attractive dwellings. The sound itself is about 300 yards wide, deep and swift — the strong fjord — whichever way the tide is running. The ferry, which has room for about 25 cars, has to manoeuvre itself through this current and run at full tilt onto the slipway to avoid being swept out to sea. Portaferry on the east bank is a small town, with a square, an elegant waterfront and another tower house set in the middle. There is also a Presbyterian church in a Greek-revival style, of a compact vigour that would not disgrace Glasgow or even Leningrad. On a hill beyond the town is an old windmill, to remind us of the grain trade. The twin peninsulas of Lecale and Ards were, and still are, among the principal granaries of Ireland, favoured by soil and by a local climate as dry and bright as Suffolk and just as given to cold winds.

One was blowing now as I turned north along the lough shore. Here every ditch runs salt and the bridges cross tidal creeks; the grass is very short and green and set around with wind-crushed gorse. The lough is wide and full of islands and sandbanks; some of the islands are inhabited and others have the remains of old houses and churches. There are old and ruined tower houses on Sketrick Island and on the causeway to Nendrum. This island, reached by a devious connecting road from one island or sandbank to another, contains the remains of Nendrum Monastery and the stump of a round tower. Today the principal inhabitants of Strangford Lough are the seals, which are plentiful and curious and entirely relaxed about human presence. There are great flocks of geese and other wandering seabirds and numerous ducks, which are permanent residents along with the herons. Strangford Lough, to geese, is what Heathrow is to holidaymakers. Sooner or later you will find yourself passing time there. Away across the water is the ridgeway of the Mourne Mountains, some five conspicuous humps and at the other end, every mile nearer, the profile of Scrabo Hill and the spike of its tower, from which I set out and which I took to be my finishing line.

I passed two villages. Kircubbin is a long and rather bleak street with a substantial Presbyterian chapel. Like many Ulster towns it seems rather uniform and even dull in its architecture, but it pays to have sharp eyes since, looking about us, we pass curious nooks and adaptations that show how one century has been grafted into another. Kircubbin was, in its small way, an industrial port built for flax, grain, potatoes and kelp bound for Liverpool, and Lancashire coal. It maintains a workaday character that distinguishes it from Greyabbey, which comes next — a neat and well-built old village beside the abbey of the same name. Like Inch Abbey, Grey was a foundation of de Courcy. In this case, Affreca Godredsdottir, coming from the Isle of Man, brought with her monks from Furness. It might be useful to think of Ards and Lecale as being part of a greater Man that Ragnhald was building for himself, for he also maintained a base on Carlingford Lough. The two abbeys, Inch and Grey, are built along the same compact lines, rather crudely, in a sort of rustic early Gothic. To my eye they reflect the English origins of the monks and their builders, who seem to have been less sophisticated and elegant in their manners than the mainly French brothers who settled at Mellifont around the same time.

The Ards Peninsula is a sort of palimpsest of the whole Irish Sea in that the traces of the overlapping clans, fiefdoms, kingdoms and social formations and their activities are here inscribed over and under one another. Around the waters of the lough are the shell-middens of the Larnian culture and the raths and cashels of the Clyde-Carlingford people who, moving into the Bronze Age, left their appropriate remnants behind them.

They in their turn gave way to the variegated Gaelic communities whose monuments are to be found on Nendrum Island and, buried under Norman walls, at Inch and Downpatrick. They are also to be found within the waters of the lough, for through the muddy flats of Greyabbey Bay run lines of stones which together worked, from the sixth century, as fish traps and tidal pens. There are also orthogonal lines of mounded stones, which acted, in the seventeenth century, as anchor points for the long fronds of kelp which, harvested and roasted, were a principal source of iodine and of fertilisers for the fields. These fields were then being enclosed and cultivated for their light sandy soils and the crops of grain, both corn and barley, and of potatoes that could feed the new and rapidly growing urban centre of Belfast. These fields were being created and tended mainly by Scottish planters; the name of Montgomery is prominent among them. In Greyabbey's ruined nave there is a carved stone memorial tablet which reads:

> Sir James by pirates shot and thereof dead 12 March 1651/2
> by them i' the sea solemnly buried.

Both Ards and the district of Lecale are the locations of landing strips and airfields from the Second World War. I am aware of six — Dundrum, Ballykinler, Bishop's

Court, Portavogie, Ballyhalbert and Newtownards. There may well be the remnants of others, just as there are squat brick buildings in a characteristic style on Killard Point. These served for the defence of much-bombed Belfast and the Irish Sea as a whole, as well as performing the function of staging posts between the United States and eastern England. Kircubbin village was also, for a while, the general headquarters of the Royal Air Force in this quarter of the sky. Ballykinler is now an army base in which there is a recently constructed 'typical Irish village', through whose streets trainee soldiers practised the arts of streetfighting and close combat. On certain days the echoless rattle of the machine gun could be heard down the sands of Dundrum as far as the summit of Slieve Donard. Bishop's Court was also, for some years, a node on the electronic network which, without regard for frontier or border, surveyed everything that moved or sparked or hummed between the North Channel and the Denmark Strait.

***

At Greyabbey the coastline and the road swing about to face north-west and, on that day, straight into the wind's eye. A low grey cloud was scurrying in, torn and ragged from the North Atlantic, and it was hiding the top of the Scrabo Tower. I pressed down and rolled forward, past the entry to Mount Pleasant, a seat of Tory grandees of the past.

For some reason, we are expected by the heritage industry to admire the houses of great families. I am never quite sure as I pass them whether or not to consider the whole matter of heritage as entirely odious. In what possible sense can I regard them as *my* past, I wonder.

> I met Murder on the way —
> he had a mask like Castlereagh —

In this mood, head down and shivering and whipping up my courage for the last long hill, I think I preferred Byron's couplet:

> So he has cut his throat at last. — He! Who?
> The man who cut his country's long ago.

Salt spray was breaking across the road as I turned the last headland to follow the long road into Newtownards.

Newtownards is the prototypical 'planter's town' of Ulster, built on a four-square plan around an elegant courthouse that would not be out of place in New England. But I was now becoming seriously tired and getting wet from the combined rain and sea spray of the last five miles. 'Go straight through and you'll make it uphill,' I told myself.

Scrabo Tower was built as a monument to the third marquis of Londonderry, who is mainly known as one of Wellington's generals at Waterloo (and in north Down as the original proprietor and builder of Newtownards). It was the inhabitants of the town who determined to erect a suitable monument to their landlord. It is, within the limits of a folly, very good. Proportioned with noble simplicity and built in a manner so austere as to be actually numb, it presents all those who can stumble up its 122 steps with an astonishing vista. As if from the nose-cone of an Atlas rocket, I swear you can see the curvature of the earth, from Ben Lomond to Snaefell and even (perhaps) the Hill of Howth. How far into Ireland you can see I am not at all certain, because the central plains lack distinctive features, but it is certainly a long way. The Mountains of Mourne and even Sperrin seem almost in your back yard. On the right day — with a cold wind from the Baltic — this is probably the longest uninterrupted view in the whole of the Islands (see Chapter 1).

The contract for the design of Scrabo Tower went, as is often the case in these matters, not to the man who won the competition, nor the man in second place, nor third, but to the fourth, because his design came within the stipulated price range. This set Charles Lanyon on the lower stages of an outstanding career in most forms of building. Lanyon went on to do most of the big buildings of nineteenth-century Belfast as well as the Antrim coastal road (which is also an achievement of great note, larger than anything equivalent in mainland Britain), and to be lord mayor of Belfast and a member of parliament.

Needless to say, the inauguration of the tower was a grand civic event. A foundation stone was laid in course on 6 March 1857 to the strains of the national anthem, 'The royal north-Down quickstep' and another military air called 'Partant pour la Syrie'. The whole matter was reported in the *Illustrated London News* (on 28 March 1857). Lanyon's tower has now become simply part of the scenery, which is what should be expected of a monument.

It was always my hope and intention to finish my journey on a day such as I had encountered six years before, when I first got the idea of this book — a day of Arctic winds and distant snow, of strong sun and stronger shade, when a light metre goes off the scale. I finished it on a day that was now miserably bleak. Moreover, as I got to the top of the long main road out of Newtownards I felt compelled to stop and ease my legs. I carefully and stiffly dismounted. Without the support of frame and wheels I fell down flat on the wet grass. I lay there a few minutes, feeling weak and foolish, until a kind lady enquired after me. Driving past, she had witnessed my collapse and wondered whether or not I had taken a heart attack.

Notes

[1]   R.F. Foster (2007) *Luck and the Irish: a brief history of change, c. 1970–2000*, London: Allen Lane.

[2]   B. Cunliffe (2001) *Facing the ocean: the Atlantic and its peoples, 8000 BC–AD 1500*, Oxford: Oxford University Press, p. vii.

[3]   *Ibid.*, p. 37.

[4]   P. McGuinness, P., A. Harrison and R. Kearney (eds) (2006) *John Toland's* Christianity not mysterious*: text, associated works, and critical essays*, Dublin: Lilliput Press. See also M.C. Jacob (1981) *The radical enlightenment: Pantheists, Freemasons and Republicans*, London: Allen and Unwin, and R. Porter (2000) *The creation of the modern world: the untold story of the British Enlightenment*, New York: Norton.

[5]   For an exploration of this phenomenon, see S. O'Toole *et al.* (eds) (2007) *Suburban to superrural*, Kinsale: Gandon and further comment in A. Jones and D. Brett (2007) *Toward an architecture: Ulster*, Belfast: Black Square, p. 48.

[6]   *Ibid.*

[7]   These points have been discussed at greater length in *ibid.*

[8]   J. Bradley (1997) *The topography and layout of medieval Drogheda*, Drogheda: Old Drogheda Society.

BIBLIOGRAPHY

Apel, J. (2001) *Daggers, knowledge and power: the social aspects of flint-dagger technology in Scandinavia 2350–1500 cal. BC*, Uppsala: Uppsala University.

Arthurson, I. (1994) *The Perkin Warbeck conspiracy 1491–1499*, Stroud: Sutton.

Ball, M.J. and J. Fife (1993) *The Celtic languages*, London: Routledge.

Barrow, G.W.S. (1988, 3rd ed.) *Robert Bruce and the Community of the Realm of Scotland*, Edinburgh: Edinburgh University Press.

Barry, T.B. (1987) *The archaeology of medieval Ireland*, London: Methuen.

Bartlett, T. and K. Jeffery (eds) (1996) *A military history of Ireland*, Cambridge: Cambridge University Press.

Bassett, S. (ed.) (1989) *The origins of Anglo-Saxon kingdoms*, London: Leicester University Press.

Belchem, J. (ed.) (2006) *Liverpool 800: culture, character and history*, Liverpool: Liverpool University Press.

Benson, C. (2001) *The cultural psychology of self: place, morality and art in human worlds*, London: Routledge.

Bijker, W.E., T.P. Hughes and T.J. Pinch (eds), *The social construction of technological systems: new directions in the sociology and history of technology*, Cambridge, MA: MIT Press.

Binchy, D.A. (1962) 'The passing of the old order' in B. Ó Cuív (ed.), *Proceedings of the International Congress of Celtic Studies held in Dublin 6–10 July 1959*, Dublin: Dublin Institute for Advanced Studies.

Bird, J.H. (1963) *The major seaports of the United Kingdom*, London: Hutchinson.

Boardman, P. (1978) *The worlds of Patrick Geddes: biologist, town planner, re-educator, peace-warrior*, London: Routledge and Kegan Paul.

Boulger, D.C. (1911) *The battle of the Boyne*, London: Martin Secker.

Bowen, I. (1908) *Statutes of Wales*, London: Unwin.

Bradley, J. (1997) *The topography and layout of medieval Drogheda*, Drogheda: Old Drogheda Society.

Bradshaw, B. and J.S. Morrill (eds) (1996) *The British problem c. 1534–1707: state formation in the Atlantic archipelago*, Houndmills: Macmillan.

Braudel, F. (S. Reynolds, tr.) (1949, repr. 1972) *The Mediterranean and the Mediterranean world in the age of Philip II*, London: Collins.

Breeze, A. (1997) *Welsh medieval literature*, Dublin: Four Courts Press.

Brett, D. (2005) *Rethinking decoration*, Cambridge: Cambridge University Press.

Brett, D. (2004) *The plain style*, Cambridge: Lutterworth Press.

Brett, D. (1996) *The construction of heritage*, Cork: Cork University Press.

Brett, D. (1992) *C.R. Mackintosh: the poetics of workmanship*, London: Reaktion Books.

Brewer, J.S. and W. Bullen (eds) (1869) *Calendar of the Carew manuscripts preserved in the Archiepiscopal Library at Lambeth, vol. 3: 1589–1600*, London, Longmans Green.

Broderick, G. (1999) *Language death in the Isle of Man: an investigation into the decline and extinction of Manx Gaelic as a community language in the Isle of Man*, Tübingen: Niemeyer.

Broderick, G. (ed. and tr.) (1979, repr. 2004) *Chronicles of the Kings of Man and the Isles*, Douglas: Manx Museum and National Trust.

Broun, D. (1999) *The Irish identity of the kingdom of the Scots in the twelfth and thirteenth centuries*, Woodbridge: Boydell Press.

Brown, D. (1991) *Human universals*, New York: McGraw Hill.

Burke, L., T. Crowley and A. Girvin (eds) (2000) *The Routledge language and cultural theory reader*, London: Routledge.

Butter, R. and D.C. Lyons (1999, 2nd ed.) *Kilmartin: Scotland's richest prehistoric landscape: an introduction and guide*, Lochgilphead: Kilmartin House Trust.

Byrne, F.J. (1973, repr. 2001) *Irish kings and high kings*, Dublin: Four Courts Press.

Campbell, B.M.S. (2003) 'Economic progress in the canal age' in D. Dickson and C. Ó Gráda (eds), *Refiguring Ireland: essays in honour of L.M. Cullen*, Dublin: Lilliput Press.

Carey, J. (1995) 'Native elements in Irish pseudohistory' in D. Edel (ed.) *Cultural identity and cultural integration: Ireland and Europe in the early middle ages*, Dublin: Four Courts Press.

Catto, M. (1994) *Art and design matters: exhibition catalogue*, Belfast: Ulster Museum and University of Ulster.

Chadwick, H.M. (1949) *Early Scotland: the Picts, the Scots and the Welsh of southern Scotland*, Cambridge: Cambridge University Press.

Chadwick, N.K. (1970) 'Early literary contacts between Wales and Ireland' in D. Moore (ed.) *The Irish Sea province in archaeology and history*, Cardiff: Cambrian Archaeological Association.

Chapman, M. (1991) *The Celts: the construction of a myth*, London: St Martin's Press.

Childs, J. (1996) 'The Williamite Wars, 1689–1691' in T. Bartlett and K. Jeffrey (eds), *A military history of Ireland*, Cambridge: Cambridge University Press.

Christensen, A.E. (1989) 'Vikings in the Irish Sea' in M. McCaughan and J. Appleby (eds), *The Irish Sea: aspects of maritime history*, Belfast: Institute of Irish Studies, Queen's University.

Colfer, B. (2004) *The Hook Peninsula: County Wexford*, Cork: Cork University Press.

Colfer, B. (2002) *Arrogant trespass: Anglo-Norman Wexford, 1169–1400*, Enniscorthy: Duffry Press.

Colles, R. (1919) *The history of Ulster from the earliest times to the present day*, London: Gresham.

Collingwood, C.C. (1828) *A selection from the public and private correspondence of Vice-Admiral Lord Collingwood: interspersed with memoirs of his life*, London: Ridgway.

Collis, J. (2003) *The Celts: origins, myths, inventions*, Stroud: Tempus.

Creighton, J. (2000) *Coins and power in late Iron Age Britain*, Cambridge: Cambridge University Press.

Crowley, T. (ed.) (1990) *The politics of language in Ireland, 1366–1922: a sourcebook*, London: Routledge.

Cubbon, M. (1983) 'The archaeology of the Vikings in the Isle of Man' in C. Fell, P. Foote, J.G. Campbell and R. Thomson (eds), *The Viking age in the Isle of Man: select papers from the ninth Viking Congress, Isle of Man, 4–14 July 1981*, London: Viking Society for Northern Research.

Cunliffe, B. (2001a) *Facing the ocean: the Atlantic and its peoples, 8000 BC–AD 1500*, Oxford: Oxford University Press.

Cunliffe, B. (2001b) *The extraordinary voyage of Pytheas the Greek*, London: Penguin Books.

Daiches, D. (1977) *Glasgow*, London: Deutsch.

Dark, P. (2000) *The environment of Britain in the first millennium AD*, London: Duckworth.

Darvill, T.C. (1987) *Prehistoric Britain*, London: Batsford.

Davies, N. (1999) *The isles: a history*, London: Papermac.

Davies, R.R. (2000) *The first English empire: power and identities in the British Isles, 1093–1343*, Oxford: Oxford University Press.

Davies, W. (1990) *Patterns of power in early Wales*, Oxford: Clarendon Press.

de Paor, L. (1993) *St Patrick's world: the Christian culture of Ireland's apostolic age*, Dublin: Four Courts Press.

Delany, D.R. (1973) *The Grand Canal of Ireland*, Newtown Abbot: David and Charles.

Dickinson, W.C. (A.A.M. Duncan, rev. and ed.) (1977, 3rd ed.) *Scotland from the earliest times to 1603*, Oxford: Clarendon Press.

Dillon, M. and N.K. Chadwick (1972, 2nd ed.) *The Celtic realms*, London: Weidenfeld and Nicholson.

Dow, J.R. (ed.) (1991) *Language and ethnicity*, Philadelphia: Benjamins.

Duffy, S. (ed.) (1997) *An atlas of Irish history*, Dublin: Gill and Macmillan.

Duke, J.A. (1937) *History of the Church of Scotland to the Reformation*, Edinburgh: Oliver and Boyd.

Durkacz, V.E. (1983) *The decline of the Celtic languages: a study of linguistic and cultural conflict in Scotland, Wales and Ireland from the Reformation to the twentieth century*, Edinburgh: John Donald.

Edel, D. (ed.) (1995) *Cultural identity and cultural integration: Ireland and Europe in the early middle ages*, Dublin: Four Courts Press.

Eliade, M. (1954) *The myth of the eternal return, or Cosmos and history*, Princeton, NJ: Princeton University Press.

Ellis, P.B. (1976) *The Boyne water: the battle of the Boyne, 1690*, London: Hamish Hamilton.

Fairclough, N. (1989) *Language and power*, London: Longman.

Farjeon, E. and H. Farjeon (1953) *Kings and queens*, Philadelphia: Lippincott.

Fell, C., P. Foote, J.G. Campbell and R. Thomson (eds) (1983) *The Viking age in the Isle of Man: select papers from the ninth Viking Congress, Isle of Man, 4–14 July 1981*, London: Viking Society for Northern Research.

Fellows-Jensen, G. (1983) 'Scandinavian settlement in the Isle of Man and north-west England' in C. Fell, P. Foote, J.G. Campbell and R. Thomson (eds), *The Viking age in the Isle of Man: select papers from the ninth Viking Congress, Isle of Man, 4–14 July 1981*, London: Viking Society for Northern Research.

Fitzpatrick, E. (2004) *Royal inauguration in Gaelic Ireland* c. *1100–1600: a cultural landscape study*, Woodbridge: Boydell Press.

Flanagan, L. (1998) *Ancient Ireland: life before the Celts*, Dublin: Gill and Macmillan.

Foster, R.F. (2007) *Luck and the Irish: a brief history of change*, c. *1970–2000*, London: Allen Lane.

Foster, S.M. (1996) *Picts, Gaels and Scots: early historic Scotland*, London: Batsford.

Frame, R. (1990) *Political development of the British Isles 1100–1400*, Oxford: Oxford University Press.

Freke, D. (1995) *The Peel Castle dig*, Douglas: Friends of Peel Castle for the Friends of Manx National Heritage.

Gantz, J. (ed.) (1976) *The Mabinogion*, London: Penguin Books.

Geddes, P. (1949) *Cities in evolution*, London: Williams and Norgate.

Gibbon, E. (1789) *The decline and fall of the Roman Empire*, London: G. Kearsley.

Giraldus Cambrensis (A.B. Scott and F.X. Martin, ed. and tr.) (1978) *Expugnatio Hibernica: the conquest of Ireland*, Dublin: Royal Irish Academy.

Graves-Brown, P., S. Jones and C. Gamble (eds) (1996) *Cultural identity and archaeology: the construction of European communities*, London: Routledge.

Griffiths, A.R. and R.S. Thomas (1987) *The making of the Tudor dynasty*, Gloucester: Sutton.

Habermas, J. (ed.) (1987) *The philosophical discourse of modernity: twelve lectures*, London: Polity Press.

Hamer, R. (tr.) (1970) *A choice of Anglo-Saxon verse*, London: Faber and Faber.

Hartley, B.R. and R.L. Fitts (1988) *The Brigantes*, Gloucester: Sutton.

Hayes-McCoy, G.A. (1969) *Irish battles*, London: Longmans.

Haywood, J. (1991) *Dark Age naval power: a reassessment of Frankish and Anglo-Saxon seafaring activity*, London: Routledge.

Head, G. (1836) *Home tour through the manufacturing districts of England in the summer of 1835*, London: Murray.

Hudson, B. (ed.) (2004) *Irish Sea studies 900–1200*, Dublin: Four Courts Press.

Huizinga, J. (1938) *Homo ludens*, Haarlem: Tjeenk Willink.

Hull, L. (2005) *The castles and bishops' palaces of Pembrokeshire*, Little Logaston: Logaston Press.

Isserlin, R.M.J. (1998) 'A spirit of improvement? Marble and the culture of Roman Britain' in R. Laurence and J. Berry (eds), *Cultural identity in the Roman Empire*, London: Routledge.

Jackson, G. and D.M. Williams (eds), *Shipping, technology and imperialism: papers presented to the third British-Dutch Maritime History Conference*, Aldershot: Scolar Press.

Jacob, M.C. (1981) *The radical enlightenment: Pantheists, Freemasons and Republicans*, London: Allen and Unwin.

James, E. (1989) 'The origins of barbarian kingdoms: the continental evidence' in S. Bassett (ed.), *The origins of Anglo-Saxon kingdoms*, London: Leicester University Press.

James, S. (1999) *The Atlantic Celts: ancient people or modern invention?* London: British Museum.

Jones, A. and D. Brett (2007) *Toward an architecture: Ulster*, Belfast: Black Square.

Jones, D. (1952) *The anathemata: fragments of an attempted writing*, London: Faber and Faber.

Jones, D. (1937) *In parenthesis: seinnyessit e gledyf ym penn mameu*, London: Faber and Faber.

Jones, G. (1968) *A history of the Vikings*, Oxford: Oxford University Press.

Kennedy, L. and P. Ollerenshaw (eds) (1985) *An economic history of Ulster, 1820–1939*, Manchester: Manchester University Press.

Kidd, C. (1999) *British identities before nationalism*, Cambridge: Cambridge University Press.

Kinsella, T. (tr.) (L. le Brocquy, illust.) (1979) *The Táin*, Oxford: Oxford University Press.

Kintyre Civic Society (2003) *The Campbeltown book*, Campbeltown: Kintyre Civic Society.

Kristeva, J. (1986) 'The revolution in poetic language' in T. Moi (ed.), *The Kristeva reader*, Oxford: Blackwell.

Kristiansen, K. (1998) *Europe before history*, Cambridge: Cambridge University Press.

Laing, L. and J. Laing (1990) *Celtic Britain and Ireland, AD 200–800: the myth of the Dark Ages*, Dublin: Irish Academic Press.

Larsen, A.C. (ed.) (2001) *The Vikings in Ireland*, Roskilde: Viking Ship Museum.

Laurence, R. and J. Berry (eds) (1998) *Cultural identity in the Roman Empire*, London: Routledge.

Lowe, E.A. (1969, 2nd ed.) *Handwriting: our medieval legacy*, Rome: Edizioni di Storia e Letteratura.

Macdonald, R.A. (1997) *The kingdom of the Isles: Scotland's western seaboard c. 1100–c. 1336*, East Linton: Tuckwell Press.

MacDougall, H.A. (1982) *Racial myth in English history: Trojans, Teutons and Anglo-Saxons*, Montreal: Harvest House.

Mackinder, H.J. (1928) 'The content of philosophical geography' in *The proceedings of the International Geographical Congress, Cambridge, July*, Cambridge: Cambridge University Press.

Mackinder, H.J. (1902) *Britain and the British seas*, London: Heinemann.

Magnusson, M. and H. Pálsson (eds and trs) (1960) *Njal's Saga*, London: Penguin Books.

Mallory, J.P. (ed.) (1992) *Aspects of the Táin*, Belfast: December Press.

Marsden, J. (2000) *Somerled and the emergence of Gaelic Scotland*, East Linton: Tuckwell Press.

Maxwell, H. (ed.) (1908) *The Chronicle of Lanercost*, Glasgow: J. Maclehose and Sons.

McCaughan, M. and J. Appleby (eds) (1989) *The Irish Sea: aspects of maritime history*, Belfast: Institute of Irish Studies, Queen's University.

McDonald, R.A. (2007) *Manx kingship in its Irish Sea setting, 1187–1229: King Rognvaldr and the Crovan dynasty*, Dublin: Four Courts Press.

McErlean, T., R. McConkey, W. Forsythe *et al.* (2002) *Strangford Lough: an archaeological survey of the maritime cultural landscape*, Belfast: Blackstaff Press for the Environment and Heritage Centre.

McGuinness, P., A. Harrison and R. Kearney (eds) (2006) *John Toland's* Christianity not mysterious*: text, associated works, and critical essays*, Dublin: Lilliput Press.

McKerral, A. (1948, repr. 2001) *Kintyre in the seventeenth century*, Edinburgh: Oliver and Boyd.

McNamee, C. (1997) *The Wars of the Bruces: Scotland, England and Ireland, 1306–1328*, East Linton: Tuckwell Press.

Mitchell, F. (1986) *The Shell guide to reading the Irish landscape*, Dublin: Country House.

Moody, T.W. and F.X. Martin (eds) (1967, repr. 2001) *The course of Irish history*, Cork: Mercier Press.

Moore, D. (ed.) (1970) *Irish Sea province in archaeology and history*, Cardiff: Cambrian Archeological Association.

Moore, F. (1996) 'Ireland's oldest bridge — at Clonmacnoise', *Archaeology Ireland* **10** (4) (winter).

Moss, M.S. (1996) 'Lagan and Clyde shipbuilding' in G. Jackson and D.M. Williams (eds), *Shipping, technology and imperialism: papers presented to the third British-Dutch Maritime History Conference*, Aldershot: Scolar Press.

Movius, H.L. (1942) *The Irish Stone Age: its chronology, development and relationships*, Cambridge: Cambridge University Press.

Mytum, H. (1995) 'Across the Irish Sea: Romano-British and Irish settlements in Wales', *Emania* **13**.

Nairn, T. (1977) *The break-up of Britain: crisis and neo-nationalism*, London: NLB.

Nelson, L.H. (1966) *The Normans in south Wales, 1070–1171*, Austin: University of Texas Press.

O'Faolain, S. (1947) *The Irish*, London: Pelican Books.

O'Hegarty, P.S. (1919) *Ulster: a brief statement*, Dublin: Maunsel.

O'Rahilly, T.F. (1946, repr. 1971) *Early Irish history and mythology*, Dublin: Dublin Institute for Advanced Studies.

O'Sullivan, P. (1986) *Geopolitics*, London: Croom Helm.

O'Toole, S. *et al.* (eds) (2007) *Suburban to superrural*, Kinsale: Gandon.

Oppenheimer, S. (2006) *The origins of the British: a genetic detective story*, London: Constable.

Orpen, G.H. (1911, repr. 1968) *Ireland under the Normans, 1169–1216, vol. 1*, Oxford: Clarendon Press.

Parker, G. (1985) *Western geopolitical thought in the twentieth century*, London: Croom Helm.

Parkinson, C.N. (1952) *The rise of the port of Liverpool*, Liverpool: Liverpool University Press.

Pettifer, A. (2000) *Welsh castles: a guide by counties*, Woodbridge: Boydell Press.

Piggott, S. (1954) *The Neolithic cultures of the British Isles: a study of the stone-using agricultural communities of Britain in the second millennium* BC, Cambridge: Cambridge University Press.

Porter, R. (2000) *The creation of the modern world: the untold story of the British Enlightenment*, New York: Norton.

Raftery, B. (1996) 'Drumanagh and Roman Ireland', *Archaeology Ireland* **10** (1) (spring).

Raftery, B. (1994) *Pagan Celtic Ireland: the enigma of the Irish Iron Age*, London: Thames and Hudson.

Richter, M. (1999) *Ireland and her neighbours in the seventh century*, Dublin: Four Courts Press.

Rodger, N.A.M. (1997) *The safeguard of the sea: a naval history of Britain 660–1649*, London: Penguin Books.

Ross, S. (1993) *The Stewart dynasty*, Nairn: Thomas and Lochar.

Sadowska, E. (1997) 'Horses led by a mare: martial aspects of the *Táin bó Cuailnge*', *Emania* **16**.

Said, E. (1978) *Orientalism*, New York: Pantheon.

Silke, J.S. (1970, repr. 2000) *Kinsale: the Spanish intervention in Ireland at the end of the Elizabethan Wars*, Dublin: Four Courts Press.

Simpson, W.D. (1935) *The Celtic Church in Scotland: a study of its penetration lines and art relationships*, Aberdeen: University Press.

Sloan, G.R. (1997) *The geopolitics of Anglo-Irish relations in the twentieth century*, London: Leicester University Press.

Smith, B. (ed.) (1999) *Britain and Ireland, 900–1300: insular responses to medieval European change*, Cambridge: Cambridge University Press.

Spenser, E. (1849) 'A view of the state of Ireland' in *The works of Edmund Spenser: with observations of his life and writings*, London: H. Washborne.

Stringer, K.J. (ed.) (1985) *Essays on the nobility of medieval Scotland*, Edinburgh: John Donald.

Swift, M. (1999) *Historical maps of Ireland*, London: Parkgate Books.

Sykes, B. (2006) *Blood of the isles: exploring the genetic roots of our tribal history*, London: Bantam.

Tacitus (1967) (R.M. Ogilvie and I.A. Richmond, eds) *De Vita Agricolae*, Oxford: Clarendon Press.

Taliesin (M. Pennar, tr.) (1988) *Poems*, Lampeter: Llanerch Enterprises.

Thomas, C. (1969) *The Iron Age in the Irish Sea province*, London: Council for British Archeology.

Traherne, T. (D. Buresh, ed.) (2002) *Waking up in heaven: a contemporary edition of Centuries of meditation*, Spencervill, MD: Hesed Press.

Wade-Evans, A.W. (tr.) (1944) *Vitae sanctorum Britanniae et genealogiae*, Cardiff: University of Wales Press Board.

Wade-Evans, A.W. (1934) *Welsh Christian origins*, Oxford: Alden Press.

Wainwright, F.T. (ed.) (1955) *The problem of the Picts*, Edinburgh: Nelson.

Walker, D. (ed.) (1976) *A history of the church in Wales*, Penarth: Church in Wales Publications.

Walker, F.M. (1996) 'The river Clyde: birthplace of an industry' in G. Jackson and D.M. Williams (eds), *Shipping, technology and imperialism: papers presented to the third British-Dutch Maritime History Conference*, Aldershot: Scolar Press.

Wallace, P.F. (2001) 'Ireland's Viking towns' in A.C. Larsen (ed.), *The Vikings in Ireland*, Roskilde: Viking Ship Museum.

Warner, R.B. (1995) 'Tuathal Techtmar: a myth or ancient literary evidence for a Roman invasion?', *Emania* 13.

Webster, B. (1997) *Medieval Scotland: the making of an identity*, London, Macmillan Press.

White, H. (1973) *Metahistory: the historical imagination in nineteenth-century Europe*, Baltimore, MD: John Hopkins University Press.

INDEX
of leading names, places and topics